T0155833

Lecture Notes in Computer Science   11495

Commenced Publication in 1973
Founding and Former Series Editors:
Gerhard Goos, Juris Hartmanis, and Jan van Leeuwen

Editorial Board Members

David Hutchison
Lancaster University, Lancaster, UK

Takeo Kanade
Carnegie Mellon University, Pittsburgh, PA, USA

Josef Kittler
University of Surrey, Guildford, UK

Jon M. Kleinberg
Cornell University, Ithaca, NY, USA

Friedemann Mattern
ETH Zurich, Zurich, Switzerland

John C. Mitchell
Stanford University, Stanford, CA, USA

Moni Naor
Weizmann Institute of Science, Rehovot, Israel

C. Pandu Rangan
Indian Institute of Technology Madras, Chennai, India

Bernhard Steffen
TU Dortmund University, Dortmund, Germany

Demetri Terzopoulos
University of California, Los Angeles, CA, USA

Doug Tygar
University of California, Berkeley, CA, USA

More information about this series at http://www.springer.com/series/7408

Simon Collart-Dutilleul · Thierry Lecomte ·
Alexander Romanovsky (Eds.)

Reliability, Safety, and Security of Railway Systems

Modelling, Analysis, Verification, and Certification

Third International Conference, RSSRail 2019
Lille, France, June 4–6, 2019
Proceedings

 Springer

Editors
Simon Collart-Dutilleul
Laboratoire IFSTTAR/ESTAS
Villeneuve d'Ascq, France

Thierry Lecomte
ClearSy
Aix en Provence, France

Alexander Romanovsky ⓘ
Newcastle University
Newcastle-upon-Tyne, UK

ISSN 0302-9743   ISSN 1611-3349   (electronic)
Lecture Notes in Computer Science
ISBN 978-3-030-18743-9   ISBN 978-3-030-18744-6   (eBook)
https://doi.org/10.1007/978-3-030-18744-6

LNCS Sublibrary: SL2 – Programming and Software Engineering

© Springer Nature Switzerland AG 2019
This work is subject to copyright. All rights are reserved by the Publisher, whether the whole or part of the material is concerned, specifically the rights of translation, reprinting, reuse of illustrations, recitation, broadcasting, reproduction on microfilms or in any other physical way, and transmission or information storage and retrieval, electronic adaptation, computer software, or by similar or dissimilar methodology now known or hereafter developed.
The use of general descriptive names, registered names, trademarks, service marks, etc. in this publication does not imply, even in the absence of a specific statement, that such names are exempt from the relevant protective laws and regulations and therefore free for general use.
The publisher, the authors and the editors are safe to assume that the advice and information in this book are believed to be true and accurate at the date of publication. Neither the publisher nor the authors or the editors give a warranty, expressed or implied, with respect to the material contained herein or for any errors or omissions that may have been made. The publisher remains neutral with regard to jurisdictional claims in published maps and institutional affiliations.

This Springer imprint is published by the registered company Springer Nature Switzerland AG
The registered company address is: Gewerbestrasse 11, 6330 Cham, Switzerland

Preface

Welcome to the proceedings of the Third International Conference on Reliability, Safety, and Security of Railway Systems: Modelling, Analysis, Verification, and Certification (RSSRail 2019). We were pleased that RSSRail 2019 took place in Lille during June 4–6, 2019, and was hosted by IFSTTAR, one of the major players in European research on transportation. The series of RSSRail conferences began in 2016 in Paris, and continued in 2017 in Pistoia. This year's conference built on the success of RSSRail 2016 and RSSRail 2017.

Development of the complex railway systems of the future faces a number of challenges:

- To improve railway system safety, security, and reliability
- To reduce production cost, time to market, and running costs
- To increase system capacity and reduce carbon emissions

And it requires integrated environments and methods that support different abstraction levels and different views, including:

- Systems architecture
- Safety analysis
- Security analysis
- Verification tools and methods.

The RSSRail 2019 conference brought together researchers and engineers interested in building critical railway applications and systems, as a working conference in which research advances are discussed and evaluated by both researchers and engineers, focusing on their potential to be deployed in industrial settings.

The conference contributed to a range of key objectives. We feel that there is a pressing need to bring together researchers and developers working on railway system reliability, security, and safety to discuss how these requirements can be met in an integrated way. It is also vital to ensure that all advances in research (both in academia and industry) are driven by real industrial needs. This can help ensure that such advances are followed by industrial deployment. Another particularly important objective is to integrate research advances into the current development processes, and make them usable and scalable. Finally, a key goal is the development of advanced methods and tools that will ensure that rail systems meet the requirements imposed both by the standards and in building the arguments for compliance.

We hope, and expect, that RSSRail 2019 successfully contributed to achieving all of these objectives.

The conference covered topics related to all aspects of reliability, safety, and security engineering for railway systems and networks, including:

- Safety in development processes and safety management
- Combined approaches to safety and security

- System and software safety analysis
- Formal modelling and verification techniques
- System reliability
- Validation according to the standards
- Safety and security argumentation
- Fault and intrusion modelling and analysis
- Evaluation of system capacity, energy consumption, cost, and their interplay
- Tool and model integration, toolchains
- Domain-specific languages and modelling frameworks
- Model reuse for reliability, safety, and security
- Modelling for maintenance strategy engineering.

This year the conference attracted 38 submissions from 14 countries. In total, 18 papers were accepted after a rigorous review process in which every paper received at least three reviews.

Three prominent researchers working on railway engineering, Airy Magnien from UIC (France), Alessandro Fantechi from the University of Florence (Italy), and Cédric Blin from Ansaldo STS (France), kindly agreed to deliver keynote talks. The volume includes one paper and two abstracts describing the research presented in the keynote talks.

We would like to thank the Program Committee members and the additional reviewers for all their efforts. We are indebted to IFSTTAR for helping with the planning and organization of this event. We would like to acknowledge the help of Newcastle University staff: Joan Atkinson, Tom Anderson, and Lisa Aston. We are very grateful to Alfred Hofmann from Springer for supporting the publication of these proceedings in the LNCS series. But, most of all, our thanks go to all the contributors and to all those who attended the conference for making this conference a success.

March 2019

Simon Collart-Dutilleul
Thierry Lecomte
Alexander Romanovsky

Organization

Conference Chairs

Simon Collart-Dutilleul   IFSTTAR, France
Thierry Lecomte   ClearSy, France
Alexander Romanovsky   Newcastle University, UK

Financial Chair

Joan Atkinson   Newcastle University, UK

Local Organization Chair

Natalie Botticchio   IFSTTAR, France

Website Design

Lisa Aston   Newcastle University, UK
Andrew McLean   Newcastle University, UK

Program Committee

Marc Antoni   UIC, France
Carlo Becheri   Alstom, Italy
Fabien Belmonte   Alstom, France
David Bonvoisin   RATP, France
Jens Braband   Siemens, Germany
Tom Chothia   University of Birmingham, UK
Fares Chucri   SNCF, France
Alessandro Fantechi   University of Florence, Italy
Francesco Flammini   Linnaeus University, Sweden
Barbara Gallina   Mälardalen University, Sweden
Frank Golatowski   University of Rostock, Germany
Anne Haxthausen   Technical University of Denmark, Denmark
Alexei Iliasov   Newcastle University, UK
Chris Johnson   University of Glasgow, UK
Hironobu Kuruma   Hitachi, Japan
Michael Leuschel   University of Düsseldorf, Germany
Jan Peleska   Verified Systems Int., Germany
Peter Popov   City University, UK
Etienne Prun   ClearSy, France
Klaus Reichl   Thales, Austria

Aryldo Russo	CERTIFER, France
Colin Snook	University of Southampton, UK
Mariëlle Stoelinga	University of Twente, The Netherlands
Kenji Taguchi	CAV Technologies, Japan
Stefano Tonetta	FBK-irst, Italy
Laurent Voisin	Systerel, France
Kirsten Winter	University of Queensland, Australia

Additional Reviewers

Abderrahim Ait Wakrime	Railenium, France
Davide Basile	ISTI, Italy
Benjamin Beichler	University of Rostock, Germany
Signe Geisler	Technical University of Denmark, Denmark
Anatoliy Gorbenko	Leeds Beckett University, UK
Sebastian Krings	University of Applied Sciences, Germany
Bjørnar Luteberget	RailComplete AS, Norway
Franco Mazzanti	ISTI, Italy
Michael Nast	University of Rostock, Germany
Hideaki Nishihara	AIST, Japan
Subeer Rangra	Alstom, France
Enno Ruijters	University of Twente, The Netherlands
Thorsten Schulz	University of Rostock, Germany
Paulius Stankaitis	Newcastle University, UK
Shunsuke Yatabe	AIST, Japan

Sponsors

CERTIFER

ClearSy

EURNEX

Newcastle University

Railenium

Systerel

SYSTRA

Wind

Abstracts of Invited Keynote Talks

RailTopoModel - A Cornerstone to Foster the Federation of Railway Digital Models

Airy Magnien

Union Internationale des Chemins de Fer, France
magnien@uic.org

Abstract. RailTopoModel (RTM) stands for a project initiated in 2013 by several European railway companies. It led to the publication of RTM 1.0 by Union Internationale des Chemins de fer (UIC) in April 2016. Its kernel addresses the issue of providing a single repository for railway infrastructure description, that is scalable, extensible, and platform-independent.

Keywords: Railway · Infrastructure · Modelling

Current developments in the RailTopoModel project (https://www.railtopomodel.org/en/) are driven by urgent business needs, namely Building Information Modelling (BIM) level 3: replicating the rail domain in IT, in the interest of prompt system certification and handover to operating and maintenance companies. This extension of the application scope to all components of the railway transport system is taking place by joining forces with the IFC Rail project coordinated by building SMART (https://www. buildingsmart.org/ifc-maritime-project/).

In parallel, UIC drives the expansion of the technical scope of RTM to operations, for the purpose of traffic planning, autonomous driving, or for disturbance recovery optimization.

Another obvious challenge is no less exciting, namely governance. Given the complexity and long life of railway systems, RTM aims at becoming one useful piece in a set of cooperating models with well-defined responsibilities and a clear evolution path.

Scientific and Technological Obstacles to Achieve the Autonomy

Cédric Blin

Ansaldo STS, France
cedric.blin@ansaldo-sts.fr

Abstract. This talk will present Ansaldo STS experience with autonomy projects and highlight the technical difficulties encountered and the technological and scientific obstacles identified, as well as the partnerships put in place to overcome them.

The new technologies brought by the digital revolution open up new opportunities for the world of transport, and the next technological era for railways is now the Autonomy.

The autonomous train has many advantages, it improves safety, performances and quality of service while reducing investment and operational costs and saving energy.

In the long term, all trains will be autonomous. However, achieving autonomy requires overcoming technical difficulties as well as technological and scientific obstacles. Therefore, the development of these complex systems requires not only innovation, but also cooperation between railways operators, industrial manufacturers as well as academic research organizations.

This talk will present Ansaldo STS experience with autonomy projects and highlight the technical difficulties encountered and the technological and scientific obstacles identified. More specifically, with regard to the autonomous freight train carried out with Railenium and SNCF, it will show how new forms of organization make it possible to better exploit innovation to meet technological challenges.

Keywords: Railway · Autonomous Trains · Innovation

The railway adventure is first and foremost a series of technological leaps that make it possible to improve mobility. Today, the new technologies brought by the digital revolution are opening up new opportunities for the world of transport, and the next technological leap for the railways is now the Autonomy.

With the autonomous train, all the advantages are added up, it improves safety, performances and quality of service and at the same time it reduces investment and operational costs while saving energy. Indeed, since machines are faster than human being and easier to coordinate, more autonomous trains will be able to follow one another on the same line. More passengers and goods can be transported while saving energy through optimized braking and acceleration. This will allow a more intensive use of infrastructures that are always expensive and often saturated, with investments well below the cost of building new tracks.

If automatic driving is operational for metro applications. For the other railways systems, the situation is much more complex, due to a diversified fleet of rolling stock, an Opened environment and network, and an infrastructure that will not be adapted. In this context, the main technological and scientific challenges that have been identified to achieve autonomy are the following:

- Geolocalization: To navigate autonomously, the train needs a geolocalization system capable of positioning it on an open network with a sufficient level of accuracy.
- Cybersecurity: Integrity and confidentiality of information circulating on networks for transportation systems is crucial, therefore it is essential to protect theses system against the growing threat of cyberattacks.
- Environmental detection: Achieving the autonomy will necessitate to provide the train with a vision of its environment. The perception system should collect the greatest amount of relevant information to allow the train to understand its environment.
- Decision-making: The train's autonomy is also its ability to make decisions; therefore, decision-making algorithm should be adapted to the context of the autonomous train to enable the system to resolve the conflicts it will face.
- System validation: Autonomous systems are so complex that it is no longer possible to test all the configurations. A virtual and representative simulation tool will have to be developed to allow massive laboratory tests.
- Safety standards: If autonomous train will increase the overall safety level of the railways system, the safety demonstration will be complex and may require an adaptation of the regulations.

However, autonomy is not limited to overcoming technological and scientific obstacles, and the arrival of autonomous trains is not only a simple market evolution but a major transformation. Since no one is able to control all its components, whether scientific, technological, industrial or economic, so that the development of a complete and operational system seems difficult to be achieved by a single actor. For railways actors, the trend is therefore towards cooperation between operators, manufacturers and public and private research organizations.

Ansaldo STS will present a feedback from experience on autonomy projects and highlight the technical difficulties encountered and the technological and scientific obstacles identified. More specifically, with regard to the autonomous freight train carried out with Railenium and SNCF, we will see how new forms of organization make it possible to better exploit innovation to meet technological challenges.

Contents

Modelling

Formal Verification

Security

Keynote Talk

Connected or Autonomous Trains?

Alessandro Fantechi[✉][iD]

Department of Information Engineering, University of Florence, Florence, Italy
alessandro.fantechi@unif.it

Abstract. In a parallel with the trends in the automotive domain, we discuss the future challenges of automation of train control, where train to infrastructure and train to train communication will support distributed control algorithms, while on board artificial intelligence will provide autonomous control decisions. Already installed systems, like ERTMS-ETCS, are actually distributed systems that span over geographical areas and are able to safely control large physical systems. But still, crucial decisions are taken at centralized places, that concentrate communications with mobile objects. Several prospected advances, aimed at increasing capacity and automation of rail transport, go in the direction of a more dynamic network connection among mobile components, in which decisions are actually taken in a distributed way.

A concept of dynamic safety envelope within which a train can safely move then emerges, built by a fusion of reliable information coming from the infrastructure and from other trains, as well as autonomously harvested by on-board "intelligent" sensors. This paper discusses some plausible scenarios in this respect and presents the basic concepts behind them.

1 Introduction

Connected cars and autonomous car driving are currently researched and experimented in view of a future where safety and full automation of car transportation are globally ensured by vehicle-to-vehicle (V2V) and vehicle-to-infrastructure (V2I) communication on one side, and by on board artificial intelligence on the other side, in one or two decades to come.

The concept of connected cars is based on availability of ubiquitous high band communication links that allow cars to negotiate the resolution of conflicts between cars either by playing distributed algorithms, or by asking help to equipment deployed along the roads and at crossings.

As an evolution of current driver assistance systems, autonomous cars elaborate instead information harvested by on-board sensors to provide the knowledge needed to an automated driver to safely proceed along a requested journey.

Connection and autonomy complement each other, and will be eventually merged in future automated cars.

When looking at railways, we can observe that the wide deployment of ERTMS-ETCS systems on high speed lines as well as on freight corridors is already a working witness to the possible achievement of high safety standards

© Springer Nature Switzerland AG 2019
S. Collart-Dutilleul et al. (Eds.): RSSRail 2019, LNCS 11495, pp. 3–19, 2019.
https://doi.org/10.1007/978-3-030-18744-6_1

by means of distributed control algorithms that span over geographical areas and are able to safely control large physical systems.

ERTMS-ETCS is known as already able to support full automation of train driving, since it provides the basic safety layer over which an automatic driving mechanism can be implemented in place, or beside, the human driver, similarly to what happens in CBTC systems of automatic metros. Hence, it can be said that a *connected trains* paradigm is already implemented in railways, and used by millions of passengers every day. Section 2 of this paper will show examples of this state of the art in which *connected trains* are at a much more advanced point w.r.t what is current practice in the automotive domain, due to the widely deployed technological instrumentation of infrastructure. But still, crucial decisions needed to guarantee safety of control are taken at centralized places (such as the ETCS Radio Block Centre - RBC), that concentrate communications with mobile objects.

Section 3 will discuss how the evolution of such technology, also pushed by the Shift2Rail Joint Initiative with the aim of a 50% increase in capacity in the railways in Europe [29], goes in the direction of a more dynamic connection among mobile components, in which decisions are actually taken in a distributed way, asking for distributed consensus algorithms.

Safety has to be preserved also by these dynamically connected trains: Sect. 4 introduces the fundamental concept of dynamic safety envelope within which a train can safely move, built by a fusion of reliable information either coming from the infrastructure and from other trains, or autonomously harvested by on-board sensors, or both.

Autonomous decisions appear to have a far less important role in train control systems, due to the strongly infrastructure-based nature of railway operations: Sect. 5 discusses where autonomous decision inherited by automotive technologies can find a role in specific operational scenarios.

2   Current *Connected Trains*

Modern "connected trains" systems, on which we will focus our discussion in the following, referring to significant examples, are indeed distributed systems, since they are composed of a network of computing *nodes* connected by communication links. Main critical control decisions are typically taken at specific nodes of the network, that collect data from the other nodes for this purpose, and are communicated to the other nodes in a master/slave fashion.

Indeed, some decisions could instead be negotiated between nodes with some specific distributed algorithm; apart from the higher complexity of this alternative, one limiting factor is that the current business policy in railway industry is centered over the independence of infrastructure managers w.r.t. train operators: the former tend to centralize control on the traffic over the infrastructure they manage, while the latter have to ask the former, and pay, for access to the infrastructure.

2.1   Centralised Control

In this section we consider some communication-based existing systems (ETCS-L2, Moving Block, Interlocking), taken as examples of centralised control over distributed systems.

ERTMS-ETCS. The increasing need to boost the volume of passenger and freight rail transport, while decreasing the cost, and the difficulties of constructing new tracks, are leading to the aim of running more trains on the existing tracks, asking for notable improvements of the operation principles of nowadays railways. The European Railway Traffic Management System (ERTMS) is an international standard that aims to answer these needs by jointly improving the interoperability, performance, reliability, and safety of modern railways.

ERTMS relies on the European Train Control System (ETCS), an Automatic Train Protection (ATP)[1] system which continuously supervises the train, ensuring that the maximum safe speed and minimum safedistance are respected. ETCS is specified at four levels of operation, depending on the role of track-side equipment and on the way the information is transmitted to/from trains. Levels 2 and 3 can indeed be considered as *connected trains* systems.

At Level 2, track-side equipment (track circuits, axle counters) is used to detect the occupancy of sections of track, determining the location of trains with a coarse granularity. This information is sent to a central unit, the Radio Block Centre (RBC), which sends to each train a Movement Authority (MA) computed by counting the free sections in front of the train (*fixed-block signalling*). The MA specifies the maximum distance that a train is allowed to travel and the maximum allowed speed depending on the track morphology (static speed profile, temporary speed restrictions, etc.). The on-board European Vital Computer (EVC) of each train uses the MA and data stored on-board (e.g., the braking capability of the train) to compute the maximum allowed speed (i.e., the braking curve or the dynamic speed profile), triggering an emergency brake whenever this limit is exceeded. Level 2 avoids track-side signalling through a continuous bidirectional communication between the train and the RBC using GSM-R (railway dedicated GSM).

Moving Block. The Level 3 of operation of the ERTMS/ETCS (ETCS-L3), currently still in development, improves upon Level 2 by removing the wayside equipment for detecting the occupancy of fixed-length tracks (fixed-block). Rather, the ETCS-L3 relies on *moving block* systems, computing the maximum distance that a train is allowed to travel based on the knowledge of the position of the rear-end of the foregoing train. In doing so, headways between trains can be considerably reduced, improving the line capacity (see Fig. 1). Although main line ETCS-L3 has not been still deployed, moving block based on continuous communication and MA computation is currently implemented in some

---

[1] For brevity, we here ignore the usual distinction between ATP and ATC (Automatic Train Control).

automatic metros, as a feature of CBTC (Communication Based Train Control) [15] systems.

In these innovative distancing systems, the traditional, simple and easily observable binary consensus information exchanged between old days electromechanical devices is replaced by more complex information (e.g. Movement Authority - MA) continuously exchanged through advanced, mostly wireless, means of communication. In such systems, safety is guaranteed not only by the proper functioning of the equipment on the ground and on board the train, but also by the accuracy and integrity of information exchanged between the ground and on board, for example speed and position information produced on board the train and Movement Authority sent to the following train.

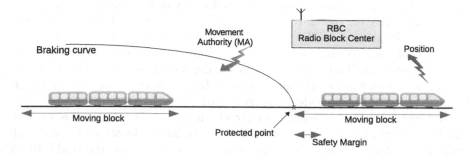

Fig. 1. Communication based moving block principle

Automated Driving - ATO. Automatic driving is typically responsibility of a so called Automatic Train Operation (ATO) system, that is responsible for driving, but still subject to a safety enforcing ATP system (such as ETCS). ATO systems of this kind are adopted by CBTC systems for automatic metros.

The ATO system manages the train running from one station (or predetermined operational stopping point) to the next, automatically adjusting the train speed with appropriate traction and braking commands. This automatic control with regard to speed and acceleration is performed by the ATO respecting the required operating conditions and the limits imposed by the ATP. The goal is to optimize the compliance to a set of possibly conflicting requirements, such as timetable respect, energy efficiency, passenger comfort, equipment durability, etc. The ATO can replace the driver also in other operations (opening and closing doors, initial train setup, etc.), making unnecessary the presence of a human operator on board. Although the ATO takes autonomous local decisions to this respect, the actual degree of train autonomy with respect to the global train control is almost null, since all the (safety-critical) decisions in a CBTC system are centralized in a Zone Controller (ZC - analogous to the RBC of ETCS). Although being the state-of-art within CBTC "closed system" solutions on urban lines, ATO implementation on main lines is still far, due to the high interoperability requirements of "open" railway systems constituted by large, complex interconnected railway networks operated by many different train types. Indeed, the automated freight heavy rail line recently opened in Australia [2] is also a closed system, with one only type of train.

Interlocking. Railway interlocking (IXL) systems are those systems that are responsible to grant to a train the exclusive access to a *route*: a route is a sequence of track elements that are exclusively assigned for the movement of a train through a station or a junction.

The instantiation of generic interlocking rules on a station topology is usually defined in a data structure named *control table*, that is specific for the station where the system resides. The control table drives the subsequent development of a centralised interlocking system. In the usual meaning of railway interlocking, we intend therefore a system that simply receives requests of reservations, and grants reservations or not on the ground of safety rules, until the reservation has been fully used (the track is again free) or has been safely revoked.

It is not a burden of the interlocking to look for alternative routes in case the requested one is busy, in order to optimise traffic throughput parameters, nor to guarantee that a train does not enter a not reserved track. These two functions, when automated, are usually responsibility of separate systems, namely Automatic Train Supervision (ATS) and ATP systems respectively.

The connection between a train and an IXL is usually either through signals that the driver must manually obey, or mediated by an ATP system: in ETCS, a MA authority including a route through a junction area is sent to a train only if the route is granted by the interlocking system controlling the junction.

2.2 Distributed Control

Railway lines are by nature geographically dispersed, so system distribution typically reflects geography: a line is divided in sections, a station is divided in zones, etc., with a separate control of each part in order to reduce complexity and equipment costs, to minimize cabling, or to obey to different authorities over the line. But within the section, or zone, the control is still centralised. A recent trend has even seen the diffusion of "multistation interlocking" systems [19], that is, a trend to centralise in a single system the interlocking functions of all the stations of a line.

An important issue in geographically decomposed and communicating systems is related to the proper interface between the different systems, avoiding proprietary interfaces and protocols that generate vendor locking, through the definition of standard interfaces and communication protocols. The whole story of ERTMS/ETCS is about this issue: interoperability between trains, infrastructures and equipment produced by different vendors and/or managed by different entities.

Indeed, one driving factor against distribution is related to maintenance costs: the dispersion of technological equipment needing a frequent maintenance over kilometers of lines hosting a continuous train traffic is a highly costly and highly risky activity. For the same reasons, if a particular functionality requires massively distributed equipments put in operation along a line, it would be an important advantage that they exhibit zero-maintenance throughout its operating life. The latter characteristic is hence a must for future systems that exploit a finer granularity of distribution, together with the capability of energy harvesting to avoid cabling as much as possible.

The centralisation trends discussed above seem to contrast the advent of pervasive, distributed intelligence to support fine grained, distributed decision systems, which are instead a general trend in advanced *cyber-physical systems* to attack complexity.

Indeed, distributed decision can already be found even in old, electromechanical signalling systems: for example the Italian BACC system (Automated Coded Currents Block) [20] is intrinsically distributed. BACC is a fixed-block ATP system based on relay technology: at any border between two sections, an alternate current, with a specific code modulation, is injected on the rails in front of the coming train: the train short circuits the rails so that no current is present on the track behind it, and an on-board equipment brakes the train if no code is detected in front. The injected code at a section border is depending on the (sensed) code of the previous section, so that the code read by the train tells how many sections are actually free in front of the train. The equipment that decides the information to be injected in the rail for delivery to the train is therefore distributed in a chain on the line: in a sense, the protection algorithm is naturally geographically distributed.

3   Future Connected Trains

In this section we discuss three possible examples of innovative systems that need a wider adoption of distributed decision.

3.1   Virtual Coupling

The availability of safe information about the position, speed, acceleration and deceleration of the preceding train, like that used in ETCS Level 3 and in CBTC, inspired the idea of an innovative method of train formation, called Virtual Coupling [7,14,30]. The concept is based on the idea of multiple trains (possibly, individual self propelling units) which run one behind the other without physical contact but at a distance comparable to mechanical coupling (see Fig. 2). The strict real-time control of the dynamic parameters of the following train with respect to the parameters of the preceding one allows the distance between trains to be minimized, therefore with consequent high capacity and high flexibility, for example in the forwarding of different segments of a train to different destinations through "run-time" composition and decomposition, without stopping the train. Although it still looks like a concept far from being implemented in reality, largely for the radical innovations needed in terms of safety and operational rules, the concept, already the object of an industrial patent in the railway domain [22], inherits some of the principles of car platooning [8], that is being experimented in the automotive domain. Virtual Coupling is one of the challenges addressed in the Shift2Rail Joint Undertaking Initiative, and well represents the limits to which the technologies upon which ETCS is based can be pushed in a next future.

Notice that in Virtual Coupling the strict cross control between coupled trains has to be negotiated locally, with a train to train communication, since it requires a precision on the relative distance between the trains that cannot be supported by ETCS-like systems.

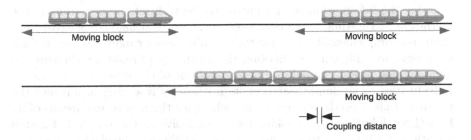

Fig. 2. The Virtual Coupling concept

3.2 Distributed Interlocking

Centralised interlockings are complex and costly to design and especially to be certified against safety guidelines. The complexity is due to the need of verifying every possible conflicting combinations of different routes through the station.

Therefore it is sensible to consider a distribution of the interlocking logic over a network of computing nodes, with a granularity pushed to the limit of one controller node for each element of the track layout. The idea of distributed interlocking has been proposed in several papers (e.g., [3,4,11]), and even patents have been issued at this regard [21,31]. In a system like this, every physical track element is equipped with a tiny computer, which knows the routes that interest the associated element, and receives and interprets route booking, release, and cancellation requests, dialoguing with the computers of adjacent elements. The overall safety of a plant of this kind can only be achieved by ensuring that the information on the routes reserved for incoming trains are properly shared in a consistent way by all distributed processors associated to the concerned elements.

A distributed mutual exclusion algorithm is played between the nodes corresponding to track elements, triggered by route requests coming from the trains or from a dispatcher [12]; the used algorithms adopted by the distributed interlocking proposals cited above differ from the point of view of the way information is allocated to nodes and trains and passed between them, but none of the proposals dares to rely directly on a distributed consensus algorithm between trains to reach a common decision about allocation of a route.

3.3   Fully Automated Train Operation

Extending the principles of ATO systems to envisage a fully automated main line train, the following principles should be considered:

– A train is given a mission in terms of:
  - starting time and location,
  - destination,
  - intermediate stops,
  - possibly, the required timetable,
  - a map of the lines to be traversed, with alternative paths if any, and with related speed limits and other local constraints.

  Whether the information is transmitted to the train at the beginning of the journey or at run-time, or section after section, or continuously asked by the train, is an implementation choice that should consider many factors, including geography, different jurisdictions, the possibility of real-time changes and different modalities adopted in different sections of the mission.
– A train tries to accomplish at best its mission by reserving in advance the resources that it needs, autonomously asking for the needed extensions of its EoA (End of Authority), or asking for the exclusive access to a route through a station or a junction to a (centralised or distributed) interlocking system.
– At any prospected conflict between trains, complex distributed consensus algorithms can be envisaged to take the role of preserving safety while optimizing resource usage and line capacity.
– A train, in case of conflict, can decide to travel through an alternative route, if available and convenient.
– The items above require the existence of (a limited set of different) standard interfaces and protocols for the exchange of information in train to infrastructure, train to train and infrastructure to infrastructure communication.
– At any time, the train can move at a maximum speed, that is below the braking curve given by the current safety envelope, and is optimal w.r.t. the objectives of timetable respect, energy efficiency, not uselessly triggering emergency brakes, etc.
– The items above related to automated driving are not safety-critical, since safety is anyway guaranteed by an underlying ATP system, such as ETCS. Different ATP systems can be however installed in different sections of the mission, and this requires adequate transition areas and mechanisms.
– At any moment, the train should release resources that were allocated to it, and have already been consumed. The sooner the resources are released, the sooner they are available to other trains, improving the capacity of the railway network. This concept is called, for interlocking system, *sequential release*. Safety concerns are raised by this issue, that should be therefore taken over by the ATP system.
– Interoperability with human-driven trains has to be guaranteed.

Again, autonomous decisions play a minor role in this picture, dominated by communication-based centralised and distributed decisions.

4   Safety Concerns

A typical concern when introducing new train control systems is that the high safety standards of railway transport are preserved.

4.1   Qualitative Safety

Safe train motion is usually defined in a qualitative manner, as the inability of a train to travel beyond a *protected point* or *EoA* (depending on the kind of of protection mechanism) established in front of the train. At any time, the span of tracks from the current train position to the protected point constitutes a *safety envelope* within which the train can freely move.

This generic notion of safety envelope has to include both the distancing from previous train (responsibility of ATP systems) along a line, and the reservation of a path in junction areas, such as stations (responsibility of interlocking). The first contribution, depending on the kind of system, is given by the number of free sections (fixed block), the distance from the preceding train (moving block), the distance and speed of the preceding train (virtual coupling). The second contribution is given by the sequence of track elements constituting the reserved route. The safety envelope can be defined as the minimum of the track spans given by these two contributions.

The guarantee of safe train motion may require other constraints as well to be satisfied by the infrastructure, such as: switches in front of the train are locked in their position so that they do not move when the train passes over them, level crossing barriers are locked in a closed position, signals show specific aspects, etc.

In general, we can look at this issue as a mutual exclusion problem: in order to proceed a train needs to have an adequate set of resources exclusively allocated to it, and the amount and characteristics of such resources define the maximum extent and speed of safe train motion. This concept is developed, limited to interlocking systems, in [12].

Notice that in such a distributed mobile system, communication timing and latencies as well as train speed have to be taken into account in the definition of the safety envelope, by adding proper safety margins that typically reduce the span of the safety envelope.

4.2   Quantitative Safety

A reference for the probabilistic quantification of safety in the railway domain is the EN50126 standard, in which functions that in case of malfunction may cause catastrophic effects are rated at SIL4 (the highest Safety Integrity Level), a level that is equated to a Tolerable Hazard Rate (THR) of 10^{-9} failures per function per operation hour.

Quantitative safety assessment should be able to provide both the probability with which a system correctly works (that is, its reliability) and the probability that the system has reacted to a possible safety threat going in a fail-safe state.

The complement of the sum of these probabilities, the unsafety, shall not exceed the THR limits defined for the SIL allocated to the function of the system. Notice that a fail-safe state in the railway signalling domain typically ends up in non providing the service, since it corresponds to some halted train, e.g. through the application of emergency braking or setting all signals to red, impacting therefore availability and capacity of the transport system (see Sect. 5.1).

Under the probabilistic perspective, considering the safety envelope concept discussed above, safety of train motion is guaranteed when it is demonstrated that the sum of the probabilities that: (i) a train goes beyond its safety envelope (e.g. the received MA), and (ii) the train is given an erroneously permissive safety envelope (e.g., a longer MA), does not exceed the THR limits.

One important aspect to be considered when distributed consensus algorithms are used for safety-critical control functions, is the fundamental result of [13]: distributed consensus cannot always be reached in presence of asynchronous, possibly faulty, communication. Evaluating the probability of not reaching consensus can provide other figures for a quantitative analysis of safety. However, the most sensible way to deal with this problem is by setting timeouts for a distributed consensus round, and to bring the system in a fail-safe state in case consensus is not reached in a useful time, again moving the problem from safety to availability.

4.3   Uncertainty

The advent of sophisticated train control system that need accurate measure of position of trains and of their speed introduce the need of coping with *uncertainty* over such measures, quantified as an error interval around the measured quantity of interest.

Uncertainty in positioning is usually managed by allowing for a longer safety margin, by assuming a maximum uncertainty threshold: in railways, positioning of a reference (say, the head) of a train is monodimensional, because it refers to a point on the line. Uncertainty makes position to stay within an interval, so safety margins have to be computed accordingly. Speed uncertainty can be handled similarly: if an error interval is known, integrating it over time gives a position uncertainty.

One cause of uncertainty of position information is given by the positioning mechanism itself. In fixed block systems, the position of a preceding train is given by the block that it currently occupies: it is not known where the train rear end actually is inside the block, and it is implicitly considered as the end of the block. In the more sophisticated positioning systems required by moving block, uncertainty is typically associated to position and speed.

A satellite positioning device, as used in avionic satellite navigation, gives, together with a position estimation a so called *protection level*, a statistical bound error computed so as to guarantee that the probability of the (unknown) real position error exceeding the protection level is smaller than or equal to a target value (called *integrity risk*). In other words, the interval (given by the protection level) around the estimated position does not contain the real position with probability less than the integrity risk. The target integrity risk can be computed in relation to the desired THR. However, a typical satellite position receiver gives a greater THR w.r.t. that of SIL4 functions, and hence sensor fusion with other odometry devices is needed to lower the THR [25].

A tramway application of these principles is reported in this volume [6], where statistical model checking is used to analysing safety-critical scenarios.

Delays in communication and the periodic, rather than continuous, nature of communications introduce another source of uncertainty: timestamps and time-out mechanisms are used in ETCS to prevent impact on safety of a missing or out-of-time MA reception, stopping the train when given uncertainty thresholds are passed (see Sect. 5.1)

4.4   Security for Safety

A further challenging aspect related to the integrity of exchanged vital data is *security*, that is the absence of intrusion by a third party to fraudulently take control of the functions of a system. This becomes increasingly important as the communication is based on open protocols at some level (internet, wireless, ...): since there is the trend to keep communication costs to an acceptable level by recurring at open protocols and media, it is believed that this aspect is by far the greatest concern for the deployment of the signalling systems whose safety is based on communication, in which security has a direct impact on the integrity of vital information.

The CENELEC standard EN50159, as well as recent developments in security and encryption techniques, attempt to mitigate this concern: the so called *cyber-physical security* research area, addressing other domains both in transportation and other pervasive computing applications, has produced also results for the railway signalling domain. Safety critical applications typically employ protection w.r.t. random corruption of communications or data, that can be strong enough to resist basic attacks. More sophisticated attacks can be countered by standard security countermeasures, which are actually used in nowadays communication-based systems: [23] shows the unfeasibility, on costs basis, of a serious attack to ETCS safety-critical communications. Security of the ETCS train to trackside protocols has been formally analysed using the ProVerif tool in [26]. [9,24] discuss how the IEC62443 standard for security of industrial automation and control systems can be applied to the railway domain by codesign of safety and security features.

A general message from this body of literature is that it is currently possible to adopt security countermeasures that make security attacks (such as counterfeiting plausible MA) with catastrophic consequences very unlikely. Rather, more concern is raised about the possibility of denying communication, which may trigger emergency braking and extensive denial of service.

On the other hand, it is not simple to give a probabilistic measure of the contribution of security issues to safety: such a measure should be obtained on the basis of assumptions on the frequency of intrusion by third parties, as well as on the basis of the capacity of the security mechanisms to counter them. Sanders in [27] discusses some possible tools and methods for quantitative predictive assessment of security for large-scale systems.

An interesting intertwining of safety and security is a recently advanced proposal of employing blockchain technology for railway control [17]. Blockchain is actually an example of distributed consensus algorithm, by which several peers agree in a secure way on some shared information. In this case, tracks or route reservation is the shared information on which involved trains are competing and need to find a consensus. This proposals is claimed to smoothly support correct accounting of infrastructure usage by train operators as well. In order for such technology to gain actual acceptance, a serious analysis of safety issues related to the probability that the consensus is not reached is needed.

4.5 Software

We deliberately leave out of this discussion software issues. It is well known that software is typically plagued with faults that can have catastrophic consequences, and that giving a quantitative evaluation of software reliability is not feasible for the required safety level. For the purpose of this paper, we assume that safety-critical software is developed and certified at SIL4 level according to EN50128 standard. We strongly advocate the adoption of formal methods in a roadmap for "zero-defect" software, in a trend championed by Shift2Rail in several projects [5].

5 Autonomy as a Mean to Performability of Automated Operation

In a parallel with the automotive domain, and inheriting autonomous cars technology, another direction of innovation is to move more and more intelligence onboard trains, to let them take autonomous decisions, with little help of ground-based infrastructure. However, the physics of train motion, that requires long stretches of free track to attain high speeds, limits the actual possibility to adopt autonomy in train control.

5.1 Performability, Availability, Capacity

As indicated by Shift2Rail [29], the primary objectives of introducing technological advances in train traffic control are not only related to an increase in the already very high safety standards of railway safety, but especially to preserve such standards while dramatically improving KPIs such as performability (often intended as adherence to expected timetables), availability of transport service and transport capacity, all attributes that in computer science terms could be tagged as "liveness properties", that often conflict with safety objectives.

On the other hand, the large number of critical computing components and the complexity of distributed algorithms increase the number of cases in which the failure of one component can bring to a fail-safe halt of a system, causing the partial or full unavailability of transport service. High reliability of each component is hence a must.

This effect is worsened by the number of communication links employed in these systems: typically, the safety layers of the communication protocols adopted in these systems exploit the principle of *positive* control to allow movement of trains: the train cannot move if no explicit consensus or MA has been received. Any serious transmission error (that is, persistent over a given period of time) eventually leads to a fail-safe state. A careful evaluation of safety characteristics of a modern, complex, signalling system cannot therefore ignore an adequate analysis of availability attributes, in order to ensure an appropriate transport capacity, with the related operation cost effectiveness, through techniques of quantitative evaluation of these attributes [28].

The already cited uncertainty sources, with the related increase in safety margins, constitute another limiting factor to capacity. A more subtle phenomenon observed in radio-based train control, such as ETCS or CBTC systems, is the indeterminate delay time in message transmission experienced when multiple trains require movement authorities and the available bandwidth of the communication link is not sufficient to guarantee correct end-to-end transmission in due time. Retries tend to clog even more the link, with the fail-safe halt as ultimate consequence. Quantitative modelling and evaluation of the ERTMS Euroradio protocol by means of Petri Net models has been studied by several authors [10,32].

5.2 Autonomy in Degraded Modes

According to what we have seen, due to the strong infrastructure-based nature of railways, autonomy would appear not to have a main role in the future of train control systems. However, in future fully automated train driving (as described in Sect. 3.3) the possibility of taking autonomous decisions in place of the driver will be essential. We briefly discuss a couple of scenarios of this kind. In both scenarios, the safety envelope in front of the train is not negotiated with the infrastructure or with other trains, but is autonomously determined.

Degraded Modes of Operation. The first scenario considers that, in order to allow trains to proceed even when a threat to safety does not allow full performance, ETCS defines degraded modes of operation, to be entered when the "Full Supervision" mode (the normal mode of operation, as described above) is no longer supported by the system, e.g., when connection is lost, and in which more responsibility is given to the driver, in different operational scenarios: Limited Supervision, Staff Responsible, OnSight, Shunting are the most relevant ones.

When an ATO system is substituting the driver, it should be able to cope with degraded modes, with no connection with any RBC or other external supervising entity. An autonomous driving system equipped with obstacle detection sensors and artificial vision may play the role of the driver, moving the train at reduced speed according to the operational procedures that are foreseen for the OnSight mode, trying to switch back to Full Supervision as soon as connection is recovered.

Light Rail Autonomous Vehicles. Tramways and light rail vehicles normally use little signalling, and safety is for most part responsibility of the human driver (on-sight driving). In this sector obstacle detection and artificial vision techniques inherited by the automotive domain, together with connection to control centers and train to train communication may be used to substitute the human driver. Autonomous trams experiments of this kind have already be shown at the last Innotrans fair [1].

A sensitive issue on autonomous driving is that advanced capabilities of autonomous decisions (such as artificial vision systems) are often based on Artificial Intelligence techniques that are not easily certifiable with a deterministic approach based on testing or formal verification, and indeed appear to be banned as *Not Recommended* by EN 50128. Possibly, the widespread adoption in automotive applications will favour the acceptance of these techniques as "proven in use" software, especially considering that trains move in a much more predictable environment than cars, hence favouring reliability of machine learning techniques.

6   Conclusions

We have shown how the state of the art of railway signalling technology envisages *connected trains* at a much more advanced point w.r.t what is current practice in the automotive domain, due to the wide instrumentation of infrastructure, and how this scenario is going to evolve when more and more automation is introduced in next generation systems. On the other hand, autonomy lags behind, but autonomous decision can take a prominent role in degraded operation, in order to improve performance of railway also in cases of safety and security threats.

In the discussion, a series of concepts that constitute open research questions have been put forward at several levels:

- distributed mutual exclusion, consensus and control algorithms;
- high reliability, zero-maintenance, low-cost, low-power computing elements;
- switch to a safety paradigm based on a real-time definition of a safety envelope in front of the train, subject to uncertainty;
- formal methods for software development;
- safety certification of AI software;
- cybersecurity issues;
- quantitative analysis of "liveness" KPIs;
- application of full autonomous driving in specific contexts.

The paper was not intended to be an exhaustive survey of the most advanced railway signalling technologies, but has only referred to some notable examples.

Several other systems have raised an important body of literature: just to name some, the ETCS variants CTCS and ETCS L3 Hybrid. We have also ignored many secondary, mostly onboard, safety-critical features, such as precise platform berthing, door opening control, speed sensors (odometry), train integrity monitors, where local autonomous decisions are favoured over communication-based ones.

As usual in the railway domain, we have assumed a conservative approach to define the safety of a railway system, according to the prescriptions of the EN5012x norms, that favour a neat separation between "liveness" and safety functions, so that the high necessary certification efforts and costs can be concentrated on the latter: less conservative approaches that collectively look at all dependability aspects are an active theoretical research area, as seen in this volume [16].

Acknowledgments. Thanks to Stefania Gnesi for her useful comments on a draft of this paper.

Work partially supported by the H2020 Shift2Rail-RIA-777561 project ASTRail and by Tuscany Region project POR FESR 2014-2020 SISTER.

References

1. Siemens mobility presents worlds first autonomous tram, 3 September 2018. https://www.siemens.com/press/en/pressrelease/?press=/en/pressrelease/2018/mobility/pr2018090290moen.htm
2. Rio Tinto completes autohaul autonomous train project, 4 January 2019. https://www.railwaygazette.com/news/news/australasia/single-view/view/rio-tinto-completes-autohaul-autonomous-train-project.html
3. Haxthausen, A.E., Peleska, J.: Formal development and verification of a distributed railway control system. IEEE Trans. Softw. Eng. **26**(8), 687–701 (2000). https://doi.org/10.1109/32.879808
4. Banci, M., Fantechi, A., Gnesi, S.: The role of formal methods in developing a distribuited railway interlocking system. In: Proceedings of Formal Methods for Automation and Safety in Railway and Automotive Systems, FORMS/FORMAT, Braunschweig, Germany, pp. 79–91 (2004)
5. Basile, D., et al.: On the industrial uptake of formal methods in the railway domain. In: Furia, C.A., Winter, K. (eds.) IFM 2018. LNCS, vol. 11023, pp. 20–29. Springer, Cham (2018). https://doi.org/10.1007/978-3-319-98938-9_2
6. Basile, D., Fantechi, A., Rucher, L., Mandò, G.: Statistical model checking of hazards in an autonomous tramway positioning system. In: Collart-Dutilleul, S., et al. (eds.) RSSRail 2019. LNCS, vol. 11495, pp. 41–58 (2019)
7. Bergenhem, C., Pettersson, H., Coelingh, E., Englund, C., Shladover, S., Tsugawa, S.: Overview of platooning systems. In: 19th ITS World Congress, Vienna, Austria (2012)
8. Bock, U., Bikker, G.: Design and development of a future freight train concept - virtually coupled train formations. In: 9th IFAC Symposium Control in Transportation Systems. IFAC, Braunschweig (2000)
9. Braband, J.: It security framework for safe railway automation. In: Mahboob, Q., Zio, E. (eds.) RAMS in Railway Systems, pp. 393–402. CRC Press (2018)

10. Carnevali, L., Flammini, F., Paolieri, M., Vicario, E.: Non-markovian performability evaluation of ERTMS/ETCS level 3. In: Beltrán, M., Knottenbelt, W., Bradley, J. (eds.) EPEW 2015. LNCS, vol. 9272, pp. 47–62. Springer, Cham (2015). https://doi.org/10.1007/978-3-319-23267-6_4

11. Fantechi, A., Gnesi, S., Haxthausen, A., van de Pol, J., Roveri, M., Treharne, H.: SaRDIn - a safe reconfigurable distributed interlocking. In: Proceedings 11th World Congress on Railway Research, WCRR, Ferrovie dello Stato Italiane, Milano (2016)

12. Fantechi, A., Haxthausen, A.E.: Safety interlocking as a distributed mutual exclusion problem. In: Howar, F., Barnat, J. (eds.) FMICS 2018. LNCS, vol. 11119, pp. 52–66. Springer, Cham (2018). https://doi.org/10.1007/978-3-030-00244-2_4

13. Fischer, M.J., Lynch, N.A., Paterson, M.: Impossibility of distributed consensus with one faulty process. J. ACM **32**(2), 374–382 (1985). https://doi.org/10.1145/3149.214121

14. Flammini, F., Marrone, S., Nardone, R., Petrillo, A., Santini, S., Vittorini, V.: Towards railway virtual coupling. In: International Transportation Electrification Conference (ITEC). IEEE, Nottingham, UK (2018). https://doi.org/10.1109/ESARS-ITEC.2018.8607523

15. Vehicular technology society: 1474.1 - standard for communications- based train control (CBTC) - performance and functional requirements. IEEE (2004)

16. Karra, S.L., Larsen, K.G., Lorber, F., Srba, J.: Safe and time-optimal control for railway games. In: Collart-Dutilleul, S., et al. (eds.) RSSRail 2019. LNCS, vol. 11495, pp. 106–122 (2019)

17. Kuperberg, M., Kindler, D., Jeschke, S.: Are smart contracts and blockchains suitable for decentralized railway control? CoRR abs/1901.06236 (2019)

18. Lecomte, T., Pinger, R., Romanovsky, A.B. (eds.): Reliability, safety, and security of railway systems. modelling, analysis, verification, and certification. In: Proceedings of First International Conference, RSSRail 2016, Paris, France, 28–30 June, 2016, LNCS, vol. 9707. Springer (2016). https://doi.org/10.1007/978-3-319-33951-1

19. Macedo, H.D., Fantechi, A., Haxthausen, A.E.: Compositional model checking of interlocking systems for lines with multiple stations. In: Barrett, C., Davies, M., Kahsai, T. (eds.) NFM 2017. LNCS, vol. 10227, pp. 146–162. Springer, Cham (2017). https://doi.org/10.1007/978-3-319-57288-8_11

20. Mayer, L., Guida, P.L., Milizia, E.: Impianti Ferroviari. CIFI (2016)

21. Michaut, P.: Method for managing the circulation of vehicles on a railway network and related system. Patent US 8820685, B2 (2014)

22. Ohmstede, H.: Method for reducing data in railway operation. Patent US 7578485 (2009)

23. Pépin, F., Vigliotti, M.G.: Risk assessment of the 3Des in ERTMS. In: Lecomte et al. [18], pp. 79–92 (2016). https://doi.org/10.1007/978-3-319-33951-1_6

24. Ponsard, C., Grandclaudon, J., Massonet, P., Touzani, M.: Assessment of emerging standards for safety and security co-design on a railway case study. In: Abdelwahed, E.H., et al. (eds.) MEDI 2018. CCIS, vol. 929, pp. 130–145. Springer, Cham (2018). https://doi.org/10.1007/978-3-030-02852-7_12

25. Rispoli, F., Neri, A., Stallo, C., Salvatori, P., Santucci, F.: Synergies for trains and cars automation in the era of virtual networking. J. Transp. Technol. **8**, 175–193 (2018). https://doi.org/10.4236/jtts.2018.83010

26. de Ruiter, J., Thomas, R.J., Chothia, T.: A formal security analysis of ERTMS train to trackside protocols. In: Lecomte, T., Pinger, R., Romanovsky, A. (eds.) RSSRail 2016. LNCS, vol. 9707, pp. 53–68. Springer, Cham (2016). https://doi.org/10.1007/978-3-319-33951-1_4

27. Sanders, W.H.: Quantitative security metrics: unattainable holy grail or a vital breakthrough within our reach? IEEE Secur. Priv. **12**(2), 67–69 (2014). https://doi.org/10.1109/MSP.2014.31

28. Schulz, O., Peleska, J.: Reliability analysis of safety-related communication architectures. In: Schoitsch, E. (ed.) SAFECOMP 2010. LNCS, vol. 6351, pp. 1–14. Springer, Heidelberg (2010). https://doi.org/10.1007/978-3-642-15651-9_1

29. Shift2Rail Joint Undertaking: Multi-annual action plan, November 2015. http://ec.europa.eu/research/participants/data/ref/h2020/other/wp/jtis/h2020-maap-shift2rail_en.pdf

30. UIC: Virtually coupled trains. http://www.railway-energy.org/static/Virtually_coupled_trains_86.php. Accessed 24 Feb 2019

31. Whitwam, F., Kanner, A.: Control of automatic guided vehicles without wayside interlocking. Patent US 20120323411, A1 (2012)

32. Zimmermann, A., Hommel, G.: Towards modeling and evaluation of ETCS real-time communication and operation. J. Syst. Softw. **77**(1), 47–54 (2005). https://doi.org/10.1016/j.jss.2003.12.039

Railways System and Infrastructure Advance Modelling

Towards a Tool-Based Domain Specific Approach for Railway Systems Modeling and Validation

Akram Idani[1,2(✉)], Yves Ledru[1,2], Abderrahim Ait Wakrime[2],
Rahma Ben Ayed[2], and Philippe Bon[2,3]

[1] Univ. Grenoble Alpes, Grenoble INP, CNRS, LIG, 38000 Grenoble, France
{Akram.Idani,Yves.Ledru}@imag.fr
[2] Institut de Recherche Technologique Railenium, 59300 Famars, France
{abderrahim.ait-wakrime,rahma.ben-ayed}@railenium.eu
[3] Univ Lille Nord de France, IFSTTAR, COSYS, ESTAS,
59650 Villeneuve d'Ascq, France
philippe.bon@ifsttar.fr

Abstract. In the railway field, graphical representations of domain concepts are omnipresent thanks to their ability to share standardized information with common knowledge about several railway mechanisms: track circuits, signalling rules... This paper proposes a domain specific approach for railway systems modeling and validation by combining the Model-Driven Engineering (MDE) paradigm and a formal method. First, an example of a graphical DSL is defined thanks to MDE tools, and then the formal B method is used to define its underlying operational semantics and to guarantee the correctness of the model's behaviour with respect to its safety properties. Our approach is assisted by the Meeduse tool which animates and visualizes execution scenarios of domain models. Starting from a given model designed in the DSL tool, Meeduse asks ProB to animate B operations and gets the reached state by means of B variables valuations. Then, it translates back these valuations to the initial DSL resulting in automatic modifications of the domain model. Our approach allows a more pragmatic domain-centric animation than current visual animation techniques since the resulting DSL tool allows domain experts, who are not necessarily trained in formal methods, to design and validate by themselves the various domain models.

Keywords: MDE · DSL · Formal methods · Visual animation

1 Introduction

In railway control and safety systems, the application of formal methods is becoming a strong requirement as recommended by CENELEC EN 50128 standard[1]. However, while formal methods provide solutions to the verification problem, human errors may lead to erroneously validate the specification, and hence

---

[1] https://standards.globalspec.com/std/13113133/en-50129.

© Springer Nature Switzerland AG 2019
S. Collart-Dutilleul et al. (Eds.): RSSRail 2019, LNCS 11495, pp. 23–40, 2019.
https://doi.org/10.1007/978-3-030-18744-6_2

to produce the wrong system. Indeed, even if formal proofs succeed, a formal specification can be wrong for two main reasons [7]: misunderstandings of the users needs or errors in the expression of these needs. In order to deal with these shortcomings, several formal tools provide graphic animation and visualization techniques [8,14,17] which help in the exploration of alternative behaviors in a step-by-step approach. This technique favours the communication between a formal methods engineer and the domain expert by using domain specific visualizations which is crucial during the validation activity.

Unfortunately, mapping a given graphical representation to the formal specification is a rather time-consuming task (several days or several weeks) and the creation of custom visualizations is often done when the formal model reaches an advanced stage during the modeling process. This is counterproductive since the identification of misunderstandings often leads to enhancements of the formal specifications which in turn impacts the implementation of the visualization. Furthermore, the domain specific visualizations are created by the formal methods engineer who would like to remedy the poor readability of his own specifications and hence, the resulting visualizations may lack of real-user perspective. In [3], Bjørner states that *before we can formulate requirements, we must understand the [application] domain*, meaning that domain specific representations are required before starting to think about formal models. In a pragmatic approach, these representations should be provided by the domain expert who has a greater knowledge of the application domain than the formal methods engineer.

In the railway domain, specific representations (textual or graphical) of domain concepts are omnipresent thanks to their ability to share standardized information with common knowledge about several railway mechanisms: track circuits, signalling rules, interlocking systems... Nowadays, there are more and more attempts to define DSL tools [12,20,22], based on these specific representations, allowing the domain expert himself to provide useful models to the software system engineer. In this paper, we propose a formal tool-based domain specific approach that defines a DSL for railroad topologies with a concrete graphical syntax and associated formal semantics. The DSL tool is developed in a well-known Model Driven Engineering paradigm (MDE) based on EMF [19] and it is intended to be used by the domain expert in order to design interesting business models. The formal part of our approach is assisted by the Meeduse tool[2] which automatically translates the DSL meta-model into an equivalent B specification [1] gathering the structure of the meta-model as well as basic operations like constructors, destructors, getters and setters. The operational semantics of the DSL are then defined using the formal B method which guarantees the correctness of the model's behavior with respect to its invariant properties. Meeduse allows the animation of underlying execution scenarios using the ProB tool [16]. Starting from a given business model, it asks ProB to animate B operations and retrieves the reached state by means of B variables valuations. Then, Meeduse translates back these valuations to the initial DSL resulting in automatic modifications of

---

[2] http://vasco.imag.fr/tools/meeduse/.

the business model which gives rise to a more pragmatic domain-centric animation than current visual animation techniques.

Section 2 provides the static semantics of a railroad DSL done thanks to the MDE paradigm. In Sect. 3, we show how our DSL is enhanced by a formal specification in order to define its operational semantics. Finally Sect. 5 draws the conclusions and the perspectives of this work.

2   A Simple Railroad DSL

The adoption of model-driven engineering (MDE) paradigms in industry is increasing because MDE is assisted by numerous tools for creating and exploiting domain models such as: EMF[3], Xtext[4], Sirius[5], GMF[6], ... These tools had several successful applications thanks to the solutions they provide for rapid-prototyping of DSLs. The application of MDE in order to define DSLs for railway systems promotes readability of these systems and enables stakeholders without experience in programming or formal languages, like certification authorities, to create the models as long as they possess domain knowledge. In MDE, the definition of a DSL follows three steps:

1. The definition of model's semantics via a meta-model which is a central arte-fact because it allows interoperability between tools such as language analysers (*e.g.* Xtext [2]), code generators (*e.g.* Acceleo [6]), and also model transformation tools (*e.g.* ATL [13]);
2. The expression of contextual constraints using the OCL language in order to enhance the DSL semantics with invariant properties which are not covered structurally by the meta-model;
3. The creation of a palette of concrete syntax elements (textual or graphical) and their relationships with the meta-model.

2.1   Meta-model Definition

Figure 1 gives a simplified meta-model of a DSL dedicated to railroad topologies and signalling systems. The DSL features three main concepts: trains (class Train), sections of a railway track (class Portion), and train movement authority (class MA) which are authorizations given to a train in order to move to a given portion. In this paper, we make some simplifying assumptions such as association between Train and Portion considering that a train occupies a single portion, and then the whole train moves instantly from one portion to another. We also assume that switches move instantly (in practice, this takes about ten seconds). These simplifications do not impact our approach and one could lift them at the price of a more complicated model.

---

[3] EMF: https://www.eclipse.org/modeling/emf/.
[4] Xtext: https://www.eclipse.org/Xtext/.
[5] https://www.obeo.fr/fr/produits/Eclipse-sirius.
[6] http://www.Eclipse.org/modeling/gmp/.

Classes Light and AutoTrStop define a signalling equipment with traffic lights (in state on or off) and automatic train stop mechanisms which may be armed or disarmed. These devices are associated to the portion where they are located.

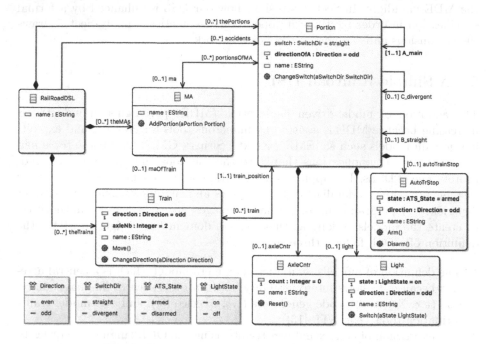

Fig. 1. Simplified meta-model of the RailRoad DSL

2.2   Concrete Syntax Definition

There exists several tools dedicated to the instantiation of meta-models. In this work we used Sirius[7] because its main advantage in comparison with other EMF-based modeling tools is its facility to define conditional styles with an OCL-like syntax. For example, the color representation of a portion would depend on three states like presented in Fig. 2: free, reserved or occupied. States, free and occupied depend on the presence or not of a train over the portion. A portion is called reserved as soon as it is concerned by a movement authority.

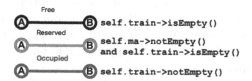

Fig. 2. Portion representations depending on OCL expressions

---

[7] https://www.obeo.fr/fr/produits/Eclipse-sirius.

The proposed concrete syntax of our Railroad DSL is inspired by graphical representations that we found in several references [9,23,24]. Figure 3 is a snapshot of the resulting DSL tool showing a railroad under construction by a domain expert where five track sections are being assembled.

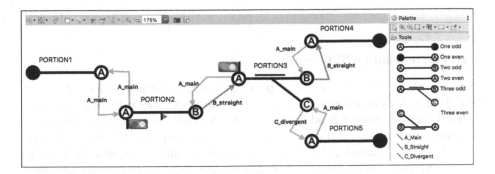

Fig. 3. Railroad under construction in a domain-specific syntax

The meta-model defines three kinds of portions depending on values of associations A_main, B_straight and C_divergent. The first kind of portions represents railroad extremities (*e.g.* portions 1, 4 and 5) and they refer only to their next portion through relation A_main. The second kind is a middle horizontal portion like portion 2 that refers to both main and straight portions by means of relations A_main and B_straight. Finally, the third kind of portions deals with switches such as portion 3 which divides into two: track B (linked to the straight portion) and track C (linked to the diverging portion). The horizontal line represents the state of the switch, pointing towards the straight (B) or diverging (C) end. It depends on values of attribute switch in class Portion. In the case of portion 3, this attribute is set to straight. Two traffic lights are introduced in this model in order to control the access to portions 2 and 3. Their graphical concrete representations depend on values of attributes state (on or off) and direction (even or odd) defined in class Light. An automatic train stop (ATS) device is also positioned on portion 2 and it is by default disarmed.

Track layout of Fig. 4 is the final model issued from Fig. 3 after hiding portion connections and where two trains, T1 and T2, are positioned respectively on portions 1 and 5. In this example, the travelling directions are odd for T1 and even for T2. Note that directions of trains and portions are independent; they don't impact each other. However, the directions of lights are relevant for train movements. Indeed, trains are concerned by lights which are oriented in the same travelling direction.

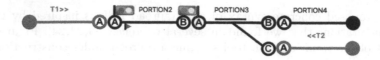

Fig. 4. A simple railroad model with two trains (Color figure online)

2.3   Contextual OCL Constraints

Meta-models are not powerful enough to represent all static semantics of a given DSL. In fact, they define context-free models which are models without any other restrictions than those defined in the meta-model and hence these models are not necessary conformant to the well-definedness rules required by the application context. In our example, the usage context of a railroad requires that tracks follow some rules such as the absence of holes, etc. In order to enhance the static semantics of our DSL, we use the OCL language which is integrated within EMF thanks to the OCLinEcore tool. Our OCL rules deal only with structural aspects of railroads, and basically they define how portions must be linked to each others. Three main invariants are defined depending on portion kinds: `AMainPortion`, `BStraightPortion` and `CDivergentPortion`.

Every portion has a successor portion (called main portion) with respect to association `A_main` in the meta-model of Fig. 1. Invariant `AMainPortion` is the well-definedness rule of this association and assesses that given two portions P1 and P2 such that P2 is the main portion of P1, then if P1 and P2 have opposite directions, then P1 must be also the main portion of P2, otherwise P1 is the straight or the divergent portion of P2. In Fig. 3 for example, PORTION1 and PORTION2 have opposite directions then every portion is the main portion of the other. Based on the same example, PORTION3 is the main portion of portions PORTION4 and PORTION5 and such that the three portions have the same direction, then none of PORTION4 and PORTION5 is the main portion of PORTION3.

```
Context Portion inv AMainPortion:
    (A_main.direction <> {direction} implies A_main.A_main = {self}) and
    (A_main.direction = {direction} implies
              A_main.B_straight = {self} or A_main.C_divergent = {self})
```

Invariants `BStraightPortion` and `CDivergentPortion` define rules for associations `B_straight` and `C_divergent`. They allow to strengthen invariant `AMainPortion` for portions which are not linked via association `A_main`. For example, if two portions P1 and P2 have opposite directions and such that P2 is the straight or the divergent portion of P1 then P1 must be either the straight or the divergent portion of P2.

```
Context Portion inv BStraightPortion:
self.B_straight -> notEmpty() implies
```

```
(B_straight.direction <> {direction} implies
    B_straight.B_straight = {self} or B_straight.C_divergent = {self})
and (B_straight.direction = {direction} implies A_main.A_main = {self})
Context Portion inv CDivergentPortion:
self.C_divergent -> notEmpty() implies
    (C_divergent.direction <> {direction} implies
        C_divergent.B_straight = {self} or C_divergent.C_divergent = {self})
    and (C_divergent.direction = {direction} implies A_main.A_main = {self})
```

The EMF platform provides a validation mechanism that checks OCL invariants provided a given input model. Figure 4 is a valid model with respect to the above invariants. This validation is interesting for the domain expert who defines informally the various management rules and who becomes able thanks to the tool to check their validity on his own models. Note that railway domain experts are not intended to write OCL expressions by themselves. In fact, the DSL tool development is the task of MDE experts who has the ability to define metamodels with associated static constraints.

2.4 Discussion

This section has shown how the MDE paradigm with associated tools is applied in order to develop a DSL for the railway domain. At this stage we didn't yet start the creation of a formal model contrary to classical techniques where the development process starts by a formal language. Our approach starts by the definition of a DSL tool like that presented in this section which allows to efficiently involve the domain expert in the development process.

Thanks to the DSL tool, the domain expert becomes able to provide various domain representations (*e.g.* Figs. 4 and 5) and also to check whether the associated contextual rules are respected or not. For example, based on the model of Fig. 4, the domain expert can informally explain that if a train T1 is located on PORTION1, it cannot move to PORTION2 due to the red light. This would allow an other train T2 located on PORTION5 to go to PORTION4 after crossing first PORTION3 and next PORTION2 where it will be able to change its direction. The straight direction of the switch allows T2 to reach PORTION4 when it comes from PORTION2. If train T1 violates the red signal the ATS should be armed automatically and the train will be stopped over PORTION2.

In general, movements of trains are more difficult to represent than this simple informal description, because in addition to the complexity of realistic railway track layouts (like that of Fig. 5) and the corresponding signalling systems, they also refer to movement authority given by traffic agents to the train drivers. In order to play useful scenarios from a domain-centric point of view, the DSL must be enhanced by behavioural aspects showing how routes are assigned to trains and how these trains can move in a safe (or unsafe) way.

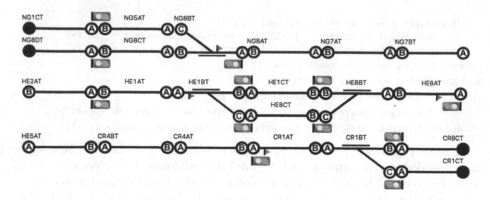

Fig. 5. Realistic example inspired by [24] (Color figure online)

3   Formal Operational Semantics

Operational semantics of our DSL are structured into several formal models which are linked using the inclusion mechanism of the B method: (*i*) a functional model which is automatically extracted from the meta-model, (*ii*) a safety-free model in which train accidents may happen, and (*iii*) a safe model applying authorization rules in order to control the train movements and avoid critical situations.

Our approach, summarized by Fig. 6, first translates the meta-model into a functional formal B specification using a UML-to-B transformation technique [10]. Then starting from a given instance of this meta-model, we apply the Meeduse tool in order to animate domain-centric scenarios based on the operational semantics defined in the formal models. The tool injects any valid instance of a meta-model into the functional specification by applying valuations to its variables. In Meeduse, animation of B specifications is done using the ProB tool [16]. Meeduse asks ProB to animate B operations and gets the new variable valuations and then it translates back these valuations to the initial graphical model

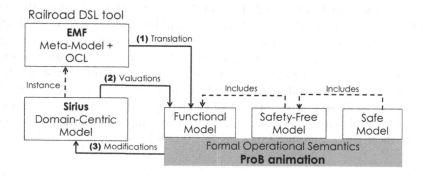

Fig. 6. Overall methodology

resulting in an automatic visual animation. Demonstration videos of Meeduse with graphical and textual DSL animation can be found at: http://vasco.imag.fr/tools/meeduse/.

3.1 Functional Formal Model

In this step we use the B4MSecure platform [10] which translates the structural aspects of the meta-model as follows:

- A meta-class *Class* gives an abstract set named *CLASS* representing possible instances and a variable named *Class* representing the set of existing instances such that existing instances belong to the set of possible instances.
- An enumeration is translated into a enumerated set (*e.g.* LightState).
- Basic types (*e.g.* integer, boolean) become B types (Z, Bool, . . .).
- Attributes and references lead to functional relations.

Figure 7 shows the declarative part of the B specification extracted from classes Train, Portion as well as the association between these classes. In this specification single valuated features are represented by partial or total functions with respect to their optional/mandatory character. For example, the **A_main** feature of a portion is single-valued and mandatory (it leads to a total function) contrary to features **B_straight** and **C_divergent** which are optional (they lead to partial functions).

MACHINE
  Functional
SETS
  PORTION ; *TRAIN* ;
  SwitchDir = { *straight, divergent* } ;
  Direction = { *even, odd* } ;
VARIABLES
  Portion, Train,
  TrainOfPortion,
  Portion_switch,
  Portion_directionOfA,
  Portion_A_main,
  Portion_B_straight,
  Portion_C_divergent,
  Train_direction

INVARIANT
  $Portion \in \mathcal{F}\ (PORTION) \wedge$
  $Train \in \mathcal{F}\ (TRAIN) \wedge$
  $TrainOfPortion \in Train \rightarrow Portion \wedge$
  $Portion\_switch \in Portion \nrightarrow SwitchDir \wedge$
  $Portion\_directionOfA \in Portion \rightarrow Direction \wedge$
  $Portion\_A\_main \in Portion \rightarrow Portion \wedge$
  $Portion\_B\_straight \in Portion \nrightarrow Portion \wedge$
  $Portion\_C\_divergent \in Portion \nrightarrow Portion \wedge$
  $Train\_direction \in Train \rightarrow Direction$

Fig. 7. Subset of the generated functional machine

The behavioural part of the functional B machine provides all basic operations such as getters, setters, constructors and destructors. For example, operation **Train_SetTrain_position** of Fig. 8 is the basic setter of feature **train_position** associated to class Train in the meta-model. This operation

```
Train_SetTrain_position(aTrain, aTrain_position) =
  PRE
      aTrain ∈ Train ∧
      aTrain_position ∈ Portion ∧
      {(aTrain ↦ aTrain_position)} ⊈ TrainOfPortion
  THEN
      TrainOfPortion := ({aTrain} ◁ TrainOfPortion)
                        ∪ {(aTrain ↦ aTrain_position)}
  END
```

Fig. 8. B Setter of feature `train_position` in class Train

puts a train (parameter `aTrain`) on any portion (parameter `aTrain_position`) provided that the portion is different from the current train position.

From our meta-model, B4MSecure produced a B specification whose length is about 900 lines with 29 variables, 73 operations for which the Atelier B prover generated 127 proof obligations that it was able to prove automatically. In fact, operations produced by B4MSecure are correct by construction with respect to the typing invariants generated automatically from the meta-model structure. The introduction of additional invariants requires improvements of operations that may violate them. There are two kinds of invariants: those about the railroad topology, and those that deal with train movements. In this work it is not necessary to use B in order to specify the well-definedness rules like those expressed in OCL. Indeed, our formal operational semantics focus on train behaviours which are operations that don't modify the railroad topology. As domain models are provided by the domain expert and validated thanks to the EMF validation mechanism based on OCL constraints, we have the guarantee that trains would not move over deficient railroads and hence we choose to keep this functional B machine as simple as possible. Train behaviours will be specified together with their corresponding invariants in the two other formal specifications defining the DSL operational semantics. The functional machine provides, on the one hand, data structures which conform to the meta-model and, on the other hand, utility operations useful for the definition of train routes and movements. Portions where accidents happen are defined by reference `accidents` in the meta-model and the corresponding B structure is variable `Portion_accidents` defined as: $Portion\_accidents \subseteq Portion$. Operation `Portion_SetAccidents` is its basic update operation (Fig. 9):

```
Portion_SetAccidents(theAccidents) =
  PRE theAccidents ∈ F (Portion)
     THEN Portion_Accidents := theAccidents
  END
```

Fig. 9. B Setter for accidents

3.2   Safety-Free Formal Model

In general, the safety of a railway system is defined by a set of operating rules that must be followed by railway agents, like stopping the train when the light is red. Unfortunately several real situations show that human errors (accidental or intentional) can lead to rule violations and hence to accidents. The safety-free operational semantics address behaviours which are uniquely governed by the laws of physics. For example, if physical devices, like ATS in our DSL, are not actioned in order to block a train, then the train has the ability to move and may induce accidents. We define the following B operations:

- **Portion_ChangeSwitch**: given a portion *aPortion* with a switch like POR-TION3 in Fig. 4 (*i.e. aPortion* $\in$ *dom(Portion_C_Divergent)*), this operation changes the switch direction (straight or divergent), or leads to an accident if the portion is occupied (*TrainOfPortion*$^{-1}$[{*aPortion*}] $\neq \emptyset$). Figure 10 shows the effect of this operation on PORTION3 starting from two different initial states: free and occupied by train T1.
- **Train_ChangeDirection**: changes the direction of a train *aTrain* from even to odd and vice-versa, or produces an accident if the train is located on a switch portion (*TrainOfPortion*(*aTrain*) $\in$ *dom(Portion_C_Divergent)*). Our DSL semantics assume that it is dangerous to change the direction of a train on a switch. A safe scenario is when the train leaves the switch portion before it changes its direction, otherwise an accident happens.
- **MA_AddPortion**: adds a movement authority *aMA* to a portion *aPortion* provided that the portion is not already concerned by a movement authority (*PortionMA*[{*aPortion*}] $= \emptyset$)[8]. Considering that *aMA* is linked to one train, this operation is useful in order to create train routes.
- **Light_Switch**: switches a light from red to green and vice-versa.
- **AutoTrStop_Arm**: arms and disarms an ATS.
- **Train_Move**: moves a train from a portion P1 to a portion P2 provided that P1 is not concerned by an accident and also the ATS (if it exists) of P2 is disarmed. This operation may produce accidents in two cases: derailment if the train tries to leave a track extremity in the wrong direction, or collision if the train enters on a portion occupied by an other train.

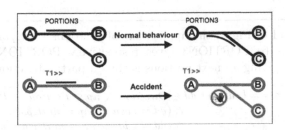

Fig. 10. Animation of operation *Portion_ChangeSwitch(PORTION3)* (Color figure online)

---

[8] *PortionMA* is a partial function mapped from the association between classes MA and Portion.

For space reasons, in the following we'll focus only on the specification of operation **Train_Move**. Given a train $aTrain$ ($aTrain \in Train$), this operation is feasible under two preconditions:

Precondition (Pre$_1$): the current portion is not concerned by an accident, *i.e.* it does not belong to set *Portion_Accidents*.

$$TrainOfPortion(aTrain) \notin Portion\_Accidents$$

Precondition (Pre$_2$): if the current portion is associated to an ATS then the ATS has a different direction than the train or it is disarmed.

$$
\begin{aligned}
&((TrainOfPortion(aTrain) \in ran(ATSOfPortion)) \Rightarrow (\\
&\quad (AutoTrStop\_direction(ATSOfPortion^{-1}(TrainOfPortion(aTrain))) \\
&\qquad\qquad\qquad\qquad\qquad\qquad\qquad \neq Train\_direction(aTrain)) \\
&\quad \vee \ (AutoTrStop\_state(ATSOfPortion^{-1}(TrainOfPortion(aTrain)))=disarmed)) \\
&)
\end{aligned}
$$

Actions of operation **Train_Move** address several situations depending on the current portion of the train and also the portion to which the train is intended to move. First we compute, based on two definitions *next_portion_odd* and *next_portion_even*, the next portion with respect to the traveling direction of a train (even or odd) and also to the portion connexions whose semantics were defined by the OCL invariants. In the following we present only *next_portion_odd* since *next_portion_even* is analog.

$$
\begin{aligned}
next\_portion\_odd == \{&p1, p2 \mid p1 \in Portion \wedge p2 \in Portion \\
\wedge \ (&p1 \notin \mathbf{dom}(Portion\_B\_straight) \\
&\Rightarrow (Portion\_directionOfA(p1) = even \wedge p2 = Portion\_A\_main(p1))) \\
\wedge \ ((&p1 \in \mathbf{dom}(Portion\_B\_straight) \wedge p1 \notin \mathbf{dom}(Portion\_C\_divergent)) \\
&\Rightarrow ((Portion\_directionOfA(p1) = odd \wedge p2 = Portion\_B\_straight(p1)) \\
&\quad \vee (Portion\_directionOfA(p1) = even \wedge p2 = Portion\_A\_main(p1)))) \\
\wedge \ (&p1 \in \mathbf{dom}(Portion\_C\_divergent) \\
&\Rightarrow ((Portion\_directionOfA(p1) = odd \\
&\quad \wedge ((Portion\_switch(p1)=straight \wedge p2 = Portion\_B\_straight(p1)) \\
&\qquad \vee (Portion\_switch(p1)=divergent \wedge p2 = Portion\_C\_divergent(p1))) \\
&\qquad \vee (Portion\_directionOfA(p1) = even \wedge p2 = Portion\_A\_main(p1))))) \\
\}&
\end{aligned}
$$

Given the railroad of Fig. 4, the application of relations *next_portion_odd* and *next_portion_even* to PORTION3 gives respectively PORTION4 and PORTION2. Relation giving all next portions is thus a partial function defined as:

$$
\begin{aligned}
next\_portion == \{&dd, np \mid dd \in Direction \wedge np \in Portion \nrightarrow Portion \\
&\wedge (dd = even \Rightarrow np = next\_portion\_even) \\
&\wedge (dd = odd \Rightarrow np = next\_portion\_odd) \}
\end{aligned}
$$

Definition (Def$_1$): *curr_portion* is the portion on which $aTrain$ is positioned:

$$curr\_portion = TrainOfPortion(aTrain)$$

Definition (Def$_2$): *nxt_port* is the portion to which *aTrain* should move:

$$nxt\_port = (next\_portion(Train\_direction(aTrain)))(curr\_portion)$$

Condition (Accident$_1$): defines a situation where the train derails.

$$(Train\_direction(aTrain) = even \wedge curr\_portion \notin \mathbf{dom}(next\_portion\_even))$$
$$\vee (Train\_direction(aTrain) = odd \wedge curr\_portion \notin \mathbf{dom}(next\_portion\_odd))$$

Condition (Accident$_2$): the next portion is already occupied by an other train.

$$\mathbf{card}(TrainOfPortion^{-1}[\{nxt\_port\}]) > 0$$

Condition (MoveAuthorization): the train enters into a portion on which it has a movement authority.

$$aTrain \in \mathbf{ran}(TrainMA) \wedge nxt\_port \in \mathbf{dom}(PortionMA) \wedge$$
$$PortionMA(nxt\_port) = TrainMA^{-1}(aTrain)$$

Operation Train_Move, presented below, moves the train from one portion to an other, by applying operation Train_SetTrain_position, or produces an accident using operation Portion_SetAccidents. If the train enters a portion for which it has a movement authority then the authority is consumed using operation MA_RemovePortionsOfMA which removes a link between a portion and a movement authority. These operations are a part of the basic operations provided by the functional B specification.

```
Train_Move(aTrain) ==
PRE
    aTrain ∈ Train ∧ (Pre₁) ∧ (Pre₂)
THEN
    LET curr_portion BE (Def₁) IN
        IF (Accident₁) THEN
            Portion_SetAccidents(Portion_Accidents ∪ {curr_portion})
        ELSE
            LET nxt_port BE (Def₂) IN
                Train_SetTrain_position(aTrain, nxt_port);
                IF (Accident₂) THEN
                    Portion_SetAccidents(Portion_Accidents ∪ {nxt_port})
                END ;
                IF (MoveAuthorization) THEN
                    MA_RemovePortionsOfMA(PortionMA(nxt_port), nxt_port)
                END
            END
        END
    END
END
```

3.3   Safe Formal Model

Operational semantics of the safety-free model allow the domain expert to visualize critical situations and simulate the corresponding scenarios in the DSL tool. In fact, in the safety-free model the driver is able to override movement authority and traffic lights. For example, given the model of Fig. 4 animation of operation Train_Move(T1), moves train T1 from PORTION1 to PORTION2 which means that the driver violated two safety rules: the red light of POR-TION2 and the entry into a portion without an authorization. Furthermore, as the ATS of PORTION2 is disarmed, the train can continue its way.

Operational semantics defined by the safe formal model apply restrictions to operations of the safety-free model in order to keep behaviours without accidents and take into account authorizations given by the railway operating rules. First, conditions (Accident$_1$) and (Accident$_2$) must be false, and then condition (MoveΛuthorization) must be true, meaning that the train cannot move if the next portion is not concerned by any movement authority or the movement authority associated to the next portion concerns an other train. In addition to the portion reservation mechanism assured by movement authority the driver must also respect signalling rules.

Condition (LightAuthorization): means that if the portion to which the train should move is concerned by a light, then this light is either oriented to the opposite direction than that of the train or it is green.

$$nxt\_port \notin \mathbf{ran}(LightOfPortion) \vee$$
$$Light\_direction(LightOfPortion^{-1}(nxt\_port)) \neq Train\_direction(aTrain) \vee$$
$$Light\_state(LightOfPortion^{-1}(nxt\_port)) = on$$

The safe version of Train_Move, named Safe_Train_Move, restricts the call to Train_Move by grouping all safety conditions in its precondition:

```
Safe_Train_Move(aTrain) ==
PRE
    aTrain ∈ Train ∧ (Pre₁) ∧ (Pre₂) ∧
    LET curr_portion BE (Def₁) IN
        not(Accident₁) ∧
        LET nxt_port BE (Def₂) IN
            not(Accident₂) ∧ (MoveAuthorization) ∧ (LightAuthorization)
        END
    END
THEN
    Train_Move(aTrain)
END
```

The safe formal model applies the same principles than those discussed for operation Train_Move, to the other operations and also introduces safety invariants such as *Portion_Accidents* = ∅, which guarantees the absence of accidents. Animation of the safe operations in Meeduse gives the possibility for the domain expert to attest whether the railway operating rules as specified in B, are valid or not. A by-product of validation through simulation is that it allows also to detect availability bugs. Indeed, it is quite easy to build a safe system, just prevent the trains and switches from moving. The use of simulation allows the domain experts to also assess the availability of the safe system. Note that validation by proofs and model-checking of the safe model is discussed in [15].

Figure 11 gives different states of the domain model (left hand side) with the list of B operations (right hand side) that can be enabled by the animator at every state. In the first state, on top of this figure, the domain expert can: (*i*) change the direction of trains TRAIN1 and TRAIN2; (*ii*) change the switch from straight to divergent; (*iii*) arm the ATS of PORTION2; and (*iv*) compose train routes using instances of operation Safe_MA_AddPortion. In this situation the light cannot be turned to green, it can only be kept to red due to the rules that we considered for this example. Animation of operation Safe_MA_AddPortion(MA2,PORTION3) followed by Safe_MA_AddPortion(MA2,PORTION2), reaches the state presented in the middle of Fig. 11 where the color of PORTION2 and PORTION3 became orange meaning that these portions are reserved for some train. In this state, operation safe_Train_Move can be enabled in order to start moving TRAIN2. Since PORTION2 and PORTION3 are reserved for TRAIN2, operation Safe_Train_Move(TRAIN2) can be animated twice which leads to the state in bottom of Fig. 11 where TRAIN2 occupies PORTION2 after consuming the authorizations provided by its route.

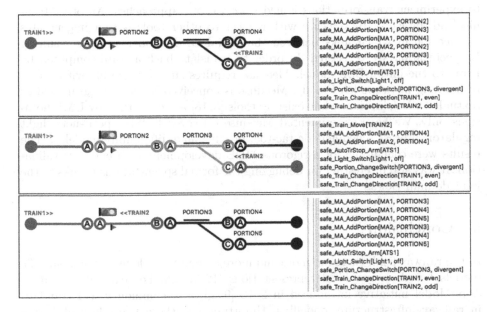

Fig. 11. Meeduse animation of a railroad model with safe operational semantics (Color figure online)

4   Related Works

This paper has shown the application of our approach and its tool support, to the railway field using a simple railroad DSL. In a more general context, besides the contributions discussed along the paper to visual animation techniques [8,14,17], our work presents an advancement in comparison with existing approaches [4,21] where DSLs are mixed with formal methods. In fact, in these works, once the formal model is defined (manually [4] or semi-automatically [21]), they don't offer any way to animate jointly the formal model and the domain model. Often translation techniques, start from a DSL definition and then they get lost in the formal process. In [21], the authors propose to use classical visual animation by applying BMotion Studio [14] to the formal specifications. Unfortunately, this is not only time consuming but also requires some additional verifications in order to address the compatibility between the initial DSL and the graphical representations used in BMotion Studio. Our approach applies well-known MDE tools for DSL creation (EMF, OCLinEcore and Sirius) and automatically manages the traceability between the formal model and the domain model.

The extraction of B specifications from a meta-model applies a UML-to-B translation technique using the B4MSecure tool [10]. The advantage of B4MSecure in comparison with other UML-to-B tools [5,18] is that it offers an extensibility facility allowing to easily add new UML-to-B rules or to modify existing rules depending on the application context. B4MSecure is an open-source MDE platform which gathers several transformations and hence it allows to experiment transformations issued from various approaches. An other technical advantage of B4MSecure with respect to other tools is that it generates a trace file in which links between the initial UML model and the resulting B specification are registered. In order to translate back a state computed by ProB to the initial DSL model, Meeduse requires such a trace file with a corresponding meta-model. Finally, Meeduse is conceived for formal (graphical or textual) DSL definition, while existing tools [5,18] are concerned by UML notations only. We have experimented Meeduse on several DSLs: petri-nets, light regulator, process scheduler, tic-tac-toe, puzzle game, lift, family model... The results were concluding for a rigorous MDE development with end-user validation. It was also interesting for debugging the formal specifications thanks to the joint domain views.

5   Conclusion

In the railway field, there are more and more attempts to define domain specific models based on graphical representations [12,20,22]. For example the Rail-TopoModel initiative introduced in 2013 [9] gives a common visual standard in railway infrastructure modelling. Unfortunately, these DSLs lack of formal operational semantics and hence they don't apply reasoning tools to address the correctness of their dynamic aspects. Our technique addresses this challenge and allows domain experts, without any knowledge in formal methods, to design railway models in a formally defined DSL and then to simulate safety-critical behaviours like those producing accidents. The SafeCap platform [11] proposes a railway DSL with formal static semantics using the EMF framework. Since Meeduse fits well to EMF-based DSLs, we think that it can contribute to this platform in order to formally specify and simulate its operational semantics.

This mix of MDE and B has several perspectives. In addition to the application to existing railway standards like ERTMS/ETCS, we plan to address multi-views modeling and interactions between various models. Indeed, a railway DSL can be better structured into several views which can be animated together in Meeduse: driver views showing train interactions with signalling systems, traffic agent views managing movement authorizations and train routes, global views...

Acknowledgments. This work is funded by the NExTRegio project of IRT Railenium. The authors would like to thank SNCF Réseau for its support. We also thank German Vega for his contributions to B4MSecure and Meeduse.

References

1. Abrial, J.-R.: The B-book: Assigning Programs to Meanings. Cambridge University Press, New York (1996)
2. Bettini, L.: Implementing Domain-Specific Languages with Xtext and Xtend. Packt Publishing, Birmingham (2013)
3. Bjørner, D.: Rôle of domain engineering in software development—why current requirements engineering is flawed !. In: Pnueli, A., Virbitskaite, I., Voronkov, A. (eds.) PSI 2009. LNCS, vol. 5947, pp. 2–34. Springer, Heidelberg (2010). https://doi.org/10.1007/978-3-642-11486-1_2
4. Bodeveix, J.-P., Filali, M., Lawall, J., Muller, G.: Formal methods meet domain specific languages. In: Romijn, J., Smith, G., van de Pol, J. (eds.) IFM 2005. LNCS, vol. 3771, pp. 187–206. Springer, Heidelberg (2005). https://doi.org/10.1007/11589976_12
5. Dghaym, D., Poppleton, M., Snook, C.: Diagram-led formal modelling using iUML-B for hybrid ERTMS level 3. In: Butler, M., Raschke, A., Hoang, T.S., Reichl, K. (eds.) ABZ 2018. LNCS, vol. 10817, pp. 338–352. Springer, Cham (2018). https://doi.org/10.1007/978-3-319-91271-4_23
6. Eclipse. Acceleo (2012). http://www.eclipse.org/acceleo/
7. Gaudel, M.C.: Advantages and limits of formal approaches for ultra-high dependability. Predictably Dependable Computing Systems. ESPRIT BASIC, pp. 241–251. Springer, Berlin (1995)
8. Hallerstede, S., Leuschel, M., Plagge, D.: Validation of formal models by refinement animation. Sci. Comput. Program. **78**(3), 272–292 (2013)
9. Hlubuek, A.: RailTopoModel and RailML 3 in overall context. Acta Polytech. CTU Proc. **11**, 16 (2017)
10. Idani, A., Ledru, Y.: B for modeling secure information systems. In: Butler, M., Conchon, S., Zaïdi, F. (eds.) ICFEM 2015. LNCS, vol. 9407, pp. 312–318. Springer, Cham (2015). https://doi.org/10.1007/978-3-319-25423-4_20

11. Iliasov, A., Lopatkin, I., Romanovsky, A.: The SafeCap platform for modelling railway safety and capacity. In: Bitsch, F., Guiochet, J., Kaâniche, M. (eds.) SAFE-COMP 2013. LNCS, vol. 8153, pp. 130–137. Springer, Heidelberg (2013). https://doi.org/10.1007/978-3-642-40793-2_12

12. James, P., Knapp, A., Mossakowski, T., Roggenbach, M.: Designing domain specific languages – a craftsman's approach for the railway domain using CASL. In: Martí-Oliet, N., Palomino, M. (eds.) WADT 2012. LNCS, vol. 7841, pp. 178–194. Springer, Heidelberg (2013). https://doi.org/10.1007/978-3-642-37635-1_11

13. Jouault, F., Allilaire, F., Bézivin, J., Kurtev, I., Valduriez, P.: ATL: A QVT-like transformation language. In: 21st ACM SIGPLAN Symposium on Object-oriented Programming Systems, Languages, and Applications, OOPSLA 2006, USA, pp. 719–720. ACM (2006)

14. Ladenberger, L., Bendisposto, J., Leuschel, M.: Visualising Event-B Models with B-Motion Studio. In: Alpuente, M., Cook, B., Joubert, C. (eds.) FMICS 2009. LNCS, vol. 5825, pp. 202–204. Springer, Heidelberg (2009). https://doi.org/10.1007/978-3-642-04570-7_17

15. Ledru, Y., Idani, A., Ben-Ayed, R., Ait Wakrime, A., Bon, P.: A separation of concerns approach for the verified modelling of railway signalling rules. In: International Conference on Reliability, Safety, and Security of Railway Systems - RssRail 2019, Lille, France, June 2019

16. Leuschel, M., Butler, M.: ProB: an automated analysis toolset for the B method. STTT 10(2), 185–203 (2008)

17. Li, M., Liu, S.: Integrating animation-based inspection into formal design specification construction for reliable software systems. IEEE Trans. Reliab. 65, 1–19 (2015)

18. Snook, C., Savicks, V., Butler, M.: Verification of UML models by translation to UML-B. In: Aichernig, B.K., de Boer, F.S., Bonsangue, M.M. (eds.) FMCO 2010. LNCS, vol. 6957, pp. 251–266. Springer, Heidelberg (2011). https://doi.org/10.1007/978-3-642-25271-6_13

19. Steinberg, D., Budinsky, F., Paternostro, M., Merks, E.: EMF: Eclipse Modeling Framework 2.0, 2nd edn. Addison-Wesley, Reading (2009)

20. Svendsen, A., Haugen, Ø., Møller-Pedersen, B.: Synthesizing software models: generating train station models automatically. In: Ober, I., Ober, I. (eds.) SDL 2011. LNCS, vol. 7083, pp. 38–53. Springer, Heidelberg (2011). https://doi.org/10.1007/978-3-642-25264-8_5

21. Tikhonova, U., Manders, M., van den Brand, M., Andova, S., Verhoeff, T.: Applying model transformation and Event-B for specifying an industrial DSL. In: MoDeVVa@ MoDELS, pp. 41–50 (2013)

22. Vu, L.H., Haxthausen, A., Peleska, J.: A domain-specific language for railway interlocking systems. In: 10th Symposium on Formal Methods for Automation and Safety in Railway and Automotive Systems, pp. 200–209, January 2014

23. Wikipedia. Railroad switch (2015). https://en.wikipedia.org/wiki/Railroad_switch

24. Winter, K., Robinson, N.J.: Modelling large railway interlockings and model checking small ones. In: ACSC, Adelaide, South Australia, February 2003, volume 16 of CRPIT, pp. 309–316. Australian Computer Society (2003)

Statistical Model Checking of Hazards in an Autonomous Tramway Positioning System

Davide Basile[1]($\boxtimes$) (iD), Alessandro Fantechi[2] (iD), Luigi Rucher[3],
and Gianluca Mandò[3]

[1] Department of Statistics, Computer Science and Applications,
University of Florence, Florence, Italy
davide.basile@unifi.it
[2] Department of Information Engineering, University of Florence, Florence, Italy
[3] Thales Italia S.p.A., Florence, Italy

Abstract. One promising option to improve performance and contain costs of current tramway signalling systems is to introduce an Autonomous Positioning System (APS) in substitution of traditional occupancy detecting sensors. APS is an onboard system that uses a plurality of sensors (such as GPS or inertial platform) and a Sensor Fusion Algorithm (SFA) to autonomously estimate the position of the tram with the needed levels of uncertainty and protection. Autonomous positioning however introduces, even in absence of faults, a quantitative uncertainty with respect to traditional sensors. This paper investigates this issue in the context of an industrial project: a model of the envisaged solution is adopted, and the UPPAAL Statistical Model Checker is used to study possible hazards induced by the substitution of legacy track circuits with on-board satellite positioning equipment.

1 Introduction

Modern computer-based, safety-critical railway signalling systems are often considered expensive both for what concerns investment costs to equip railway lines, and for the costs of their accurate maintenance.

Substitution of costly occupancy sensors (such as track circuits or axle counters) by on-board positioning platforms based on satellite positioning is one promising option to contain such costs; such alternative has however to preserve, or even improve, the safety level of consolidated sensor technologies. This option is one of the themes under the Multiannual Programme of the Shift2Rail Joint Initiative [19] (Innovation Programme 2, Technical demonstrator 2.4 "Fail-Safe Train Positioning, including satellite technology") and is the subject of several research projects.

The SISTER project, funded by Tuscany Region, has focused on a scaled down objective at this respect, that is, substituting track circuits installed on

© Springer Nature Switzerland AG 2019
S. Collart-Dutilleul et al. (Eds.): RSSRail 2019, LNCS 11495, pp. 41–58, 2019.
https://doi.org/10.1007/978-3-030-18744-6_3

tramway lines with an integrated on-board solution including satellite positioning and an inertial navigation platform. In such applications, track circuits are adopted for detecting track occupancy for an *interlocking* system to be able to grant free routes through the junction to incoming trams. Notice that while in the prospected railway applications satellite positioning is mainly proposed for train distancing purposes (e.g. within the ERTMS/ETCS framework), in the case of tramways safe distancing responsibility is left to the human driver, and track occupancy is used only for determining safe routes through a junction.

The substitution principles are based on computing on board of a tram its current location on the basis of received satellite signals to be fused through complex mathematical algorithms with other information (e.g. IMU (Inertial Measurement Unit), odometry, radar and other different sensor data), and to communicate this information to the interlocking system in order to know which track sections are occupied. Satellite positioning comes however with uncertainty, enhanced in urban environments by buildings along the tramway tracks, which create the so-called "urban canyons". This is known as the *multi-path problem* in signal reception, i.e., interferences due to waves refraction and reflection. These problems could in principle generate false track section occupancy detections, or miss some true track section occupancy, with obvious consequences on the safety of the overall system.

For this reason, the SISTER project has developed a safety assessment procedure, particularly focused on the added hazards introduced by satellite positioning uncertainties. In this paper, we address such hazards by means of a formal model of the SISTER system, in which Stochastic Timed Automata are used to enable reasoning on the probability of events, by means of UPPAAL SMC, a Statistical Model Checker. Our primary interest is to investigate whether some particular hazard may actually occur, and the relation of their probability of occurrence with respect to the known uncertainty sources.

In the paper, we first describe the system and how substitution impact on its principles of operations (Sect. 2); after a short background section (Sect. 3), the formal model is presented (Sect. 4), and the conducted analysis (Sect. 5) shows how it was possible by the formal modelling and tools adopted to detect a hazard which was not previously considered. Finally, related work is in Sect. 6 while conclusion and future work are in Sect. 7.

2   Description of the System

The goal of the SISTER project is to provide a new localization system that replaces the old positioning devices such as track circuits and axle counters with virtual ones. A major advantage of adopting such solution is to reduce the cost of maintenance of ground-based equipment. Moreover, the deployment of such equipment suffers by physical constraints, especially in the urban environment in which a tramway is built: these constraints can be overcome by equipment virtualization, freely optimizing the position and number of virtual devices.

The new localization system is based on a proprietary sensor fusion algorithm developed by Thales, which we consider to be a black box. This algorithm calculates the (virtual) position of the tram based on different sensors including satellite tracking, IMU, odometer. The position is provided together with an estimate of the uncertainty. This is of help for reducing the satellite uncertainty when, for example, a tram is traversing a gallery and the satellite signal is not available.

In this paper we will focus on the satellite-based positioning and we assume the positioning information in terms of current point on a line and of a related uncertainty estimation: for the purpose of studying rare, but possible hazards, we take a pessimistic approach about uncertainty estimation. The positioning information is communicated periodically (for example, at a frequency of 10 Hz) by a tram to the relevant interlocking (IXL) and to the operations control centre (OCC).

A first, upward compatible, solution proposal is aimed at leaving unchanged the configuration parameters of the existing system, i.e. the position and number of tram detectors on the ground are exactly the same of their virtual counterpart. This solution still takes into account physical installation constraints that are no longer necessary, but does not require modification and a consequent new certification of the specific IXL application.

Figure 1 shows the principles of operation of the legacy system vs. the new solution, when a tram is approaching a junction. Notice that in tramway systems junctions are relatively simple, and traffic over the line between two junctions is not subject to signalling. A local IXL system is used instead for guaranteeing a safe transit through a junction: when approaching a junction, a tramway has to ask for a route among those available through the junction: this is automated in the legacy solution by reading a *Tag* and consequently asking the local IXL for a route. The route is assigned by IXL on the basis of the occupancy of *Track Circuits (TC)* (green ones are free, the red one is busy), points are set according to the route, and the protecting signal is set to green. Notice that it is driver's responsibility to drive safely through the assigned route, respecting signals. Although very simple, the example junction layout of Fig. 1 can be considered representative enough of the few different junction layouts that are typically considered in a tramway system.

In the satellite-based solution, shown in the lower part of Fig. 1 the tram knows its position, and compares it with an onboard map listing the *Virtual Tags (VT)* coordinates on the network. If the position matches a VT, a connection is established with the local IXL (that is, the IXL controlling the junction area referred by the VT), requesting a route to tram's destination. The connection establishes a communication session in which a tram periodically communicates its position to IXL, which maps the received position on *Virtual Track Circuit (VTC)* coordinates, to know about track occupancy. Indeed, in order to keep the legacy IXL unchanged, connection and VTC mapping are performed by a wrapper layer that interfaces to IXL. Route, points and signals setting is the same as in the legacy solution. The connection session terminates when a tram leaves the junction area.

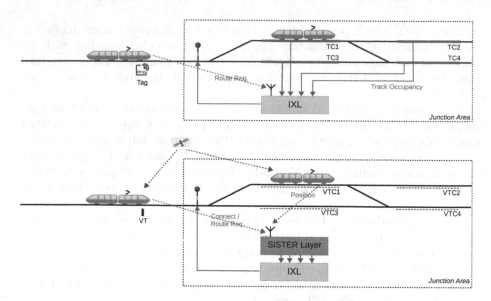

Fig. 1. Substituting track circuits with satellite positioning (Color figure online)

Notice that the correct mapping of position to VTC is a safety-critical function, rated SIL4, as are the other IXL functions. On the converse, the position-to-VT mapping is not considered safety critical. Indeed, the failure to connect to an IXL does not open any protecting signal, and there are no safety threats.

Communication with OCC by trams and IXLs (not depicted in Fig. 1) is aimed at monitoring and performing high level functions of traffic regulation. Being not safety critical, OCC will not be modelled in Sect. 5. Notwithstanding its safety-critical nature, the IXL is not modeled either, because it is considered a legacy system, already certified at SIL4, which is not changed at all in this solution.

In the following, we assume that position information (i.e. coordinates of tram, VT and VTC) are actually unidimensional, i.e., are mapped over positions on a line (representing the route a tram is following). Indeed, the current setting of points (for track branches) is assumed to be performed according to the assigned route allowing therefore precise positioning information at this respect. In particular, the experiments that will be discussed in Sect. 5 do not require multiple routes assigned to several trams. Hence, abstracting away from two dimensional space is of help for improving performances and complexity factors.

Virtual Tags and Virtual Track Circuits are two new components of the SISTER system.

- *Virtual Track Circuits* (VTC) correspond to location ranges (track sections) within a virtual map on the ground system (i.e., interlocking, operations centre): they are hence considered as intervals.

– *Virtual Tags* (VT) are similar but are only available on the map of each tram. Traditional tags could be seen as points on the line. However, in order to properly compare the satellite-based position with the tag position, it is safer to define a VT as a (shorter) interval as well.

In both cases, the detection (i.e. if a tram occupies a VTC or has read a VT), will be implemented through a function (called *LocationReferencing*) that will compare the coordinates of the tram with the map, where both VTC and VT are identified by intervals $[a, b]$.

3 Background

Statistical Model Checking (SMC) [2,16,17] is concerned with running a sufficient number of (probabilistic) simulations of a system model to obtain statistical evidence (with a predefined level of statistical confidence) of the quantitative properties to be checked. SMC offers advantages over exhaustive (probabilistic) model checking. Most importantly: SMC scales better, since there is no need to generate and possibly explore the full state space of the model under scrutiny, thus avoiding the combinatorial state-space explosion problem typical of model checking, and the required simulations can be easily distributed and run in parallel. This comes at a price: contrary to (probabilistic) model checking, exact results (with 100% confidence) are out of the question. Another advantage of SMC is its uptake in industry: compared to model checking, SMC is very simple to implement, understand and use.

UPPAAL SMC [14] is an extension of UPPAAL [10], a well-known toolbox for the verification of real-time systems modelled by (extended) timed automata, which was introduced specifically for modelling and analysing cyber-physical systems. UPPAAL SMC models are stochastic timed automata. These are finite state automata enhanced with real-time modelling through *clock* variables. Moreover, their stochastic extension replaces non-determinism with probabilistic choices and time delays with probability distributions (uniform for bounded time and exponential for unbounded time). These automata may communicate via (broadcast) channels and shared variables.

UPPAAL SMC allows to check (quantitative) properties over simulation runs of an UPPAAL SMC model (i.e. a network of stochastic timed automata). These properties must be expressed in a dialect of the Metric Interval Temporal Logic (MITL) [12]. In particular, we will use the query P(<>[t, t'] ap) that denotes the probability that a random simulation run of a model M reaches a configuration satisfying the atomic proposition ap in the interval of time that goes from t to t' time units.

A drawback of SMC is that it can have difficulties in efficiently observing rare events. Being based on a large number of simulation runs, which can however be not exhaustive, rare events can be found in only a small fraction of runs, or even in no one at all. Since we are interesting in evaluating the probability of occurrence of particular hazards related to positioning uncertainty, we easily run in this problem. To avoid this, we artificially inflate the probability of occurrence of such hazards, so to be able to observe them in some run (see Sect. 5).

4   Formal Model

The two main entities modelled are the On-board Computer (OBC – one for each tram) and the Interlocking (IXL – one for each junction area). This model abstracts away from other intermediary entities. Global constants are used in the model to instantiate various quantities, as for example, the number of trams, the number of IXLs, the number of VT and VTC (of each IXL). Indeed, thanks to the template mechanism of UPPAAL, this model is highly configurable and many operative scenarios (and specific applications) can be modelled and analysed. The model and experiments are available at https://github.com/davidebasile/rssrail2019.

Description of the Components. Each OBC, uniquely identified by its identifier, is modelled as a set of automata that are composed together. They are called OBC_PL (used to simulate the protection level, see below), OBC_SendPosIXL (used to periodically send the position to the IXL when connected), OBC_Drive (used to simulate the tram movement), OBC_Mitigation (used to collect the various alerts for entering a degraded mode and actuating the mitigations), OBC_IXLConnectionSupervision (used to issue connection requests to the IXL and monitoring the connection). A special automaton, OBC_VT, is used to check periodically if a VT has been read. OBC_VT takes as parameters its unique identifier, the interval $[a, b]$ on the map, and the identifier of the IXL to be read by a tram.

Each IXL has its unique identifier, that is a parameter of the automata whose composition builds the IXL module. The automata are: IXL_Connect (used for serving the connection request from a tram), IXL_ReceivePos (used to collect the positions of trams and update the IXL status), IXL_Lsafemargin_Supervision (used to check if PL exceeds the maximum limit allowed, see below), IXL_Mitigation (used to trigger mitigations in case of an alert), IXL_Disconnect (used for disconnecting a tram once it has released its assigned route). The IXL_Disconnect automaton takes in input as parameters also the identifier of the last VTC involved in the assigned route, and a boolean condition stating whether the disconnection occurs when the corresponding VTC is occupied or when it is freed (in the legacy system these are called *release conditions*). Finally, IXL_VTC is an automaton used to model a VTC. It takes as parameters its unique identifier, its location interval $[a, b]$ and the identifier of the IXL that includes it. Note that all the IXL components we modelled are part of the SISTER layer shown in Fig. 1. Indeed, we do not model nor analyse the legacy system, but only the SISTER layer. Thus we abstract from, e.g., how route requests are managed by the IXL.

4.1   Formalising Virtual Track Circuits

Due to the complexity of the model, the analysis will be limited to the main aspects involved in changing from the legacy system to the new SISTER system.

First, the function for checking if a VTC is occupied is formally defined. Let L_v be the virtual coordinates of a tram (i.e. the positioning data calculated by the algorithm on board the tram), and let L be its actual coordinates (in a given moment of time). As a first contribution, we argue that the safety must be guaranteed assuming the presence of an error ε between L_v and L such that $L = L_v \pm \varepsilon$. If such uncertainty is ignored, potential hazards are introduced, as it will be described in Sect. 5.

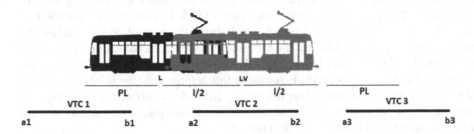

Fig. 2. Example of the protection level PL reducing the capacity of the network

These safety requirements are inspired by their aeronautical counterparts [1, 18]. In particular, the actual error is unknown, hence an uncertainty ε is introduced which is an aleatory variable that follows a Normal distribution with average zero (denoted φ_{0,σ^2}). The Sensor Fusion Algorithm periodically provides L_v and φ_{0,σ^2}. The *protection level* (PL) is a statistical bound error computed from L_v and φ_{0,σ^2} so as to guarantee that the probability of the (unknown) real position error exceeding PL is smaller than or equal to a target value (called *integrity risk* (IR)). In other words, the interval $[L_v - \mathrm{PL}, L_v + \mathrm{PL}]$ contains the real position with probability greater or equal to $1 - IR$ (e.g. $1 - 10^{-9}$). The *alert limit* (AL) is the maximum value of PL allowed. Finally, the *time-to-alert* (TTA) is the maximum allowable time elapsed in which $PL > AL$ before an alert is issued and a degraded operation mode is entered.

In this paper, these quantities are either abstracted away or they are global constants and global variables to be instantiated. For simplicity, it is assumed that the satellite receiver is located in the centre of the tram and hence L_v is centered in the tram. The location L_v is refreshed in the automaton OBC_Drive according to a constant travelling speed. More importantly, to simulate the behaviour of the SFA, the automaton OBC_PL selects non-deterministically and periodically a value of PL from a given interval. Hence, we completely abstract away from the way in which PL is calculated and consider the Sensor Fusion Algorithm as a black box which provides both L_v and PL.

Let l be the length of the tram, then the corresponding VTC is occupied if $LocationReferencingVTC(L_v, \text{PL}, a, b) = true$ (where a and b identify the interval associated with the VTC); otherwise it is free, formally:

$$LocationReferencingVTC(L_v, \text{PL}, a, b) = (a - \text{PL} - \frac{l}{2} \leq L_v) \wedge (L_v \leq b + \text{PL} + \frac{l}{2}) \quad (1)$$

With virtual positioning, an uncertainty about the real position of the trams is thus introduced. This implies an approximation of the number of occupied VTC.

Example 1. Figure 2 shows a vehicle that physically (black tram) occupies VTC 1 and VTC 2, but virtually (grey tram) also VTC 3. Indeed in this example $L_v - \text{PL} < L < L_v$ and the physical position is behind the virtual one, but inside the protection level PL provided by the virtual position. Note that, in case PL would be ignored, VTC 1 would be erroneously considered free (i.e. a false negative). Through PL this false negative is removed but a false positive is introduced (i.e. VTC 3 is detected occupied but it is free). Indeed, *LocationReferencingVTC* computes an *over-approximation* of the real track occupancy and in this example will evaluate true for all the three intervals.

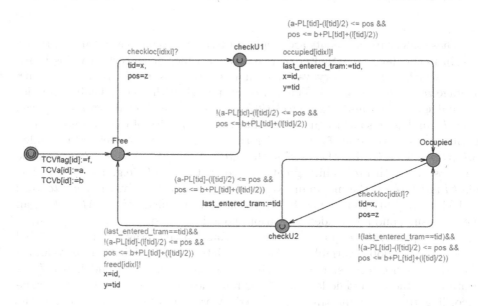

Fig. 3. The template automaton IXL_VTC.

We are now ready to describe the automaton IXL_VTC that implements the logic described above and in Sect. 2. The model is depicted in Fig. 3. We remark that UPPAAL allows to define templates: the parametric automata will be instantiated in the declaration phase by assigning constant parameters to the instances. As previously stated, the VTC template takes as input a unique identifier *id*, a unique *idixl* IXL identifier, two integers *a, b* which identify the track section where the VTC is positioned. The VTC has two main states: *Free* and *Occupied*, which intuitively identify the occupation and release status of the VTC. The initial transition assigns the respective parameters to globally shared variables. Both the initial state and the remaining two states are marked as *urgent* states, i.e. instantaneous states in which the system spends zero units of time. These states are used to divide different operations that are performed in sequence, but at the same time.

Each transition of an automaton in UPPAAL can contain a guard, a send (!) or receive (?) signal and an update of variables. From state *Free*, a transition is triggered by the reception of a signal on the channel *checkloc[idixl]*?, a signal coming from the relevant IXL to check the position received by a tram against the VTC. UPPAAL does not primitively allow value-passing, hence buffer variables (named *x*, *y* and *z*) are used to transmit data together with the signal. The *tid* variable stores the unique tram identifier for which the occupation is to be controlled. Likewise, the variable *pos* will contain the position of the tram *tid*. This transition is divided into two possible behaviours through the intermediate urgent state. In particular, it returns to the *Free* state in the event that *LocationReferencing* evaluates to false (conditions expressed in the transition guards). Otherwise, two operations are performed: firstly a signal is sent to the interlocking to acknowledge the occupation of the VTC via *occupied[idixl]*!, then the tram identifier is stored in a temporary variable and both the VTC and tram identifiers are written to the output buffer, to be used for further operations, and the status reached is *Occupied*.

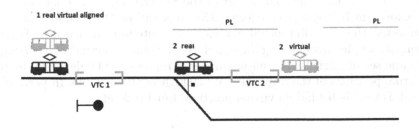

Fig. 4. A critical scenario where a tram is derailed if the protection level PL is ignored

From state *Occupied* a transition is triggered similarly to the transition that exits the *Free* state. However, there are three different conditions exiting the urgent state. In the case where *LocationReferencing* evaluates to true, the target state remains *Occupied*: the tram has not yet freed the VTC. In this case the temporary identifier of the last tram entered is updated. In the event that *LocationReferencing* evaluates to false, there are two possibilities. If the tram that has freed the VTC is the same stored in the temporary variable, this means that it was the last tram to have occupied the VTC. The VTC goes to the *Free* state. Otherwise, some other trams are still potentially occupying the *VTC* (recall the presence of an uncertainty), so the VTC remains in the *Occupied* state.

5   Formal Analysis of Virtual Track Circuits

In this section, the formal analysis of the model (in particular the VTC template) will be described.

We anticipate that, thanks to the formalization and analysis, some defects in the previous SISTER specification have been identified and fixed.

Three Hazards and Three Mitigations. As discussed in Sect. 2, in the initial specification the substitution of physical devices with virtual ones was considered enough to preserve the safety of the legacy system. In what follows, three different hazards will be analysed through the formal model, and mitigations will be proposed. These hazards are a result of particular set-ups of parameters, which at this stage of development of the system have to be considered plausible in order to cover worst case scenarios.

These hazards will be analysed on a safety critical scenario depicted in Fig. 4. In this scenario there are two trams and two VTCs. Tram 2 is traversing its assigned route whilst Tram 1 is waiting at a red signal for its route to be assigned by IXL. VTC 1 is used to detect the occupation of a route, whilst VTC 2 is used to detect the release of a route. It is assumed that a tram is disconnected instantaneously from the IXL when it has released its assigned route, hence the events route release and disconnection are coupled. Our analysis will focus on the event disconnection that is part of the SISTER layer, and not the route release, an event belonging to the legacy IXL application. Once Tram 2 has been disconnected, the IXL will proceed to create the route to be assigned to Tram 1. Creating a route involves moving the switch (that Tram 2 is actually traversing in Fig. 4) and setting signals. The misalignment is represented by depicting in grey the virtual positions of the trams and in black their physical one. In particular, in Fig. 4 Tram 2 is behind its virtual position, but inside PL.

Table 1. Set-up of experiments and their results

	Formula	Protection level	Release condition	Result
Exp 1	2	[200, 250]	Free	[0.995, 1]
Exp 2	3	[200, 250]	Free	[0,0.005]
Exp 3	3	[200, 250]	Occupied	[0,995, 1]
Exp 4	3	[0, 50]	Occupied	[0.158198, 0.168198]
Exp 5	3	[0, 250]	Free	[0.0221134, 0.0321134]
Exp 6	3	(Use alert limit)	Free	[0, 0.005]

Table 2. Performances of the experiments

	Verification/kernel/elapsed time used	Resident/virtual memory usage peaks
Exp 1	293,657 s/0,172 s/293,888 s	145.536 KB/310.060 KB
Exp 2	782.938 s/0.078 s/783.69 s	75,736 KB/165,432 KB
Exp 3	144.328 s/0.109 s/144.519 s	142,188 KB/300,160 KB
Exp 4	563.391 s/0.11 s/563.782 s	176,944 KB/468,928 KB
Exp 5	1,364.172 s/0.062 s/1,366.364 s	242,432 KB/601,588 KB
Exp 6	1,604.281 s/0.047 s/1,605.323 s	74,316 KB/164,548 KB

In all the experiments discussed in this section, it will be assumed that the tram is travelling at constant speed of 5 m/s (18 km/h) and its length is 50 m. Additionally, VTC 1 has interval [350, 450] (meters) and the time upperbound (for each simulation) is of 150 s, that is, enough for the tram to cover 750 m and traverse the whole junction area. More importantly, the system is assumed to be working in nominal operation conditions in the sense of Stanford Diagram, (i.e. the alert limit is considered to be greater than the protection level and the protection level greater than the position error), so excluding unavailability conditions and/or misleading information provided.

Finally, the analysed formulae will detect "bad" scenarios, hence their value should be closer to zero. A summary of the various experiments, their parameters and their results is in Table 1.

Set-Up of the Experiments. In the experiments, UPPAAL SMC academic version 4.1.19 (rev. 5649) has been used. During the experiments, the statistical parameters have been tuned (for all evaluated properties) to the values displayed in Figs. 5 and 6. This set-up allowed to quickly evaluates the various experiments with a confidence that was sufficient thanks to the "inflated" values of PL. In particular, this set-up required the model-checker to perform 119830 simulations for each experiment to reach confidence 0.995. Table 2 reports the performances for the experiments, run on a machine with Processor Intel(R) Core(TM) i7-8700 CPU at 3.20 GHz, 3192 Mhz, 6 Core(s), 12 Logical Processor(s) with 16 GB of RAM, running 64-bit Windows Version 10.0.17134 Build 17134.

Experiment 1. This experiment will evaluate the first hazard by assuming that the function *LocationReferencing* does not consider any misalignment between L and L_v (as it was in the original specification), and that the route is released when VTC 2 is freed (i.e. release condition of VTC 2 is set to free). In this case, the route assigned to Tram 2 is released because it has virtually (and erroneously) freed VTC 2. Indeed, the virtual position of Tram 2 is already beyond VTC 2, whilst its physical position is behind it. Hence, the route required by Tram 1 can be created. The IXL proceeds to move the switch, with the consequent possible derailment of Tram 2. This critical scenario can be detected by the formula:

$$\mathrm{Pr}(<> [0, 150](L + 1/2 < \mathtt{VTCa}) \&\&(L_v - 1/2 > \mathtt{VTCb})) \tag{2}$$

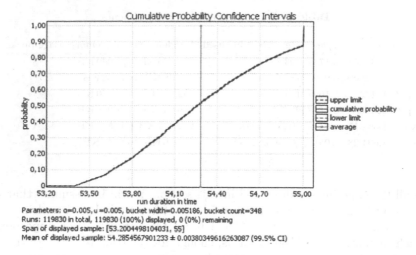

Fig. 5. Plot for formula detecting Hazard 1

This formula evaluates the probability that, within 150 time units, there exists a configuration in which the tram has not yet (physically) reached VTC 2, but virtually (that is, by adding PL) it has already passed it. In experiment it is assumed that L is the actual location of Tram 2 whilst its virtual one is $Lv = L + PL$, i.e. the gap between the two positions is the worst allowed by the integrity risk. It will also be assumed that PL varies non-deterministically between 200 and 250 m, i.e. a worst-case scenario with a large PL. Moreover, l is the length of Tram 2, $VTCa$ and $VTCb$ are the parameters $[a, b]$ of an instantiation of template IXL_VTC. Of course the value of such formula strictly depends on the instantiation of the parameters.

For this particular experiment the statistical model checker evaluates the value of the formula to be in the interval $[0.995, 1]$ with confidence 0.995. In Fig. 5 it is shown how the probability switches to one as soon as 55 time units have passed. Indeed, after 55 s the tail of the tram will be at 250 m. By summing up the smallest possible PL (i.e. 200 m) the estimated position will be beyond 450 m, that is, enough to fully traverse VTC 2 and so satisfy $Lv - l/2 > VTCb$.

Experiment 2. The mitigation to the first hazard, already described in Sect. 4, will be evaluated. It consists in using a *LocationReferencing* function where a protection level PL is considered. To evaluate the proposed mitigation, the following formula will be used:

$$\text{Pr}(<> [0, 150](\text{IXLD\_0.Disconnecting}\&\&(Lv + 1/2 < \text{VTCa}))) \tag{3}$$

In this formula, IXLD_0 is an instantiation of the template IXL_Disconnect. Moreover, it is still assumed that the physical position L is such that $Lv - PL \leq L \leq Lv$. This formula evaluates the probability that, within 150 time units, there exists a configuration in which Tram 2 has been disconnected (and hence has released its route) (state $IXLD\_0.Disconnecting$ is reached) but it has not yet reached VTC 2 (and therefore it could be still traversing a junction) (i.e. $(L + l/2 < L_v + l/2 < VTCa))$.

The value of PL in this case is the same of Formula 2. The statistical model checker evaluates the value of Formula 3 to be in the interval $[0, 0.005]$ with confidence 0.995. Indeed, with this set-up of parameters, this hazard becomes unlikely, even in the presence of a non-negligible PL.

Experiment 3. In this experiment the second hazard is detected whilst the first mitigation is applied by slightly changing the scenario. In particular, apart from applying the first mitigation, the release condition of VTC 2 is set to occupied. This means that the route is released as soon as Tram 2 occupies VTC 2. The statistical model checker evaluates the value of Formula 3 to be in the interval $[0.995,1]$ with confidence 0.995. An intuitive explanation of the causes of such hazard follows: due to the introduction of PL in *LocationReferencing* (see Formula 1), the tram is "stretched" in such a way that VTC 2 can be occupied virtually, before than physically. It must be noted that this hazard is not triggered by a wider PL. Indeed, even in the presence of a small PL the hazard is likely to happen, as discussed in the next experiment.

Experiment 4. In this experiment the second hazard is further evaluated. The value of PL will be (non-deterministically) updated periodically selecting a value in the interval $[0, 50]$ meters. The statistical model checker evaluates Formula 3 to be in the interval $[0.158198, 0.168198]$ with confidence 0.995.

Experiment 5. The second mitigation consists in removing the occupied release condition and force a route to be released only after the last VTC involved (in this case VTC 2) is completely traversed. Since in Experiment 2 the release condition is free, this mitigation has been already evaluated to be effective. Note that this mitigation violates the assumption made by the initial specification (see Sect. 2), and in particular that the configuration parameters of the legacy system should remain unchanged in the new system. Indeed, all VTC must have release condition set to free.

In this experiment the third hazard is finally discussed. This hazard is possible even if the two previous mitigations above take place (i.e. consider PL and remove the occupied release condition). In particular, this new hazard can be observed if the instantiation of parameters is such that PL can vary from 0 to 250 (due for example to bad weather conditions). In this experiment, it is assumed that PL varies in the interval $[0, 250]$ meters. Now the statistical model checker evaluates Formula 3 to be in the interval $[0.0221134, 0.0321134]$ with confidence 0.995.

Figure 6 shows the probability distribution of Formula 3 for this experiment. It can be observed that, similar to Fig. 5, the mean of the displayed sample is 48.38 s, that is, when the tram approaches VTC 2. Moreover, the variation of values of PL can be observed in the probability distribution that "jumps" from zero to the target value periodically, according to the fact that in this model a new position is communicated and a new PL is computed every 5 s. This can be intuitively explained as follows: since the values of PL can vary from 0 to 250 m, the length of the tram can be "stretched" and "shrinked" quickly (every 5 s) and in such a way that VTC 2 may switch from occupied (when the tram is stretched because of an higher PL) to free (when the tram is shrinked because of a small PL), even if the tram has not yet physically reached VTC 2. When IXL detects VTC 2 to switch from occupied to free it proceeds to release the route and disconnects Tram 2.

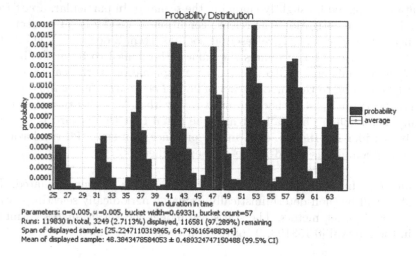

Fig. 6. Plot for Experiment 5

Experiment 6. In the last experiment a third (and final) mitigation is proposed. It is possible to mitigate such hazard by substituting the protection level with the alert limit in the *LocationReferencing* function. Indeed, whilst the protection level PL varies dynamically (and this variation may potentially lead to hazards as explained above), the alert limit is fixed. Moreover, in case PL exceeds the alert limit the system will enter a degraded mode, where due operations will take place to restore normal conditions. By applying the third mitigation (in the implementation of *LocationReferencing* function in the VTC template), and by considering again PL in the interval [0, 250] meters and the alert limit set-up to 300 m (so that the results are not tampered by a degraded mode), the statistical model checker evaluates Formula 3 to be in the interval [0, 0.005] with confidence 0.995.

Remarks. The analysis described in this section has proved that the adoption of formal methods (in this particular case statistical model checking) may be of help for detecting in the early design phase of a system potentially critical bugs in the specification. Whilst the first hazard has been noted prior to the formalisation step (and indeed the mitigation is already present in the model), the other two were noticed only after the analysis has been carried on. By altering the probability of hazards (i.e. worst values of PL in our case) we have been able to detect such hazards and evaluate the corresponding mitigations even without using higher accuracy levels of the statistical model checker, and even more without actually visiting the whole state space of the system (which is up to millions of states).

The adoption of a state-machine formalism has also been of help in sharing results with the industrial partners of this project.

We wish to stress that our aim was not a quantitative evaluation of dependability attributes of the proposed system. Indeed, we used SMC as a fast tool to enlighten possible hazards in the design of a safety-critical system affected by uncertainty: the obtained probability values for the hazards are not realistic, but call for a further accurate quantitative evaluation that could be used to demonstrate that their probability of occurrence is well below any reasonable risk level, and a possible refinement of the system specification.

It can be observed that the experiments take a substantial amount of time, and so they may appear to be not scalable to larger designs. On the other hand, SMC does not need to exhaustively visit the state-space of the model, which in our case is very large, so that a conventional model checking approach could result to be even less scalable. However, the studied hazards were related to the substitution of the track circuits with autonomous positioning, and did not include malfunctioning of legacy components, such as the IXL system, whose safety is considered already assessed. Indeed, the substitution principles studied on an example junction are actually quite independent from the junction itself and from its size. Moreover, if deemed necessary, the experiments can be independently repeated for each junction of a line, with an execution time growing linearly with the number of junctions.

6   Related Work

Statistical model checking, and UPPAAL SMC in particular, has been applied to other case studies belonging to the transport domain [4,9,13].

In the European Horizon 2020 Shift2Rail project ASTRail (SAtellite-based Signalling and Automation SysTems on Railways along with Formal Method and Moving Block Validation), formal methods and tools are evaluated on a moving block signalling scenarios [6]. In this context, UPPAAL SMC has also been used to model and analyse the ASTRail specification, as discussed in [5].

Two different formalisations, stochastic hybrid automata and Stochastic Activity Networks (SAN) have been compared in [7] regarding their capability to evaluate the reliability of systems of rail road switch heaters and their energy consumption, with the aim of comparing and tuning different policies of energy consumption, according to the case study presented in [3].

Stochastic Petri net (SPN) models have been used as well in the context of dependability evaluation of railway signalling systems: Evaluation of the probability of emergency stops due to GSM-R failures is notably addressed in [21], a result later extended in [11, 20], showing the capability of SPNs for evaluating dependability attributes.

A separate task in the SISTER project has been related to detection, through installed radars, of unavailability of track sections, for example due to obstruction of stuck cars. In the last RSSRail conference [15], we presented an Integer Linear Programming (ILP) model for addressing route planning inspired to the SISTER system [8]. Traditionally, ILP models are used to statically plan routes to meet their time-schedule. The presented model instead works at run-time as mitigation in case some track section is detected unavailable. Routes of all vehicles are recomputed up to their next target station, so to avoid obstructed tracks, guaranteeing safety and optimising the overall time-schedule.

7   Conclusion and Future Work

In this paper a formal evaluation of hazards in the SISTER project has been carried on. The goal of the SISTER project is the substitution of physical positioning devices with virtual ones in tramway lines. Such devices are safety-critical, and the new system calls for a rigorous analysis with state-of-the-art techniques.

Starting from natural language requirements and operative scenarios provided by the industrial partners, we formalised the functioning of the SISTER system through stochastic timed automata and UPPAAL SMC. The result is a parametric formal model for a *generic application*, to be instantiated with parameters of a *specific application*. Such model is thus highly reusable and different operational scenarios can be evaluated.

Through the formal analysis it has been possible to detect hazards in the informal specification that were not considered in the first specification. The output of the analysis is a refined specification where proper mitigations are in place. Moreover, the new specification is described through a state-machine formalism, and it is ready to be used in the first stage of development of the system.

Future Work. As future work we are planning to formalise other entities that have not been considered so far, e.g. the operation control centre. Whilst in this paper the analysis has been focussed on improper route release due to bad positioning errors, other critical aspects need to be analysed. For example, in case the alert limit is exceeded proper alarms must be issued within specific time units to not incur in hazardous scenarios. Generally, wireless communication must be monitored and proper mitigations have to be in place in case of failures in the communications. Finally, we aim at refining the model for generating PL, which is now non-deterministic, into a model that computes PL starting from the error distribution φ_{0,σ^2}.

Aknowledgements. This work has been partially supported by the Tuscany Region project POR FESR 2014-2020 SISTER "SIgnaling & Sensing Technologies in Railway application".

References

1. https://gssc.esa.int/navipedia/index.php/Integrity#Protection_Level
2. Agha, G., Palmskog, K.: A survey of statistical model checking. ACM Trans. Model. Comput. Simul. **28**(1), 6:1–6:39 (2018)
3. Basile, D., Di Giandomenico, F., Gnesi, S.: Tuning energy consumption strategies in the railway domain: a model-based approach. In: Margaria, T., Steffen, B. (eds.) ISoLA 2016. LNCS, vol. 9953, pp. 315–330. Springer, Cham (2016). https://doi.org/10.1007/978-3-319-47169-3_23
4. Basile, D., Di Giandomenico, F., Gnesi, S.: Statistical model checking of an energy-saving cyber-physical system in the railway domain. In: Proceedings of the 32nd Symposium on Applied Computing (SAC 2017), pp. 1356–1363. ACM (2017)
5. Basile, D., ter Beek, M.H., Ciancia, V.: Statistical model checking of a moving block railway signalling scenario with UPPAAL SMC. In: Margaria, T., Steffen, B. (eds.) ISoLA 2018. LNCS, vol. 11245, pp. 372–391. Springer, Cham (2018). https://doi.org/10.1007/978-3-030-03421-4_24
6. Basile, D., et al.: On the industrial uptake of formal methods in the railway domain. In: Furia, C.A., Winter, K. (eds.) IFM 2018. LNCS, vol. 11023, pp. 20–29. Springer, Cham (2018). https://doi.org/10.1007/978-3-319-98938-9_2
7. Basile, D., Di Giandomenico, F., Gnesi, S.: On quantitative assessment of reliability and energy consumption indicators in railway systems. In: Kharchenko, V., Kondratenko, Y., Kacprzyk, J. (eds.) Green IT Engineering: Social, Business and Industrial Applications. SSDC, vol. 171, pp. 423–447. Springer, Cham (2019). https://doi.org/10.1007/978-3-030-00253-4_18
8. Basile, D., Giandomenico, F.D., Gnesi, S.: Dependable dynamic routing for urban transport systems through integer linear programming. In: Fantechi et al. [15], pp. 221–237
9. ter Beek, M.H., Legay, A., Lluch Lafuente, A., Vandin, A.: A framework for quantitative modeling and analysis of highly (re)configurable systems. IEEE Trans. Softw. Eng. (2018)
10. Behrmann, G., et al.: UPPAAL 4.0. In: Proceedings of the 3rd International Conference on the Quantitative Evaluation of SysTems (QEST 2006), pp. 125–126. IEEE (2006)
11. Biagi, M., Carnevali, L., Paolieri, M., Vicario, E.: Performability evaluation of the ERTMS/ETCS - level 3. Transp. Res. Part C: Emerg. Technol. **82**, 314–336 (2017)
12. Bulychev, P., David, A., Larsen, K.G., Legay, A., Li, G., Poulsen, D.B.: Rewrite-based statistical model checking of WMTL. In: Qadeer, S., Tasiran, S. (eds.) RV 2012. LNCS, vol. 7687, pp. 260–275. Springer, Heidelberg (2013). https://doi.org/10.1007/978-3-642-35632-2_25
13. Ciancia, V., Latella, D., Massink, M., Paškauskas, R., Vandin, A.: A tool-chain for statistical spatio-temporal model checking of bike sharing systems. In: Margaria, T., Steffen, B. (eds.) ISoLA 2016. LNCS, vol. 9952, pp. 657–673. Springer, Cham (2016). https://doi.org/10.1007/978-3-319-47166-2_46
14. David, A., Larsen, K.G., Legay, A., Mikučionis, M., Poulsen, D.B.: UPPALL SMC tutorial. Int. J. Softw. Tools Technol. Transf. **17**(4), 397–415 (2015)

15. Fantechi, A., Lecomte, T., Romanovsky, A.B. (eds.): RSSRail 2017. LNCS, vol. 10598. Springer, Heidelberg (2017)

16. Larsen, K.G., Legay, A.: Statistical model checking past, present, and future. In: Margaria, T., Steffen, B. (eds.) ISoLA 2014. LNCS, vol. 8803, pp. 135–142. Springer, Heidelberg (2014). https://doi.org/10.1007/978-3-662-45231-8_10

17. Legay, A., Delahaye, B., Bensalem, S.: Statistical model checking: an overview. In: Barringer, H., et al. (eds.) RV 2010. LNCS, vol. 6418, pp. 122–135. Springer, Heidelberg (2010). https://doi.org/10.1007/978-3-642-16612-9_11

18. Legrand, C., Beugin, J., Conrard, B., Marais, J., Berbineau, M., El-Miloudi, E.K.: Approach for evaluating the safety of a satellite-based train localisation system through the extended integrity concept. In: Proceedings of ESREL 2015 - European Safety and Reliability Conference (2015)

19. Shift2Rail Joint Undertaking: Multi-Annual Action Plan, 26 November 2015. http://ec.europa.eu/research/participants/data/ref/h2020/other/wp/jtis/h2020-maap-shift2rail_en.pdf

20. Vicario, E., Sassoli, L., Carnevali, L.: Using stochastic state classes in quantitative evaluation of dense-time reactive systems. IEEE Trans. Softw. Eng. **35**(5), 703–719 (2009)

21. Zimmermann, A., Hommel, G.: Towards modeling and evaluation of ETCS real-time communication and operation. J. Syst. Softw. **77**(1), 47–54 (2005)

Performance Evaluation of Metro Regulations Using Probabilistic Model-Checking

Nathalie Bertrand[1], Benjamin Bordais[2], Loïc Hélouët[1(✉)], Thomas Mari[2],
Julie Parreaux[2], and Ocan Sankur[1]

[1] Univ. Rennes, Inria, CNRS, IRISA, Rennes, France
{nathalie.bertrand,loic.helouet}@inria.fr, ocan.sankur@irisa.fr
[2] ENS Rennes, Rennes, France
{Julie.Parreaux,Benjamin.Bordais,Thomas.Mari}@ens-rennes.fr

Abstract. Metros are subject to unexpected delays due to weather conditions, incidents, passenger misconduct, etc. To recover from delays and avoid their propagation to the whole network, metro operators use regulation algorithms that adapt speeds and departure dates of trains. Regulation algorithms are ad-hoc tools tuned to cope with characteristics of tracks, rolling stock, and passengers habits. However, there is no universal optimal regulation adapted in any environment. So, performance of a regulation must be evaluated before its integration in a network.

In this work, we use probabilistic model-checking to evaluate the performance of regulation algorithms in simple metro lines. We model the moves of trains and random delays with Markov decision processes, and regulation as a controller that forces a decision depending on its partial knowledge of the state of the system. We then use the probabilistic model checker PRISM to evaluate performance of regulation: We compute the probability to reach a stable situation from an unstable one in less than d time units, letting d vary in a large enough time interval. This approach is applied on a case study, the metro network of Glasgow.

1 Introduction

Urban Train Systems (UTS) play an increasing role in modern cities: they provide connections from work to residential areas, and have become a key element for economical and environmental concerns. Usually, UTS are operated by private or semi-public companies, whose role is to provide services with contractualized performance. A typical demand of local authorities is to guarantee departures with a high pace (for instance one train every two minutes) during peak hours to avoid networks congestion, and then ensure punctual/regular departures at lower pace for the rest of the day. Form a contractual point of view, performance is often specified in terms of Key Performance Indicators [12] (or KPIs for short). KPIs are measures for trains punctuality, passenger comfort, average trip times, etc. They are evaluated a posteriori from weekly or

© Springer Nature Switzerland AG 2019
S. Collart-Dutilleul et al. (Eds.): RSSRail 2019, LNCS 11495, pp. 59–76, 2019.
https://doi.org/10.1007/978-3-030-18744-6_4

monthly logs recorded during operation of the network. Failing to meet fixed quality objectives may result in financial penalties.

A normal behavior of a train in a metro network is a succession of arrivals at stations and departures, usually scheduled at precise dates, or cadenced according to chosen departure rates at each station. Operators often rely on an a priori schedule called a *timetable*, that fulfills the KPI objectives if realized properly. Now, even during a normal day of operation, departures and arrivals of trains cannot match exactly such a precise schedule: trains are frequently delayed, due to passenger misbehavior, weather conditions, incidents on tracks, etc. Further, incidents are not independent: as trains have to maintain security distances, a primary delay on a train rapidly propagates to the following trains. To recover from delays and eventually meet quality objectives, UTS are equipped with *regulation algorithms*. Regulation algorithms consider the state of the network (train positions, delays w.r.t. a timetable, etc.), and compute advices to adapt trains dwell times or speeds. Several strategies such as trying to recover delays, sticking to existing timetables, or trying to equalize distances between trains.

It is well known that there is no *universal and optimal* regulation algorithm: efficiency of a particular regulation depends on the targeted KPI objective, on the topology of a line, on the number of trains in the network, and even on passenger behavior. It is hence important to evaluate and compare performance of several algorithms to provide the most adapted solution in a given situation. Evaluation of regulation is hence often seen as a performance evaluation question.

In this work, we use the probabilistic model checker PRISM [10] to evaluate the performance of regulation schemes. We model UTS as Markov decision processes (MDPs for short) [5], and regulation algorithms as controllers that make decisions in MDPs (i.e. implement a strategy). The approach is the following: a metro network is seen as a finite number of discrete locations. The behaviors of trains are modeled as processes which maintain discrete variables memorizing their positions, and have probabilistic guarded transitions, that randomly increment the position of a train. Regulation is also specified as a process whose decisions synchronize with the rest of the system to allow or prevent some transitions of trains. The overall behavior of the network is a form of product between processes, with safety constraints (trains shall not collide), which gives a Markov Decision Process. The accuracy of the model is chosen by appropriately discretizing time and space, and choosing probabilities to define models with sensible distributions of trips durations. We then study performance of regulation in a ring network equipped with a simple regulation algorithm with PRISM. More precisely, we initialize the system in a highly perturbed state (some significant delays have occurred), and compute the probability to get back to a *stable* situation (i.e. a situation in which the network has recovered from delay) in less that d time units, letting d vary in a significant time interval. Getting back to a normal situation in less than d time units is encoded with a PCTL formula [6].

The results obtained show that one can obtain the exact values of probabilities for fleets of 4 trains with a reasonable discretization factor. For larger fleets and larger discretization factors, one has to rely on statistical model checking techniques. Another lesson learned is that without regulation, the probability to recover from a delay by chance is close to zero.

Model checking of railway systems has already been addressed in a Boolean setting, mainly with safety objectives (see for instance [7]). Verification of railway crossing, for instance, is a standard case study for model-checkers (see for instance [3]). Boolean verification mainly addresses safety issues (critical sections must not be violated), but usually cannot address quantitative properties, such as the time needed to recover from a primary delay. These quantitative notions are often addressed using simulation tools dedicated to performance evaluation. To evaluate a regulation policy, one can design a model of an UTS, and simulate a large sample of runs representing operation days with incidents, and derive statistics. Dedicated tools address railway systems modeling at a microscopic or macroscopic level. Macroscopic tools such as NEMO [8] use abstract models (a graph representing the network), and do not consider details such as adherence of trains to tracks, passenger flows. They are mainly used by infrastructure managers. On the other hand, tools working at microscopic level (e.g. Opentrack [11]) consider every detail of rail systems: characteristics of rolling stocks and tracks, weather conditions... Then, simulation steps compute the evolution of the network during a fixed time period (typically, one second). However, micro-steps simulation is time and space consuming. Microscopic and macroscopic approaches used for mainline trains can be adapted for metros, but metro networks have two characteristics that need to be considered: first they embed regulation algorithm, and second, decisions have to be made in a few seconds to avoid delays and their propagation. This makes a big difference, for instance, with macroscopic models of mainlines, where track occupancy schedules can be easily maintained in case of short delay impacting only a few trains. The SimMETRO tool [9] is specialized for simulation of metro systems. It includes regulation schemes, and was used to simulate performance of regulation in the Boston Metro network. The work in [2] uses a macroscopic simulation approach based on a Petri Net variants to model metro system equipped with regulation. The approach presented in this paper is a quantitative and macroscopic one, based on model checking. When the considered model is of reasonable size, the values computed are exact values, and hence provide strong performance guarantees. However, as subway systems are complex, their state space can rapidly exceed the limits of standard model-checkers that compute exact probabilities of properties from an explicit representation of the state space of the system. Even in this case, Statistical Model Checking can be used to obtain these probabilities, but only with a confidence interval.

This paper is organized as follows: Sect. 2 describes the Glasgow metro network, that will be used as a case study to illustrate our approach. Section 3 defines the formal material used later in the paper, namely Markov Decision Processes and PCTL properties, and shows how to use them to evaluate Performance in a regulated metro network. Section 4 gives experimental results, and comments them these results. Section 5 concludes this work and gives some perspectives. Due to lack of space, some technical elements are not detailed in this paper, but can be found in an extended version available at [4].

2　A Case Study: A Metro Network in Glasgow

The usual behavior of metros is the following. A metro travels at a given speed between two stations, and then dwells in station for a predetermined duration. Commercial speed of metros usually lies between 30 and 40 km/h. When the dwell time has expired, the doors close, and the train leaves for the next station. This is where some incident may delay a train: doors may not close well, usually when passengers try to alight while doors are closing. This can result in delays of several seconds w.r.t. the expected departure date.

We consider the metro line of Glasgow [1], a bi-directional ring of 10.5 km with 15 stations, depicted in Fig. 1. Train can travel both clockwise and counterclockwise, using distinct tracks in separate tunnels; therefore, we only study a unidirectional line. The ring has no intersection with other lines. Completing a full round trip takes approximately 24 min. Several trains are used to provide optimal service: if 4 trains are in use, then a metro leaves a station every 6 min. The planned service is one metro every 4 min at peak hours and every 6 to 8 min otherwise. The average dwell time in stations is around 30 s.

Fig. 1. A schema of the subway line of Glasgow

Ideally, providing a high quality service requires to maintain the network in a *stable* configuration, i.e. a situation where distances between consecutive trains are approximately equal (up to some small deviations appearing when trains stop or suffer delays of a few seconds). Such situations are ideal to enforce arrivals and departures at a regular pace. As in the Glasgow network the expected service is one train every 6 min, maintaining such balanced situations is a good way to fulfill the fixed quality objectives. However, networks do not remain in stable configurations without external help. As delays tend to accumulate, one may face the following situation: a train that is delayed arrives late at the next station, which increase the size of the crowd, and results in new door incidents, and penalizes the late train with an additional delay. Usually, as people tend to rush in trains as soon as they arrive in station, fewer passengers will enter the next train alighting at this station. This situation repeats all along the line, causing delays. As trains cannot overtake, accumulation of delays results in a bunching phenomenon, i.e. in a situation where a crowded train is followed closely by almost empty trains. Regulation should avoid such situation and improve KPIs.

A regulation is an algorithm that gives advice to trains: these pieces of advice can be about changing the speed between two stations or the dwell time at a station, depending on the global state of the network. The range of values that can be returned by a regulation algorithm are of course bounded: there is a minimal and maximal running speed for trains, and similarly, a minimal dwell time allowing a sufficient number of passengers to leave trains or alight. In complex line topologies, a standard way to address regulation is to build precomputed timetables, and to try to stick as much as possible to these schedules. Of course, timetables are never realized exactly as specified, they are simply idealized schedules. A standard regulation called *hold-on* technique tries to return to this schedule by reducing dwell times and increasing trains speeds when a delay is measured. In the case of rings such as Glasgow network, the most relevant objective is to maintain a constant duration between arrivals at each station. Considering that characteristics of rolling stocks allow all trains to have the same speed ranges, this pace objective can be addressed as a distance objective, by requiring trains to maintain equal spacing among them. In practice, as distances between stations in metro networks are short, changing train speeds has little impact on delay recovery. We will hence consider regulation policies that change dwell times in stations in order to equilibrate distances among trains.

For the Glasgow network, we will build a stochastic model encompassing train behaviors, the possible perturbations, a regulation algorithm, then study the performance of this algorithm with a probabilistic model checker. To achieve this objective, we will compute the probability to reach a stable situation from an unstable one in less than d minute, letting d vary in interval $[0; 250]$.

3   Models

Unpredictable external events can affect the durations of dwelling and of trips from one station to the next one: it is natural to model them using probabilities. These events delay trains, and as explained in Sect. 2, regulation policies are then used to recover from primary delays and avoid their propagation to the whole network. Given the current state of the system, an appropriate regulation decision is chosen from a set of possible options and given as instructions to the trains. To represent a metro system, we thus need a model that combines probabilities (for the unpredictable events) and non-determinism (for the choice of regulation decisions), hence we choose Markov decision processes (MDP). In this section, we first define the mathematical model of MDP. Then we provide a model of a generic ring metro line with several trains as an MDP with parameters. We explain how to tune the values of the parameters for the Glasgow case study, to reflect the number of trains in the network and the average trip durations. Finally, we define properties on this instantiated MDP model, that are of particular interest to evaluate the performances of regulation policies.

64   N. Bertrand et al.

3.1 Markov Decision Processes

Definition 1. *A* Markov decision process *(MDP) is a tuple* $\mathcal{M} = (S, s_0, \mathsf{Act}, \delta, AP, \ell)$, *where S is a set of states, s_0 is the initial state, Act is a finite set of* actions, $\delta : S \times \mathsf{Act} \times S \to [0, 1]$ *is the probabilistic transition function such that for every $s \in S$ and $\alpha \in \mathsf{Act}$, $\sum_{s' \in S} \delta(s, \alpha, s') \in \{0, 1\}$, AP is a set of atomic propositions, and $\ell : S \to 2^{AP}$ is the labeling function.*

An action $\alpha \in \mathsf{Act}$ is *enabled in state s* if $\sum_{s' \in S} \delta(s, \alpha, s') = 1$. The semantics of a Markov decision process $\mathcal{M} = (S, s_0, \mathsf{Act}, \delta, AP, \ell)$ operates in discrete time as follows: from some state $s \in S$, when an enabled action α is chosen, the probability to be in s' at the next time instant is $\delta(s, \alpha, s')$. Actions in $\mathcal{M}$ thus model the possible choices one has to guide the system. A *path* in an MDP is a finite or infinite alternating sequence of the form $s_0.\alpha_0.s_1\alpha_1.s_2 \ldots$ such that, for every $i \geq 0$, $\delta(s_i, \alpha_i, s_{i+1}) > 0$, that is, the probability to reach s_{i+1} from s_i when choosing action α_i is positive. We denote by $\mathcal{P}ath^{\mathcal{M}}$ (resp. $\mathcal{P}ath_{\mathit{fin}}^{\mathcal{M}}$) the set of all paths (resp. all finite paths) of $\mathcal{M}$. Figure 2 is an example MDP, with $S = \{s_a, s_1, s_2, s_{\mathsf{goal}}\}$, $s_0 = s_a$, $\mathsf{Act} = \{\alpha, \beta\}$, and $AP = \{a, goal\}$, and $\ell(s_a) = \{a\}$, $\ell(s_1) = \ell(s_2) = \emptyset$ and $\ell(s_{\mathsf{goal}}) = \{goal\}$. The transition relation of this MDP is given by: $\delta(s_a, \alpha, s_1) = 1$, $\delta(s_1, \alpha, s_2) = 0.3$, $\delta(s_1, \alpha, s_a) = 0.7$, $\delta(s_2, \alpha, s_a) = 0.5$, $\delta(s_2, \alpha, s_2) = 0.5$, $\delta(s_1, \beta, s_1) = 0.5$, $\delta(s_1, \beta, s_2) = 0.1$, $\delta(s_1, \beta, s_{\mathsf{goal}}) = 0.4$, $\delta(s_2, \beta, s_a) = 0.9$, $\delta(s_2, \beta, s_{\mathsf{goal}}) = 0.1$, $\delta(s_{\mathsf{goal}}, \beta, s_{\mathsf{goal}}) = 1$ and $\delta(s, \gamma, s') = 0$ for all other states s, s' and action $\gamma \in \mathsf{Act}$.

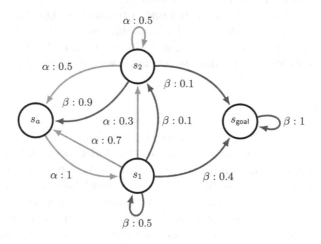

Fig. 2. An example MDP

Given an MDP, a policy resolves the non-determinism by choosing an enabled action after each history of states and actions seen so far, that is for every finite path of $\mathcal{M}$. Formally,

Definition 2. *A* policy *for the MDP $\mathcal{M} = (S, s_0, \mathsf{Act}, \delta, AP, \ell)$ is a function* $\sigma : \mathcal{P}ath_{\mathit{fin}}^{\mathcal{M}} \to \mathsf{Act}$.

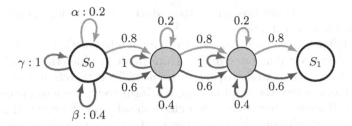

Fig. 3. Part of the MDP model for a train, representing the journey between stations S_0 and S_1 and with two intermediate locations.

Given an MDP $\mathcal{M}$, each policy σ defines a probability measure on infinite paths of $\mathcal{M}$ originating from initial state s_0, that we write $\mathbb{P}^\sigma_\mathcal{M}$. Reasonable sets of paths A are measurable: one can write $\mathbb{P}^\sigma_\mathcal{M}(A)$ for the probability that a sampled path of $\mathcal{M}$ starting from s_0 and following σ belongs to A.

3.2 An MDP Model for the Glasgow Network

As argued earlier, MDPs are well suited to model random events occurring in a metro, as well as non-determinism for the choice of the regulation decision. However, MDPs are discrete models, whereas metro networks are continuous systems, both in space and time. We thus propose to approximate their behavior with a fine enough discretization of space and time. In this discrete model, each state of the MDP will indicate the trains positions, and if some trains are stopped their remaining dwell time. Each discrete step in the MDP model corresponds to changes (in the positions and remaining dwell times) occurring during a fixed delay. To obtain a relevant model, we associate a position to each station, but we also consider intermediate positions between two stations, i.e. we discretize the distance between two stations by adding k intermediate positions between two consecutive stations of the network. The number of intermediate positions is one of the parameters of the model that need to be fixed a priori. We will call *location* either a station or one of these intermediate positions.

As for regulation policies, the interesting elements to consider are arrival and departure dates, and train positions. The behavior of each train T_i traveling in the network can then be seen as an individual MDP $\mathcal{M}_i$, in which states are locations of the network, and actions are regulation decisions. In this MDP, train T_i applies an action $\alpha \in \mathsf{Act}_{\mathcal{M}_i}$ (that represents a regulation decision), and moves to the next location in the network with some probability p_α, or stays at its current position with probability $1 - p_\alpha$.

Figure 3 represents the MDP model of the individual behavior of a train between two stations S_0 and S_1, with two intermediate points. At each location (that correspond to states of the MDP), there are three possible actions, representing the three different target speeds. Action α, labeling green transitions represents the behavior of the trains when running at their standard speed, action β (blue transitions) symbolizes the reduced speed mode, and action γ (red transitions) the stopped mode.

In the following, we will restrict to train models with the three possible running modes α, β, γ illustrated in Fig. 3: one mode in which the train is running at its standard commercial speed, one mode in which it travels at reduced speed, and a last mode where the train is stopped. Intuitively, the intermediary mode will be used if some other train is too close ahead, and the stopped mode will be used to avoid collisions. However, the model easily extends to an arbitrary number of target speeds, but at the cost of an increased the number of actions and transitions in the model.

The overall behavior of the metro network is also an MDP, obtained as a product $\bigotimes \mathcal{M}_i \otimes \mathcal{M}_R$ of all individual MDP models for each train and of regulation, with safety constraints. An important constraint is that the product forbids two trains (or more) to be at the same location at the same moment. This safety requirement can be easily be implemented as a constraint on the enabled transitions in each state of the product MDP. For example, if a train T_i is in location x and at the same instant another train T_j is in the next location, i.e. $x + 1$, then all transitions that send T_i in location $x + 1$ are forbidden. This restriction guarantees that trains never collide.

In our MDP model for each train, probabilities attached to transitions allow one to reflect the time a train will take to travel from a station S_i to the next station S_{i+1}. For each action α, β, γ, at each step, a train can stay at its current location with probabilities $p_\alpha, p_\beta, p_\gamma$, respectively, or go to the next location with probabilities $1 - p_\alpha, 1 - p_\beta, 1 - p_\gamma$. The parameters $p_\alpha, p_\beta, p_\gamma$ must be adjusted to reflect the speed instructions (normal, reduced, 0). To simplify our model, we will assume that the distance between two consecutive stations is the same in the whole network. The distance Δ_d between two consecutive locations is hence also uniform, and depends on the number k of intermediate positions. Each step in the execution of a MDP symbolizes elapsing of a fixed duration Δ_t. We will explain how to choose Δ_t once the probability parameters are fixed.

First of all, let us consider the speed induced by the choice of a particular action by regulation. In our model, we want the speed induced by action α to be the usual speed of trains, and the speed corresponding to action β to be a lower speed occurring when trains slow down for safety reasons (if the next train is too close), finally γ corresponds to stopping the train. Start for example with action α. The probability of going to the next location in one step under action α is set to $p_\alpha = 0.8$. In every location of the network, the probability to stay in there under action α during m steps is thus $(1 - p_\alpha)^m$, and the probability to move to the next location exactly at the mth step is $(1 - p_\alpha)^{m-1} \times p_\alpha$. More generally, the number of steps needed to move to the next location follows a geometric law, whose expected value is $\mathbb{E}_\alpha = \dfrac{1}{p_\alpha}$. With the parameters of Fig. 3, $\mathbb{E}_\alpha = \dfrac{1}{0.8} = 1.25$, so that in average, it takes 1.25 steps to go from a location to the next one, assuming the regulation decision is always α.

The standard speed v_α of a train traveling at speed given by regulation instruction α is obtained by dividing the distance Δ_d between two successive locations by the average time needed to go from a location to the next one under action α. The first parameter Δ_d can be easily computed as soon as k, the number of intermediary locations, is fixed. In the Glasgow line, the total length of the network is 10.5 km, and there are 15 stations. So the distance between two consecutive stations is $\Delta_d = 10500/15 \cdot k$. Similarly, for a geometric law of parameter p_α, the expected number of discrete steps to move from one station to the next one is $\mathbb{E}_\alpha \cdot k$. We know that the total duration of a round trip in the Glasgow line is 1440 s, including a dwell time of 30 s at each station. Hence the total running time in seconds is $t_{tot} = 1440 - (30 \times 15) = 990$. The time needed to move from a station to another, in seconds, is thus $t_{stat} = 990/15 = 66$. Fixing parameter k, we should have $\mathbb{E}_\alpha . k . \Delta_t = 66$. If we choose to have $k = 5$ locations between two stations, we obtain $\Delta_d = 140$ m and $\Delta_t = 10.56$ s. We finally obtain the commercial speed $v_\alpha = \dfrac{\Delta_d}{E_\alpha \times \Delta_t} = p_\alpha . \dfrac{\Delta_d}{\Delta_t} \approx 10.6 \text{ m·s}^{-1} \approx 38.2 \text{ km·h}^{-1}$.

In a similar way, we can compute the average speed of trains when their behavior is dictated by regulation instruction β. The expected number of steps needed to go from a location to the next one is now $\mathbb{E}_\beta = 1/p_\beta$. We hence have $v_\beta = p_\beta \cdot \dfrac{\Delta d}{\Delta t}$. If $p_\beta = 0.6$ as in the model of Fig. 3, we obtain a reduced speed $v_\beta \approx 7.95 \text{ m·s}^{-1} \approx 28.6 \text{ km·h}^{-1}$. Finally, for action γ that represents the instruction not to move, the speed is obviously $v_\gamma = 0$. All in all, using three types of actions, associated each with a probability to move one location forward in the next step, we were able to model three regulation instructions for the speed of trains.

Notice that as soon as the discretization constant k is known, the value of Δ_d follows from the length of the line. Similarly, considering that the dwell time in stations, the total duration of a round trip are known, it suffices to choose the value of p_α to obtain the value of Δ_t. As we had no data on round trip durations in Glasgow, we have chosen a value for p_α such that the distribution of trip durations in our model matches statistics recorded for a track portion in another line with similar characteristics. We refer interested reader to the extended version of this paper [4] to see how this fitting was performed, and how value $p_\alpha = 0.8$ was chosen to model duration of trips from a station to the next one at standard commercial speed.

3.3 Integrating a Regulation Policy in the Model

Regulation policies decide which instruction to give to the trains, given their positions (and possibly other useful data). In this work, we assume that a *signaling system* is used to determine the safe speed of running trains at every step. We also consider that trains run at their usual commercial speed whenever this speed is allowed. We thus consider regulation policies that only choose the dwell times at stations, that is, determining whether a given train should leave the station early or continue waiting.

The signaling system works as follows. Between two stations, trains travel at their commercial speed (following α-transitions) if there is no train too close ahead, at reduced speed (β-transitions) if the train ahead is close, and stop moving to prevent collision or if they have to stay longer in a station.

A regulation policy aims at avoiding delays or recovering from them. In a train networks, delay can be interpreted as a difference between an arrival/departure date and the expected date of realization of this event in a pre-computed timetable. However, in metros like Glasgow, emphasis is put on regularity of departures, not on precise schedules. To formalize delays, we compute, for each state q of the MDP representing the whole network, a function $bal_q : 1..nb_{\text{trains}} \to \mathbb{R}$ that measures whether time intervals between trains are similar or not in state q. In a state q, let us call $pos(q,i)$ a number between 0 and $k.15 - 1$ denoting the position of train i in sate q. Then, for a particular train i, we define: $bal_q(i) = \dfrac{d_q(i, i+1)}{d_q(i-1, i) + d_q(i, i+1)}$ where $d_q(i,j)$ measures the difference between the position of trains T_i and T_j in sate q. It has to be noted that bal_q cannot be equal to 0 nor 1 since two trains cannot be in the same location.

An ideal situation is when $\alpha_q(i) = 0.5$ for every train T_i in the network, which means that each train is positioned precisely in the middle of the space delimited by its predecessor and its successor. Maintaining this equilibrium is a way to guarantee regularity of service. However, it cannot be achieved unless the movements of trains are quasi synchronous, which is too much requiring, as distances between trains always vary due to dwell in stations. We will say that the position of train T_i is *balanced* in state q if $\alpha_q(i) \in [0.4, 0.6]$, and unbalanced otherwise. We say that the current state of the network is balanced if all train positions are balanced. As this definition only depends on the current state, one can attach an atomic proposition **balanced** to every balanced state of the global MDP. Similarly, we can associate a tag **collision** to a state if $pos(q,i) = pos(q,j)$ for some $i \neq j \in 1..nb_{\text{trains}}$, that is to represent that a collision occurs.

We can now define our regulation policy as a linear function $\mathsf{Dwell} : [0, 1] \to [20, 40]$ applies from the value $bal_q(i)$ for every train T_i. In each state of the system, when a train T_i arrives in station, the regulation algorithm imposes a dwell time of $\mathsf{Dwell}(bal_q(i))$ to train T_i. If $bal_q(i)$ is close to 1, the train has to leave the station early, and if it is close to 0, it has to dwell in station for a longer duration than the nominal dwell time. Due to the discretization of time, the dwell duration in station depends on the interval to which $bal_q(i)$ belongs and not the exact value of $bal_q(i)$. For instance, with $\Delta_t \simeq 5\ s$, the dwell time was set as follows:

$$\text{Dwell}(v) = \begin{cases} 4 \times \Delta_t & \text{if } v \in [0.875, 1] \\ 5 \times \Delta_t & \text{if } v \in [0.625, 875] \\ 6 \times \Delta_t & \text{if } v \in [0.375, 0.625] \\ 7 \times \Delta_t & \text{if } v \in [0.125, 375] \\ 8 \times \Delta_t & \text{if } v \in [0, 0.125] \end{cases} \quad (1)$$

Similarly, if $\Delta_t = 10s$, we have set $\text{Dwell}(v) = 2 \times \Delta_t$ if $v \in [0.667, 1]$, $\text{Dwell}(v) = 3 \times \Delta_t$ if $v \in [0.334, 0.666]$ and $\text{Dwell}(v) = 4 \times \Delta_t$ if $v \in [0, 0.333]$.

3.4 Logical Properties for MDP

The overall objective of our experiment is to assess the performances of regulation policies from a metro model. To do so, we use relevant quantitative properties. For example, we evaluate the probability of a regulation policy to recover from a delay in less than 30 min. This can be done by writing "from initial state, the MDP reaches a balanced state within 30 min" as a property φ in logics, and then computing the probability of this event in the MDP given the policy σ corresponding to the regulation at hand. One can also evaluate the maximum probability for this event when σ ranges over all possible regulation policies. Such an optimal policy σ can be computed: we have $\mathbb{P}^\sigma_{\mathcal{M}}(\varphi) = \max_\tau \mathbb{P}^\tau_{\mathcal{M}}(\varphi)$ where τ ranges over a finite number of policies (see the extended version [4] for details). Typically, we will denote this value by $\mathbb{P}^{\max}_{\mathcal{M}}(\varphi)$.

The mentioned property φ is usually written using a formula $F^{\leq 30}$balanced in linear temporal logics [13]. Such a property φ is a *bounded reachability property*: the aim is to reach a given set of states (here the balanced ones) within a given number of steps (or seconds). We are also interested in (unbounded) *reachability properties*, such as F collision that expresses that eventually a collision occurs, yet with no time bound. For our metro system, we aim at proving that under all regulation policies the probability of F collision is 0, showing that collisions are impossible. This constraint can be expressed as $\max_\tau \mathbb{P}^\tau_{\mathcal{M}}(F \text{ collision}) = 0$, or in a more compact way $\mathbb{P}^{\max}_{\mathcal{M}}(F \text{ collision}) = 0$.

To compute such optimal probabilities, we use the probabilistic model checker PRISM [10]. We describe our metro model as processes in the PRISM language: each train is a process, whose state encodes the position of the train in the network. Regulation is also a process. The underlying semantics of these processes is the MDP depicted in Sect. 3.2. A first sanity check for our PRISM model is thus to verify that the safety requirement is met, i.e. that the resulting MDP $\mathcal{M}$ for the network behavior (obtained as the product of processes for trains) satisfies the formula $\mathbb{P}^{\max}_{\mathcal{M}}(F \text{ collision}) = 0$. Then to evaluate the efficiency of a regulation algorithm, we will compute values such a $\mathbb{P}^{\max}_{\mathcal{M}}(F^{\leq q} \text{ balanced})$ for q a given number of steps. This value is the maximal probability, among all regulation policies, i.e. considering choices of actions that are not decided by regulation, that the system recovers a balanced situation within q steps (or equivalently within $q \times \Delta_t$ seconds). We will also measure $\mathbb{P}^\sigma_{\mathcal{M}}(F^{\leq q} \text{ balanced})$ to evaluate efficiency of a policy σ. Letting the system start from an unbalanced state, we can compute this probability for different values of q and obtain performance measures for a regulation algorithm.

4   Experimental Results

We performed several experiments with PRISM on the MDP models we constructed for the Glasgow metro. The objective was to evaluate the value of quantitative formulas given in Sect. 3.4 to study performances of the simple regulation algorithm (balancing of trains positions on the ring) defined in Sect. 3.3. Usually, PRISM explicitly builds the MDP resulting from the processes description, and then computes the values for the properties to check by value iteration (see [5] for a description of the algorithms). As an alternative to the explicit MDP construction, in case the model is too large (in terms of state space, and transition table) to be stored, PRISM can perform *statistical model checking* (SMC), i.e., generate on the fly a set of sample runs, to approximate, with a given confidence, the values one aims at computing.

For our case-study, the size of the MDP depends on the discretization factor k, and on the number of trains running in the system. The tests we performed were conducted for two discretization values ($k = 5$ and $k = 10$) and two possible number of trains ($\mathsf{nb}_{\mathsf{trains}} = 4$ and $\mathsf{nb}_{\mathsf{trains}} = 6$). As described in Sect. 3.2, all processes representing trains were designed with three distinct possible speeds α, β, γ, corresponding respectively to standard commercial speed, reduced speed, and train stopped. These speeds were modeled using intermediary locations as in Fig. 3, with probabilities $p_\alpha = 0.8, p_\beta = 0.6, p_\gamma = 0$.

As initial state of our MDP, we chose a very unbalanced configuration, in which trains occupy consecutive stations, with no free location between them. This configuration is certainly the worst for the network. We then computed three probabilities, for increasing values of q, the bound on the number of steps to recover a balanced configuration. We first consider the policy σ_{bal} defined in Sect. 3.3, which chooses dwell times for each train in order to move the train to the middle of the previous and the next train. This probability is thus denoted $\mathbb{P}_{\mathcal{M}}^{\sigma_{\mathsf{bal}}}(F^{\leq q}\ \mathsf{balanced})$. Second, we computed the maximum probability when the policy ranges over all possible ones. This is written as $\mathbb{P}_{\mathcal{M}}^{\mathsf{max}}(F^{\leq q}\ \mathsf{balanced})$. Note that when computing this probability, PRISM also determines *how to optimize this value*, and returns a policy. Third, we defined a fixed regulation policy σ_{fix} which always picks the dwell time of 30 s regardless of the current state. This probability is thus denoted $\mathbb{P}_{\mathcal{M}}^{\sigma_{\mathsf{fix}}}(F^{\leq q}\ \mathsf{balanced})$. This choice corresponds to an absence of regulation policy. We expect that σ_{fix} should perform worse than σ_{bal} since the latter makes clever choices to equilibrate distances.

Obviously, the size of the models increases with the discretization factor k and with the number of trains. With the smallest values $k = 5$ and $\mathsf{nb}_{\mathsf{trains}} = 4$, PRISM was not able to build the complete state space of the model, and hence could not compute that optimal policy. A standard technique to overcome this limit is to use abstraction. Abstraction allows to consider some states as equivalent, and then perform model checking on a quotient (w.r.t. equivalence classes)

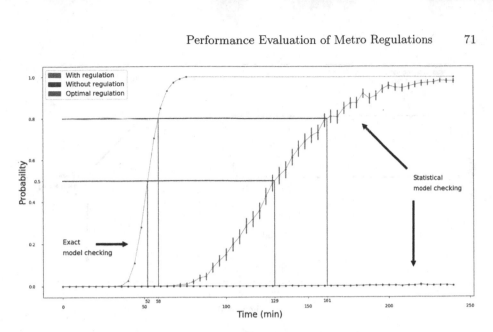

Fig. 4. Probability to recover from a delay with nb$_{trains}$ = 4 and $k = 5$

of the original MDP (which is then smaller). We have used a sound abstraction of states up to a rotation of positions in the network. Indeed, in the Glasgow ring, the dwell time decided for a train only depends on the distance to the predecessor and successor, and not on the visited station. This abstraction allowed to reduce the state space of the original MDP, while preserving values of the formulas (as behaviors of trains and the balanced property of states are equivalent up to rotation). We do not detail here the formal definition of abstraction *up to rotation*, and refer interested readers to the extended version [4] for details.

The Table 1 below shows the effect of abstraction on the size of the MDP computed by PRISM, for a discretization $k = 5$, with and without abstraction. Abstraction up to rotation reduces the number of states by a factor 1000 for 3 trains, and allows PRISM to compute explicitly and MDP for 4 trains, which is not possible without abstraction. However, even with abstraction, taking as discretization factor $k = 10$ or a fleet of 6 trains exceeded the size of models for which PRISM can return an exact value for a simple property. With these parameters, one necessarily have to rely on SMC.

Table 1. Size of the MDP models in terms of number of states and transitions ($k = 5$)

Model number of trains	Before abstraction	After abstraction
Three trains	2.1×10^8 states	3.5×10^5 states
	3.4×10^9 transitions	8.3×10^5 transitions
Four trains	Not built in PRISM	2.0×10^7 states
		5.7×10^7 transitions

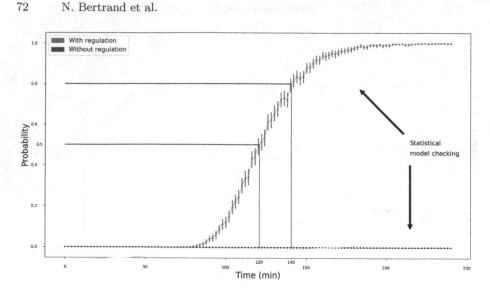

Fig. 5. Probability to recover from a delay with $nb_{trains} = 4$ and $k = 10$

We can now show the results obtained from our experiment. Figure 4 shows the probability to return to a balanced state in x minutes when starting from a very unbalanced situation. Absiscae represents time elapsed, and ordinates the probability. The green curve is the exact value of the probability computed from the MDP (an MDP - quotiented by the rotation abstraction- was explicitly built by PRISM) when an optimal policy is used to regulate trains. The red curve is the result obtained with our simple regulation policy σ_{bal}, and the blue curve the results obtained when constant time regulation σ_{fix} is used. For the red and blue series of measures, statistical model checking had to be used. Indeed, introducing a particular regulation scheme may require the use of additional information in states and increases the size of the underlying MDP. Note that on the figure, as the results are obtained with statistical model checking, the probabilities in the red and blue curse are not given as a single point but as an interval. This figure shows that the best possible choices when doing regulation cannot do better than returning to a balanced state with probability 0.5 in 52 min, and with probability 0.8 in 58 min. The regulation policy σ_{bal} needs respectively 129 min and 161 min to reach probabilities 0.5 and 0.8. One can however notice that this regulation improves the performance of the metro network, as the regulation σ_{fix} that sticks to standard dwell times of 30 s in stations has a probability to return to a balanced state that stays close to 0.

Let us now compare these results with the curves obtained for $k = 10$ and $nb_{trains} = 4$ (Fig. 5) and for $k = 10$ and $nb_{trains} = 6$ (Fig. 6). As explained before, these values do not allow PRISM to compute and store the whole state space of the MDP and hence to obtain the green curve representing results achieved with an optimal policy. However, measures for regulation σ_{bal} or σ_{fix} can still be obtained with statistical model checking. We can now discuss the effect of

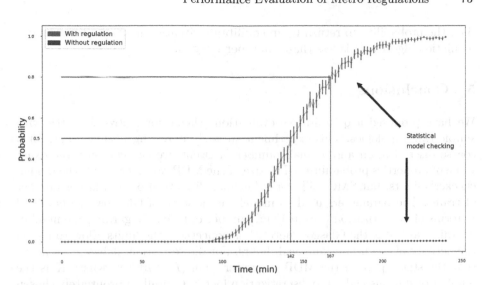

Fig. 6. Probability to recover from a delay with nb$_{\text{trains}}$ = 6 and k = 10

discretization by comparing the red curve in Figs. 4 and 5. One can notice that the global shape of the curve is the same, but that with a discretization factor of 10, it takes 120 min (instead of 129) to return to a balanced state with probability 0.5. Similarly, it takes a slightly smaller time (140 min instead of 161) to get back to a balanced state with probability 0.8. This can be explained by several facts. First, when choosing a rough discretization, one gives regulation the ability to take fewer choices, and starting from less precise information than with a finer discretization. A second aspect is that trains reduce their speed when they approach their predecessor (i.e. the number of locations between the two trains is low), and stop when moving to the next location would cause a collision. So, with a coarse discretization, trains will slow down and stop more frequently, which will delay the date of recovery.

Let us compare the curves of Figs. 5 and 6, respectively obtained with values (k = 10, nb$_{\text{trains}}$ = 4) and (k = 10, nb$_{\text{trains}}$ = 6). Returning to a balanced situation take a longer time with 6 trains than with 4: the network needs 142 min instead of 120 to get back to a balanced state with probability 0.5, and 167 min instead of 140 to return to a balanced state with probability 0.8. Indeed, each train introduces randomness in the system, and increasing the number of trains increases the probability to move to an unbalanced state.

Let us now address the time needed by PRISM to compute the curves. We recall that the green curve in Fig. 4 is the exact probability to reach a stable configuration in x steps achievable with an optimal regulation scheme, for k = 5 and nb_{trains} = 4. Each point in this curve took less than 1 hour to compute on an average laptop. For statistical model checking, with a confidence level of 99%, the time needed to compute each interval in the red curves of Figs. 4, 5 and 6 (i.e., the probability to return to an equilibrate situation in x minutes with our regulation algorithm) is less than 2 min per interval.

5   Conclusions

We have proposed a quantitative evaluation scheme for metro networks with simple ring topologies. This experiment showed interesting results. First, for a coarse discretization and a small number of trains, we can compute the exact value of properties probabilities. The size of the MDP rapidly exceeds the model-checker's limits, but SMC still works for finer discretization and larger number of trains. The parameters used to model the network of Glasgow are bounded in terms of discretization ($k \leq 10$) and number of trains. Regarding the number of trains, as far as the Glasgow network is concerned, the limits allow to model the activity of the network at peak hours. For discretization, it has to be noted that the state space of the MDP is greater than $(K \times k)^{nbtrains}$ where K is the number of stations and k the discretization factor. Overall, appropriately chosen parameters allow to obtain a fair estimation of the distribution of time needed to return to normal situations. The durations obtained may seem rather high (on the average 150 min), but the initial state of simulation is the worst possible situation for the network. A natural extension of this work is to consider the time needed to recover from less severe perturbations (e.g. when a single train is delayed).

One advantage when working with explicitly built MDP models in PRISM, is that computing the optimal value for a formula also gives a finite memory strategy to reach this optimal. However, these strategies are state-based, and cannot be interpreted immediately as a regulation algorithm. An interesting issue is hence to understand better the output of quantitative model checkers to be able to synthesize efficient strategies in terms of user-understandable rules. Another possible extension for this work is to consider more complex topologies, and more complex regulation techniques, for instance network topologies with forks and joins where trains complete distinct trips, networks with parking locations allowing to remove a train from the network or insert it at the most appropriate moment to improve performance of the network...

This work also helped to discover strengths and weaknesses of generic model-checking techniques. Undoubtedly, generic model checking tools such as PRISM have flexible enough input languages to model complex systems such as regulated metro networks. They also build on solid theory to obtains values for probabilistic properties. However, they also have some weaknesses. First of all, as already mentioned in the paper, the MDP of a metro network, even for a simple topology such as the Glasgow ring is huge. This has an impact on the applicability of exact techniques such as value iteration, that need to build a complete state space to obtain results. With respect to this drawback, abstraction techniques can help reducing the size of MDPs. In this paper, the reduction used is a symmetry, and is an exact abstraction: the value of a property checked on the abstract model is exactly the value of the property on the original model. Exact reductions via symmetries work mainly for ring-like lines, but should be more difficult to obtain, and less efficient for other topologies. Then, one can rely on other techniques that group sets of states into equivalence classes, but at the cost of an approximation in the obtained results.

Discretization is a factor that increases a lot the state space considered by model-checkers. The choice of the discretization levels chosen for the experiment were mainly guided by the will to model accurately the distributions of transit times between stations. Hence, shapes of network topologies do not impact too much the discretization level of a model. However, the discretization level is an important parameter of our models: when discretization increases, the distribution of transit times that can be obtained approach a Gaussian distribution. Further, if discretization is too coarse, the space between two intermediate locations may cover more than one block. As a consequence, information about block occupation ahead a train is pessimistic, and trains may have to brake more often in the simulated model that in the real network, which decreases the performances of the simulated system. Hence, a rather high level of discretization is preferable to model realistic train movements (at least intermediate locations should not cover several blocks). It should be noted, however, that improving discretization by a factor c results is a blowup of $c^{nb_{trains}}$ of the size of the MDP.

We hence face several generic difficulties that are inherent to model-checking tools (and not only to PRISM): a very precise model leads to a state space explosion, which disallows computation of exact values for probabilities. To overcome this problem, one can reduce the discretization level of the model, and obtain pessimistic results for the performance of regulation. The other possibility is to find a good abstraction, but as long as an abstraction is not exact, this leads to a loss of precision in the results. The other possibility is to use statistical model checking. As shown in this paper, SMC allows to deal with models of larger sizes (in our case 6 trains and a discretization factor of 10, i.e., a system with more than 10^{13} states), but computes a confidence interval. It shall be noted that the precision of the confidence interval can be set in most SMC tool by choosing a confidence level. Of course, the computation time needed to obtain small confidence intervals increase with the required confidence, but the loss of precision when using SMC for performance evaluation from a faithful model can be controlled. All these consideration advocate for the use of SMC for evaluation of regulation in metro networks. Another possible approach is to use SMC with continuous representations of train trajectories instead of discrete positions. This is the approach followed in [2]. The price to pay here is that evolution of the system over time is not discretized and one has to compute the next occurrence date of events (arrival, departure, braking...). This calculus can also become costly when the size of the model grows.

References

1. Glasgow subway webpage (2018). http://www.spt.co.uk/subway/
2. Adeline, B., Dersin, P., Fabre, E., Hélouët, L., Kecir, K.: An efficient evaluation scheme for KPIs in regulated urban train systems. In: Fantechi, A., Lecomte, T., Romanovsky, A. (eds.) RSSRAIL 2017. LNCS, vol. 10598, pp. 195–211. Springer, Heidelberg (2017). https://doi.org/10.1007/978-3-319-68499-4_13
3. Behrmann, G., David, A., Larsen, K.G.: A tutorial on UPPAAL 4.0 (2006)
4. Bertrand, N., Bordais, B., Hélouët, L., Mari, T., Parreaux, J., Sankur, O.: Performance evaluation of metro regulations using probabilistic model-checking (draft). In: Preprint of RSSRAIL 2019 HAL (2019). hal.inria.fr/hal-02065365
5. Forejt, V., Kwiatkowska, M., Norman, G., Parker, D.: Automated verification techniques for probabilistic systems. In: Bernardo, M., Issarny, V. (eds.) SFM 2011. LNCS, vol. 6659, pp. 53–113. Springer, Heidelberg (2011). https://doi.org/10.1007/978-3-642-21455-4_3
6. Hansson, H., Jonsson, B.: A logic for reasoning about time and reliability. Formal Aspects Comput. **6**(5), 512–535 (1994)
7. Haxthausen, A.E., Peleska, J.: Formal development and verification of a distributed railway control system. IEEE Trans. Softw. Eng. **26**(8), 687–701 (2000)
8. Kettner, M., Sewcyk, B., Eickmann, C.: Integrating microscopic and macroscopic models for railway network evaluation. In: Association for European Transport (2003)
9. Koustopoulos, H.N., Wang, Z.: Simulation of urban rail operations: model and calibration methodology. In: Transport Simulation, Beyond Traditional Approaches, pp. 153–169 (2009)
10. Kwiatkowska, M., Norman, G., Parker, D.: PRISM 4.0: verification of probabilistic real-time systems. In: Gopalakrishnan, G., Qadeer, S. (eds.) CAV 2011. LNCS, vol. 6806, pp. 585–591. Springer, Heidelberg (2011). https://doi.org/10.1007/978-3-642-22110-1_47
11. Nash, A., Huerlimann, D.: Railroad simulation using opentrack. In: Computers in Railways IX, pp. 45–54 (2004)
12. UITP (International Association of Public Transports). Metro service performance indicators, a UITP information sheet (2011)
13. Pnueli, A.: The temporal logic of programs. In: 18th Annual Symposium on Foundations of Computer Science FOCS 1977, pp. 46–57. IEEE (1977)

Scheduling and Track Planning

Automated Planning of ETCS Tracks

Stefan Dillmann[✉][iD] and Reiner Hähnle[iD]

Department of Computer Science, Technische Universität Darmstadt,
Darmstadt, Germany
{dillmann,haehnle}@cs.tu-darmstadt.de

Abstract. Planning of railway tracks at Deutsche Bahn (DB) so far is
done manually by planning experts with the help of CAD tools. This
incurs substantial cost and planning time which is exacerbated by the
complex planning rules laid down in ETCS regulations mandatory for
new tracks. In a project performed for DB Netz AG we explore the
possibility of automating a large part of the ETCS rail track planning
process. We report on our experience in building a prototypic automated
ETCS planning tool. It takes a standardized object-oriented track model
as input and provides output in the same format with all required ETCS
track elements placed at their correct position. The tool can be integrated
into manual planning processes and allows manual fine-tuning. Our approach uses algorithmic sequencing of formalized planning rules based on
the knowledge and best practices obtained from experienced track planners. The result of the planning tool can be visualized for the purpose
of conformance checking with the ETCS planning rulebooks to simplify
the certification process. A model-based, domain-specific test coverage
criterion has been developed to validate correctness and completeness of
the algorithmic rendering of the rules.

1 Introduction

The introduction of the European Train Control System (ETCS) in Germany
poses a formidable challenge to the responsible infrastructure provider DB Netz
AG. On the one hand, important trans-European corridors such as Rotterdam-
Genoa pass though Germany and require an ETCS upgrade to allow interoperability. On the other hand, vendor support for the existing national LZB safety
system ends and must be replaced in the near future. Therefore, a large number
of ETCS tracks must be planned in coming years.

At present, the planning process is performed mostly by hand. Only limited
tool support is available, essentially assisting in the mere drawing process by
providing symbol libraries and CAD tools (lower layer in Table 1). All necessary signalling elements are placed onto the plan individually and their correct
position is calculated manually. Neither can drawing tools check whether the
plan is compliant to the ETCS rules [5]: this is established in a complex review

---

The work reported in this paper was supported by DB Netz AG in project FORMETCS,
part of the Innovationsallianz TU Darmstadt/Deutsche Bahn AG.

ⓒ Springer Nature Switzerland AG 2019
S. Collart-Dutilleul et al. (Eds.): RSSRail 2019, LNCS 11495, pp. 79–90, 2019.
https://doi.org/10.1007/978-3-030-18744-6_5

Table 1. Information layers of the planning domain

Layer	Type of Information	Tool Capability	Type of Tool	Example
Pragmatics	Algorithmic	Automation	Planner, Validator	EPLAN
Semantics	Function, Purpose	Interoperability	OODB, XML	ProSig
Factual	Geometry, Id	Draw, Visualize	CAD	AutoCAD

procedure. Therefore, currently the planning of an ETCS compliant track is a time-consuming, expensive, and error-prone process.

In the last years DB Netz AG has been developing the XML-based interchange standard PlanPro [9] for rail tracks. PlanPro started to be rolled out in commonly used commercial planning tools such as ProSig.[1] In addition to the mere layout and identification of signalling elements, PlanPro contains semantic information (middle layer in Table 1) about their function and purpose. For example, it can group signals, switches, and other track elements that belong together. Technically, PlanPro consists of an object-oriented model with an associated XML-based linearization schema. PlanPro makes it possible for different tools to *interoperate* in a semantics-preserving manner. This is the basis for the partial automation of the planning process described in this paper.

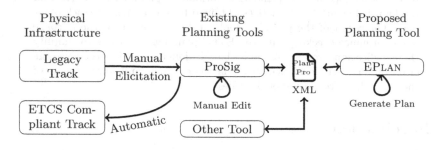

Fig. 1. Usage schema of EPLAN

To assist planners, we were asked by DB Netz AG to develop the tool EPLAN for automated generation of valid ETCS plans based on the PlanPro XML format, see Fig. 1 on the right. EPLAN takes as input a legacy track layout and additional information such as block definitions and a legacy (conventional) signalling system represented as a PlanPro XML file. It then automatically computes the components required for ETCS compliance and determines their positions according to ETCS planning rules (top layer in Table 1, on the right in Fig. 1). The new components are added to the existing PlanPro XML file which can be processed by other tools. This interoperability has important advantages:

---

[1] http://www.ivv-gmbh.de/de/prosigr.html.

- As EPLAN starts with a given track layout with optional conventional signalling, it is ideally suited for upgrading legacy tracks with ETCS components
  in parallel to persisting national systems.
- Its PlanPro output can be further processed in editing tools such as ProSig,
  allowing manual fine-tuning and adjustment of generated plans.
- Existing PlanPro-compatible tools can be used to generate the input for our
  tool and process its output, for example, to generate data tables for the plan
  review process.
- Since the PlanPro format is intended as the future interchange standard for
  digital planning of signalling systems at DB, our tool can easily be integrated
  into any designated planning workflow.

In this paper we describe the architecture and design of EPLAN, as well as
some strategies for testing and validation. In Sect. 2 we give a very compact
account of ETCS planning rules, in Sect. 3 we describe the PlanPro data model
[9], in Sect. 4 we document how we arrived at the planning algorithms and give
implementation and performance details. In Sect. 5 we lay down our validation
and verification strategy, finally we discuss related work and conclude.

2   ETCS Planning Rules

The main planning rulebook for all signalling systems in the German railway
network is Ril (Richtlinie) 819 [5]. It is divided into several submodules. Most
important for our case are module 819.1344 for executive planning of ETCS
Level 2 and module 819.1348 for ETCS Level 1. Both require that an interlocking
system (including routes, block definitions, possibly signals) has already been
planned. They define several types of data points (balise groups with a specific
meaning and a common set of included packets) and according placement rules.
Placement is relative to a reference point, in most cases a signal[2].

Most distances relevant for placement are defined as intervals, i.e. a minimum
and maximum allowed distance to the reference point, inside which the final
position can legally vary. For example, a data point of type 23 must be placed
300 m in front of a main signal with an allowed deviation of ±50 m. The interval
boundaries may depend on conditions, such as the distance to other objects. It
is also possible to specify that within a certain area around particular objects
no data point is placed. In this case, alternative placement instructions apply.

If the placement intervals of two data points intersect, then these data points
should be merged to reduce the total number of required balises. In some cases
the placement rules specify already how this can be achieved. For example, if two
signals facing in opposite direction have a distance between 350 m and 700 m, the
data points of type 23 for both signals (as described above) can be merged into
a single one, placed at the center between both signals. In cases where merging

---

[2] If a track is planned without signals, the ETCS stop marker boards Ne 14 [4] are
used as reference points instead.

rules are not explicitly stated, it is up to the planner to detect these situations manually and to optimize the plan accordingly.

All rules are described in a declarative manner. They constitute a set of conditions that any final plan must satisfy as a whole. The rules do not include an algorithm to obtain a valid plan starting from a blank sheet of paper (or from a given legacy layout). Experienced track planners have elaborated strategies in which order to place data points. They perform their task as an iterative process: data points are placed onto the plan until it is not possible to place any further data point without violating the rules (we provide more details on this in Sect. 4.1 below). Then it is necessary to backtrack, adjust a suitable data point position, and re-try until the plan is complete and valid—a time-consuming and tedious task.

It is important to realize that the rules in [5] are mere guidelines, representing the state of the art, and do not have the status of a law. This entails that it is possible to deviate from the rules if they cannot possibly be fulfilled for a given track layout. However, in this case a "proof of equal safety" must be provided, attesting that the probability of a safety-critical situation is not higher as if the rules had been satisfied. This can be a complex task, hence satisfying the rules drastically simplifies the certification process and normally is by far preferable.

3   The PlanPro Data Model

Prerequisite for automated plan generation is a digital track model that contains sufficient semantic information about the function of track elements and their relation. As explained in Sect. 1, we use the PlanPro object model [9] developed by DB Netz for the planning of digital interlocking systems.

PlanPro is an object-oriented model. It defines classes that contain objects corresponding to all elements of a signalling system: the track layout (as nodes and edges), switches (with their mechanical and electrical components), signals, block definitions, train control system components (PZB magnets, ETCS balises, etc.), and train detection devices [3]. All objects have properties, including an id (for referencing), a position, and, where applicable, a direction, build type, etc. The classes in PlanPro form a hierarchy. As usual in OO models, properties common to subclasses are factored out to their superclass to render the description succinct. For example, all objects with a geographical location inherit from a parent PointObject, where the properties for position information are declared.

The PlanPro Model makes it possible to store track plans in some form of OO database (see Table 1), which in the simplest case can be just a sequence of property lists. Cross referencing between PlanPro objects is realized by referencing an object id, which is a 128 bit UUID conforming to RFC 4122 [6]. There is an XML schema for the PlanPro object model that allows to linearize it for (XML) file-based interchange (export and import).

PlanPro was originally intended as a data storage and exchange format between different planning stages (for example, planners and component providers or planners and certifiers). The main use case so far is to generate from the PlanPro model the layout plans and data tables for the review process. An automation of the planning task was not intended when the format was developed. Therefore, one objective of our work is to evaluate whether the PlanPro model contains sufficient information and hence is usable for automated planning.

4 From Planning Rules to Planning Program

4.1 Elicitation of Planning Algorithm

Our starting point is a digital track layout in PlanPro format, possibly with legacy signalling, and the ETCS planning rules in paper form. One planning approach is to formalize the rules, for example, as logic constraints and then use a logic programming language to start a systematic, complete search over all rules applicable to the given track layout. Such an unguided search is bound to be inefficient, because the rules embody few semantic constraints which leads to a very high branching factor. In addition, even when exhaustive search generates a valid track plan, the result would be not necessarily perceived as "good" or intuitive by a human expert. It would also be not straightforward to incorporate optimization (for example, minimizing the balise count) into such an approach.

> **⚲ Key Insight 1:**
> We decided to replace exhaustive search with a heuristically guided construction algorithm, informed by the experience and strategy of the human planners. Put differently, instead of formalizing the rulebooks, we formalize the heuristic knowledge of human planners.

The data in the rulebooks are merely used to compute the position, where an object must be placed and to verify each single construction step. This is not formalized as a rule, but incorporated into the placement algorithm. This is possible, because, even though there is a large number of rules in Ril 819, there is only a relatively small number of placement constructions that are used over and over again. Hence, only a small fraction of the content of the rulebook, namely that relating to automatic placement, had to be formalized in algorithmic form.

Obviously, such a heuristic approach only works in a highly specific domain, where the heuristic knowledge of the human expert is sufficiently explicit. It was not obvious from the beginning whether this is the case. Therefore, we conducted a series of interviews with experienced ETCS track planners from DB Engineering & Consulting. The goal was to find out how a planner constructs a plan from scratch and the order in which each single step is performed. We needed to establish whether the heuristic knowledge of the planners is sufficiently structured and explicit to be rendered algorithmically. We also wanted to know which tasks should be automated and which are better performed manually.

> **🔍 Key Insight 2:**
> The track planners proceed in a highly structured manner whereby the planning process is divided into clearly distinguishable sequential phases among which no backtracking occurs. This structure reflects an implicit hierarchy among the track elements to be placed that is not obvious from the rulebooks.

The following staged approach for ETCS Level 2 planning can be formulated, which makes the planning heuristics explicit:

1. Start with the placement of data points located directly at main signals or that have a fixed distance to them. This includes the data point types 20, 21 which disallow a train to proceed in Staff Responsible (SR) mode and the positioning data point type 23, always located 300 m in front of a signal.
2. Place the positioning data points type 28 for Start-of-Mission (SoM) areas providing position information for starting trains. Each SoM area contains up to eight separate data points (up to 14 single balises) and their position depends on the distance to a signal and a following switch, as well as on the track speed. The rules contain many variations and special cases which makes manual placement laborious and error-prone. The relevant rules also prescribe combinations with the second location data point in front of signals (data point type 24) which is also placed at this stage.
3. Place data point type 24 as standalone where no combination with type 28 is possible.
4. Place the Temporary Speed Restriction (TSR) data points (type 26), restricting speed when approaching a signal in SR mode. Their position depends on the track gradient and they must be repeated when another signal resides between them and the related signal.
5. Place TSR Revocation data points (type 37) on all branches after data point type 26 that do not lead to the guarded signal.
6. Place positioning data points (type 25) for route detection on faulty switches. For this the shortest possible route after a switch must be calculated and all data points already existing on it must be taken into account. Data point 25 is only placed if the existing data points cannot determine the used route. Manual calculation of these positions is a complex and error-prone task.
7. Place positioning data points (type 25) between any already placed data points that have a distance of more than 1800 m. This is needed to reduce the uncertainty of train position reports.

In 1–7 the list of PlanPro objects is traversed until a potential reference point is found. From there positions where data points have to be placed are calculated, the objects are created and added. For example, in 7 the list of already placed data points is traversed, their neighbors are determined and distances calculated. If a distance is above 1800 m, the path is repeatedly divided into smaller subsegments of equal length, with new data points of type 25 in between them, until no more gaps above 1800 m are present.

It was decided not to consider other data points at this time: they can either be easily placed manually, or are only relevant in special cases, or they require input external to the model. For example, the transition area between ETCS and national systems must be defined by the planner or the ordering party. For ETCS Level 1 (mode Limited Supervision), we only place those data points at main and presignals that correspond to PZB track magnets. Level 1 is a proof of concept for now—more extensive support will be realized at a later stage.

4.2 Tool Implementation

EPLAN is realized as a console application written in JAVA. All necessary planning parameters, such as the ETCS level, input and output files, etc., are provided as command line parameters. As mentioned in Sect. 2, the ETCS planing rules require an already planned interlocking system which must be part of the input PlanPro file. Main signals or legacy train control systems are not needed, however. The output file contains the new ETCS components like data points, any other information from the input file remains *unchanged*. The overall control flow is as follows:

1. Command line arguments are parsed.
2. The PlanPro XML file is loaded, its content parsed and stored as an hierarchical DOM tree [11].
3. For each item 1–7 described in Sect. 4.1, an algorithmic construction for placement of track elements is implemented. It accesses the complete DOM tree to calculate placement parameters (such as distances to specific objects). The new data points are created as DOM nodes and added to the tree.
4. The resulting DOM tree is written out as a PlanPro XML file.

The placement algorithm accesses several helper functions. These operate on the DOM tree and provide functionalities such as tracking graph traversal, distance calculation between two objects, or calculation of positions with a relative distance to an object considering all possible track branches. These functions are used in the placement algorithms to evaluate placement conditions and to calculate the positions of the data points.

Performance. The planning tool consists of over 2,000 lines of JAVA code. The PlanPro input files we use for evaluation can have a size of over 25 MB, contain up to 3,900 objects with more than 35,000 attributes (including Base64-encoded binary data as specified in RFC 4648). This corresponds to a complete layout for a typical mid-sized station with eight tracks, 140 signals, 30 switches, and 75 train detection components. The generation of a track plan in this case takes ca. 5 s. All real ETCS plannings we have seen so far have a comparable size, so we do not expect performance issues for a real-life application.

Evaluation. We presented the generated plans of small to medium-sized stations to planning experts who confirmed that the placement of track elements is reasonable and correct up to minor adjustments.

5   Validation and Verification

5.1   General Considerations

A perfect V & V strategy for our setting would require to (i) *validate* that all rules in [5] have been correctly interpreted and formalized (ii) formally *verify* that the planning tool implements them correctly and produces only ETCS-compliant plans.Given that for the foreseeable future all created plans must pass a review process before they are approved for construction, and it is far from clear whether certification of a fully verified tool is possible or even wished by the responsible authorities, the above vision seems over-ambitious.[3]

Our priority at this point is to get a usable prototype out into the production environment as soon as possible. We are able to afford weaker demands on correctness, because errors in the generated plan will be detected and corrected in the review process, just as for manually generated plans. However, to achieve an acceptable level of trust (and, therefore, usability) it is important to minimize the need for manual modification of generated plans. Here it is important to realize that only the plan reviewers have the knowledge to tell whether a plan is correct or not. But reviewers can only evaluate *final* planning results, not individual planning steps. Therefore, it is not useful to specify separate correctness properties for the various stages of the planning algorithm at this time. Instead we pursue a two-pronged approach focusing on final plans: To help planners *validating* generated plans we developed a visualization tool (following section). To *verify* the EPLAN tool we use a *domain-specific test coverage criterion*: a set of generated test plans that cover all possible planning cases is submitted for review. This allows to infer correctness of the algorithms from the correctness of the reviewed plans relative to coverage (Sect. 5.3).

5.2   Visualization and Data Analysis Tool

Raw XML output is unintuitive and must be rendered in a human-readable format to amenable for review.

> **⚲ Key Insight 3:**
> From our discussions with the planners we learned that visualization and interactive querying of generated track plans is essential for effective validation.

Unfortunately, the currently available tools that can process data in Plan-Pro format have been designed for planning conventional signalling systems and do not yet support PlanPro data with ETCS Level 2 objects. Therefore, we developed our own PlanPro visualization tool. It is capable of generating a track layout plan from a PlanPro XML file. The layout contains all objects with a geographical position (signals, data points, train detection components, etc.). It is

---

[3] Still, it is clearly of great interest to *validate* a suitable formalization of the rulebooks (item (i) above), because it minimizes errors in the generated plans and increases trust on side of the planners who use it. This activity is currently pursued in the FORMETCS project and will be reported in a follow-up paper. In Sect. 6.1 we report on an automated verification tool for manually created plans.

designed to resemble the track overview plans employed in certification reviews and provides sufficient information on the generated plan, including the positions of the components relative to each other. Figure 2 shows two screenshots from the PlanPro visualization tool, demonstrating the changes EPLAN makes to a given track layout. Figure 2a is the basic track plan with conventional signalling given as input to EPLAN. Figure 2b shows the same plan after the execution of EPLAN, where the ETCS Level 2-compliant placement of new track elements is shown as yellow circles.

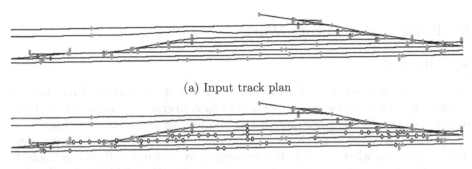

(a) Input track plan

(b) Track plan after placement of ETCS elements with EPLAN

Fig. 2. Screenshots from the PlanPro visualization tool.

All objects, including logical objects without position (telegrams, signal aspects, etc.), can be separately listed and queried. The tool allows interactive inspection of object attributes as well as search for object ids. A feature to calculate the distance between two arbitrary selected, placeable objects is included. This distance measurement is a common (and tedious) task in a plan review process. Correctly computed distances are crucial for safety, so the implementation of this function is a prime candidate for formal verification, see Sect. 6.2.

5.3 Rule Coverage

Rulebook [5] is organized into placement rules for each data point type. Each placement rule has several conditions, forming branches and subrules within the main rule. However, not all available rules need to be applied to place a specific data point—the rules that are triggered depend on the planning situation and, as explained above, the placement algorithm constitutes no one-to-one implementation of the rules.

> **🔍 Key Insight 4:**
> Generic, code-based test coverage criteria [2] are unsuitable for programs such as EPLAN whose output is a complex DOM object. Like for compilers and other code transformers, it is more adequate to define a *domain-specific* test criterion and build an according test suite.

To increase trust in the correctness of an automated planning process, all possible subrules must be selected at least once in a scenario of the set suite. We call this *rule coverage*. For each test scenario an *expected* generated plan is constructed that must be approved by the certifier once. A test *oracle* can be constructed from it simply by comparing the expected plan for each test scenario with the actually generated plan (modulo renaming and DOM tree traversal sequence). This is the basis, for example, for automated regression testing.

Another way to view our testing strategy is as an instance of model-based testing [10], where the (formalized) rulebook [5] plays the role of the model.

6 Related and Future Work

6.1 Related Work

There is a large body of work on formal models and verification of interlocking systems, generally on *dynamic* aspects of railway operation. This is not the focus of our project which is about automated planning of *static* infrastructure.

We are not aware of much work on automated ETCS-compliant track planning. Closest to what we do is the Norwegian NFR project RailCons[4], jointly pursued by University of Oslo and the company RailCOMPLETE AS. The latter markets a CAD-based infrastructure planning tool similar to ProSig, which extends AutoCAD with railway-specific semantic data. In the project the program has been extended with additional semantic information, based on the standardized Railway Markup Language railML[5] and stored directly in the Auto-CAD files. The railML model can be extracted from the CAD files and verified against formalized planning rules [8]. In contrast to our approach they encode rulebooks into a generic logic programming language. They evaluate their approach with track data from a real construction project and show that non-trivial properties can be verified in seconds. The RailCons project is *complementary* to our work in being about automated rule-based *verification* of manually created plans. In FORMETCS we automate, at least partially, the *planning* process. The RailCons model seems to be somewhat more abstract than ours and the rules used for verification seem to be incomplete. Specifically, ETCS regulations are mentioned as future work in [8].

6.2 Future Work

As a next step, a real ETCS track in operation in the DB network will be re-planned with our tool and the results will be compared by the DB planning team. This is a further step towards verification of the algorithmic rendering in EPLAN. It will also demonstrate that our tool is usable for a real life scenario. For use in production it will be necessary to provide support for ETCS Level 1.

---

[4] https://www.mn.uio.no/ifi/english/research/projects/railcons.
[5] https://www.railml.org.

A companion project to FORMETCS is FORMBAR[6], where the rulebooks for the *operation* of trains are formalized in an executable model [7] that permits simulation as well as static cost estimation. It would be desirable to connect both projects: First one generates with EPLAN different variants of a track plan (for example, ETCS Level 1 and 2). These are then evaluated with the FORMBAR tool for relative performance in various traffic load situations. This would allow to base decisions in capacity planning *at the track planning stage* on fine-grained, highly realistic, dynamic models.

As mentioned in Sect. 5.1, while it makes limited sense to formally verify or even specify EPLAN as a whole, it is desirable to verify the most safety-critical and error-prone parts such as distance calculations. Formal verification of this kind of JAVA code is completely feasible [1].

7   Conclusion

We presented a concept for automating large parts of the planning process for rail tracks, in particular with respect to the ETCS Level 2 regulations. We concentrated on well-structured aspects, where the application of placement rules is governed by explicit heuristics and no or little search is involved. Our work proved that the PlanPro model contains sufficient information to be used in automated planning.

We took great care that the automated planner can be integrated into the existing workflow and tool chains. We found that the capability to visualize, inspect and interact with the generated plans is essential.

We designed a pragmatic validation and verification strategy based on visualization and automatable, model-based testing with a domain-specific test criterion. Formal validation and verification is possible as future work.

Acknowledgments. We are very grateful to the planning team of DB Engineering & Consulting in Karlsruhe for being generous with their time and expertise. We thank the reviewers for their suggestions that helped to improve the final version of this paper.

References

1. Ahrendt, W., Beckert, B., Bubel, R., Hähnle, R., Schmitt, P., Ulbrich, M. (eds.): Deductive Software Verification-The KeY Book: From Theory to Practice. LNCS, vol. 10001. Springer, Heidelberg (2016). https://doi.org/10.1007/978-3-319-49812-6
2. Ammann, P., Offutt, J.: Introduction to Software Testing. Cambridge University Press, Cambridge (2008)
3. DB Netz AG: PlanPro-Glossar 1.8.0. http://confluence.plan-pro.org/display/G180/Index
4. Deutsche Bahn AG, Frankfurt: Richtlinie 301: Signalbuch
5. Deutsche Bahn AG, Frankfurt: Richtlinie 819: LST-Anlagen planen

---

[6] https://formbar.raillab.de/en/about-2.

6. ISO: Standard on Generation and registration of Universally Unique Identifiers (UUIDs) and their use as ASN.1 Object Identifier components (2005). ISO/IEC 9834-8:2005

7. Kamburjan, E., Hähnle, R., Schön, S.: Formal modeling and analysis of railway operations with active objects. Sci. Comput. Program. **166**, 167–193 (2018)

8. Luteberget, B., Johansen, C.: Efficient verification of railway infrastructure designs against standard regulations. Formal Methods Syst. Des. **52**(1), 1–32 (2018)

9. Maschek, U., Klaus, C., Gerke, C., Uminski, V., Girke, K.J.: PlanPro: Durchgängige elektronische Datenhaltung im ESTW-Planungsprozess. Signal+Draht **104**(9), 22–26 (2012)

10. Utting, M., Legeard, B.: Practical Model-Based Testing - A Tools Approach. Morgan Kaufmann, Burlington (2007)

11. W3C: Document Object Model DOM 4, November 2015. https://www.w3.org/TR/dom/

The Recent Applications of Machine Learning in Rail Track Maintenance: A Survey

Muhammad Chenariyan Nakhaee[1]([⊠]), Djoerd Hiemstra[1],
Mariëlle Stoelinga[2,3], and Martijn van Noort[4]

[1] Data Science, University of Twente, Enschede, The Netherlands
{m.cnakhaee,d.hiemstra}@utwente.nl
[2] Formal Methods and Tools, University of Twente, Enschede, The Netherlands
m.i.a.stoelinga@utwente.nl
[3] Software Science, Radboud University Nijmegen, Nijmegen, The Netherlands
[4] ProRail, Utrecht, The Netherlands
martijn.vannoort@prorail.nl

Abstract. Railway systems play a vital role in the world's economy and movement of goods and people. Rail tracks are one of the most critical components needed for the uninterrupted operation of railway systems. However, environmental conditions or mechanical forces can accelerate the degradation process of rail tracks. Any fault in rail tracks can incur enormous costs or even results in disastrous incidents such as train derailment. Over the past few years, the research community has adopted the use of machine learning (ML) algorithms for diagnosis and prognosis of rail defects in order to help the railway industry to carry out timely responses to failures. In this paper, we review the existing literature on the state-of-the-art machine learning-based approaches used in different rail track maintenance tasks. As one of our main contributions, we also provide a taxonomy to classify the existing literature based on types of methods and types of data. Moreover, we present the shortcomings of current techniques and discuss what research community and rail industry can do to address these issues. Finally, we conclude with a list of recommended directions for future research in the field.

Keywords: Rail track · Machine learning · Maintenance · Deep learning

1 Introduction

Railway systems are one of the most important means of transportation and play a crucial role in the world's economy [1]. Compared to other means, railways provide a more comfortable experience. Besides, they are more affordable, which make them one the most popular way of commuting. Railway tracks are one of the most important components of railway systems. However, the continuous impact of repetitive passing of trains, high railroad network velocity, axle loads and environmental conditions cause rail deterioration. The presence of even a small flaw in rail tracks might introduce more severe defects and broken rails which can lead to huge maintenance costs and reduce the reliability and availability of the system [2]. But more importantly, broken rail track

© Springer Nature Switzerland AG 2019
S. Collart-Dutilleul et al. (Eds.): RSSRail 2019, LNCS 11495, pp. 91–105, 2019.
https://doi.org/10.1007/978-3-030-18744-6_6

can lead to train derailments which subsequently endanger the safety of the passengers and train crews [3]. For example, over the past decade, around one-third of all railroad accidents in the US have been caused by track related defects [4]. Thus, to avoid risks and system disruptions, rail tracks need to be monitored and maintained regularly [5, 6]. However, railway track maintenance is one of the most expensive maintenance activities in railway engineering. For instance, the estimates reveal that approximately each year half of the maintenance budget in the Netherlands is spent only on railway track maintenance activities [7]. Therefore, to reduce the costs and risk associated with rail track failures and to improve the safety and maintenance operations novel techniques and approaches should be developed and be adopted.

Nowadays due to the rapid technological advances and the extensive deployment of low-cost connected devices and sensors, the industrial Internet of Things (IoT) plays an increasing role in the effective implementation of maintenance strategies across a wide range of industries [8]. The railway industry has also embraced the integration of connected devices, sensors and big data technologies to improve their daily maintenance operations [9]. Over the past two decades, machine learning (ML) has revolutionized a wide range of fields such as computer vision, natural language processing, and speech recognition. With the explosion in the amount of data collected by advanced monitoring devices such as wireless sensor networks or high resolution video cameras which are being widely used to inspect critical railway infrastructure, machine learning is also gaining in popularity to improve the operations and reliability of railway systems, and to minimize the daily maintenance costs and risks [10].

To address this demand from the rail industry, a great deal of research has been done over the past few years and various machine learning models have been employed for condition monitoring of rail tracks. Although the application of machine learning for maintenance has been reviewed in other domains such as machine health monitoring [8] and wind turbines [11], to the best of our knowledge no other paper has surveyed the existing literature on the application of machine learning in the rail track maintenance. The aim of this paper is to provide a thorough literature review on current machine learning techniques used for the condition monitoring of rail tracks while also discussing drawbacks of these methods along with what researchers and industry can do to improve the performance and trustworthiness of existing approaches.

This paper is organized as follows: In Sect. 2, the paper introduces different paradigms of machine learning. Section 3 discuss what kinds of flaws can be observed in rail tracks and which types of tools are utilized to inspect rail defects. Section 4, explores the existing machine learning algorithms used in the context of rail track maintenance. In Sect. 5, we describe the shortfalls of current techniques and present a set of new research directions. Finally, in Sect. 6 we present our conclusion.

2   A Brief Introduction to Machine Learning

An ML algorithm usually defined as an algorithm that can learn the underlying patterns from data without being explicitly programmed by human experts. Supervise learning algorithms are a subset of ML models that can learn to predict a target variable from a set of predictive variables also called as features or attributes. On the other hand, unsupervised learning techniques try to infer the inherent structure or represent the input data into a more compressed and interpretable way without being provided with labeled datasets. For instance, principal components analysis (PCA) which is one of the most widely-used unsupervised techniques, takes a dataset stored as a set of potentially correlated variables and compress the dataset by generating a set of new variables that have no linear correlation. Machine learning techniques can also be divided into shallow algorithms and deep algorithms. The main distinction between shallow and deep learning algorithms is in their level of representation. Shallow learning-based techniques use hand-crafted features, manual feature extraction/selection techniques and algorithms such as Support Vector Machines (SVM) [12], Decision Trees [13] and Random Forests [14] for learning the mapping between predictive variables and the target [8]. Moreover, this set of algorithms often use structured datasets such as tables as an input. For example, a decision tree algorithm incrementally learns a set of decision- rules represented as decision nodes and leaf nodes from a dataset that has multiple rows and columns. At each decision node, the decision tree algorithm splits the observations into smaller subsets based on a feature in the dataset that gives higher homogeneity among observations in each subset. A random forest algorithm is an ensemble of multiple decision trees. In each iteration of a random forest algorithm, a decision tree model is trained on a subset of features and a subset of data samples. Then, the algorithm aggregates the outputs of individual trees to make a prediction. Random forests can be an extremely powerful machine learning technique since they add an extra randomness element to a simple decision tree and they combine the predictions of multiple decision trees.

However, deep learning algorithms rarely require hand-engineered features and they can learn the representation directly from the data (e.g. raw images). For this reason, deep learning is sometimes referred to as "representation learning" [15]. This property partially eliminates the need for feature engineering, which gives deep learning algorithms an edge over shallow learning algorithms. Over the past couple of years, the research community has also taken advantage of deep learning for rail defect inspection and monitoring. Even some researchers believe deep learning may become a potential element in the ultimate fully automated rail inspection systems [6].

Convolutional neural networks (CNN) are a special case of deep artificial neural networks (ANN) which have been especially used for computer vision tasks. In CNN models, the fully connected layers in normal neural networks are replaced by convolutional layers. The main difference between the fully-connected and convolutional layer is that in a convolutional layer each neuron is not connected to all neurons in the previous and next layers and the weights are shared between groups of layers [16]. It has been shown that this difference give CNNs a unique property. The early layers of CNNs store low-level feature like edges and curves, while the last layers of a CNN contain the information about the more complex features such as eyes [17]. This is considered to be an interesting characteristic of CNNs as it gives the CNN the ability to use the knowledge (weights) learnt from solving a problem to solve a new problem, also widely known as transfer learning. For example, the weights of a CNN trained on a very large dataset such as ImageNet database [18] can be used to train a new CNN network for detecting tumors in medical applications [19]. CNNs have been successfully applied to various computer vision problems and even beat both humans and the existing algorithms in tasks such as image classification and object detection [20, 21]. In the following section we can also see a surge in the number of publications that trained CNNs to recognize faults in rail tracks.

Besides CNNs there are other classes of deep learning algorithms which have been widely used in the literature to predict time series data [22]. For example, long short-term memory (LSTM) networks, a variant of recurrent neural networks (RNNs) [23], can learn the long-term temporal dependencies by utilizing special mechanisms called memory cells [24]. Lately LSTM networks have shown promising results in predicting the remaining useful life of industrial equipment using IoT data [25].

3   Rail Track Data

The rail inspection data can differ based on different rail defects and measurement methods. In addition, rail data can be stored as structured, semi-structured and unstructured formats. These differences determine which kind of processing techniques and algorithms are more suited for a certain problem. For instance, rail track data such as records of previous maintenance activities collected by human operators can be stored as a structured table and later used by shallow learning algorithm such as random forests. On the other hand, deep learning algorithms are the natural choice for dealing with unstructured data like images. Therefore, in this section we draw a distinction between different defects and data sources which later will be used in our proposed taxonomy.

3.1   Type of Rail Track Faults

Rail defects can develop and grow in different parts of a railway track and therefore they have been categorized in different ways by the researchers. However, in general, rail track defects can be divided into structural defects and track geometry irregularities [1]. Track geometry defects such as rail misalignments are characterized by undesirable deviation of rail geometric parameters from their designed value. Structural defects describe the structural degradations of rail track components such as rail, ballast and fasteners [26]. However, It should be noted that not only track geometry irregularities are responsible for train accidents and directly impact the safety of the rail network but they can also lead to the birth of structural defects [4, 27]. More information on different geometry defects can be found in [28]. Readers can also refer to [29] to find a more complete overview of different structural rail track defects.

3.2   Rail Inspection Methods and Tools

Numerous non-destructive methods and tools are utilized in the rail industry to inspect the condition of rail tracks and data collection. These techniques include manual inspection, ultrasonic devices, high resolution video cameras, 3D-laser cameras, eddy current inspection, magnetic flux leakage etc. A more comprehensive description and comparison of rail inspection tools and methods can be found in [10, 30]. While each method can be used to detect failures in different parts of the rail track and collect specific information about the condition of the rail, not all of them have been used in machine learning literature. However, in recent years, visual inspection systems and particularly video cameras have become one of the most important and effective inspection tools for automatic and flexible rail track monitoring [2]. Video cameras mounted on specialized trains can capture high-resolution images of rail tracks from different angles. In that case, a large number of images are collected which later can be used to train machine learning algorithms to detect anomalies in the rail track. However, large scale deployment of video cameras can present some technical challenges as they require a key infrastructure for efficient storage and processing of streaming data. For instance, each year video cameras collect roughly 10 terabytes of image data in the Dutch railway system [31]. Moreover the existence of some residuals such as oil and dust which might be present in the collected images can have a negative impact on the performance of machine learning algorithms [32].

4 Machine Learning for Track Defect Detection

In this section, we summarize different machine learning techniques adopted by researchers to help the rail industry overcome its maintenance challenges. The current literature has been divided into two major classes of techniques based on the taxonomy we have presented throughout the paper (Table 1). The first group represents the experiments that were carried out with shallow learning algorithms and the second group specifically includes deep learning-based approaches. Further, Table 1 offers more information on other parts of our taxonomy.

4.1 Shallow Learning-Based Algorithms for Rail Track Maintenance

Before 2012 and when deep learning made its first breakthrough in the field of computer vision by AlexNet [33], researchers mainly used complex features extracted manually from images and then trained a shallow learning algorithm such as SVM for image classification and object detection [15]. Likewise, in classical defect detection literature and before the emergence of deep learning techniques, various feature extraction and transformation techniques such as histogram of oriented gradients (HoG) have been applied to image datasets [34]. For instance, Xia et al. [35] extracted Haar-like features to detect broken fasteners in the railway network by an AdaBoost algorithm. To reduce the dimensionality of the input data, Santur et al. [36] first applied various feature extraction techniques such as PCA, kernel principal component analysis (KPCA), singular value decomposition (SVD) and histogram match (HM) techniques to a dataset which comprised a number of non-defective image and an artificially generated image dataset of non-defective images. Next, they trained a random forest algorithm on a set of extracted features. They concluded that features created by PCA provided the most accurate result. Gao et al. [37] merged three different data sources in what they described as 'combined systems method' which comprised of ultrasonic, eddy current and surface imaging video measurements. Then they fed the features extracted from applying a clustering algorithm on their database to an SVM algorithm for detecting squats. Sadeghi et al. [38] employed four neural network models with each with one hidden layer to predict the defect density of rail tracks which was defined as the fraction of a rail segment that is defective. To train the neural network models they combined various attributes such as track quality index of gauges collected through manual inspection.

In the case of rail geometry defects, using a subset of RAS Problem Solving Competition 2015 dataset, Hu et al. [39] attempted to use an SVM algorithm to forecast when a less severe track defect will develop into a more severe type of defect. Famurewa et al. [40] presented a systematic data methodology for rail condition monitoring which consists of descriptive, diagnostic, predictive, and prescriptive steps. As a part of their descriptive and diagnostic strategy, the authors aimed their attention to detect anomalous patterns in sharp curves using PCA algorithm and data acquired by manual inspection from the Swedish railway network. Jiang et al. [41] proposed a hybrid approach to recognize rolling contact fatigue from data obtained in laser ultrasonic experiments. In their proposed approach, the measurement signals were decomposed into a new set of features using a wavelet packet transform (WPT). Next, to reduce the dimensionality of data and to remove the effect of correlated features. Similarly, to better understand and visualize high dimensional track geometry data into a more compressed representation, Lasisi et al. [4] applied PCA, a well-known dimensionality reduction algorithm, to a dataset of 31 features collected from a section of US Class I railway network. KPCA, a nonlinear variant of PCA technique, was applied to new features. Finally, the output of the KPCA algorithm was used as an input to an SVM model to detect four kinds of surface defects.

Lee et al. [42] made use of artificial neural networks (ANNs) and SVM algorithms to predict track quality index (TQI) based on simulation data generated from various important track parameters such as type of curvatures. They concluded that while the ANN algorithm slightly performs better that the SVM algorithm, the difference between these two algorithms is mostly insignificant. Furthermore, they stated that at least two years of data is required for more stable predictions.

In some real-world cases, the railway defect dataset might consist of only positive (defective) and unlabeled observations which essentially means that the conventional classification metrics cannot be computed accurately. Motivated by this problem, Hajizadeh et al. [43] introduced a new metric called Positive and Unlabeled Learning Performance (PULP) to assess the performance of classifiers on datasets with only defective observations. They tested their proposed metric on a rail vibration datasets using two SVM models and stated that a model with a better PULP performance can detect more failures compared to a model with inferior PUPL performance. In another similar work, Hajizadeh et al. [44] proposed a semi-supervised technique which added the unlabeled observations to the training dataset to improve the balance between the two classes of squat defects and non-defects.

4.2 Deep Learning-Based Algorithms for Rail Track Maintenance

One of the earliest attempts to employ deep learning techniques for rail defect detection was carried out by Soukup et al. [45]. They designed a CNN network with two layers to distinguish defective and non-defective cases using photometric stereo images. Since they had a relatively small dataset, and the methodology appeared to be vulnerable to over-fitting, sparse autoencoders and data augmentation were also used in their experiment to tackle this issue. After the successful implementation of CNNs for rail defect detection, other researchers gradually started to apply CNNs to other image databases. In [46], Gibert et al. applied a CNN network with 4 convolutional layers to a set of manually annotated images collected on US Northeast Corridor and classified rail track materials. Then they used the trained parameters of the CNN model for defect detection and semantic segmentation of railroad ties. As an extension of their previous research and based on their proposed approach in [47] which used an SVM to classify fastener defects, Gibert et al. [6] designed and trained a custom CNN architecture with five convolutional layers on the same dataset to categorize the condition of rail fasteners as missing, broken or good. To make their machine learning model more robust against unusual situations, they also used data augmentation and used re-sampling to add more hard-to-classify images to their training dataset.

To provide a tool for automatic defects detection in rail surface, Faghih-Roohi et al. [34] trained 3 different-sized CNN architectures on a manually labeled image dataset collected from approximately 700 km of rail tracks in the Netherlands. Based on the results of their experiment, they concluded that the deepest architecture outperforms the other two models on the multi-class classification of squat defects. The designed architecture for the medium-sized CNN network proposed in this paper is shown in Fig. 1. Jamshidi et al. [31] also classified squat defects with different levels of severity using a simple CNN architecture and a real-world image dataset. They also assessed the visual growth of a defect and its severity using an image database. However, the interesting contribution of their work is that not only they used image data for squat defect classification but they also analyzed crack growth using data collected from ultrasonic measurements and then combined it with image analysis results to provide a failure risk model.

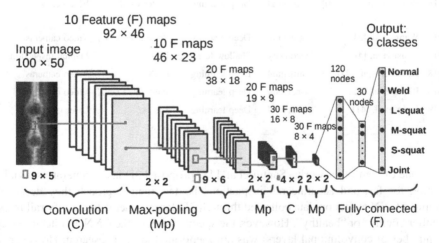

Fig. 1. Illustration of the medium-sized CNN network proposed in [34]

Table 1. An overview of current ML publications for rail track maintenance

Year	Authors	Defect type	ML class	ML algorithm	Data Source
2010	Xia et al. [35]	Structural	Shallow learning	Ada-Boost	Video cameras
2012	Sadeghi et al. [38]	Structural	Deep learning	ANN	Manual inspection
2014	Soukup et al. [45]	Structural	Deep learning	CNN/ Autoencoders	Photometric sensors
2014	Hajizadeh et al. [43]	Structural	Shallow learning	SVM	Video cameras
2015	Gibert et al. [6]	Structural	Shallow learning	SVM	Video cameras
2015	Gibert et al. [46]	Structural	Deep learning	CNN	Video cameras
2016	Hajizadeh et al. [44]	Structural	Shallow learning	SVM	Video cameras
2016	Hu et al. [39]	Geometry	Shallow learning	SVM	Manual inspection
2016	Faghih-Roohi et al. [34]	Structural	Deep learning	CNN	Video cameras
2017	Santur et al. [36]	Structural	Shallow learning	PCA/KPCA/ SVD/HM/ Random forest	Video cameras
2017	Gibert et al. [6]	Structural	Deep learning	CNN	Video cameras
2017	Santur et al. [48]	Structural	Deep learning	CNN	3D-laser cameras
2017	Famurewa et al. [40]	Geometry	Shallow learning	PCA	Manual inspection
2017	Jamshidi et al. [31]	Structural	Shallow learning	CNN	Ultrasonic/ Video cameras
2018	Gao et al. [37]	Structural	Shallow learning	SVM	Ultrasonic/ Eddy current/ Video cameras
2018	Lee et al. [42]	Geometry	Shallow learning	ANN	Simulation
2018	Santur et al. [49]	Structural	Deep learning	CNN	Video cameras
2018	Rauschmayr et al. [50]	Structural	Deep learning	Faster R-CNN/ GAN	Video cameras
2018	Wang et al. [51]	Structural	Deep learning	Pre-trained CNN	Video cameras
2018	Lasisi et al. [4]	Geometry	Shallow learning	PCA	Manual inspection
2018	Jamshidi et al. [27]	Structural	Deep learning	CNN	Video cameras
2018	Ritika et al. [52]	Geometry	Deep learning	Pre-trained CNN	Video cameras
2019	Jiang et al. [41]	Structural	Deep learning	KPCA/ SVM	Laser ultrasonic

In one of their other works, Santur et al. [48] proposed 3D laser cameras as a viable solution for fast and accurate rail inspection. To test their approach they described training a CNN model on data collected through 3D laser cameras to classify rail tracks as either "faulty" or "healthy". However, the specification of the CNN architecture (e.g. the number of convolutional layers) was not mentioned in their research. However, in their next experiment, Santur et al. [49] used normal video cameras and proposed a three-stage pipeline with a blur elimination step and trained a three-layers CNN model.

As a part of a more comprehensive big data-oriented methodology, Jamshidi et al. [27] in their recent analysis, trained a CNN network on both Axle Box Acceleration (ABA) inspection data and a manually labeled image dataset collected from a specific section of the Dutch rail network. In the other major contribution of this paper, the output of deep learning model, designed to classify the state of rail tracks as a normal, light squat defect and sever squat defect, was later used along with input from analysis of degradation factors and domain experts to define an optimal maintenance strategy.

Lately, the research community has also adopted more advanced deep learning techniques in railway engineering. For instance, to reduce the maintenance expense and enhance the safety of Swiss Federal Railways (SBB) system, Rauschmayr et al. [50] employed several state-of-the-art deep learning algorithms to detect defect and to locate the defective parts on the tracks. First of all, by using a pre-trained faster R-CNN model, they segmented track surfaces and clamps to identify anomalies. Then they made use of Generative Adversarial Networks (GAN) to cluster normal and anomalous observations. In this case, if an observation does not belong to certain clusters, more likely it will be a defect. Further, they discussed the feasibility of this approach as an alternative to replace the manual labeling. Wang et al. [51] also performed an experiment with two well-known deep learning architectures and transfer learning, known as AlexNet and ResNet, to recognize fasteners defects using a hand-annotated image dataset acquired from two separate lines of rails in the US. They concluded that the pre-trained ResNet not only achieved more accurate and reliable results, but it could generalize well on classification of different track lines. To detect geometry defects, Ritika et al. [52] applied several data augmentation techniques to generate artificial images with sun kinks defects. Then, they used a pre-trained Inception V3 CNN architecture to identify sun kinks in rail tracks.

5 Discussion

As one can observe in Table 1, deep learning algorithms have been the most extensively used technique for the detection of structural defects. That has happened thanks to the large-scale usage of video cameras by the industry which subsequently provides the research community with a vast amount of data to experiment with more advanced methods. The table further demonstrates the extensive applications of shallow learning techniques for geometry irregularities. Yet the current state of the literature on the applications of machine learning in rail track maintenance suffers from a few shortcomings. To accelerate the machine learning research progress and machine learning adoption in the railway systems, it is the responsibility of both the research community and the industry to focus on what they can do to address for these shortcomings:

- **Small number of defective observations:** One major property of rail defects datasets is the highly skewed distribution of defective and non-defective classes. In general, a substantial majority of observations belong to the non-defective components while only a slim portion of observations are in fact defective (often less than 1 percent). This can negatively affect the performance of machine learning models as they often favor the majority class [53]. In machine learning literature, various techniques have been proposed to deal with imbalanced datasets. For instance, under-sampling and over-sampling are the two most common approaches used to mitigate the effect of the imbalanced number of classes on training machine learning algorithms [54]. However, in rail maintenance literature only a few number of attempts have been made to address the class imbalance problem or to study the effectiveness of current techniques on rail data. The only known research concerning this issue are carried out by Hajizadeh et al. [44]. Thus, the research community needs to focus more on developing or applying new techniques for overcoming the problem of imbalanced observations in rail defect datasets.

- **Availability of labeled datasets:** The performance of machine learning models heavily depends on the availability and quality of a sufficiently large and labeled dataset. However, while due to the huge amount of measurements most of the time the size of a dataset is not a problem, the presence of enough labeled samples can pose a more serious challenge. Especially this issue becomes more visible in image datasets since manual labeling of the rail track images is a labor-intensive and expensive process, and requires a high level of expertise and domain knowledge. As a result, often the existing datasets cannot satisfy the amount of data needed for machine learning systems. Although several research papers have been published and a few tools have been developed to partially automate the dataset labeling problem, these issues have been overlooked by researchers in the rail domain and in the intelligent maintenance community. So far, only Rauschmayr et al. [50] and Hajizadeh et al. [44] have tried to develop techniques to automatically label rail images.

- **Lack of a public benchmark dataset:** There are several well-known public datasets that have been widely used and studied as a benchmark for comparing different techniques and approaches in other maintenance domains [55]. However, only a few small datasets are available for rail track defects and often the datasets used by researches are proprietary and not sharable. This issue makes training, evaluating and comparing the results of machine learning algorithms more challenging. Thus, as long as there is no public dataset available, not all machine learning researchers outside the rail industry can contribute to the research progress in this domain which subsequently could slow down the progress and stifle the innovation in the domain. Therefore, it is necessary that the rail industry grants the academia access to the rail track data.

- **Explainability of machine learning models:** As mentioned at the beginning of this section, a significant number of papers published in rail maintenance domain exploited CNN models and recommended the use of CNNs for automatic defect detection in real-world scenarios. However, CNNs are considered to be black-box models and are not inherently interpretable. In other words, the machine learning researcher is not able to explain how a CNN model came up with its predictions or prove its trustworthiness to the end user [56]. So far the question of how we can trust ML models has not been addressed by the research community. Therefore, developing accurate black-box machine learning algorithms should not be the only goal but actually how these algorithms classify defects needs to be taken into consideration.

- **Combining domain knowledge with machine learning models:** How defects evolve, which factors contribute to the degradation of rail track components and domain expert knowledge can significantly influence the effective scheduling of rail maintenance operations [27]. For instance, rail track areas with a high concentration of light squats can be fixed by a grinding process. However, if these light squats develop into more severe defects, not only a replacement is needed to fix rail track faults, but the risk of more serious damages also increases [57]. Fault tree analysis (FTA) is a powerful model-based method for risk assessment of complex systems. Fault trees have been used by a vast array of industries, to model how malfunctions in system components lead to the failure of the system [58]. ML techniques can be used together with fault trees to better learn how a system fails [59].

6 Conclusion

This paper has reviewed major machine learning techniques for fault detection. First of all, we have found that especially in the past few years, deep learning algorithms have become the prevailing tool for identifying structural rail defects. Similarly, the results of our survey show that video cameras are the most popular data source for machine learning applications.

However, the current research publications are exposed to a number of shortcomings that we have highlighted throughout our paper. Data quality issues such as highly imbalanced datasets, limitation of manual labeling process and the absence of a comprehensive public database for training and evaluating different approaches is slowing down the progress on the side of research community. The issues related to explaining how an algorithm identifies defects which is absolutely necessary to earn the trust of the industry and incorporating the domain knowledge in ML approaches hinder the progress on the deployment side of ML research. To overcome these shortcomings several research directions and suggestions have been proposed. We believe that the research community needs to focus more on issues including data quality, explainability and trustworthiness of machine learning algorithms and combining the expert knowledge with their machine learning models while the industry should provide the academia the access rail track datasets to facilitate the progress of ML research and to encourage more researchers to contribute and improve the existing methods.

Acknowledgment. This research is supported by ProRail and the Netherlands Organization for Scientific Research (NWO) under the Sequoia project.

References

1. Sharma, S., Cui, Y., He, Q., Mohammadi, R., Li, Z.: Data-driven optimization of railway maintenance for track geometry. Trans. Res. Part C: Emerg. Technol. **90**, 34–58 (2018)
2. Zhuang, L., Wang, L., Zhang, Z., Tsui, K.L.: Automated vision inspection of rail surface cracks: a double-layer data-driven framework. Transp. Res. Part C Emerg. Technol. **92**, 258–277 (2018). https://doi.org/10.1016/j.trc.2018.05.007

3. Liu, X., Saat, M., Barkan, C.: Analysis of causes of major train derailment and their effect on accident rates. Transp. Res. Rec. J. Transp. Res. Board. **2289**, 154–163 (2012). https://doi.org/10.3141/2289-20

4. Lasisi, A., Attoh-Okine, N.: Principal components analysis and track quality index: a machine learning approach. Transp. Res. Part C Emerg. Technol. **91**, 230–248 (2018). https://doi.org/10.1016/j.trc.2018.04.001

5. Durazo-Cardenas, I., et al.: An autonomous system for maintenance scheduling data-rich complex infrastructure: fusing the railways' condition, planning and cost. Transp. Res. Part C Emerg. Technol. **89**, 234–253 (2018). https://doi.org/10.1016/j.trc.2018.02.010

6. Gibert, X., Patel, V.M., Chellappa, R.: Deep multitask learning for railway track inspection. IEEE Trans. Intell. Transp. Syst. **18**, 153–164 (2017). https://doi.org/10.1109/TITS.2016.2568758

7. Zoeteman, A., Dollevoet, R., Li, Z.: Dutch research results on wheel/rail interface management: 2001–2013 and beyond. Proc. Inst. Mech. Eng. Part F J. Rail Rapid Transit. **228**, 642–651 (2014). https://doi.org/10.1177/0954409714524379

8. Zhao, R., Yan, R., Chen, Z., Mao, K., Wang, P., Gao, R.X.: Deep learning and its applications to machine health monitoring: a survey, **14**, 1–14 (2016). https://arxiv.org/abs/1612.07640

9. Thaduri, A., Galar, D., Kumar, U.: Railway assets: a potential domain for big data analytics. Proc. Comput. Sci. **53**, 457–467 (2015). https://doi.org/10.1016/j.procs.2015.07.323

10. Li, Q., Zhong, Z., Liang, Z., Liang, Y.: Rail inspection meets big data: methods and trends (2015)

11. Stetco, A., et al.: Machine learning methods for wind turbine condition monitoring: a review. Renew. Energy. **133**, 620–635 (2018). https://doi.org/10.1016/j.renene.2018.10.047

12. Widodo, A., Yang, B.S.: Support vector machine in machine condition monitoring and fault diagnosis. Mech. Syst. Signal Process. **21**, 2560–2574 (2007). https://doi.org/10.1016/j.ymssp.2006.12.007

13. Sun, W., Chen, J., Li, J.: Decision tree and PCA-based fault diagnosis of rotating machinery. Mech. Syst. Signal Process. **21**, 1300–1317 (2007). https://doi.org/10.1016/j.ymssp.2006.06.010

14. Cerrada, M., Zurita, G., Cabrera, D., Sánchez, R.V., Artés, M., Li, C.: Fault diagnosis in spur gears based on genetic algorithm and random forest. Mech. Syst. Signal Process. **70–71**, 87–103 (2016). https://doi.org/10.1016/j.ymssp.2015.08.030

15. Lecun, Y., Bengio, Y., Hinton, G.: Deep learning. Nature **521**, 436–444 (2015). https://doi.org/10.1038/nature14539

16. LeCun, Y., et al.: Backpropagation applied to handwritten zip code recognition. Neural Comput. **1**, 541–551 (1989)

17. Zeiler, M.D., Fergus, R.: Visualizing and understanding convolutional networks. In: Fleet, D., Pajdla, T., Schiele, B., Tuytelaars, T. (eds.) ECCV 2014. LNCS, vol. 8689, pp. 818–833. Springer, Cham (2014). https://doi.org/10.1007/978-3-319-10590-1_53

18. Russakovsky, O., et al.: ImageNet large scale visual recognition challenge. Int. J. Comput. Vis. **115**, 211–252 (2015). https://doi.org/10.1007/s11263-015-0816-y

19. Kim, S., Kim, W., Noh, Y.K., Park, F.C.: Transfer learning for automated optical inspection. In: International Joint Conference on Neural Networks (IJCNN), May 2017, pp. 2517–2524 (2017). https://doi.org/10.1109/ijcnn.2017.7966162

20. Karpathy, A.: What I learned from competing against a convnet on imagenet (2014). http://karpathy.github.io/2014/09/02/what-i-learned-from-competing-against-a-convnet-on-imagenet

21. Hu, J., Shen, L., Albanie, S., Sun, G., Wu, E.: Squeeze-and-excitation networks, pp. 1–14 (2017). https://doi.org/10.1109/CVPR.2018.00745

22. Lipton, Z.C., Kale, D.C., Elkan, C., Wetzel, R.: Learning to Diagnose with LSTM Recurrent Neural Networks. 1–18 (2015). https://arxiv.org/abs/1511.03677
23. Lipton, Z.C., Berkowitz, J., Elkan, C.: A critical review of recurrent neural networks for sequence learning, pp. 1–38 (2015). https://arxiv.org/abs/1506.00019
24. Hochreiter, S., Urgen Schmidhuber, J.: Ltsm. Neural Comput. **9**, 1735–1780 (1997). https://doi.org/10.1162/neco.1997.9.8.1735
25. Zhang, W., et al.: LSTM-based analysis of industrial iot equipment. IEEE Access. **6**, 23551–23560 (2018). https://doi.org/10.1109/ACCESS.2018.2825538
26. Ghofrani, F., He, Q., Goverde, R.M.P., Liu, X.: Recent applications of big data analytics in railway transportation systems: a survey. Transp. Res. Part C Emerg. Technol. **90**, 226–246 (2018). https://doi.org/10.1016/j.trc.2018.03.010
27. Jamshidi, A., et al.: A decision support approach for condition-based maintenance of rails based on big data analysis ★. Transp. Res. Part C **95**, 185–206 (2018). https://doi.org/10.1016/j.trc.2018.07.007
28. Soleimanmeigouni, I., Ahmadi, A., Kumar, U.: Track geometry degradation and maintenance modelling: a review. Proc. Inst. Mech. Eng. Part F J. Rail Rapid Transit. **232**, 73–102 (2018)
29. Alahakoon, S., Sun, Y.Q., Spiryagin, M., Cole, C.: Rail flaw detection technologies for safer, reliable transportation: a review. J. Dyn. Syst. Meas. Control **140**, 020801 (2017). https://doi.org/10.1115/1.4037295
30. Papaelias, M.P., Roberts, C., Davis, C.L.: A review on non-destructive evaluation of rails: state-of-the-art and future development. Proc. Inst. Mech. Eng. **222**, 367–384 (2008). https://doi.org/10.1243/09544097JRRT209
31. Jamshidi, A., et al.: A big data analysis approach for rail failure risk assessment. Risk Anal. **37**, 1495–1507 (2017). https://doi.org/10.1111/risa.12836
32. Santur, Y., Karaköse, M., Akın, E.: Condition monitoring approach using 3D-modelling of railway tracks with laser cameras (2017)
33. Krizhevsky, A., Sutskever, I., Hinton, G.E.: ImageNet classification with deep convolutional neural networks. In: Pereira, F., Burges, C.J.C., Bottou, L., Weinberger, K.Q. (eds.) Advances in Neural Information Processing Systems, vol. 25, pp. 1097–1105. Curran Associates, Inc. (2012)
34. Faghih-Roohi, S., Hajizadeh, S., Nunez, A., Babuska, R., De Schutter, B.: Deep convolutional neural networks for detection of rail surface defects. In: Proceedings International Joint Conference on Neural Networks (IJCNN), October 2016, pp. 2584–2589 (2016). https://doi.org/10.1109/ijcnn.2016.7727522
35. Xia, Y., Xie, F., Jiang, Z.: Broken railway fastener detection based on adaboost algorithm. In: Proceedings - 2010 International Conference Optoelectronics and Image Processing, ICOIP 2010, vol. 1, pp. 313–316 (2010). https://doi.org/10.1109/icoip.2010.303
36. Santur, Y., Karakose, M., Akin, E.: Random forest based diagnosis approach for rail fault inspection in railways. In: 2016 National Conference on Electrical, Electronics and Biomedical Engineering (ELECO) (2017)
37. Gao, S., Szugs, T., Inspection, E., Ahlbrink, R.: Use of combined railway inspection data sources for characterization of rolling contact fatigue (2018)
38. Sadeghi, J., Askarinejad, H.: Application of neural networks in evaluation of railway track quality condition. J. Mech. Sci. Technol. **26**, 113–122 (2012). https://doi.org/10.1007/s12206-011-1016-5
39. Hu, C., Liu, X.: Modeling track geometry degradation using support vector machine technique (2016)

40. Famurewa, S.M., Zhang, L., Asplund, M.: Maintenance analytics for railway infrastructure decision support. J. Qual. Maint. Eng. **23**, 310–325 (2017). https://doi.org/10.1108/JQME-11-2016-0059

41. Jiang, Y., Wang, H., Tian, G., Yi, Q., Zhao, J., Zhen, K.: Fast classification for rail defect depths using a hybrid intelligent method. Optik (Stuttg). **180**, 455–468 (2019). https://doi.org/10.1016/j.ijleo.2018.11.053

42. Lee, J.S., Hwang, S.H., Choi, I.Y., Kim, I.K.: Prediction of track deterioration using maintenance data and machine learning schemes. J. Transp. Eng. Part A Syst. **144**, 4018045 (2018). https://doi.org/10.1061/JTEPBS.0000173

43. Hajizadeh, S., Li, Z., Dollevoet, R.P.B.J., Tax, D.M.J.: Evaluating classification performance with only positive and unlabeled samples. In: Fränti, P., Brown, G., Loog, M., Escolano, F., Pelillo, M. (eds.) S+SSPR 2014. LNCS, vol. 8621, pp. 233–242. Springer, Heidelberg (2014). https://doi.org/10.1007/978-3-662-44415-3_24

44. Hajizadeh, S., Núñez, A., Tax, D.M.J.: Semi-supervised rail defect detection from imbalanced image data. IFAC-PapersOnLine. **49**, 78–83 (2016). https://doi.org/10.1016/j.ifacol.2016.07.014

45. Soukup, D., Huber-Mörk, R.: Convolutional neural networks for steel surface defect detection from photometric stereo images. In: Bebis, G., et al. (eds.) ISVC 2014. LNCS, vol. 8887, pp. 668–677. Springer, Cham (2014). https://doi.org/10.1007/978-3-319-14249-4_64

46. Giben, X., Patel, V.M., Chellappa, R.: Material classification and semantic segmentation of railway track images with deep convolutional neural networks. In: Proceedings International Conference Image Processing ICIP, December 2015, pp. 621–625 (2015). https://doi.org/10.1109/icip.2015.7350873

47. Gibert, X., Patel, V.M., Chellappa, R.: Robust fastener detection for autonomous visual railway track inspection. In: 2015 IEEE Winter Conference on Applications of Computer Vision, pp. 694–701 (2015)

48. Santur, Y., Karaköse, M., Akin, E.: A new rail inspection method based on deep learning using laser cameras (2017)

49. Santur, Y., Karakose, M., Akin, E.: An adaptive fault diagnosis approach using pipeline implementation for railway inspection. Turk. J. Electr. Eng. Comput. Sci. **26**, 987–998 (2018). https://doi.org/10.3906/elk-1704-214

50. Rauschmayr, N., Hoechemer, M., Zurkirchen, M., Kenzelmann, S., Gilles, M.: Deep Learning Of Railway Track Faults using GPUs Swiss Federal Railways (SBB) Swiss Center for Electronics and Microtechnology (CSEM) (2018)

51. Dai, P., Du, X., Wang, S., Gu, Z., Ma, Y.: Rail fastener automatic recognition method in complex background. In: Tenth International Conference Digital Image Processing (ICDIP) 2018, vol. 314, p. 1080625 (2018). https://doi.org/10.1117/12.2503323

52. Ritika, S., Rao, D.: Data augmentation of railway images for track inspection (2018)

53. García, V., Sánchez, J.S., Mollineda, R.A.: On the effectiveness of preprocessing methods when dealing with different levels of class imbalance. Knowl.-Based Syst. **25**, 13–21 (2012). https://doi.org/10.1016/j.knosys.2011.06.013

54. He, H., Garcia, E.A.: Learning from imbalanced data. IEEE Trans. Knowl. Data Eng. **21**, 1263–1284 (2009). https://doi.org/10.1109/TKDE.2008.239

55. Nectoux, P., et al.: PRONOSTIA : an experimental platform for bearings accelerated degradation tests. In: IEEE International Conference on Prognostics and Health Management, pp. 1–8 (2012)

56. Ribeiro, M.T., Guestrin, C.: Why should I trust you ? Explaining the predictions of any classifier (2016)

57. Jamshidi, A., Nunez, A., Li, Z., Dollevoet, R.: Maintenance decision indicators for treating squats in railway infrastructures. In: Transportation Research Board 94th Annual Meeting (2015)
58. Ruijters, E., Stoelinga, M.: Fault tree analysis: a survey of the state-of-the-art in modeling, analysis and tools. Comput. Sci. Rev. **15–16**, 29–62 (2015). https://doi.org/10.1016/j.cosrev.2015.03.001
59. Nauta, M., Bucur, D., Stoelinga, M.: LIFT: learning fault trees from observational data. In: McIver, Annabelle, Horvath, Andras (eds.) QEST 2018. LNCS, vol. 11024, pp. 306–322. Springer, Cham (2018). https://doi.org/10.1007/978-3-319-99154-2_19

Safe and Time-Optimal Control
for Railway Games

Shyam Lal Karra[✉], Kim Guldstrand Larsen, Florian Lorber, and Jiří Srba

Department of Computer Science, Aalborg University,
Selma Lagerløfs Vej 300, 9220 Aalborg East, Denmark
kgl@cs.aau.dk

Abstract. Railway scheduling is a complex and safety critical problem
that has recently attracted attention in the formal verification community. We provide a formal model of railway scheduling as a stochastic
timed game and using the tool UPPAAL STRATEGO, we synthesise the
most permissive control strategy for operating the lights and points at
the railway scenario such that we guarantee system's safety (avoidance of
train collisions). Among all such safe strategies, we then select (with the
help of reinforcement learning) a concrete strategy that minimizes the
time needed to move all trains to their target locations. This optimizes
the speed and capacity of a railway system and advances the current
state-of-the-art where the optimality criteria were not considered yet.
We successfully demonstrate our approach on the models of two Danish railway stations, and discuss the applicability and scalability of our
approach.

1 Introduction

Railway networks are complex safety critical systems where one has to guarantee safety despite the unpredictable behaviour of external factors influencing the
system operation. This unpredictable behaviour arises from the fact that the
durations taken by trains to change positions in the railway network are influenced by human operators as well as other factors like weather conditions etc. In
addition to that, trains can move concurrently on multiple independent tracks
and it becomes hard to manually control the lights and points (switches) in
order to avoid trains collisions or derailment. This becomes particularly important, once we try to increase the throughput in the railway network and minimize
the train travel times, as this requires more concurrency where dangerous situations can be easily overlooked by a human operator. There is hence a clear
demand on the employment of automatic methods that will assist with a safe
and time-optimal operation of a railway network, and this is the main focus of
our paper.

We shall first introduce our railway scheduling problem by an example. An
instance of the problem is given in Fig. 1 and consists of two *trains*, each travelling
in a given (and fixed) direction. At any moment, each train is placed on a

© Springer Nature Switzerland AG 2019
S. Collart-Dutilleul et al. (Eds.): RSSRail 2019, LNCS 11495, pp. 106–122, 2019.
https://doi.org/10.1007/978-3-030-18744-6_7

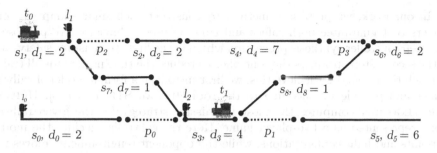

Fig. 1. A railway network with two trains t_0 and t_1, four points p_0, p_1, p_2 and p_3, nine sections $s_0 \ldots s_8$ and three lights l_0, l_1 and l_2.

clearly identified part of a track called *section*. In our example, the train t_0 is located at the section s_1 and travels from the left end-point of the section to its right end-point, assuming that the duration of such a move has some predefined probabilistic distribution with the expected value of 2 time units. Similarly, the train t_1 starts at the right end-point of section s_3 and moves in the right-to-left direction with the expected travel time of 4 time units to cross section s_3. Sections are connected with *points* (switches), like the point p_0 that depending on its *mode* can connect the section s_3 with either the section s_7 as depicted in our figure, or with the section s_0. Ends of sections can be guarded by *lights* that signal to the trains whether they are allowed to leave a given section and move to the connected section (depending on the mode of the points). We assume that passing a point is instantenious and that trains follow the light signals (i.e. never pass a light that is red).

The *railway scheduling problem* (also known as dynamic routing problem) is given by a track layout together with the initial positions of trains in the network and the target positions (sections) for each train. The role of the controller is to operate the lights and points such that the trains move to their target positions in a safe way (without the possibility of a collision, under the assumption that they respect the lights), while at the same time optimizing the time it takes before all trains arrive to their target sections.

Returning to our example, let us assume that the target section for the train t_0 is s_6 and that the trains t_1 aims to reach s_0. Note that we can change the points so that both trains simply drive straightforward and reach the target sections without the risk of a crash. However, the controller has an alternative choice for the train t_0 to navigate it through the sections s_7, s_3 and s_8 instead, where the expected arrival time is shorter than passing through the section s_4. Now, the optimal strategy depends on the fact how fast the train t_1 leaves the section s_3. If it does so early (depending on the respective stochastic distribution), then it is worth for the controller to direct the train t_0 along the faster route that includes the section s_3, otherwise (in case t_1 is for some reason delayed) it is more time-optimal to guide the train t_0 in the straight line.

In our work, we propose a method to construct such smart/adaptive controllers that guarantee both safety and time optimal behaviour. We propose a two-step controller synthesis procedure, which in the first step ensures safety, and in the second step optimises the controller to reduce the time needed for all trains to reach their goals. To achieve this, we first introduce a formal model of railway games and provide its encoding to the tool UPPAAL STRATEGO [6]. UPPAAL STRATEGO first computes the most permissive strategy for the given railway game represented as a two-player game. Here the controller decides the modes of points and light configurations, while the opponent (environment) moves the trains around in the network, respecting the lights guarding each section. The speed of the trains in this game is completely unconstrained, meaning that they may stay in a section forever or move immediately to the other end of the section without any time contraints. This guarantees that the synthetised strategy is safe, irrelevant of the speed of the trains (including the possibility that a train breaks and does not move at all). The tool UPPAAL STRATEGO is able to synthesise the most permissive strategy that includes *all* safe operations of the railway network. In the second step, we add stochastic behaviour to the trains so that they take a random amount of time for crossing a section which is chosen according to the rates for a given probabilistic distribution associated with the train and the concrete section in the network. From all safe strategies, we then (again using UPPAAL STRATEGO) select the fastest one by employing reinforcement learning. This provides us with the control strategy that is (near) time-optimal and provably safe.

Our main contributions can be summarized as follows:

- We generalize previous attempts to solve the train scheduling problem by allowing for concurrent moves of trains and we extend the existing railway models with stochastic information about the expected times for trains to travel along a section.
- We provide both the untimed and timed semantics for a railway network that allows us to argue about safety and time-optimality and we show their encoding in the model of stochastic timed automata.
- We explain the application of the tool UPPAAL STRATEGO for solving network scheduling problems and by means of two existing railway stations in Aalborg and Lyngy, we prove that the tool is able to compute safe and near-optimal control strategies.

Related Work. Railway safety was studied e.g. in [3,5,14,16] with a focus on model checking of safety properties in railway networks, however, these approaches do not consider controller synthesis.

The work in [12] considers controller synthesis problem for the railway scheduling problem and the safety condition by translating it to strictly alternating two-player game and provides a number of abstractions in order to reduce the state space of the underlying game graph. In [10] this approach has been explored with the use of on-the-fly controller synthesis techniques, however, these approaches do not allow for concurrent train moves in order to reduce the complexity of the problem. The controller synthesis problem for railway network safety and deadlock avoidance was addressed in [9] by its modelling in Petri nets. In [11] automatic generation and verification of formal safety conditions from an interlocking tables of a relay interlocking system are discussed. However, none of these approaches consider the timing aspects in combination with controller synthesis and to the best of our knowledge, our work is the first one that synthetizes a schedule that is both safe and time-optimal at the same time.

UPPAAL STRATEGO has been used in several case studies, where first a safe strategy is generated, and then an optimization step is performed. Examples include adaptive cruise control [13] and the intelligent control of traffic lights [8]. While the approach for the controller synthesis used in this paper is similar to these works, it is applied to a completely new area, which requires an efficient modeling of problem and nontrivial effort in order to boost the performance of the tool, including the use of a new learning method recently implemented in UPPAAL STRATEGO.

2 Formal Definition of Railway Games

We first introduce a game graph that is used to give the semantics to our railway scheduling problem. A *game graph* is a tuple $\mathcal{G} = \langle V, \longrightarrow, \cdots\rightarrow, v_0, Bad, Goal \rangle$ where V is a finite set of vertices, $\longrightarrow \subseteq V \times V$ is the set of controller transitions, $\cdots\rightarrow \subseteq V \times V$ is the set of environmental transitions, $v_0 \in V$ is the initial vertex, $Bad \subseteq V$ is the set of bad vertices where controller loses and $Goal \subseteq V$ is the set of vertices controller aims to eventually reach.

Given a game graph $\mathcal{G}$, a *run* is a finite or infinite sequence $\rho = \langle v_0, v_1, v_2, \ldots \rangle$ of vertices such that either $v_i \longrightarrow v_{i+1}$ or $v_i \cdots\rightarrow v_{i+1}$ for every relevant i. A run ρ is a *maximal run* if it is either infinite or $\rho = \langle v_0 \ldots v_k \rangle$ and there is no v_{k+1} such that $v_k \longrightarrow v_{k+1}$ or $v_k \cdots\rightarrow v_{k+1}$. The set of all maximal runs starting at the vertex v_0 is denoted by $MaxRuns(v_0)$.

A controller *strategy* $\sigma : V \hookrightarrow V$ is a partial function such that for every $v \in V$ we have $v \longrightarrow \sigma(v)$ or $\sigma(v)$ is undefined in case that v has no outgoing controllable transitions. Given a strategy σ, the outcome of the game under σ from the vertex v_0 is defined as the set of all possible maximal runs that follow the strategy σ, formally

$$Outcome^{\sigma}(v_0) =$$
$$\{\langle v_0, v_1, \ldots \rangle \in MaxRuns(v_0) \mid v_i \cdots\rightarrow v_{i+1} \text{ or } \sigma(v_i) = v_{i+1} \text{ for all } i\}.$$

A run $\rho = \langle v_0, v_1, \ldots \rangle$ is called *safe* if there is no i such that $v_i \in Bad$. A strategy σ is a *safe strategy* if all the runs from $Outcome^{\sigma}(v_0)$ are safe. A strategy σ is a *winning strategy* if it is safe and for every run $\rho = \langle v_0, v_1 \ldots \rangle \in Outcome^{\sigma}(v_0)$ there is an i such that $v_i \in Goal$.

2.1 Railway Topology

We are now ready to formalise the railway topology. A *railway topology* is a tuple $R = (S, P, L, \gamma, E)$ where $S = \{s_0, s_1 \ldots s_m\}$, $P = \{p_0, p_1 \ldots p_r\}$

and $L = \{l_0, l_1, l_2 \ldots l_t\}$ are the sets of sections, points and lights, respectively. Each section $s \in S$ has two ends denoted by $s.left$ and $s.right$ and each point p has three ends $p.up$, $p.down$, $p.main$. We shall use the notation $S^{ends} = \{s.left, s.right \mid s \in S\}$ and $P^{ends} = \{p.up, p.down, p.main \mid p \in P\}$. The injective function $\gamma : L \to S^{ends}$ assigns each light to a section. A light at a left (right) end of a section can only control a train moving on that section in the direction right to left (left to right). Finally, the connectivity of the sections and points is represented by undirected edges E such that $E \subseteq [V]^2$ where $V = P^{ends} \cup S^{ends}$ and $[V]^2 = \{Z \subseteq V \mid |Z| = 2\}$ satisfying

- if $e_1 \neq e_2$ then $e_1 \cap e_2 = \emptyset$ for all $e_1, e_2 \in E$,
- $\{s.left, s.right\} \notin E$ for each section $s \in S$, and
- for each $p.z \in P^{ends}$ there is an $s.x \in S^{ends}$ such that $\{p.z, s.x\} \in E$.

In other words, each end can connect to at most one other end, we allow point ends to connect only to section ends and section-loops as well as isolated point ends are not allowed.

2.2   Untimed Semantics of Railway Games

Consider a railway topology $R = (S, P, L, \gamma, E)$. We shall define its associated game graph for a given number of trains $T = \{t_0, t_1 \ldots t_{k-1}\}$. The vertices of the game graph consist of configurations where each train is located at a section end and has a direction in which it is moving. For each point $p \in P$, a mode $up/down$ is associated with it in the configuration, indicated by $p.mode$. Finally, for each light $l \in L$, there is a colour $red/green$ associated with it in a given configuration. The underlying semantics is given as a game graph $\mathcal{G}_R = \langle C, \longrightarrow, \cdots\cdots\rangle, c_0, Bad, Goal\rangle$ defined in the rest of this section.

Configurations. The set of configurations is $C \subseteq (S^{ends} \times \{left, right\})^T \times \{up, down\}^P \times \{red, green\}^L$ so that a configuration $c \in C$ is a triple of three functions of the form (pos, mod, col) where

- $pos : T \to S^{ends} \times \{left, right\}$ stores the location and direction of each train $t \in T$. For each train $t \in T$, $pos(t)$ is an ordered pair of the form $(pos^1(t), pos^2(t))$ where $pos^1(t)$ indicates the section end in which t is currently located and $pos^2(t)$ indicates the train direction,
- $mod : P \to \{up, down\}$ records the mode of each point, and
- $col : L \to \{red, green\}$ remembers the current lights setting.

We assume a given initial configuration c_0 with the initial placement of all trains and a fixed color lights and modes of points, as well as a set of goal configurations $Goal$ where all trains are in their target sections and the positions of points and light colors can be arbitrary. The set Bad contains all configurations where two trains are located on the same sections, formally $Bad = \{(pos, mod, col) \in C \mid$ there is $t, t' \in T$ where $t \neq t', pos^1(t) = s.x$ and $pos^1(t') = s.y$ for some $x, y \in \{left, right\}\}$.

Transitions. We shall first define a function $nextSec : \left(S^{ends} \times (P \rightarrow \{up, down\})\right) \rightarrow S^{ends}$ that, given the modes of points, determines what are the neighbouring sections in the network (we assume that $x, y \in \{left, right\}$ and $z \in \{main, up, down\}$):

- $nextSec(s.x, mod) = s'.y$ if $\{s.x, s'.y\} \in E$
- $nextSec(s.x, mod) = s'.y$ if there exists a $p \in P$ such that $\{s.x, p.z\} \in E$ and
  - $z = main$ and $mod(p) = up$ such that $\{p.up, s'.y\} \in E$, or
  - $z = main$ and $mod(p) = down$ such that $\{p.down, s'.y\} \in E$, or
  - $z = down$ or $z = up$ such that $\{p.main, s'.y\} \in E$
- $nextSec(s.x, mod) = s.x$ otherwise.

Let $c = (pos, mod, col)$ be a configuration from C. We shall also define a set of movable trains $movableTrains(pos, col) \subseteq T$ that, given the position of trains and colours of all lights, returns the set of all trains (if any) that are at the end of their sections and their corresponding lights (if any) are green in colour. Formally, $movableTrains(pos, col) = \{t \in T \mid pos(t) = (s.x, x)$ where $x \in \{left, right\}$ and $col(l) = green$ for all $l \in L$ such that $\gamma(l) = s.x\}$.

We are now ready to define the controllable and environmental transitions in the graph.

Controllable Transitions: These are transitions modelling the moves made by the controller in the game. Whenever there is a train at the end of a section, the controller can change the modes of points and the colours of lights, with the restriction that if a train is moving in a section where there is green light, it is not allowed to suddenly change it to red (as instanteniously stopping a moving train is not a realistic behaviour). The controller move is finished by placing all movable trains to the connected sections, unless there is a train that can crash to another train, in which case this train moves alone and the crash is detected by the fact that the target configuration belongs to the set Bad. Formally, we write $(pos, mod, col) \longrightarrow (pos', mod', col')$ if

- there exists a $t \in T$ such that $pos(t) = (s.x, x)$ where $x \in \{left, right\}$,
- for every $t \in T$ where $pos(t) = (s.y, x)$ for $x, y \in \{left, right\}$ if for every light $l \in L$ where $\gamma(l) = s.x$ holds $col(l) = green$ then $col'(l) = green$,
- and moreover
  - if there is $t \in movableTrains(pos, col')$ s.t. $nextSec(pos^1(t), mod') = pos(t')$ for some $t' \in T \setminus \{t\}$ then $pos'(t) = \left(nextSec(pos^1(t), mod'), pos^2(t) \right)$ and for every other $t' \in T \setminus \{t\}$ we have $pos'(t') = pos(t')$,
  - otherwise $pos'(t) = \left(nextSec(pos^1(t), mod'), pos^2(t) \right)$ for every $t \in movableTrains(pos, col')$ and $pos'(t') = pos(t')$ for every other t'.

Environmental Transitions: Finally, we can define the transitions controlled by the environment modelling the uncertainty whether the trains move along the sections and what set of trains move concurrently. We define $(pos, mod, col) \dashrightarrow (pos', mod, col)$ if

- *movableTrains*(pos, col) = $\emptyset$,
- for every $t \in T$ either $pos'(t) = pos(t)$, or $pos'(t) = (s.y,y)$ provided that $pos(t) = (s.x,y)$ for $x, y \in \{left, right\}$), and
- $pos \neq pos'$.

The first condition guarantees that if there are some movable trains at the end of the sections, then they move to their neighbouring sections (by means of controllable transitions). The second condition gives the environment the freedom to decide any subset of trains that (concurrently) arrive at the ends of their respective sections and the last conditions guarantees that at least one train moves in order to guarantee progress (we want to avoid environmental self-loops as the game will not have any winning strategy in this case). Notice that the environment cannot influence the modes of points nor the setting of lights.

Example 1. The railway network shown in Fig. 1 is in the initial configuration $c_0 = (pos, mod, col)$ where $pos(t_0) = (s_1.left, right)$, $pos(t_1) = (s_3.right, left)$, and $mod(p_0) = mod(p_1) = up$, $mod(p_2) = mod(p_3) = down$, and say that $col(l_0) = col(l_1) = col(l_2) = red$. There are no controllable transitions in c_0 as no trains are at the ends of the sections, i.e., *movableTrains*(pos, col) = $\emptyset$. However, the environment can move either the train t_0 from $s_1.left$ to $s_1.right$ or the train t_1 from $s_3.right$ to $s_3.left$, or both of them at the same time. Suppose it is the second case and the train t_1 arrives at $s_3.left$. Now the controller can swap the mode of p_0 and set the light l_2 to green, which implies that the train t_1 moves to $s_0.right$. Now it is the environmental turn and say that the train t_0 arrives to $s_1.right$. The controller can safely set the light l_1 to green and without any further control, also the train t_0 eventually arrives to its target section s_6.

2.3   Stochastic Semantics for Railway Games

In the railway game provided in the previous section, the movement of trains along sections has been purely discrete with no information about the timing of these movements. In this section we refine this view by assuming that the time it takes a train t to pass a section s is given by a distribution $\mu_{t,s}$. Here we shall assume that the passage-time distributions are given by exponential distributions. Choosing exponential distributions simplifies the technical presentation due to the memoryless property of exponential distributions, however, in UPPAAL STRATEGO there is a support for several other distributions as well as for the possibility to make the distribution parameters depend on weather conditions and other external factors (see [7]). However, assuming only knowledge about the expected passage-time, exponential distribution is anyway the most appropriate choice in terms of entropy.

A stochastic railway game for a set of trains T is a tuple (S, P, L, γ, E, R), where (S, P, L, γ, E) is a railway game and $R : T \times S \rightarrow \mathbb{R}_{\geq 0}$ provides for each train $t \in T$ and each section S the rate $R(t, s)$ of an exponential distribution being the passage-time distribution $\mu_{t,s}$. We recall that for an exponential distribution with rate r, the density of passage-time d is $r \exp^{-r \cdot d}$, and the probability that the passage-time will be less than d is $1 - \exp^{-r \cdot d}$. Also, the expected passage-time is $\frac{1}{r}$. Finally, given two trains t_1 and t_2 with passage-time rates r_1 and r_2, the probability that t_1 completes its passage first is $\frac{r_1}{r_1+r_2}$.

In the full railway game, various trains (all the ones that are not stopped by a red light at the end of a section) are independently moving along different sections simultaneously with the passage-times given by exponential distributions with rates prescribed by R. One of these trains will reach its end first[1]. This calls for a stochastic refinement of the uncontrolled train transitions of the railway game. Consider the untimed train transition $(pos, mod, col) \dashrightarrow (pos', mod, col)$, where train t – non-deterministically choosen between the moving trains – is the unique train reaching the end of its section s, i.e. $pos(t) \neq pos'(t)$. In the stochastic refinement we will assign a density δ for this transition happening at time d. Now let $M \subseteq T$ describe the set of trains moving excluding the winning train t. Also for $t' \in M$, let $s(t')$ denote the section along which t' is moving. Then a timed train transition is of the form:

$$(pos, mod, col) \dashrightarrow_\delta^d (pos', mod, col)$$

where d is a passage-time and δ is given by:

$$\delta = R(t, s) \cdot \exp^{-R(t,s)\cdot d} \cdot \prod_{t' \in M} \exp^{-R(t',s(t'))\cdot d}$$

In the above the first two terms of the product – $R(t, s) \cdot \exp^{-R(t,s)\cdot d}$ – is the density that train t passes section s in d time-units. However, the density δ of the train transition must also reflect that t is the first train to reach the end of its section. This is expressed by the last product term. Note that $\exp^{-R(t',s(t'))\cdot d}$ is the probability that train t' has not completed the passage of its section $s(t')$ in d time-units. Due to the assumed independence of the passage-times of trains, the product among all these equals the probability that no other moving train but t has reached the end of its section before d.

The above notion of density of a timed train transition extends to densities on finite timed runs by simple multiplication of the densities of the timed train transitions appearing in the run. Now constrained by a strategy σ, the railway game becomes fully stochastic as the non-deterministic choices of the controller are resolved by the strategy. Hence – by integration and addition – the densities on runs determine a probability measure $\mathbb{P}_\sigma$ on sets of outcomes under σ. In particular, for a given strategy σ we may determine the probability of the set of runs leading to a crash of two trains. If no crash under the strategy can occur, we may determine the expected time until all trains have reached their goal.

Example 2. Reconsider the railway network from Fig. 1. Assume that all lights are green (sounds dangerous, and it is!). A possible control strategy σ_1 could try to avoid disaster by turning point p_2 up once any of the two trains reached the end of the initial section. However, there is still a possibility of crash as train t_1

---

[1] The event that two or more trains reach the end of their sections simultaneously has measure zero and may be ignored.

may complete both sections s_3 and s_7 before train t_0 completes section s_1. The following shows that the probability of this is $\frac{2}{9}$.

$$\begin{aligned}
\mathbb{P}_{\sigma_1}(Crash) &= \mathbb{P}_{\sigma_1}(t_1 \text{ completes } s_3 \text{ and } s_7 \text{ before } t_0 \text{ completes } s_1) \\
&= \mathbb{P}_{\sigma_1}(t_1 \text{ completes } s_3 \text{ before } t_0 \text{ completes } s_1) \cdot \\
&\quad \mathbb{P}_{\sigma_1}(t_1 \text{ completes } s_7 \text{ before } t_0 \text{ completes } s_1) \\
&= \frac{\frac{1}{4}}{\frac{1}{4}+\frac{1}{2}} \cdot \frac{\frac{1}{1}}{\frac{1}{1}+\frac{1}{2}} = \frac{1}{3} \cdot \frac{2}{3} = \frac{2}{9}
\end{aligned}$$

Example 3. Again consider the railway network from Fig. 1. In this scenario we assume that all lights are initially red (sounds better from a safety point of view). Here we consider a safety strategy σ_2, where whenever a train (t_1 respectively t_0) reaches its end the corresponding light (l_2 respective l_1) is turned green and at the same time the corresponding point (p_0 respective p_2) is moved (down respectively up). This strategy guarantees safety, so the probability of the two trains crashing is 0. The expected time until both trains are at their goal location under σ_2 is 13 as seen by:

$$\begin{aligned}
\mathbb{E}_{\sigma_2}[Goal] &= \max\left\{\mathbb{E}_{\sigma_2}[t_1 \text{ in goal}], \mathbb{E}_{\sigma_2}[t_0 \text{ in goal}]\right\} \\
&= \max\{4+2, 2+2+7+2\} = 13
\end{aligned}$$

Example 4. As a final example, consider yet again the railway network from Fig. 1. Let us first consider that t_0 is the first train to reach the end of its section. The optimal strategy σ_o for the controller is now to move p_2 up, and drive straight for the goal, with an expected time of 13. If, however, t_1 is the train to reach its end first, t_0 can move through the sections s_7, s_3, s_8, with an expected time of 8. The expected time for both trains to reach their goal under this strategy is 12.3, as calculated below.

$$\begin{aligned}
\mathbb{E}_{\sigma_o}[Goal] &= \max\{\mathbb{E}_{\sigma_o}[t_1 \text{ in goal}], \mathbb{E}_{\sigma_o}[t_0 \text{ in goal}]\} \\
&= \max\Big\{4+2, \mathbb{P}_{\sigma_o}(t_0 \text{ completes } s_1 \text{ before } t_1 \text{ completes } s_3) \\
&\qquad \cdot (2+2+7+2) + \\
&\qquad \mathbb{P}_{\sigma_o}(t_0 \text{ completes } s_1 \text{ after } t_1 \text{ completes } s_3) \\
&\qquad \cdot (2+1+4+1+2)\Big\} \\
&= \max\left\{4+2, \frac{7}{9} \cdot 13 + \frac{2}{9} \cdot 10\right\} = 12.3
\end{aligned}$$

3   Railway Games in UPPAAL STRATEGO

After having introduced the theoretical foundations of our untimed railway game and its stochastic extension, we shall discuss the encoding of our approach into timed automata in the UPPAAL-style and use the tool UPPAAL STRATEGO [6] to synthesise (near) time-optimal and safe control strategies.

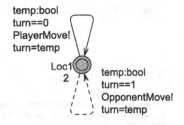

Fig. 2. An example of a timed game automaton of the tool UPPAAL STRATEGO

3.1 Translation to Timed Game Automata

UPPAAL STRATEGO uses timed game automata as models, which are an extension of timed automata [2]. Timed automata extend finite state machines with a number of real-valued clocks that enable them to measure the progress of time. The automata used by UPPAAL are extended further, by allowing for additional model features, e.g. C-like syntax, explained below. Timed game automata additionally divide transitions into controllable and uncontrollable transitions. Figure 2 provides an example of a timed game automaton in UPPAAL STRATEGO, containing all feature used in the presented models. The automaton consists of one location (*Loc1*), which contains an exponential rate (*2*) determining how long we have to stay in that location before performing a transition. The transition on top is controllable, denoted by the solid line. The controller can only execute the transition, if the turn variable is currently 0. The transition sends a signal (*PlayerMove!*) to other automata (run in parallel and not showed in the figure) when executed. Finally, the controller can choose a value for the variable *temp*, which will be assigned to the global variable *turn*. If it assigns the value 1, its the opponent's turn, which means it can execute the transition below (dotted line). Before such a transition is executed, we again delay according to the exponential rate of the location, and the opponent can choose to keep broadcasting on the channel *OpponentMove!* until it decides to change the value of *turn*.

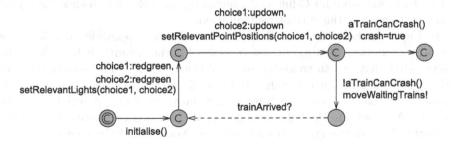

Fig. 3. Controller of a railway game modelled as a timed automaton

When encoding our railway games into UPPAAL STRATEGO, we applied two main optimizations in order to reduce the state space of the games. One

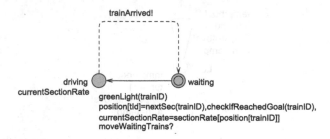

Fig. 4. A train in a railway game modelled as a timed automaton

optimization was inspired by [12], and it separates lights and points into relevant and irrelevant sets. Only lights that are on sections currently occupied by a train are considered relevant for the controller. The same applies to points, that is, only points connected to occupied sections are relevant. When the controller moves, it can only change the configuration of currently relevant lights/points. All other lights/points are set to their default values (red/down). The second optimization is a static analysis of the railway network. For each train we perform an exploration of the connectivity in railway network and collect all the sections it may visit in order to be still able to reach its target section. If a mode of a given point leads to a section from which it is not feasible to move the train to its target location, we remove this mode choice from the controller for this specific train. This further reduces the state-space that UPPAAL STRATEGO needs to explore during the controller synthesis. Both optimizations do not change the existence of winning strategies nor remove any time-optimal strategies. Another optimization was to enforce green light for at least one train, every time the controller sets the lights. This will ensure progress by forcing at least one train to move at any given point.

Figures 3 and 4 show a (simplified) example of the used timed automata models[2]. The models are split into one automaton for the controller, and one automaton for each train. Only one template of the trains is shown. In addition, the UPPAAL files contain C-line code, including variables for storing the layout of the stations, and the current configuration.

In Fig. 3 we show the controller: the controller is responsible for initializing the railway station (setting all the variables for the layout), before the game starts. After that, it can chose the mode of the relevant lights, setting them to either green or red. Then it can set the mode of the relevant points. In this example, we consider only two trains, hence only two lights/points need to be set here. After setting the lights and points, if there is a possibility for a crash, the controller sets the crash variable to true. Note that if the controller has a winning strategy, this will never occur. If no train can crash, all trains that are waiting for green light are notified that the configuration changed. When these

---

[2] Our experiment files can be found online at http://people.cs.aau.dk/~florber/ TrainGames/ExperimentFiles.rar.

steps are done, the controller waits for a train to arrive at the end of a section, at which point it will be able to change the settings again.

Figure 4 illustrates a train: initially, trains are starting at the end of a section, waiting to pass to the next section. If the train receives the signal that the configuration was changed (*moveWaitingTrains?*) and is has green light now, it can move to the next section and start driving there. When a train moves to the next section, several variables are updated. First, the train updates its current position according to the *nextSec* function, then it checks whether it reached its final destination, and finally it updates its rate to the rate of the section it is currently driving on. If it reaches the end of the section, it will signal this to the controller, which is done via sending the *trainArrived!* signal. The duration until a train reaches the end of a section is given by the rate of the current section, which in the figure is illustrated next to the driving location.

In Fig. 5 is an excerpt of the *nextSec* function implemented in case of the railway network shown in Fig. 1 which either reports a crash or returns the next section end of the train, depending on the settings of points and lights. For example, if the current position of the train is $s_1.right$ (stored in the variable *pos*), the train is going towards the right, the light l_1 is green and point p_2 is in *down* mode, the train ends up in $s_7.left$. Now if s_7 is already occupied then it results in a crash otherwise the position of the train is updated accordingly.

```
section_End nextSec(int tId){
    ⋮

    pos=currentPosition[tId];
    if(pos == s1.right and dir == right)
        if(colour[1] == green)
            if(mode[2]= down)
                if(sectionOccupied[7] == false) pos=s7.left;
                else crash=true;
            else
                if(sectionOccupied[2] == false) pos=s2.left;
                else crash=true;
        else
            pos=s1.right;
    ⋮

    return pos;
}
```

Fig. 5. Fragment of UPPAAL C-code for changing a train position

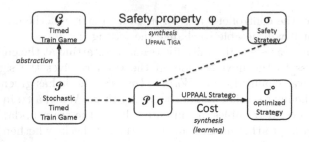

Fig. 6. Overview of the functionality of UPPAAL STRATEGO

3.2 UPPAAL STRATEGO

UPPAAL STRATEGO [6] combines the two branches UPPAAL TIGA [4] and UPPAAL SMC [7]. UPPAAL TIGA provides an on-the-fly algorithm for synthesis of reachability and safety objectives for timed games. UPPAAL SMC provides statistical model-checking for stochastic timed games. The workflow of UPPAAL STRATEGO which combines the two tools can be seen in Fig. 6. To run UPPAAL STRATEGO, one has to define queries for the model checker. We used two types of queries to generate the strategies.

The query below synthesises the safe strategy. It asks the model checker for a control strategy, such that the Boolean variable crash is always false.

```
strategy safe = control:A[] not crash
```

The optimization of our strategy with machine learning requires the specification of a cost function. In our case, the cost is given by the time passing, while there is a reward for bringing a train to its destination. We simulate for at most 151 time units (or until all trains exited), thus we set the reward to 150, such that exiting the train is always of higher priority than ending fast. This optimization is performed while adhering to the safe strategy. The query is given below.

```
strategy opt = minE  (time - 150*(exited[0])) [<=151]:
<> (time>=150 || exited[0]) under safe
```

The second step does not provide necessarily the time-optimal strategy (as the problem is in general undecidable), however, by the use of reinforcement learning it approaches the optimal solution and works convincingly in practice.

4 Experiments

We shall now present the experiments and results we achieved using UPPAAL STRATEGO. We analyzed two Danish railway stations, Aalborg and Lyngby. The railway layout for Lyngby was based on the layout presented by Kasting et al. [12] that we extended by the rates associated to each section. The layout used for Aalborg is based on a track plan found online [1] where we considered

Table 1. Specifics about the Lybgy and Aalborg station

Station	# Sections	# Lights	# Points	# Trains
Lyngby	11	14	6	2 to 5
Aalborg	26	41	14	2 to 5

the main tracks, disregarding the cargo tracks. We assumed that each entry to a point is guarded by a light. The rates for both stations were estimated by using Google Maps to figure out the length of the sections, and assuming that trains drive with 80 kmh outside of the station, and 40 kmh in the proximity of the platforms. To achieve that all rates are higher than 1, the rates of Lyngby were multiplied by 66, and all rates in Aalborg by 20. Thus, one time unit in an experiment with Lyngby/Aalborg below corresponds to 66/20 s, respectively.

4.1 Setup

We considered the problem with 2, 3, 4 and even 5 trains concurrently moving at the station in order to explore the scalability of our approach. The initial and final locations for the trains in the Lyngby station were chosen similarly to [12]. The trains in Aalborg are placed in a way to make their travel as complex as possible, i.e., they always have to travel from one side to the other, taking several points and cross each others paths. The models with less than 5 trains were produced by removing trains from the complete model with a maximum number of trains. The specifics about the stations can be found in Table 1, showing that Aalborg is about twice the size of Lyngby. The experiments were executed on AMD Opteron 6376 processor running at 2,3 Ghz with 10 GB memory limit.

4.2 Results

In Table 2 we report on the time to compute the safety strategy. The runtime for computing the strategy depends on the size of the station and, as expected, it grows exponentially with the number of trains (Aalborg with 5 trains timed out). This means that for this high number of trains, the proposed approach is at the moment infeasible without further state-space reductions. However, even at the larger stations like Aalborg, in reality there should rarely be more than three trains approaching the station at the same time.

Table 2. Time (in seconds) for computing the most permissive safe strategy

Station	2 Trains	3 Trains	4 Trains	5 Trains
Lyngby	0.04	0.16	3.37	55.93
Aalborg	0.24	16.57	858.91	timeout

Table 3. Strategy optimization, including the runtime of safe strategy synthesis (in seconds), and the expected time until all trains reach their destinations

Station	Aal2	Aal3	Aal4	Aal5	Lyn2	Lyn3	Lyn4	Lyn5
UPPAAL runtime	650.53	1501.46	3990.49	—	66.79	143.86	244.38	382.33
Expected time	1.8	2.62	2.65	—	1.06	2.6	2.27	2.72

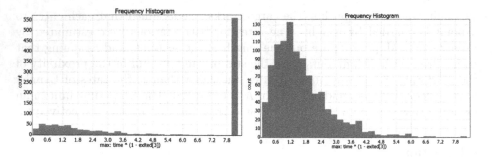

Fig. 7. 1000 random runs on Lyngby, the right plot is under the optimized strategy

In Table 3 we investigate how UPPAAL STRATEGO performs in optimizing the constructed safe strategy. We use a currently unpublished learning method of UPPAAL STRATEGO relying on Q-learning [15]. We use 50 iterations and each of 1000 runs for learning the strategies for Lyngby, and 5000 runs for Aalborg, as the increased state-space requires a higher learning effort. We report the time needed to produce the safe strategy plus to its optimization in UPPAAL STRATEGO, the expected time until all trains reach their goals under the synthesised strategies where e.g. Aal3 means the Aalborg station with 3 trains. The expected time was computed by simulating 2000 random runs under the strategy. The presented values are an average computed from repeating the experiments 20 times. The stochastic nature of the trains can of course influence the observed timed behaviour, and lead to small time fluctuations in the expected time.

Figure 7 shows the frequency histogram of the arrival times of the train number 4 during 1000 simulations on Lyngby with 5 trains, where the unoptimized safe strategy is on the left side and the guided optimized strategy is on the right side. The x-axis represents the train arrival time in minutes and the y-axis the number of times the train arrived at the given time. Clearly, the unguided strategy has a majority of simulation where the train did not arrive within 8 min, whereas the optimized strategy makes the train number 4 to arrive on average in 1.6 min.

5 Conclusion

We presented a game-theoretic approach for controlling of a railway network as a two player game between the controller (setting up the lights and modes of points) and the environment (moving the trains). Our approach guarantees safety (absence of trains simultaneously entering the same section) by computing the most permissive safe strategy in the untimed game. This strategy is further optimized in the model enhanced with stochastic semantics, approximating the time trains use to travel across a section, in order to optimize the speed of trains arriving to their target sections.

The main novelty of the proposed approach is the support for concurrently moving trains and the synthesis of (near) time-optimal controllers that are safe. Both these steps can be automatically realized in our tool UPPAAL STRATEGO. This is an important step towards reflecting the behaviour of trains in reality. Our approach was demonstrated and evaluated on two Danish railway stations, using different number of trains. The experiments clearly show the feasibility of our approach, however, for one of the stations, the highest number of trains led to a timeout, highlighting also the limitations of our current implementation.

In the future work, we shall work on improving the performance of our tool and on applying reduction techniques in order to decrease the size of the state-space, similarly as it was done in [10] for the untimed and strictly alternating game. We will also look at the scheduling problem where each train has a pre-defined route like in [11]; this is a realistic assumption and it will likely reduce the complexity of the control synthesis. Furthermore, we can without any effort use cost functions of different types e.g. to prioritize or penalize certain trains depending on their importance. For further evaluation of our strategies, we plan on making it easier to extract them from our tool, so that they can be applied to simulations in other software or control directly model trains in a demonstrator that we plan to build. Finally, in our railway model we made a few simplifying assumptions that we plan to relax in our future work. For example, we shall add a travel time through a point (at the moment we assume that it is instantaneous) and make sure that points are not operated while trains are passing over them in order to prevent derailment.

Acknowledgments. We would like to thank to Peter G. Jensen for his support with the experiments and advice on UPPAAL STRATEGO. We also thank the anonymous reviewers for their detailed comments and in particular for pointing out a problem in our original formal model that could have made the constructed controller potentially unsafe. The research leading to these results has received funding from the project DiCyPS funded by the Innovation Fund Denmark, the Sino Danish Research Center IDEA4CPS and the ERC Advanced Grant LASSO. The fourth author is partially affiliated with FI MU, Brno, Czech Republic.

References

1. Danish railway station plans. https://www.sporskiftet.dk/wiki/danske-spor-og-stationer-sporplaner-og-link/. Accessed 14 Jan 2019
2. Alur, R., Dill, D.L.: A theory of timed automata. Theor. Comput. Sci. **126**(2), 183–235 (1994)

3. Aristyo, B., Pradityo, K., Tamba, T.A., Nazaruddin, Y.Y., Widyotriatmo, A.: Model checking-based safety verification of a Petri net representation of train interlocking systems. In: 2018 57th Annual Conference of the Society of Instrument and Control Engineers of Japan (SICE), pp. 392–397, September 2018

4. Behrmann, G., David, A., Larsen, K.G.: A tutorial on UPPAAL. In: Bernardo, M., Corradini, F. (eds.) SFM-RT 2004. LNCS, vol. 3185, pp. 200–236. Springer, Heidelberg (2004). https://doi.org/10.1007/978-3-540-30080-9_7

5. Cimatti, A., Giunchiglia, F., Mongardi, G., Romano, D., Torielli, F., Traverso, P.: Formal verification of a railway interlocking system using model checking. Formal Aspects Comput. **10**(4), 361–380 (1998)

6. David, A., Jensen, P.G., Larsen, K.G., Mikučionis, M., Taankvist, J.H.: Uppaal stratego. In: Baier, C., Tinelli, C. (eds.) TACAS 2015. LNCS, vol. 9035, pp. 206–211. Springer, Heidelberg (2015). https://doi.org/10.1007/978-3-662-46681-0_16

7. David, A., Larsen, K.G., Legay, A., Mikučionis, M., Poulsen, D.B.: Uppaal SMC tutorial. Int. J. Softw. Tools Technol. Transfer **17**(4), 397–415 (2015)

8. Eriksen, A.B., et al.: Uppaal stratego for intelligent traffic lights. In: 12th ITS European Congress (2017)

9. Giua, A., Seatzu, C.: Modeling and supervisory control of railway networks using Petri nets. IEEE Trans. Autom. Sci. Eng. **5**(3), 431–445 (2008)

10. Hansen, M.R.: On-the-Fly Solving of Railway Games (work in progress). Waldén, M. (ed.), p. 34 (2017)

11. Haxthausen, A.E.: Automated generation of formal safety conditions from railway interlocking tables. STTT **16**(6), 713–726 (2014)

12. Kasting, P., Hansen, M.R., Vester, S.: Synthesis of railway-signaling plans using reachability games. In: Proceedings of the 28th Symposium on the Implementation and Application of Functional Programming Languages, IFL 2016, pp. 9:1–9:13. ACM, New York (2016)

13. Larsen, K.G., Mikučionis, M., Taankvist, J.H.: Safe and optimal adaptive cruise control. In: Meyer, R., Platzer, A., Wehrheim, H. (eds.) Correct System Design. LNCS, vol. 9360, pp. 260–277. Springer, Cham (2015). https://doi.org/10.1007/978-3-319-23506-6_17

14. Petersen, J.L.: Automatic verification of railway interlocking systems: a case study. In: Proceedings of the Second Workshop on Formal Methods in Software Practice, FMSP 1998, pp. 1–6. ACM, New York (1998)

15. Watkins, C.J.C.H., Dayan, P.: Q-learning. Mach. Learn. **8**(3), 279–292 (1992)

16. Winter, K.: Model checking railway interlocking systems. In: Proceedings of the Twenty-fifth Australasian Conference on Computer Science, ACSC 2002, vol. 4, pp. 303–310. Australian Computer Society Inc., Darlinghurst (2002)

Safety Process and Validation

A Tool-Supported Model-Based Method for Facilitating the EN50129-Compliant Safety Approval Process

Faiz Ul Muram[1], Barbara Gallina[1]([✉]), and Samina Kanwal[2]

[1] School of Innovation, Design and Engineering, Mälardalen University,
Västerås, Sweden
{faiz.ul.muram,barbara.gallina}@mdh.se
[2] National University of Sciences and Technology, Islamabad, Pakistan
saminakanwal5231@gmail.com

Abstract. Compliance with the CENELEC series is mandatory during the planning of as well as development of railway systems. For compliance purposes, the creation of safety plans, which define safety-related activities and all other process elements relevant at the planning phase, is also needed. These plans are expected to be executed during the development phase. Specifically, EN 50129 defines the safety plan acceptance and approval process, where interactions between the applicant and the certification body are recommended: after the planning phase, to ensure the compliance between plans and standards, and after the development phase, to ensure the effective and not-deviating-unless-justified execution of plans. In this paper, we provide a tool-supported method for facilitating the safety approval processes/certification liaison processes. More specifically, the facilitation consists in guidance for modelling planned processes and the requirements listed in the standards in order to enable the automatic generation of baselines, post-planning processes and evidence models, needed during the execution phase and change impact tracking for manual monitoring of the compatibility between plans and their execution. The applicability of the proposed method is illustrated in the context of EN 50126-1 and EN 50129 standards.

Keywords: EN 50129 · EN 50126-1 · Safety management ·
Safety processes · Regulatory compliance · Safety plans ·
Model transformation

1 Introduction

In the context of railway systems engineering, the Comité Européen de Normalisation Electrotechnique (CENELEC) standard series defines a set of norms as well as a set of processes to be followed. Process planning is one of these processes, which involves development of safety plans, which define: the units of work (such as phases, activities, tasks), expected to be executed during the

© Springer Nature Switzerland AG 2019
S. Collart-Dutilleul et al. (Eds.): RSSRail 2019, LNCS 11495, pp. 125–141, 2019.
https://doi.org/10.1007/978-3-030-18744-6_8

development; a set of methods to be used; work products to be taken as input or produced as output; involved roles, expected to take responsibility for the execution of the work. In avionics, DO-178C [19], the de-facto standard for airborne software development defines the *certification liaison process*, where the interactions (Stages of Involvement-SOI) between the applicant and the certification body are expected to take place throughout the life-cycle of a project. In particular, the first interaction (SOI#1) is expected to take place after the planning phase to ensure that plans are compliant with DO-178C objectives. The second interaction (SOI#2) is expected to take place after the execution phase to assess the project-specific implementation against the approved plans and the DO-178C requirements (i.e., to ensure that the activities to be undertaken are fully congruent). Similarly, in the context of railway systems, the EN 50129 standard [10] defines the reviews (safety acceptance and approval process), which shall be carried out at appropriate stages in the life-cycle. For the safety plan approval, a checklist of activities and items shall be produced in compliance with the CENELEC standard series. The review of the safety plan after each safety life-cycle phase is also recommended.

For getting the approval of safety plans from the certification body, the compliance between the safety plans and the CENELEC standard series requirements should be shown. Furthermore, for the getting the approval for the evidence produced during the development, compatibility between the executed process and the planned process should also be shown. Therefore, it is necessary to provide a reference between the safety plans and the CENELEC standard series requirements as well as a reference between the executed process (including the corresponding evidence) and the planned process. Managing manually such traceability is a tedious and challenging task because of the large amount of information, which needs to be handled. Also, since most of the exiting approaches used to document process models representing plans are natural language-based, the automation of such task is hindered. To facilitate the approval process and more specifically the automatic management of process-related compliance information, in this paper, we provide a novel tool-supported method, which consists of: guidance for modelling (in compliance with the Process Engineering Metamodel (SPEM) 2.0 [18], and more specifically with its reference implementation, implemented in EPF (Eclipse Process Framework) Composer[1]) safety plans and the requirements listed in the standards in order to enable the execution of our proposed model transformation for generating baselines, post-planning processes and evidence models (in compliance with Common Assurance and Certification Metamodel (CACM) [4], implemented in OpenCert[2], which enables the evolution and traceability of models during the development phase), needed during the systems development phase. The transformation is achieved by using Epsilon Transformation Language (ETL)[3]. Specifically, a set of ETL transformation rules are used to transform the CENELEC standard series requirements into the

---

[1] https://www.eclipse.org/epf/.
[2] https://www.polarsys.org/proposals/opencert.
[3] https://www.eclipse.org/epsilon/doc/etl/.

baseline models and diagrams; whereas the safety processes are transformed into the first-view of post-planning processed and evidence models. By automatically generating baseline and evidence models within an environment that supports traceability, this model transformation facilitates the compliance demonstration and thus the plan and its substantiation's approval. Moreover, once the modelling of the standards is completed, process engineers might dedicate their time to the manual production of portions of expected outputs/deliverables that strictly require human intervention. The applicability of the proposed method is illustrated for EN 50126-compliant design specification [9] and EN 50129-compliant safety plan acceptance and approval process [10], focusing on the safety demonstration for a generic product (i.e. independent of application).

The rest of this paper is organized as follows: Sect. 2 presents essential background information. Section 3 describes the tool-supported model-based method for the transformation of standard compliant planned process models to baseline, post-planning process and evidence models. Section 4 illustrates the application of our approach for CENELEC EN 50126 and EN 50129 standards. Section 5 presents the related work. Finally, Sect. 6 concludes the paper and presents future research directions.

2 Background

This section recalls the background information on which the presented work is based: in particular, Sect. 2.1 recalls the necessary information regarding the CENELEC standard series. Section 2.2 presents the process modelling language used in this paper. Section 2.3 recalls basic information about EPF Composer. Section 2.4 recalls essential information about CACM metamodel and the OpenCert tool. Finally, Sect. 2.5 recalls basic information regarding model-driven engineering principles and techniques.

2.1 CENELEC Series

The CENELEC series is a set of standards, which contains requirements and recommendations concerning processes to be followed during the planning, development, deployment and maintenance of the railway systems. EN 50126-1 [9] is part of the CENELEC series. EN 50126-1 provides a fourteen-phase life-cycle process, known as the RAMS process, for developing railway systems by focusing on Reliability, Availability, Maintainability and Safety. The verification and validation activities take place throughout each phase of life-cycle process. In this paper, we limit our attention to Phase 6 (Design and Implementation). The main objective of this phase is to design the sub-systems and components in conformity with RAMS requirements. This phase includes general tasks (e.g., planning, design and development, design analysis and testing, implementation, and verification and validation) and the safety tasks (e.g., preparation and application of safety cases, and the justification of safety related decisions). The verification tasks associated with this phase include the verification of design and realisation of sub-systems and components against RAMS requirements, future life-cycle plans, competence of all personnel, methods, tools and techniques used in this phase, and verification of safety case design and application etc. Each task is associated with the expected output/deliverable or artefacts showing the evidences of requirements. EN 50129 [10], also part of the CENELEC series, defines the three conditions that shall be satisfied in order that a safety-related electronic railway system/sub-system/equipment can be accepted as adequately safe for its intended application. These three conditions are: (1) evidence of quality management (including quality planning and organisational structures) to be documented in the quality management report; (2) evidence of safety management, expected to be consistent to the RAMS process recommended in EN 50126-1 and expected to be documented in the Safety Management Report; and (3) evidence of functional and technical safety. This paper facilitates the satisfaction of the first two conditions.

2.2 Process Engineering Metamodel

SPEM 2.0 [18] is the Object Management Group's (OMG) standard. SPEM 2.0 provides the necessary concepts for modelling, documenting, interchanging, and presenting systems and software development processes. The conceptual framework of SPEM 2.0 consists of *Method Content* and the *Process*. *Method Content* allows users to define reusable process content, i.e., partially ordered *tasks*, *work products* (which can be a type of artifact, deliverable, or outcome), *roles* and *guidances*, and the *Category* such as *disciplines*, *role sets*, *domains* and *tools*. *Process* describes the systematic development processes as sequences of *phases* and *milestones* for the specific types of projects. To define a *process*, tasks can be grouped to form an *activity* and a set of nested activities can be grouped into *iteration* (to indicate that the set can be repeated more than once). A process can be a *capability pattern*, which describes reusable clusters of activities or a *delivery process*, which describes a complete end-to-end project life-cycle. Table 1 shows the main structural elements for defining the process in SPEM 2.0.

Table 1. Process modelling elements in SPEM 2.0

Delivery Process	Capability Pattern	Activity	Iteration	Phase	Milestone	Task
Role	Work Products	Guidance	Practice	Role Sets	Tool	Disciplines

SPEM 2.0 supports variability management in the *Method Content* package, which allows elements to modify or reuse elements in other content packages

without directly modifying the original content. SPEM 2.0 defines five types
of variability relationships: *not assigned* (na)—the default value, *contributes*,
replaces, *extends*, and *extends and replaces* [18]. In the scope of this paper, we
consider *Extends* variability and *Contributes* variability.

2.3 Modelling Standards and Safety Plans in EPF Composer

EPF Composer is an extensible process framework, based on the Unified Method
Architecture (UMA) metamodel, which covers most of the SPEM 2.0 [18] concepts, needed for our purposes. It is worth to highlight that EPF Composer
has been recently ported from Eclipse Galileo 3.5.2 to Eclipse Neon 4.6.3 in the
context of the AMASS project [13]. As presented in [6,16] and [3], based on
Mc Isaac's approach [14] conceived for the commercial version of EPF Composer, EPF Composer can be used to model standards and safety plans, as well
as to show that plans comply with standards. In EPF Composer, *method plugins* are containers of process related information (i.e., Method Content and
Processes), while a *configuration* is a selection of sub-sets of library content
to be shown in the browsing perspective. To model the requirements listed in
the standards, the guidance type *Practice* can be customized with an icon in
a separate plugin *(customized_icon)*. The *standard requirements plugin* captures
the standard's requirements and has the variability relationship *Extends* with
the previously mentioned *customized_icon* plugin. Requirements can be nested
(i.e., a requirement inside another requirement to respect the nesting existing
in the standards), as shown in Fig. 1a. The *process lifecycle plugin* defines the
process life-cycle (i.e., content elements, categories and processes), as shown in
Fig. 1b. To define the mapping, standard requirements are copied in *mapping
requirements plugin*. These copied requirements have a variability relationship
Contributes with original requirements modelled in *standard requirements plugin*.
In addition, the links between process elements (such as tasks) to each "standard requirement" have been established through "references" tab. The mapped
requirements can be grouped in *Custom Categories* to facilitate their visualization in the browsing perspective. To do so, a Custom Category, named *Mapped
Requirements*, is created in the *mapping requirements plugin* and all requirements
are assigned through the "Assign" tab. Figure 1c shows the mapped requirements
in EPF Composer.

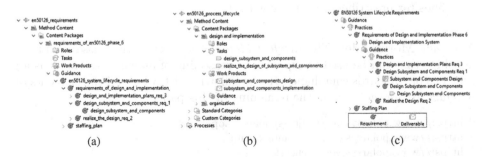

(a)   (b)   (c)

Fig. 1. A cut of the EN 50126-compliant models in EPF Composer-focus on Phase 6

2.4   CACM and OpenCert Within the AMASS Platform

Common Assurance and Certification Metamodel (CACM) is created for the AMASS platform. CACM consists of several packages/metamodels. More specifically, CACM incorporates: (1) the *System Component Metamodel*, which is based on the modelling language (CHESSML) [7], to support the specification of system-specific details and decisions; (2) the *Assurance Case Metamodel*, which is based on the Structured Assurance Case Metamodel (SACM) [17], to support the modelling assurance cases; (3) the *Compliance Management Metamodel* group, which, in turn, consists of several metamodels such as *Process Definition Metamodel*—based on the UMA metamodel, *Assurance Project Definition, Baseline Definition Metamodel* and etc. These metamodels focus on what is planned to be done in a project. The *Evidence Management Metamodels* group based on three OpenCert metamodels: *Artifact Metamodel, Executed Process Metamodel* and *Traceability Metamodel* (AssuranceAsset). These metamodels deal with what has actually been done.

Three tools compose the AMASS platform: EPF Composer, OpenCert[4] and CHESS Toolset[5]. The interested reader may refer the AMASS platform presentation, hosted within the new OpenCert space[6].

In this paper, we focus on *Baseline Definition Metamodel, Artifact Metamodel, Executed Process Metamodel* of OpenCert tool. The main elements of metamodels and their semantics are given in the following subsections.

Baseline Definition Metamodel. The *Baseline Definition Metamodel* (BDM) defines what is planned to be complied with a concrete standard, in a specific assurance project. In the following list, we recall the BDM elements used in the remaining of this paper:

- *BaseFramework* is a main container to model the concepts against which safety and system engineering aspects of a given system are developed and assessed.
- *BaseActivity* is the first-class modelling entity of process specifications, which describes a phase, activity or tasks depending on the activity granularity level defined in a standard or company process. The base activity can be decomposed into one or more fine-grained base activities, called *subActivity*.
- *BaseRequirement* specifies the criteria (e.g., objectives) that a base framework defines (or prescribes) to comply with it.

Artefact Metamodel. The *Artefact Metamodel* specifies the classes and relationships that can be used to support the reasoning of managed artefacts as an evidence of standards compliance. In the following list, we recall the elements of *Artefact Metamodel* used in the remaining of this paper:

---

[4] https://www.polarsys.org/projects/polarsys.opencert.
[5] https://www.polarsys.org/chess/index.html.
[6] https://www.polarsys.org/opencert/.

- *ArtefactModel* defines the root element of a model representing a set of Arte-facts.
- *ArtefactDefinition* specifies a distinguishable abstract unit of data to manage in an assurance project, which represents the whole life-cycle resulting from the evolution, in different versions of Artefacts. In particular, it is a template of a work product involved in an activity.
- *Artefact* describes the instance of artefacts characterised for a version and a set of resources modelling tangible artefact resources or files. An Artefact can be composed of other artefacts or artefact parts.

Executed Process Metamodel. The *Executed Process Metamodel* supports the specification of process-specific compliance needs that might have to be considered in an assurance project, such needs include not only the activities to execute, but also artefacts to manage. In the following list, we recall the elements of *Executed Process Metamodel* used in the remaining of this paper:

- *ProcessModel* is a container of root elements to model a set of Process elements. The Process model corresponds to the actual execution of a process with data related to the results to the process.
- *Activity* models a unit of work performed in a product life-cycle. An Activity is a specification of an activity already executed.
- *Person* models individuals that are involved in a product life-cycle.
- *Tool* models software tools used in a product life-cycle.
- *Organization* corresponds to the groups of people (e.g., companies, societies, associations, etc.) that are involved in a product life-cycle.
- *Technique* is used in the Activity to generate the produced Artefacts.

2.5   Model-Driven Engineering

As summarised in [11], Model-driven Engineering (MDE) is a model-centric software development methodology aimed at raising the software at different levels of abstraction and increasing automation in software development. For automation purposes, model-to-model transformation is used to refine models. In particular, model-to-model transformation transforms the source model (compliant with one metamodel) into a target model compliant with the same or a different metamodel. A standard transformation can be defined as a set of rules to map source to the target. A transformation can be defined by using transformation languages. Epsilon Transformation Language (ETL)[7] is a hybrid, rule-based model-to-model transformation language and provides the enhanced flexibility to transform arbitrary number of source models to an arbitrary number of target models. An ETL transformation is typically organised in modules *ETLModule* and each module can contain any number of transformation rules *TransformationRule* and *Epsilon Object Language (EOL) operations*.

---

[7] See https://www.eclipse.org/epsilon/doc/etl/.

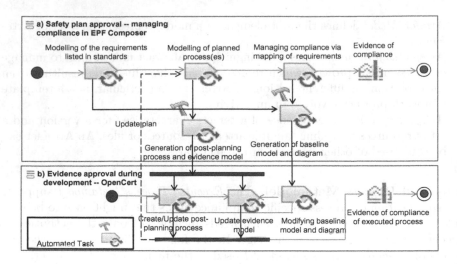

Fig. 2. Overview of the proposed method for facilitating the safety approval process

3   Tool-Support Model-Based Method

In this section, we present our tool-supported model-based method for facilitating the safety approval process. The overview, given in SPEM2.0, of our method is illustrated in Fig. 2. As the activity diagram illustrates, for getting the approval of the safety plans, the compliance between the safety plans and the CENELEC series requirements has to be shown. All this is done in EPF Composer by modelling the requirements, the plans, and the compliance (shown, in this paper, via a simple mapping between standards requirements and safety plans through references in EPF Composer as shown in Sect. 2.3, see Fig. 1. Alternatively, compliance could be explained via argumentation as presented in [16], where process-based arguments (model and diagram) can be derived automatically from process models. Next, the compliant evidence is given to the certification body for approval, afterwards OpenCert tool is used for the execution of the process (safety plan).

For facilitating the compliance between the executed process (including the corresponding evidence) and the planned process, the transformations of standards requirements and planned process from EPF Composer into baselines, post-planning process and evidence models into OpenCert are performed. In particular, the requirements modelled in EPF Composer as "Practice" under the Content Packages are proceeded to generate the baseline model and diagram using implemented *Baseline Generator plugin* (see Sect. 3.1); while the delivery process modelled in EPF Composer is proceeded to generate an evidence model and a process model in OpenCert by using *Process and Evidence Models Generator plugin* (see Sect. 3.2). These transformations help process engineers to get the baseline model and diagram, a first version of their post-planning process model and evidence model, which enables the evolution and traceability of models during the development phase. The baseline model and diagram, post-planning process and evidence models are generated locally as well as in the CDO[8] (Connected Data Objects) repository. CDO is a development-time model repository as well as a run-time persistence framework, which offers transactions with save points, change notifications, queries, transparent temporality, and etc. OpenCert supports engineers to update or evolve the models during the development phase (Fig. 2b) and evidence of compliance is provided for review.

3.1 Generating Baseline Model from Standard Requirements

In this subsection, we explain how we generate the baseline model and diagram from standard requirements for providing the convincing justification to the certification body about compliance means. For this, the mapping between standard requirements compliant with SPEM/UMA and baseline elements compliant with BDM (part of CACM) has been implemented. In order to get the nested requirements and differentiate between them (for example, which process element (i.e., phase, activity, task) is mapped to a standard requirement), we retrieve the information from the *mapping requirements plugin* through "activityReferences" and "contentReferences". The main mapping between these metamodels is described in Table 2. In particular, the *ContentPackage* that contains the requirements is mapped into a *BaseFramework*, whereas the top-level requirement *Practice* related to the Delivery Process or Capability pattern is mapped to the *BaseActivity*. These requirements are decomposed into sub-requirements associated to phases, in turn, for each phase all sub-requirements associated to activities and so on; until the sub-requirements associated to tasks are reached we mapped them into *BaseRequirements* in the Baseline model. Id, name and description of requirements are mapped into Id, name and description of baseline elements.

Table 2. Mappings concepts of requirements

SPEM/UMA	BDM
ContentPackage	BaseFramework
Practice (top-level requirement)	BaseActivity
subPractice (requirement associated to Phase/Activity)	subActivity
subPractice (requirement associated to Task)	BaseRequirement
Id, name and description	Id, name and description

---

[8] http://www.eclipse.org/cdo/.

Algorithm 1. Generating Baseline Model

Input: UMA: ContentPackage, ProcessComponent, Baseline Definition Metamodel, Executed Process Metamodel
Output: BaseFramework
while $childPackages.isTypeOf.ContentPackage =$ "CoreContent" **do**
  $BaseFramework \leftarrow getElementsByTagName(uma : ContentPackage)$
  Transform
  $(BaseFramework \leftarrow ContentPackage)$;
  // Map all three attributes for all elements <element>.id,
    <element>.name, <element>.briefDescription
  for $contentElements.isTypeOf(uma : Practice)$ **do**
    for $activityReferences$ **in** $Practice.activityReferences$ **do**
      $(BaseActivity \leftarrow Practice)$;
      for $subPractice$ **in** $Practice.subPractices()$ **do**
        for $activityReferences$ **in** $subPractices.activityReferences$ **do**
          $(subActivity \leftarrow subPractice)$;
        end for
        // subPractices linked with role, task, work product
        for $contentReferences$ **in** $subPractices.contentReferences$ **do**
          $(BaseRequirement \leftarrow subPractice)$;
        end for
      end for
    end for
  end for
end while

The mapping is achieved by using ETL, in particular, a *Baseline Generator plugin* has been implemented in the AMASS platform, which automatically transforms the requirements into baseline model and diagram. The generated baseline model and diagram are visualized via the Baseline editor in OpenCert. The generated baseline model and diagram are also stored in the CDO Repository. Algorithm 1 shows the skeleton of generation of baseline model and diagram.

3.2   Generating Post-planning Processes and Evidence Models

In this subsection, we present our algorithmic solution for the generation of the post-planning process and the evidence model in OpenCert, from the planned process, modelled in EPF Composer. The mapping is focused on the *Work Breakdown Structure* of Delivery Process in EPF Composer. In particular, a Delivery Process in EPF Composer is contained in the metamodel class *ProcessComponent* which provides additional information to the process description like its version, authors or team profiles required for the execution of the process. However, the user does not explicitly require creating a ProcessComponent in the EPF Composer; they are automatically created each time a delivery process or capability pattern is created. The main mappings between UMA/SPEM and CACM Executed Process and Artefact metamodels are described in Table 3. OpenCert provides the Assurance Process and Evidence Model wizard to visualise generated process model and evidence model, respectively.

Table 3. Mappings concepts of process and artefacts

SPEM/UMA	Executed process and aretfact metamodels
ProcessComponent	ProcessModel, ArtefactModel
CapabilityPattern	Activity
Activity, Phase, Iteration, TaskDescriptor, Milestone	subActivity
RoleDescriptor	Person
Guideline, Practice	Technique
ToolMentor	Tool
RoleSet, TeamProfile	Organization
WorkProductDescriptor	ArtefactDefinition, Artefact
Id, name and description	Id, name and description

In general, evidences are specified and managed by evidence models. Within this model, objects for Artefacts and Artefact Models can be created. The semantics of *ArtefactDefinition* and *Artefact* are slightly different in CACM and UMA metamodels. In the case of CACM, *ArtefactDefinition* is a template of a work product involved in an activity, whereas an *Artefact* represents the specific work product involved in the activity which uses particular template. On the other

---

Algorithm 2. Generating Post-planning Process and Evidence Model
___

Input: UMA: ProcessComponent, Executed Process Metamodel, Aretfact Metamaodel
Output: ProcessModel, ArtefactModel
while $ProcessComponent.isTypeOf(DeliveryProcess)$ **do**
    $ProcessModel \leftarrow getElementsByTagName(uma : ProcessComponent)$
    Transform
    $(ProcessModel \ \& \ ArtefactModel \leftarrow ProcessComponent)$;
    for all CapabilityPattern **do**
        $(Activity \leftarrow CapabilityPattern)$;
        // Map all three attributes for all elements <element>.id,
        <element>.name, <element>.briefDescription
        if $CapabilityPattern \ breakdownElements.isTypeOf(Phase)! = null$ **then**
            for $Phase$ **in** $CapabilityPattern.breakdownElements.isTypeOf(Phase)$ **do**
                $(Activity \leftarrow Phase)$;
            end for
        end if
        if $Activity.getTaskDescriptors(Activity.breakdownElements)! = null$ **then**
            for $TaskDescriptors$ **in** $Activity.getTaskDescriptors(Activity.breakdownElements)! = null$ **do**
                $(Activity \leftarrow TaskDescriptors)$;
                if $TaskDescriptor.WorkProductDescriptor! = null$ **then**
                    for $WorkProductDescriptor$ **in** $TaskDescriptor.WorkProductDescriptor$ **do**
                        Call **operations** getexternalInput(); getoptionalInput(); getmandatoryInput();
                        getoutput();
                        $(ArtefactDefinition \ \& \ Artefact \leftarrow WorkProductDescriptor)$;
                    end for
                end if
            end for
        end if
    end for
end while

hand, in UMA, *Artifact* is an element that belongs to the Method Content package and *WorkProductDescriptor* is an instantiation of an artefact in the context of an activity. Therefore, an ArtefactDefinition and an initial version of Artefact are generated from the WorkProductDescriptor, shown in Table 3. The mapping is achieved by using ETL, in particular, *Process and Evidence Generator* plugin has been implemented in the AMASS platform. Algorithm starts by searching the ProcessComponent if it is the type of Delivery Process and considers the *Work Breakdown Structure* (decomposed) linked elements such as phases, activities etc. Algorithm 2 shows the skeleton of our transformation.

4   An Illustrative Example

In this section, we apply our tool-supported method to show how it facilitates the safety plan acceptance and approval process defined in the EN 50129 standard. Our focus is on the safety demonstration for a generic product (i.e. independent of application) as indicated in EN 50129, Part 5.5.2. Moreover, our focus is limited to Phase 6 (Design and Implementation) of the EN 50126-RAMS life-cycle, which must be taken into consideration for the definition of the portion of the safety plan regarding design and implementation. Based on that, we model: the custom practice for representing a generic requirement modelling element, the requirements from that phase (which inherit from the generic requirement), the portion of the safety plan, which is expected to comply with those requirements, and the compliance (achieved via a mapping through references in *mapping requirements plugin*). The basic compliance between the requirements listed in the Phase 6 (Design and Implementation) of EN 50126 standard and planned process is shown in Fig. 3b.

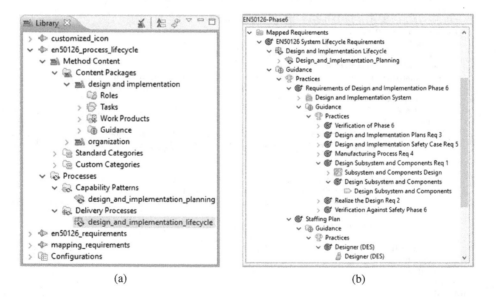

(a)   (b)

Fig. 3. Mapping of planned process and standards in EPF Composer

This modelling activity is performed in EPF Composer by following the guidelines mentioned in Sect. 2.3. As a results, as shown in Fig. 3a, four EPF Composer plugins are created. Concerning the plan, we model: activities, work products, methods, roles, etc. Concerning roles, since EN 50126 is less prescriptive than EN 50128 [8], we have decided to borrow from EN 50128 to plan the responsibilities and competence required at system design level. Due to space limits, the complete visualization of the result of our modelling activity cannot be shown. The interested reader can access the complete EPF Composer project regarding Phase 6 [15].

The OpenCert tool allows users to model baselines as requirements. Instead of manually creating the baselines, the baseline model and diagram are automatically generated from the ContentPackage using our *Baseline Generator plugin* (see Sect. 3.1). Figure 4 shows generated baseline model and diagram, compliant to the BDM that are visualised in baseline editor in OpenCert. The generated baseline model and diagram are also stored in the CDO Repository.

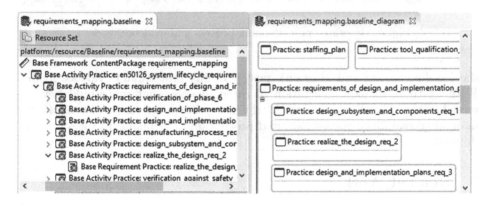

Fig. 4. Generated baseline model and diagram

Finally, for the getting the approval for the evidence produced during the development, compatibility between the executed process and the planned process has also to be shown or the deviations should be tracked and explained. For this, the safety plans compliant with the EN 50126 requirements (including the work products) modelled in EPF Composer are transformed into post-planning process and evidence model in OpenCert. Specifically, the transformation is performed using the *Process and Evidence Models Generator* plugin by right-clicking on ProcessComponent (i.e. delivery process) from the EPF Composer (see Sect. 3.2). The generated evidence model listing all the artefacts to be produced during the execution phase. The generated post-planning process and evidence model can evolve during the life-cycle. Figure 5 shows generated post-planning process and evidence model in OpenCert. The generated models are also stored in the corresponding in the CDO Repository under "PROCESSES" and "EVIDENCE" folder. Both transformations took few seconds to generate

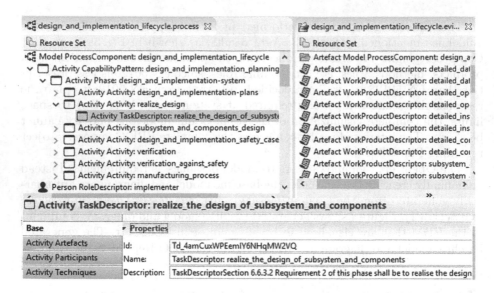

Fig. 5. Generated post-planning process and evidence model

the baseline (model and diagram), post-planning process and evidence model. Without the automatic generation of these models, engineers would have to model them manually from scratch which requires huge effort, also managing manual traceability between executed process and the planned process is very difficult.

5   Related Work

In the literature, as far as we know, no work has addressed the facilitation of the safety plan acceptance and approval process (/certification liaison process) during both phases: planning and execution. However, in the literature, several works exist on execution of process models and on transformations from models created in technological spaces for process definition to models derived within technological spaces for their execution/exchange (Gallina et al. [12] propose an extension of SPEM 2.0, called S-TunExSPEM, for modelling and exchanging safety processes; Bendraou et al. [5] present a model-driven approach, which includes the mapping between UML4SPM, used for the definition of software processes, and WS-BPEL, used for process execution; Alajrami et al. [2] propose and extension of SPEM2.0, called EXE-SPEM for enabling process models execution on the Cloud). In addition, Adedjouma et al. [1] present an approach that transforms the text-based standards to a tree-like structure relying upon the JSON transducer, and then from the JSON tree-like structure to a graphical BPMN model for easy visualisation and navigation. In Adedjouma et al.'s approach non-textual standard elements such as figures, tables are formatted manually by the user. Our work does not automate the digitalisation of the standards yet. However, it provides full guidance for their manual digitalisation, including complex recommendation tables, which populate the standards. Schoitsch et al. [20] propose the certification process in DECOS (Dependable Embedded Components and Systems), which is implemented in a modular way and uses the concept of generic safety cases. The proposed approach is supported by the Generic Test Bench to generate the safety cases by providing generic v-plans for safety standards, documentation support in order to generate the validation report from the completed v-plans and built-in user guidance in terms of a help file. As compared to these works, our tool-supported method facilitates the safety approval process by offering a browsing perspective of compliance management, within EPF Composer during the planning phase and within OpenCert via the evidence management during the execution phase. Our method supports the modelling of plans in compliance with the standards and the automatic generation of post-planning process (including corresponding evidence) required for the execution phase.

6 Conclusion and Future Work

EN 50129-compliant safety plan acceptance and approval process (similar to the DO-178C-compliant certification liaison process) requires the interaction between the applicant and the certification body in order to get approval first for the plans and then for the evidence (which represents the substantiation of the plans). This process is delicate and time consuming due to the necessity of showing that all pieces of evidence produced comply with the CENELEC standard series. In this paper, we have presented a tool-supported method for facilitating such process. Specifically, our method supports: the modelling of the standards, the modelling of the plans in compliance with the standards, the automatic generation of corresponding process-related representations needed for the execution phase and for impact-change tracking. As a consequence, it facilitates the compliance demonstration during the planning phase and the manual review of the safety plan after the execution of each safety life-cycle phase to track alterations or extensions. We have illustrated the usage of our method for facilitating the approval of a portion of an EN 50126/9-compliant safety plan targeting the design specification.

At the current stage of development, our method automatically generates the process-related representations needed for the execution phase. However, in case of alterations and/or extensions made during the execution phase, back transformation from the executed processes to the planned processes is not supported yet. As future work, we intend to investigate the back-propagation of the changes. Based on our gathered experience, such propagation could be achieved by defining similar transformation rules, as presented in this paper, but on the opposite directions. We also intend to conduct a proper evaluation of the approach to achieve a quantitative measurement of the gain that users might get via application of our method. To do that, we will not only consider a generic safety plan, but we will consider its instantiation at a specific project level for the design and implementation of a real subsystem. This in-depth evaluation is planned to be carried out in the context of the AMASS case study 6 (Automatic Train Control Formal Verification) in cooperation with Alstom.

Acknowledgment. This work is supported by EU and VINNOVA via the ECSEL Joint Undertaking under grant agreement No. 692474, AMASS project. We thank Inmaculada Ayala for her contribution on requirements modelling using customised elements in EPF Composer.

References

1. Adedjouma, M., Pedroza, G., Smaoui, A., Dang, T.K.: Facilitating the adoption of standards through model-based representation. In: Proceedings of the 23rd International Conference on Engineering of Complex Computer Systems (ICECCS 2018), Melbourne, Australia, 12–14 December 2018 (2018)
2. Alajrami, S., Gallina, B., Romanovsky, A.: EXE-SPEM: towards cloud-based executable software process models. In: 4th International Conference on Model-Driven Engineering and Software Development, MODELSWARD, pp. 517–527 (2016)
3. AMASS: AMASS User guidance and Methodological framework (2018). https://www.amass-ecsel.eu/sites/amass.drupal.pulsartecnalia.com/files/D2.5_User-guidance-and-methodological-framework_AMASS_Final.pdf. Accessed 5 Mar 2018
4. AMASS: AMASS platform validation D2.9 (2019). https://www.amass-ecsel.eu/sites/amass.drupal.pulsartecnalia.com/files/documents/D2.9_AMASS-platform-validation_AMASS_Final.pdf. Accessed 5 Mar 2019
5. Bendraou, R., Jezéquél, J.-M., Fleurey, F.: Combining aspect and model-driven engineering approaches for software process modeling and execution. In: Wang, Q., Garousi, V., Madachy, R., Pfahl, D. (eds.) ICSP 2009. LNCS, vol. 5543, pp. 148–160. Springer, Heidelberg (2009). https://doi.org/10.1007/978-3-642-01680-6_15
6. Castellanos Ardila, J.P., Gallina, B., Ul Muram, F.: Enabling compliance checking against safety standards from SPEM 2.0 process models. In: 44th Euromicro Conference on Software Engineering and Advanced Applications, SEAA 2018, Prague, Czech Republic, 29–31 August 2018, pp. 45–49 (2018). https://doi.org/10.1109/SEAA.2018.00017
7. CHESS-Team: CHESSML (2018). https://www.polarsys.org/chess/start.html
8. European Commitee for Electrotechnical Standardization (CENELEC): EN 50128 - railway applications - communication, signalling and processing systems - software for railway control and protection systems (2011)
9. European Commitee for Electrotechnical Standardization (CENELEC): EN 50126–1: railway applications - the specification and demonstration of reliability, availability, maintainability and safety (RAMS), part 1 generic RAMS process (2017)
10. European Commitee for Electrotechnical Standardization (CENELEC): EN50129: railway applications - communication, signalling and processing systems - safety related electronic systems for signalling (2018)
11. Gallina, B.: A Model-driven safety certification method for process compliance. In: 2nd International Workshop on Assurance Cases for Software-Intensive Systems, joint event of ISSRE, Naples, Italy, 3–6 November 2014, pp. 204–209. IEEE (2014). https://doi.org/10.1109/ISSREW.2014.30

12. Gallina, B., Pitchai, K.R., Lundqvist, K.: S-TunExSPEM: towards an extension of SPEM 2.0 to model and exchange tunable safety-oriented processes. In: Lee, R. (ed.) Software Engineering Research, Management and Applications. Studies in Computational Intelligence, vol. 496, pp. 215–230. Springer, Heidelberg (2014). https://doi.org/10.1007/978-3-319-00948-3_14
13. Javed, M.A., Gallina, B.: Get EPF Composer back to the future: a trip from Galileo to Photon after 11 years. EclipseCon, Toulouse, France, 13–14 June (2018). http://www.es.mdh.se/publications/5091-Get_EPF_Composer_back_to_the_future_A_trip_from_Galileo_to_Photon_after_11_years
14. McIsaac, B.: IBM rational method composer: standards mapping. Technical report, IBM Developer Works (2015)
15. Muram, F.U., Gallina, B.: EPF Composer Library for EN 50126-9 compliant process authoring, limited to Phase 6 (2019). https://www.dropbox.com/sh/1o7cf12nqvmyvqc/AACi0EZymqzbQJKinutcNAzsa?dl=0. Accessed 5 Mar 2019
16. Muram, F.U., Gallina, B., Rodriguez, L.G.: Preventing omission of key evidence fallacy in process-based argumentations. In: 11th International Conference on the Quality of Information and Communications Technology (QUATIC), Coimbra, Portugal, 4–7 September 2018, pp. 65–73. IEEE (2018). https://doi.org/10.1109/QUATIC.2018.00019
17. Object Management Group (OMG): Structured Assurance Case Metamodel (SACM), Version 2.0 (2018). https://www.omg.org/spec/SACM/2.0. Accessed 5 Mar 2019
18. OMG: Software & Systems Process Engineering Metamodel Specification (SPEM), Version 2.0 (2008). http://www.omg.org/spec/SPEM/2.0/. Accessed 5 Mar 2019
19. RTCA Inc: Software Considerations in Airborne Systems and Equipment Certification, RTCA DO-178C (EUROCAE ED-12C), Washington DC (2011)
20. Schoitsch, E., Althammer, E., Sonneck, G., Eriksson, H., Vinter, J.: Modular certification support - the DECOS concept of generic safety cases. In: 2008 6th IEEE International Conference on Industrial Informatics, pp. 258–263, July 2008. https://doi.org/10.1109/INDIN.2008.4618105

Efficient Data Validation for Geographical Interlocking Systems

Jan Peleska[1]([✉]), Niklas Krafczyk[1], Anne E. Haxthausen[2], and Ralf Pinger[3]

[1] Department of Mathematics and Computer Science, University of Bremen, Bremen, Germany
{peleska,niklas}@uni-bremen.de
[2] DTU Compute, Technical University of Denmark, Kongens Lyngby, Denmark
aeha@dtu.dk
[3] Siemens Mobility GmbH, Braunschweig, Germany
ralf.pinger@siemens.com

Abstract. In this paper, an efficient approach to data validation of geographical interlocking systems (IXLs) is presented. It is explained how configuration rules for IXLs can be specified by temporal logic formulas interpreted on Kripke structure representations of the IXL configuration. Violations of configuration rules can be specified using formulas from a well-defined subset of LTL. By decomposing the complete configuration model into sub-models corresponding to routes through the model, the LTL model checking problem can be transformed into a CTL checking problem for which highly efficient algorithms exist. Specialised rule violation queries that are hard to express in LTL can be simplified and checked faster by performing sub-model transformations adding auxiliary variables to the states of the underlying Kripke structures. Further performance enhancements are achieved by checking each sub-model concurrently. The approach presented here has been implemented in a model checking tool which is applied by Siemens for data validation of geographical IXLs.

Keywords: Data validation · Interlocking systems · LTL · CTL · Model checking

1 Introduction

Background. Railway interlocking systems (IXLs) are designed according to different paradigms [13, Chap. 4]. Two of the most widely used are (a) *route-based interlocking systems* and (b) *geographical interlocking systems*. The former are based on predefined routes through the rail network and use interlocking tables specifying safety conflicts between different routes and the point positions and signal states to be enforced before a route may be entered by a train. For design type (b), routes through the railway network can be allocated dynamically by indicating the starting and destination points of trains intending to traverse

© Springer Nature Switzerland AG 2019
S. Collart-Dutilleul et al. (Eds.): RSSRail 2019, LNCS 11495, pp. 142–158, 2019.
https://doi.org/10.1007/978-3-030-18744-6_9

the railway network portion controlled by the IXL under consideration. In the original technology, electrical relay-based circuits were applied, whose elements and interconnections were designed in one-to-one correspondence with those of the physical track layout. The electric circuit design ensured dynamic identification of free routes from starting point to destination, the locking of points and setting of signals along the route, as well as on neighbouring track segments for the purpose of flank protection. In today's software-controlled electronic interlocking systems, instances of software components "mimic" the elements of the electric circuit. Typically following the object-oriented paradigm, different components are developed, each corresponding to a specific type of physical track element, such as points, track sections associated with signals, and others with axle counters or similar devices detecting trains passing along the track. Similar to connections between electric circuit elements, instances of these software components are connected by communication channels reflecting the track network. The messages passed along these channels carry requests for route allocation, point switching and locking, signal settings, and the associated responses acknowledging or rejecting these requests. The software components are developed for re-use, so that novel interlocking software designs can be realised by means of configuration data, specifying which instances of software components are required, their attribute values, and how their communication channels shall be connected.

IXL design induces a distinguished verification and validation (V&V) step which is called *data validation*. For route-based IXLs, its main objective is to ensure completeness and correctness of interlocking tables. For geographical IXLs, the objective is to check whether the instantiation of software components is complete, each component is equipped with the correct attribute values, and whether the channel interconnections are adequate. The data validation objectives are specified by means of rules, and the rule collection is usually quite extensive (several hundreds), so that manual data validation would be a cumbersome, costly, and error-prone task. Also, manually programmed checking software is not a satisfactory solution, since the addition of new rules would require frequent extensions of the code. These extensions are costly, since data validation tools need to be validated according to tool class T2, as specified in the standard [5].

Previous Work. This paper is a follow-up contribution to [9], where a solution to the data validation problem for geographical IXLs by means of bounded model checking (BMC) had been presented.[1] During practical evaluation of the results described there, it turned out that the BMC approach was highly effective as a bug-finder: if violations of configuration rules were present, these were uncovered effectively and within acceptable running time. The configuration experts from Siemens, however, criticised that the tool would not prove the *absence* of

---

[1] The text of the previous paragraph describing the general problem and the more detailed description in Sect. 2 have been reproduced here in slightly modified form from [9], in order to make the present paper self-contained.

configuration errors. Typical for BMC algorithms, the running time of the checks sometimes increased exponentially with the search depth, so that an exploration of the model up to its *recurrence diameter*[2] would have resulted in unacceptable running time and storage consumption.

Main Contributions. As a consequence of the experiences gained with the application of BMC technology described in [9], an alternative approach has been elaborated and implemented in a new data validation tool, the *DVL-Checker* (Data Validation Language Checker). The new approach is described in the present paper, and it is based on the following key insights which, to our best knowledge, have not been explored before for the purpose of IXL data validation.

1. Exploiting known results about the temporal logic LTL, it is shown that violations of safety-properties can be represented by a syntactic subset of LTL which is denoted as *data validation language (DVL)*. This ensures that violations of IXL configuration rules can be specified using this subset.
2. Exploiting known results about LTL and CTL, we show how LTL formulae ϕ representing safety violations (so-called *DVL-queries*) can be translated to CTL formulae $\Phi(\phi)$, such that CTL model checking of $\Phi(\phi)$ is an *over-approximation* for LTL model checking of ϕ in the sense of abstract interpretation. This means that the absence of witnesses[3] for CTL formula $\Phi(\phi)$ implies the absence of solutions for LTL formula ϕ, which proves that no rule violation specified by ϕ is present.
3. For CTL, highly efficient and well-explored global model checking algorithms can be applied. These have complexity $O(|f| \cdot (|S| + |R|))$, where $|f|$ is the number of sub-formulae in CTL formula f, $|S|$ is the size of the state space, and $|R|$ is the size of the transition relation. Moreover, the application of CTL model checking is generally more efficient than that of LTL model checking, since the latter represents an NP-hard problem [6, Section 4.2] which is PSPACE-complete [16].
4. A decomposition of the complete IXL configuration into sub-models corresponding to directed routes through the railway network allows for (1) significant reduction of false alarms that might result from the fact that CTL checking for witnesses of $\Phi(\phi)$ is an over-approximation of LTL checking for ϕ[4], and (2) significant speed-up of the checking process by processing sub-models concurrently.

Related Work. Data validation for railway interlocking systems is a well-established V&V task in railway technology. At the same time, it is a very

---

[2] The recurrence diameter denotes the number of steps to be performed by a BMC algorithm to achieve exhaustive model exploration [3].

[3] A *witness* is a sequence of states fulfilling a temporal logic formula.

[4] This reduction of false alarms is achieved because the sub-models corresponding to directed routes do not contain as many branches as the full network, and it is well known that on linear paths, LTL and corresponding CTL formulas are equivalent.

active research field, since the complexity of today's IXL configurations requires a high degree of automation for checking their correctness. There seems to be an agreement among the research communities that hard-coded data validation programs are inefficient, due to the large number of rules to be checked and the frequent adaptations and extensions of rules that are necessary to take into account the requirements of different IXLs. These observations are confirmed by numerous publications on IXL data validation, such as [1,7–10].

It is interesting to point out that some V&V approaches for IXLs do not explicitly distinguish between data validation and the verification of dynamic IXL behaviour; this is the case, for example, in [4,10]. We agree, however, with [7], where it is emphasised that data validation should be a separate activity in the IXL V&V process. This assessment is motivated by the analogy with software verification, where the correctness of static semantics – this corresponds to the IXL configuration data – is verified before the correctness of dynamic program behaviour – this corresponds to the dynamic IXL behaviour – is analysed.

As observed in [2], data validation approaches based on the B tool family seem to be the most widely used both in industry and academia in Europe, we name [1,7,8,10] as noteworthy examples for this fact.

The methodology and tool support described in the present paper differs significantly from the B methodology: whereas the methods based on the B family require specifications in first-order logic and perform verification by theorem proving or constraint (model) checking, our approach is based on temporal logic and CTL model checking. Moreover, our methodology strictly specialises in geographical interlocking systems, while – in principle – the B-methods can be applied to any type of IXL technology. Our more restricted approach, however, comes with the advantage that rule specifications are simpler to construct than in B, since temporal logic formulae do not require quantification over variables. Moreover, the sub-model construction technique used in our methodology ensures that the proper verification by CTL model checking is always fully automatic and fast, whereas the B-approaches may require interactive user support during theorem proving [8].

Overview. In Sect. 2, the data validation approach to geographical IXLs is explained from an engineering perspective. The mathematical foundations required to enable automated complete detection of IXL configuration rule violations are elaborated in Sect. 3. This is done without any reference to the intended application. The latter is described in Sect. 4, where the application of the mathematical theory to IXL data validation is presented in detail. In Sect. 5, a conclusion is presented.

A more detailed technical report containing all formal definitions, theorems, proofs, and algorithms on which the DVL-Checker is based can be found in [14].

2 Data Validation for Geographic Interlocking Systems

As indicated above, the software controlling geographical interlocking systems consists of objects communicating over channels, each instance representing a

physical track element or a related hardware interface. A subset of these channels
– called *primary channels* in the following – reflect the physical interconnection
between neighbouring track elements which are part of possible routes, to be
dynamically allocated when a request for traversal from some starting point to
a destination is given (Fig. 1). Other channels – called *secondary channels* –
connect certain elements s_1 to others s_2, such that s_1 and s_2 are not necessarily
neighbouring elements on a route, but s_2 may offer flank protection to s_1, when
some route including s_1 should be allocated. Since geographical interlocking
is based on request and response messages, each channel for sending request
messages from some instance s_1 connected to an instance s_2 is associated with a
"response channel" from s_2 to s_1. Primary channels are subsequently denoted by
variable symbols a, b, c, d, while secondary channels are denoted by $e, f, g, \ldots$.
Only points and diamond crossings use c-channels, and d-channels are used by
diamond crossings only.

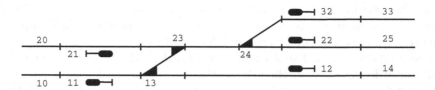

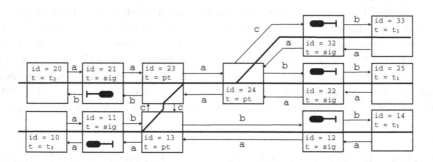

Fig. 1. Physical layout, associated software instances and channel connections.

For signals, the driving direction they apply to is along channel a. For points,
the straight track (point position "+") is always represented by the channel
connections from a to b and vice versa, and the diverging track (point position
"−") always from a to c and vice versa. The stems of a point are denoted
by *A,B,C-stems* according to the channels associated with the stem. The entry
into/exit from the track network controlled by the interlocking systems is always
marked by *border elements* of a special type. In Fig. 1, these types are denoted
by the fictitious identifiers t_1 and t_3. Some track sections may be crossed in both
directions, so a border element may serve both as entry and exit element. This
is discussed in more detail in the context of sub-model creation in Sect. 4.

All software instances are associated with a unique *id* and a type *t* corresponding to the track element type they are representing. Depending on the type, a list of further attributes $a_1, \ldots, a_k$ may be defined for each software instance. By using default value 0 for attributes that are not applicable to a certain component type, each element can be associated with the same complete list of attributes. Each valuation of a channel variable contains either a default value 0, meaning "no connection on this channel", or the instance identification *id* > 0 of the destination instance of the channel.

Data validation rules state conditions about admissible sequences of element types and about admissible parameters.

Example 1. A typical pattern of data validation rules checks the existence of expected follow-up elements for an element of a given type.

Rule 1. From channel *a* of an element of type *sig* pointing in downstream direction, an element of the same type with its *b*-channel pointing upstream is found, before a border element of type t_1 or t_3 is reached.

Every rule can be transformed into a *rule violation condition*. For Rule 1, the violation would be specified as

Violation of Rule 1. From channel *a* of an element of type *sig* pointing in downstream direction, no element of the same type with its *b*-channel pointing upstream is found, before a border element of type t_1 or t_3 is reached.

The configuration in Fig. 1 violates Rule 1, because, for example, the path segment $\pi_1 = s_{21}.s_{23}.s_{24}.s_{22}.s_{25}$ contains the follow-up element s_{22}, but this points with its *a*-channel towards signal 21. Practically, this means that the signal with id 22 does not point into the expected driving direction, so the expected route exit signal along π_1 is missing. An example of a path segment which is consistent with this rule is $\pi_2 = s_{32}.s_{24}.s_{23}.s_{13}.s_{11}.s_{10}$. $\square$

Example 2. Another typical pattern of data validation rules refers to the element types that are required or admissible in certain segments of a route marked by elements of specific type.

Rule 2. Between channel *a* of an element of type *sig* and channel *b* of the associated downstream element of the same type *sig*, there must be at least one element of type t_3.

The corresponding rule violation can be specified as

Violation of Rule 2. Between channel *a* of an element of type *sig* and channel *b* of the associated downstream element of type *sig*, there does not exist any element of type t_3.

The configuration in Fig. 1 violates this rule, because the path segments connecting the signals of type *sig* do not contain any element of type t_3. $\square$

3   Logical Foundations

In this section, the logical foundations of the model checking method for data validation are summarised. The underlying theory is described without references to their practical application in the IXL context; the latter is explained in Sect. 4. A comprehensive description of these foundations can be found in [14].

Kripke Structures. A *State Transition System* is a triple $TS = (S, S_0, R)$, where S is the set of *states*, $S_0 \subseteq S$ is the set of *initial states*, $R \subseteq S \times S$ is the *transition relation*. The intuitive interpretation of R is that a state change from $s_1 \in S$ to $s_2 \in S$ is possible in TS if and only if $(s_1, s_2) \in R$. A *Kripke Structure* $K = (S, S_0, R, L, AP)$ is a state transition system (S, S_0, R) augmented with a set AP of *atomic propositions* and a *labelling function* $L : S \to 2^{AP}$ mapping each state s of K to the set of atomic propositions valid in s. Furthermore, it is required that the transition relation R is *total* in the sense that $\forall s \in S : \exists s' \in S : (s, s') \in R$. It is assumed that AP always contains the truth values `false`, `true`.

A *computation* of a state transition system (or a Kripke structure) is an infinite sequence $\pi = s_0.s_1.s_2 \cdots \in S^\omega$ of states $s_i \in S$, such that the start state is an initial state, that is, $s_0 \in S_0$, and each pair of consecutive states is linked by the transition relation, that is, $\forall i > 0 : (s_{i-1}, s_i) \in R$. The terms *path* or *execution* are used synonymously for computations. In the context of this paper, state spaces S consist of *valuation functions* $s : V \to D$ mapping variable names from V to their actual values in D. For the context of this paper, it suffices to consider $D = \text{int}$, because all configuration parameters used for the interlocking systems under consideration may be encoded as integers. For the Boolean values `true`, `false`, the integer values $1, 0$ are used, respectively.

First Order Formulae and Their Valuation. Given a Kripke Structure K with variable valuation functions $s : V \to \text{int}$ as states, expressions are evaluated in the usual way by replacing free variables v with their actual value $s(v)$ in this state. We write $s \models f$ for an unquantified first-order expression, if and only if f becomes true when replacing all symbols v by $s(v)$. Atomic propositions are constructed by composing variables, constants, or arithmetic expressions using comparison operators. An *(unquantified) first-order formula* f over V is a logical formula with atomic propositions over V, composed by logical operators $\neg, \wedge, \vee$.

Linear Temporal Logic LTL. Given a Kripke structure with state valuations over variables from V, we use unquantified first-order LTL with the following syntax.

– Every unquantified first-order formula over V as specified above is an unquantified first-order LTL formula.
– If f, g are unquantified first-order LTL formulae, then $\neg f$, $f \wedge g$, $f \vee g$, $\mathbf{X}f$ (*Next*), $\mathbf{G}f$ (*Globally*), $\mathbf{F}f$ (*Finally*), $f\mathbf{U}g$ (*Until*), and $f\mathbf{W}g$ (*Weak Until*) are also unquantified first-order LTL formulae.

Operators $\mathbf{X}$, $\mathbf{G}$, $\mathbf{F}$, $\mathbf{U}$, and $\mathbf{W}$ are called *path operators*. The models of LTL formulae are infinite paths $\pi = s_0.s_1.s_2. \cdots \in S^\omega$; we write $\pi \models_{\text{LTL}} f$ if formula

f holds on path π according to the semantic rules specified in Table 1.[5] We use notation $\pi^i = s_i.s_{i+1}.s_{i+2}\ldots$ to denote the path segment of π starting at element $\pi(i)$. A Kripke structure K fulfils LTL formula f ($K \models_{\text{LTL}} f$) if and only if every computation of K is a model of f.

Table 1. Semantics of LTL formulae.

$\pi^i \models_{\text{LTL}} \textbf{true}$ for all $i \geqslant 0$

$\pi^i \not\models_{\text{LTL}} \textbf{false}$ for all $i \geqslant 0$

$\pi^i \models_{\text{LTL}} f$ iff $\pi(i) \models f$ if f is an unquantified first-order formula over V

$\pi^i \models_{\text{LTL}} \neg\varphi$ iff $\pi^i \not\models_{\text{LTL}} \varphi$

$\pi^i \models_{\text{LTL}} \varphi \wedge \psi$ iff $\pi^i \models_{\text{LTL}} \varphi$ and $\pi^i \models_{\text{LTL}} \psi$

$\pi^i \models_{\text{LTL}} \varphi \vee \psi$ iff $\pi^i \models_{\text{LTL}} \varphi$ or $\pi^i \models_{\text{LTL}} \psi$

$\pi^i \models_{\text{LTL}} \mathbf{X}\varphi$ iff $\pi^{i+1} \models_{\text{LTL}} \varphi$

$\pi^i \models_{\text{LTL}} \mathbf{G}\varphi$ iff $\pi^{i+j} \models_{\text{LTL}} \varphi$ for all $j \geqslant 0$

$\pi^i \models_{\text{LTL}} \mathbf{F}\varphi$ iff there exists $j \geqslant 0$ such that $\pi^{i+j} \models_{\text{LTL}} \varphi$

$\pi^i \models_{\text{LTL}} \varphi\mathbf{U}\psi$ iff there exists $j \geqslant 0$ such that $\pi^{i+j} \models_{\text{LTL}} \psi$ and

   $\pi^{i+k} \models_{\text{LTL}} \varphi$ for all $0 \leqslant k < j$

$\pi^i \models_{\text{LTL}} \varphi\mathbf{W}\psi$ iff

   $\pi^{i+k} \models_{\text{LTL}} \varphi$ for all $k \geqslant 0$,

   or there exists $j \geqslant 0$ such that $\pi^{i+j} \models_{\text{LTL}} \psi$ and

   $\pi^{i+k} \models_{\text{LTL}} \varphi$ for all $0 \leqslant k < j$

Safety Properties. A *safety property* P is a collection of computations $\pi \in S^\omega$, such that for every $\pi' \in S^\omega$ with $\pi' \notin P$, the fact that π' does *not* fulfil P can already be decided on a finite prefix of π'. It has been shown in [15] that every safety property P can be characterised by a *Safety LTL* formula f, so that the computations in P are exactly those fulfilling f. The Safety LTL formulae are specified as follows [15, Theorem 3.1]:
(1) Every unquantified first-order formula is a Safety LTL-formula. (2) If f, g are Safety LTL-Formulae, then so are $f \wedge g$, $f \vee g$, $\mathbf{X}f$, $f\mathbf{W}g$, and $\mathbf{G}f$.

Observe that in these safety formulae, the negation operator must only occur in first-order sub-formulae. Suppose that a safety property P is specified by Safety LTL formula f. When looking for a path π *violating* f, the violation

---

[5] The operators $\vee$, $\mathbf{G}$, $\mathbf{F}$, $\mathbf{U}$ are redundant and can be expressed using the remaining LTL operators alone. Therefore, they are sometimes introduced as syntactic abbreviations. For the purpose of this paper, however, it is better to represent their semantics in an explicit way.

$\pi \models_{\mathrm{LTL}} \neg f$ can be equivalently expressed by a formula containing only first-order expressions composed by the operators $\wedge, \vee, \mathbf{X}, \mathbf{U}$. This is stated in the following theorem proven in [14].

Theorem 1. *Let f be a Safety LTL formula. Then $\neg f$ can be equivalently expressed using first-order expressions composed by operators $\wedge, \vee, \mathbf{X}, \mathbf{U}$.*   □

Safety Violation Formulae on Finite Paths. It will be explained in Sect. 4 how IXL configurations may be interpreted as Kripke structures. This interpretation needs one relaxation of the Kripke structure definition $K = (S, S_0, R, L, AP)$: we admit state transition systems (S, S_0, R) whose transition relation is no longer total. This leads to finite computations, because some states do not possess any post-states under R.

From Theorem 1 above we know that the LTL formulae we are interested in – these express safety violations – can be represented by $\wedge, \vee, \mathbf{X}, \mathbf{U}$. For these operators, the LTL semantics can be easily extended to finite computations by declaring the evaluation result to be **false** if the end of the path has been reached before the truth of the formula could be shown. The LTL semantics on finite computations has been investigated in [3], we only need a simplified version thereof, because it will only be applied to acyclic sub-models of IXL configurations.

Computation Tree Logic CTL. While LTL formulae have computations of Kripke structures as models, CTL has trees of computations as models. As a consequence, two new *path quantors* are introduced in addition to the path operators already known from LTL: quantors $\mathbf{E}$ and $\mathbf{A}$ denote existential and universal path quantification, respectively. The CTL syntax is defined by the following grammar, where f denotes unquantified first-order formulae as specified above, formulae ϕ are called *state formulae*, and formulae ψ are called *path formulae*.

$$\text{CTL-formula} ::= \phi$$
$$\phi ::= f \mid \neg\phi \mid \phi \vee \phi \mid \phi \wedge \phi \mid \mathbf{E}\psi \mid \mathbf{A}\psi$$
$$\psi ::= \phi \mid \neg\psi \mid \psi \vee \psi \mid \psi \wedge \psi \mid \mathbf{X}\phi \mid \mathbf{F}\phi \mid \mathbf{G}\phi \mid \phi\mathbf{U}\phi \mid \phi\mathbf{W}\phi$$

According to this grammar, the path operators $\mathbf{X}, \mathbf{F}, \mathbf{G}, \mathbf{U}, \mathbf{W}$ can never be prefixed by another temporal operator in CTL. Only pairs consisting of a path quantifier and a temporal operator can occur in a row.

The semantics of CTL formulae is explained using a Kripke structure K, specific states s of K and computations π of K. We write $K, s \models_{\mathrm{CTL}} \phi$ to express that ϕ holds in state s of K. We write $K, \pi \models_{\mathrm{CTL}} \psi$ to express that ψ holds along path π through K. For CTL formulae ϕ we say ϕ *holds in the Kripke model K* and write $K \models_{\mathrm{CTL}} \phi$ if and only if $K, s_0 \models_{\mathrm{CTL}} \phi$ holds in every initial state s_0 of K. The semantics of the subset of CTL formulae we are interested in is specified in Table 2, where f denotes unquantified first-order formulae, ϕ, ϕ_i denote state formulae, and ψ, ψ_j denote path formulae. First-order formulae are interpreted just as in LTL.

Table 2. Semantics of CTL subset required for data validation.

$K, s \models_{\text{CTL}} f$	iff	$s \models f$ for any unquantified first-order formula f
$K, s \models_{\text{CTL}} \phi_1 \vee \phi_2$	iff	$K, s \models_{\text{CTL}} \phi_1$ or $K, s \models_{\text{CTL}} \phi_2$
$K, s \models_{\text{CTL}} \phi_1 \wedge \phi_2$	iff	$K, s \models_{\text{CTL}} \phi_1$ and $K, s \models_{\text{CTL}} \phi_2$
$K, s \models_{\text{CTL}} \mathbf{E} \psi$	iff	there is a path π from s such that $K, \pi^i \models_{\text{CTL}} \psi$
$K, \pi^i \models_{\text{CTL}} \phi$	iff	$K, \pi(i) \models_{\text{CTL}} \phi$
$K, \pi^i \models_{\text{CTL}} \psi_1 \vee \psi_2$	iff	$K, \pi^i \models_{\text{CTL}} \psi_1$ or $K, \pi^i \models_{\text{CTL}} \psi_2$
$K, \pi^i \models_{\text{CTL}} \psi_1 \wedge \psi_2$	iff	$K, \pi^i \models_{\text{CTL}} \psi_1$ and $K, \pi^i \models_{\text{CTL}} \psi_2$
$K, \pi^i \models_{\text{CTL}} \mathbf{X} \psi$	iff	$K, \pi^{i+1} \models_{\text{CTL}} \psi$
$K, \pi^i \models_{\text{CTL}} \psi_1 \mathbf{U} \psi_2$	iff	there exists $j \geq 0$ such that $K, \pi^{i+j} \models_{\text{CTL}} \psi_2$ and $K, \pi^{i+k} \models_{\text{CTL}} \psi_1$ for all $0 \leqslant k < j$

Over-Approximation of LTL Safety Violation Formulae by CTL. Full LTL and CTL have different expressiveness, and neither one is able to express all formulae of the other with equivalent semantics [6]. It can be shown, however, that any safety violation specified by an LTL formula f on a path π can also be detected by applying CTL model checking to a translated formula $\Phi(f)$ on any Kripke structure K containing π as a computation. This is, however, an *over-approximation*, in the sense that witnesses for $\Phi(f)$ in K will not always correspond to single paths π where $\pi \models_{\text{LTL}} f$ holds. It will be shown in Sect. 4 how the choice of sub-models significantly reduces the number of such false alarms.

Recalling from Theorem 1 that any safety violation can be specified using first-order formulae and operators $\wedge, \vee, \mathbf{X}, \mathbf{U}$, we specify a partial transformation function $\Phi : \text{LTL} \rightarrowtail \text{CTL}$ as follows, where f denotes a first-order formula and ψ_1, ψ_2 denote formulas containing path operators.

$$\Phi(f) = f$$
$$\Phi(\psi_1 \wedge \psi_2) = \Phi(\psi_1) \wedge \Phi(\psi_2) \qquad \Phi(\psi_1 \vee \psi_2) = \Phi(\psi_1) \vee \Phi(\psi_2)$$
$$\Phi(\mathbf{X}\psi_1) = \mathbf{EX}(\Phi(\psi_1)) \qquad \Phi(\psi_1 \mathbf{U}\psi_2) = \mathbf{E}(\Phi(\psi_1)\mathbf{U}\Phi(\psi_2))$$

With this transformation at hand, the following theorem states that the absence of witnesses for $\Phi(f)$ in K guarantees the absence of a rule violation f on π.

Theorem 2. *Let π be any path and f an LTL formula specifying a safety violation on π. Let K be a Kripke structure over state space S containing π as a computation. Then $\pi \models_{\text{LTL}} f$ implies $K \models_{\text{CTL}} \Phi(f)$.* $\square$

With Theorem 2 at hand, we can apply the classical CTL model checking algorithms from [6] with small modifications related to first-order expressions, the resulting algorithms are specified in [14]. There, it is also shown that the algorithms are sound and complete for Kripke structures with finite computations. The algorithms have running time $O(|f| \cdot (|S| + |R|))$, where $|f|$ is the number of sub-formulae in CTL formula f, $|S|$ is the size of the state space, and $|R|$ is the size of the transition relation. As a consequence, the running time is affected by the model size in a linear way only, while model size may affect the running time of BMC in an exponential way. The running time is also lower than using LTL model checking algorithms directly, since the latter are PSPACE-complete [16].

4   Model Checking of IXL Configurations

IXL Configurations as Kripke Structures. The configurations for geographical IXLs described in Sect. 2 give rise to Kripke structures $K = (S, S_0, R, L, AP)$ with variable symbols from some set V as follows (symbol d denotes int-values).

$$V = \{id, t\} \cup C \cup A$$
$$C = \{c \mid c \text{ is a primary or secondary channel symbol}\}$$
$$A = \{a \mid a \text{ is an attribute}\}$$
$$S = \{s : V \to \text{int} \mid \text{There exists a configuration instance with}$$
$$\text{id, type, channel, and attribute valuation } s\}$$
$$S_0 = S$$
$$R = \{(s, s') \mid \exists c \in C : s(c) = s'(id)\}$$
$$AP = \{id = d \mid \exists s \in S : s(id) = d\} \cup \{t = d \mid \exists s \in S : s(t) = d\} \cup$$
$$\{c = d \mid c \in C \land \exists s \in S : s(c) = d\} \cup$$
$$\{a = d \mid a \in A \land \exists s \in S : s(a) = d\}$$
$$L : S \to 2^{AP}; \quad s \mapsto \{v = d \mid v \in V \land s(v) = d\}$$

Each K-state in S is represented by a valuation function s mapping id, type, channel, and attribute symbols to corresponding integer values, such that there is a configuration element with exactly these values. The atomic propositions consist of all equalities $v = d$, where v is a symbol of V and d an integer value occurring for v in at least one configuration element. Every K-state is an initial state, because configuration rules are checked from any element as starting point. Two elements s, s' are linked by the transition relation whenever s has a channel c connected to s'; this is expressed by $s(c)$ carrying the id of s'. The labelling function maps each state s exactly to the propositions $v = s(v)$, $v \in V$ that are valid in this state. Using the state valuation rules specified in Sect. 3, this can be equivalently expressed by $L(s) = \{v = d \mid s \models v = d\}$.

With the Kripke structure at hand, IXL configuration rules can be expressed by LTL Safety formulas, so rule violations may be expressed in LTL using first-order formulas and operators $\land, \lor, \mathbf{X}, \mathbf{U}$, as shown in Sect. 3. Specifying rule violations on Kripke structure K representing a complete IXL configuration, however, is quite complicated, because most rules refer to routes traversed in a certain driving direction, whereas K's transition relation connects any pair of configuration elements linked by any channel. This results in computations that do not correspond to any "real" route through the network.

Example 3. The Kripke structure corresponding to the configuration shown in Fig. 1 has a path $s_{10}.s_{11}.s_{13}.s_{23}.s_{21}.s_{20}$, because all elements in this sequence are linked by some channel a, b, c. This path, however, cannot be realised as a train route, due to the topology of points s_{13} and s_{23}. □

In [9], this problem has been overcome by using existentially quantified LTL with rigid variables as introduced in [12]. Apart from the fact that quantified LTL formulae are harder to create and understand, this would not allow for the over-approximation by means of CTL as described in Sect. 3. Therefore, we will now introduce sub-models of full configuration models where the problem of infeasible paths no longer occurs.

Sub-models. The *border elements* of an IXL configuration can be identified by the fact that only one of the main channels a, b is connected to another element, while the other channel is undefined. Element 20 in Fig. 1, for example, is a border element, because it has channel a connected to element 21, while channel b remains unconnected. Points or diamond crossings are never used as border elements, so only channels a, b need to be considered when identifying them in the Kripke structure K representing the complete configuration. Each border element introduces a well-defined driving direction specified by the channel which is defined and, therefore, "points into" the network specified by the configuration.

A sub-model is now created for every border element s_b as a Kripke structure $K(s_b)$ according to the following rules.

1. The driving direction corresponds to the direction specified by the defined channel a or b of border element s_b.
2. The sub-model is induced by the largest acyclic directed graph G with initial element s_b, such that
   - each element which is reachable in driving direction is part of this graph,
   - for points entered by their B-stem or C-stem, the only continuation is via the element connected to the points' A-stem,
   - for points entered by their A-stem, the continuations are via the elements connected to the points' B-stem or C-stem,
   - for diamond crossings entered via A, B, C, D-stem, the only possible continuations are via elements connected to the D, C, B, A-stems, respectively.
   - The graph expansion stops when an element is reached for the second time.
   - The graph expansion stops when a border element is reached by its defined channel, so that no outgoing channel is available.
3. The states of $K(s_b)$ are the nodes of G.

4. Every state is an initial state.
5. The transition relation of $K(s_b)$ contains all pairs of states (s, s'), such that there exists an edge from s to s' in G.
6. Every element of the sub-model is equipped with additional attributes $dirA$, $dirB$, $dirC$, $dirD$ with value 1 if its respective channel a, b, c, or d points in driving direction; otherwise the attribute carries value 0.
6. Further auxiliary attributes are added to each sub-model state as described in Sect. 4 below.

Example 4. The complete IXL configuration depicted in Fig. 1 has border elements $s_{10}, s_{20}, s_{33}, s_{25}, s_{14}$. The sub-model resulting from border element s_{33} is shown in Fig. 2, together with the new auxiliary attributes $dirA, \dots$ (the meaning of attribute $pCnt$ is explained in Sect. 4 below). Element s_{33} induces the driving direction along its channel a; since it is a border element, its channel b is not linked to another element. □

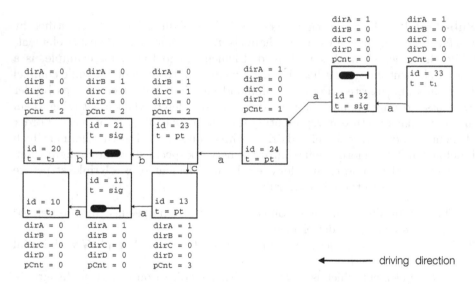

Fig. 2. Sub-model created from border element s_{33} in Fig. 1.

Specifying Rule Violations on Sub-models. The description of rule violations in LTL becomes rather straightforward when specified for sub-models; this is illustrated in the following examples.

Example 5. The rule violation specified in Example 1, when applied to a sub-model as the one depicted in Fig. 2, may be expressed in unquantified first-order LTL as $\phi_1 \equiv t = sig \wedge dirA = 1 \wedge \mathbf{X}\big((t \neq sig \vee dirA = 0)\mathbf{U}(t = t_1 \vee t = t_3)\big)$. This LTL formula is translated via Φ defined in Sect. 3 into CTL formula $\Phi(\phi_1) \equiv t = sig \wedge dirA = 1 \wedge \mathbf{EX}\Big(\mathbf{E}\big((t \neq sig \vee dirA = 0)\mathbf{U}(t = t_1 \vee t = t_3)\big)\Big)$. The only witness for $\Phi(\phi_1)$ in the sub-model shown on Fig. 2 is the path $s_{32}.s_{24}.s_{23}.s_{21}.s_{20}$, and this is also a witness for ϕ_1, so the CTL over-approximation does not produce any false alarms in this case. □

Example 6. The rule violation specified in Example 2, when applied to a sub-model, may be expressed in unquantified first-order LTL as $\phi_2 \equiv t = sig \wedge dirA = 1 \wedge \mathbf{X}(t \neq t_3\mathbf{U}(t = sig \wedge dirA = 1))$. This LTL formula is translated via Φ defined in Sect. 3 into CTL formula $\Phi(\phi_2) \equiv t = sig \wedge dirA = 1 \wedge \mathbf{EX}\big(\mathbf{E}(t \neq t_3\mathbf{U}(t = sig \wedge dirA = 1))\big)$. It is easy to see that for the sub-model shown in Fig. 2, the only witness is given by path $s_{32}.s_{24}.s_{23}.s_{13}.s_{11}$, so, again, there are no false alarms possible for this rule violation. □

Query Simplification by Auxiliary Parameters. We have seen that auxiliary attributes can be introduced during sub-model creation, in order to facilitate the construction of rule violation formulae. Moreover, these attributes may be used to speed up the checking process.

Example 7. Another typical pattern of data validation rules restricts the number of elements of a certain type that may be allocated between two elements of another type. The following fictitious rule illustrates this pattern (the real rules are slightly more complex and refer to other element types).

Rule 3. From channel a of a signal of type *sig* pointing in downstream direction, no more than k points $(t = pt)$ are allowed, before the corresponding signal with type *sig* and channel b pointing in upstream direction is reached.

Violation of Rule 3. From channel a of a signal of type *sig* pointing in downstream direction, more than k points $(t = pt)$ are encountered, before the corresponding signal with type *sig* and channel b pointing in upstream direction is reached. □

In principle, rule violations as the one specified in Example 7 could be specified using *Counting LTL*, an extension of LTL allowing to check whether a path fulfils constraints referring to the number of states fulfilling certain properties [11]. Checking Counting LTL formulae, however, is EXPSPACE-complete, and therefore, we cannot expect to find model checking algorithms for Counting LTL that are as efficient as the CTL-algorithms presented above.

Instead, a new auxiliary attribute $pCnt$ is introduced during sub-model creation. In every state of the sub-model, this attribute contains the number of points encountered in driving direction so far. It is reset to 0, as soon as a downstream signal is reached. This is illustrated in Fig. 2.

Example 8. With auxiliary attribute $pCnt$ at hand, the violation of Rule 3 from Example 7 is specified in LTL as $\phi_3 \equiv t = sig \wedge dirA = 1 \wedge \mathbf{X}((t \neq sig \vee dirA = 0)\mathbf{U}pCnt > k)$. Translated to CTL, this results in

$$\Phi(\phi_3) \equiv t = sig \wedge dirA = 1 \wedge \mathbf{EX}\Big(\mathbf{E}((t \neq sig \vee dirA = 0)\mathbf{U}pCnt > k)\Big)$$

Assuming that $k \geqslant 3$, there are obviously no witnesses for $\Phi(\phi_3)$ in the sub-model from Fig. 2. For $k = 2$, checking $\Phi(\phi_3)$ results in witness $s_{32}.s_{24}.s_{23}.s_{13}$, and again, this is also a witness for the LTL formula ϕ_3.   □

By analogy with the example shown here, further auxiliary attributes are added by the DVL-Checker during sub-model creation.

Parallelisation. The concept to use sub-models for verifying DVL-queries allows for parallelisation of checking activities. The concurrent checking process receives file names of the DVL-query and the IXL configuration model to be verified. After the query and the configuration have been successfully parsed, all jobs to be performed are placed into a queue. A job consists of a triple (query, id, direction), where id is the identification of a border element. Attribute direction is A or B, depending on whether channel a or b of the border element is defined.

A predefined number of worker threads process these jobs concurrently, until the job queue is empty. Each thread pops a job from the (thread-safe) queue and creates the sub-model identified by id and direction. After that, the CTL checker functions are executed, and any witness found in the sub-model for the given query is written to the output interface.

Evaluation. The efficiency of the CTL model checking algorithms in combination with the parallelisation allows for checking queries interactively, because the results are obtained in less than five seconds on standard PC hardware, even for the largest configurations used by Siemens. No false alarms have been encountered with the DVL-queries checked so far on the IXL configurations provided by Siemens.

The bounded model checking version used before as described in [9] could also produce witnesses for faulty configurations in acceptable time (less than 10 s), but was unable to prove the *absence* of errors, due to running time that was exponential in the length of the search paths and very high memory consumption.

5   Conclusion

We have presented an efficient model checking approach for data validation of geographical interlocking systems, which is fast enough to uncover violations of configuration rules or prove the absence of rule violations directly while design-ing the IXL configuration. The checking speed has been achieved by translating LTL formulae specifying rule violations to CTL formulae and using the "clas-sical" global CTL model checking algorithms. It has been shown that for the class of LTL formulae specifying rule violations, CTL model checking is an over-approximation for the (slower) alternative checking for witnesses of LTL formu-lae directly. Therefore, the absence of CTL witnesses proves the absence of path segments fulfilling the original rule violation formula specified in LTL. Further speed-up has been achieved by running checks concurrently on configuration sub-models augmented by auxiliary attributes, instead of performing a single check on the full model.

The concepts and algorithms presented here have been implemented in the DVL-Checker tool which is used by Siemens for the validation of IXL configurations in new interlocking systems provided by Siemens for Belgian railways.

During the checks performed so far, no false alarms due to CTL over-approximation have been observed. It is planned to implement an automated detection of potential false alarms in the future: when CTL model checking results in an alarm for some rule violation $\Phi(\phi)$, it can be checked whether one of the finite paths π through the sub-model fulfil the original LTL formula ϕ. Since each sub-model is an acyclic directed graph, the paths π can be enumerated with low effort, and the LTL checks can also be parallelised. For checking the validity of ϕ on a finite path, the linear encodings of bounded LTL described in [3] are very efficient.

References

1. Badeau, F., Doche-Petit, M.: Formal data validation with event-B. arXiv:1210.7039 [cs], October 2012
2. Basile, D., et al.: On the industrial uptake of formal methods in the railway domain. In: Furia, C.A., Winter, K. (eds.) IFM 2018. LNCS, vol. 11023, pp. 20–29. Springer, Heidelberg (2018). https://doi.org/10.1007/978-3-319-98938-9_2
3. Biere, A., Heljanko, K., Junttila, T., Latvala, T., Schuppan, V.: Linear encodings of bounded LTL model checking. Log. Methods Comput. Sci. 2(5) (2006). arXiv: cs/0611029
4. Celebi, B.T., Kaymakci, O.T.: Verifying the accuracy of interlocking tables for railway signalling systems using abstract state machines. J. Mod. Transp. 24(4), 277–283 (2016). https://doi.org/10.1007/s40534-016-0119-1
5. CENELEC: EN 50128:2011 Railway applications - Communication, signalling and processing systems - Software for railway control and protection systems (2011)
6. Clarke, E.M., Grumberg, O., Peled, D.A.: Model Checking. The MIT Press, Cambridge (1999)
7. Fredj, M., Leger, S., Feliachi, A., Ordioni, J.: OVADO. In: Fantechi, A., Lecomte, T., Romanovsky, A. (eds.) RSSRail 2017. LNCS, vol. 10598, pp. 87–98. Springer, Cham (2017). https://doi.org/10.1007/978-3-319-68499-4_6
8. Hansen, D., Schneider, D., Leuschel, M.: Using B and ProB for data validation projects. In: Butler, M., Schewe, K.-D., Mashkoor, A., Biro, M. (eds.) ABZ 2016. LNCS, vol. 9675, pp. 167–182. Springer, Cham (2016). https://doi.org/10.1007/978-3-319-33600-8_10
9. Haxthausen, A.E., Peleska, J., Pinger, R.: Applied bounded model checking for interlocking system designs. In: Counsell, S., Núñez, M. (eds.) SEFM 2013. LNCS, vol. 8368, pp. 205–220. Springer, Cham (2014). https://doi.org/10.1007/978-3-319-05032-4_16
10. Keming, W., Zheng, W., Chuandong, Z.: Formal modeling and data validation of general railway interlocking system. WIT Trans. Built Environ. 181, 527–538 (2018)

11. Laroussinie, F., Meyer, A., Petonnet, E.: Counting LTL. In: Markey, N., Wijsen, J. (eds.) TIME 2010–17th International Symposium on Temporal Representation and Reasoning, Paris, France, 6–8 September 2010, pp. 51–58. IEEE Computer Society (2010). https://doi.org/10.1109/TIME.2010.20
12. Manna, Z., Pnueli, A.: The Temporal Logic of Reactive and Concurrent Systems - Specification. Springer, New York (1992). https://doi.org/10.1007/978-1-4612-0931-7
13. Pachl, J.: Railway Operation and Control. VTD Rail Publishing, Mountlake Terrace (2002)
14. Peleska, J., Krafczyk, N., Haxthausen, A.E., Pinger, R.: Efficient data validation for geographical interlocking systems. Technical report, Embedded Systems Testing Benchmarks Site, 13 Jan 2019. http://www.informatik.uni-bremen.de/agbs/jp/papers/dvl2019.pdf
15. Sistla, A.P.: Safety, liveness and fairness in temporal logic. Formal Aspects Comput. 6(5), 495–511 (1994). https://doi.org/10.1007/BF01211865
16. Sistla, A.P., Clarke, E.M.: The complexity of propositional linear temporal logics. J. ACM 32(3), 733–749 (1985). https://doi.org/10.1145/3828.3837

Formal Model Validation Through Acceptance Tests

Tomas Fischer[1](✉) and Dana Dghyam[2]

[1] Thales Austria GmbH, Vienna, Austria
tomas.fischer@thalesgroup.com
[2] ECS, University of Southampton, Southampton, UK
dd4g12@ecs.soton.ac.uk

Abstract. When formal systems modelling is used as part of the development process, modellers need to understand the requirements in order to create appropriate models, and domain experts need to validate the final models to ensure they fit the needs of stakeholders. A suitable mechanism for such a validation are acceptance tests.

In this paper we discuss how the principles of Behaviour-Driven Development (BDD) can be applied to (i) formal modelling and (ii) validation of behaviour specifications, thus coupling those two tasks. We show how to close the gap between the informal domain specification and the formal model, thus enabling the domain expert to write acceptance tests in a high-level language matching the formal specification.

We analyse the applicability of this approach by providing the Gherkin scenarios for an Event-B/iUML-B formal model of a 'fixed virtual block' approach to train movement control, developed according to the Hybrid ERTMS/ETCS Level 3 principles specified by the EEIG ERTMS Users Group and presented as a case study on the 6. International ABZ Conference 2018.

Keywords: Formal methods · Validation · Acceptance tests · Event-B · iUML-B · Gherkin · Cucumber

1 Introduction

A fully proven formal model is still pointless if it does not represent the customer's needs. Therefore formal models must be thoroughly validated in order to show that they capture useful functionality. Although today's formal methods tools offer great verification[1] support through techniques like automated theorem proving and model checking, their assistance with the model validation[2] is basically limited to the model visualization and animation [12]. This leaves the interpretation of the results to the user, so it remains essentially a manual task, e.g. expert review, which is tedious, time consuming and error prone. Rigorous

---

[1] Ensuring that the developers *build the thing right*.
[2] Ensuring that the developers *build the right thing*.

© Springer Nature Switzerland AG 2019
S. Collart-Dutilleul et al. (Eds.): RSSRail 2019, LNCS 11495, pp. 159–169, 2019.
https://doi.org/10.1007/978-3-030-18744-6_10

tracing of model elements to the requirements solves the problem only partially, as it can only represent static relationships, but not the dynamic behavior of a model.

One widely-used and reliable validation method is acceptance testing, which, assuming adequate coverage, can provide assurance that a system (in our case embodied by the formal model) does indeed represent the informal customer requirements. Acceptance tests describe a sequence of stimulation steps involving concrete data examples to test the functional responses of the system and can be thus considered to be a definitive specification of the behavioural requirements of a system. The high level nature of acceptance tests, which are both human-readable and executable, makes their verification and validation possible with much less effort than directly ensuring the correspondence of formal specification and informal requirements [4].

Behavior-driven development (BDD) methodology [15] combines the general techniques and principles of test-driven development with ideas from domain-driven design and object oriented methods. It advocates that tests should be written first, describing desired functionality. Then the actual functionality should be implemented (or as in our case, a model should be created) to match the formulated requirements. Our approach is to combine BDD principles with formal methods in order to validate a formal model using scenarios written in the Gherkin language [19].

The remainder of the paper is structured as follows. In Sect. 2 we give a brief overview of an Event-B/iUML-B formal model of a 'fixed virtual block' approach to train movement control. In Sect. 3 we provide a short description of the Gherkin notation and Cucumber framework and demonstrate the validation of the presented Event-B/iUML-B models using Gherkin acceptance tests. In the same section we analyse discovered problems and challenges and suggest future improvements. In Sect. 4 we summarise the benefits of the presented approach for validating formal models and outline how the proposed method and tools will integrate into the process being developed in the ENABLE-S3 project.

2   Hybrid ERTMS/ETCS Level 3

In this paper we use the Event-B model of a hybrid ERTMS/ETCS Level 3 (HL3) [8] specification presented in [7] as an example. HL3 is a 'fixed virtual block' approach to train movement, where the trackside train detection (TTD) derived from wayside equipment is augmented by information obtained from information sent by trains[3] The hardware derived TTD section is divided into a fixed number of virtual sections (VSS). A train movement controller called the Radio Block Centre (RBC) manages the Movement Authority (MA) granted to each train in mission. This granted MA is the permission for a train to move safely to a specific location avoiding train collisions. However, in order for the RBC to grant a MA it needs to know which sections are free. The status of the

---

[3] Trains may or may not be specially equipped with the necessary equipment, hence the term hybrid.

virtual sections is calculated by the Virtual Block Detector (VBD) depending on the information it receives from the environment:

- Track occupancy received from the trackside.
- Position reports and integrity confirmations received from the trains.
- Timer expiry.

The state of a VSS can be one of the four states:

- *Free*: there is no train on the section.
- *Unknown*: there might be zero or more trains on the section.
- *Ambiguous*: there might be one or more trains on the sections.
- *Occupied*: there is one train on the section.

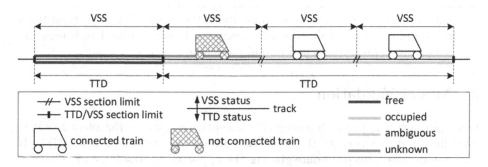

Fig. 1. Section conventions (taken from [8])

The RBC uses free sections to calculate the MA, while the other states are necessary for example to mitigate against possible roll-back of disconnected trains, and to optimise the use of sections in a safe manner (Fig. 1).

The transitions from one state to the other can only happen under certain conditions, which are represented as guards in the Event-B model. The VSS state machine is fully connected and the transition table in the specification presents 12 transitions, some of which decomposed into different alternatives. Additionally, we also explicitly model the start and the completion of the statemachine run. There are also explicit events to model the expiry of started timers.

For example take transition #T4A which has only one condition: "TTD is free". However, in Event-B this event is modelled as follows:

```
event T4A_unknown_free refines T4_unknown_free
any vss // generated class instance
where
  @isin_unknown: vss ∈ unknown
  @grd1: Sections∼(vss) ∉ occupiedTTD
  @grd2: startVSSUpdate = TRUE
  @grd3: vss ∉ updatedVSS
then
  @act1: updatedVSS := updatedVSS ∪{vss}
  @leave_unknown: unknown := unknown \{vss}
  @enter_free: free := free ∪{vss}
  @act_disconnectProp: disconnectPropagationTimer(vss) := Idle
  @act_integProp: integrityLossPropagationTimer(vss) := Idle
end
```

Such events can be difficult to validate due to the complexity of the conditions which are difficult to explain to domain experts, hence the need to bridge the gap between domain experts and formal modelling experts.

3   Model Validation

Our approach was to create executable acceptance tests on the plain Event-B level first and to switch to the visual and thus easier to comprehend iUML-B level afterwards. This procedure gives us the opportunity to solve some low-level technical challenges (described in more detail later in this chapter) first and then to deal with the gap between the domain model and the formal model.

3.1   Acceptance Tests for Event-B Models

Gherkin. Gherkin [19] is a language that defines lightweight structures for describing the expected behaviour in plain text as a collection of features, readable by both domain experts and developers, yet still automatically executable.

A feature is a description of one single piece of business value, best structured as a story "*As a* «role» *I want* «feature» *so that* «business value»", which gives an answer to three fundamental questions – *who* requires *what* and *why.*

The features contain a list of scenarios, every scenario representing one use case. In the simplest case the scenario also contains the test data and thus represents an individual test case. A scenario outline describes a group of similar usage scenarios and contains placeholder for the particular test data specified as a list of examples, each data set representing one individual test case.

Each scenario consists of steps describing the interaction with the system under test: "Given «preconditions»When «interaction»Then «postconditions»", providing an initial state for the test, test input (execution trigger) as well as expected output, the observable outcome shall be compared with.

Cucumber. Cucumber is a framework for executing acceptance tests written in Gherkin language and provides Gherkin language parser, test automation as well as report generation. In order to make such test cases automatically executable, the user must supply the actual step definitions providing the gluing code, which implements the interaction with the System Under Test (SUT).

Compound steps may encapsulate complex interaction with a system caused by a single domain activity, thus decoupling the features from the technical interfaces of the System Under Test (SUT). This defines a new domain-related testing language, which may simplify the feature description. The description of the business functionality shall, however, still be contained in the features.

Event-B. Event-B [2,9] is a formal method for system development, supported by the Rodin Platform (Rodin) [3], an extensible open source toolkit. A machine in Event-B corresponds to a transition system where *variables* represent the state and *events* specify the transitions.

Cucumber for Event-B. In the scope of this project we have developed Cucumber for Event-B as a custom Cucumber extension, which allows to execute Gherkin scenarios on an Event-B model. It is a collection of step definitions providing means for the Event-B state space traversal:

Given *machine with "*≪formula≫*"*
  Setup constants with the given constraints and initialize the machine.
When *fire event "*≪name≫*" with "*≪formula≫*"*
  Fire the given event with the given parameters constraints.
Then *event "*≪name≫*" with "*≪formula≫*" is enabled/disabled*
  Check if the given event with the given parameters constraints is enabled/disabled.
Then *formula "*≪formula≫*" is TRUE/FALSE*
  Check if the given formula evaluates to TRUE or FALSE.

An essential property of acceptance tests is reproducibility. The user shall assure that the tested machine is deterministic and, if not, refine it further.

Cucumber for Event-B can be found under https://github.com/tofische/cucumber-event-b and has been released under Eclipse Public License 2.0.

Environment Definition. Let us deal with the very basic scenario of a train entering the controlled section.[4]

---

[4] Please note that the provided example is only a snippet of an end-to-end test scenario, which checks the functionality from the end user's perspective.

```
Background:
  Given machine
  When fire event "VBD_start_vss_update"
  And fire event "4A_unknown_free" with "vss=VSS11"
  And fire event "4A_unknown_free" with "vss=VSS12"
  And fire event "4A_unknown_free" with "vss=VSS21"
  And fire event "4A_unknown_free" with "vss=VSS22"
  And fire event "4A_unknown_free" with "vss=VSS23"
  And fire event "4A_unknown_free" with "vss=VSS31"
  And fire event "4A_unknown_free" with "vss=VSS32"
  And fire event "4A_unknown_free" with "vss=VSS33"
  And fire event "VBD_vss_update_complete"

Scenario: Enter HL3 area
  When fire event "ENV_enter_HL3_area" with "tr=TRAIN1"
  And fire event "VBD_start_vss_update"
  And fire event "1A_free_unknown" with "ttd=TTD10 & vss=VSS11"
  And fire event "1A_free_unknown" with "ttd=TTD10 & vss=VSS12"
  And fire event "self_free" with "vss=VSS21"
  And fire event "self_free" with "vss=VSS22"
  And fire event "self_free" with "vss=VSS23"
  And fire event "self_free" with "vss=VSS31"
  And fire event "self_free" with "vss=VSS32"
  And fire event "self_free" with "vss=VSS33"
  And fire event "VBD_vss_update_complete"
  Then is TRUE formula "free = {VSS21,VSS22,VSS23,VSS31,VSS32,VSS33}"
  Then is TRUE formula "occupied = {}"
  Then is TRUE formula "ambiguous = {}"
  Then is TRUE formula "unknown = {VSS11,VSS12}"
  When fire event "ENV_start_of_mission" with "tr=TRAIN1"
  # ...
```

This example reveals the fact, that there are two kinds of events which must be treated differently. The environment events represent some relevant change in the environment and are thus triggered from outside of the modeled system (in our case through the tests). The system events on the other side represent the reaction of the modeled system to the external stimulus and shall therefore be considered as an implementation detail not prescribed by the acceptance tests.

The acceptance tests being of black box nature shall contain environment events only. Nevertheless, when running the tests, the system must be given the opportunity to fire all internal events according to the assumed execution strategy. For our purposes run to completion semantic is sufficient – after an environment event (according to the test scenario) fires, the particular step definitions shall automatically trigger all enabled internal events until the system stabilizes and only environment events are enabled. However, this requires some kind of naming convention (e.g. event name prefix) which allows the steps to distinguish the event kind (environment from system).

The previous example would be then reduced to the following snippet, including domain events only:

Scenario: Enter HL3 area
  When *fire event* "ENV_enter_HL3_area" *with* "tr=TRAIN1"
  And *fire event* "ENV_start_of_mission" *with* "tr=TRAIN1"
  # ...

Event Selection. During the refinement process an event is often decomposed into different alternatives, e.g. ENV_exit_HL3_area into ENV_exit_HL3_area and ENV_exit_HL3_area_free_ttd. The acceptance tests shall not be aware of this decomposition, so that they may reference an abstract event, ENV_exit_HL3_area in this case. The step definitions shall then descend the refinement hierarchy and select an appropriate enabled concrete event. This process is deterministic as long as all concrete refinements of one abstract event are disjunct, otherwise the event selection fails and the model must be adjusted. In order to utilize this capability it might be necessary to rename decomposed events so that they can be clearly distinguished from the refined abstract ones.

Timeouts. While unsolicited environment events (caused by some unexpected change in the environment) may occur at any time, answers to previously issued system commands shall happen within a defined time period, otherwise the system shall assume an error in the environment and process an appropriate corrective action.

There are several techniques how to model time. If both events (answer and timeout) are enabled simultaneously, the environment (in our case the acceptance tests) must be able to choose, which situation happens. This approach simplifies the model, however the acceptance tests must be aware of the timeout names.

  # ...
  When *fire event* "VBD_ghost_timer_expires" *with* "ttd=TTD10"
  # ...

Another possibility is to consider the timeouts as an internal model concept, and only trigger the time progress (ticks) by the environment. However, the explicit notion of time clutters the model and has therefore been omitted from our model and left for further analysis.

Data. While the event parameters are often simple values, the attribute values may have complex types. This raises the issue of how to describe such data for the setup of constants on one side and for the attribute value checks on the other side. We want to represent the data in a table form, but we have to overcome different viewpoints: class instance groups the values of all attributes (row by row), while in Event-B one variable represents the value of one attribute for all instances (column by column). This is still an open point left for future work.

There is no technical difference between attributes and associations. However, there is a logical distinction between an attribute and an association, which shall be respected by the test language.

3.2   Acceptance Tests for iUML-B Models

iUML-B. Customer requirements are typically based on a domain model, which is often expressed in terms of entities with attributes and relationships. State-machines and activity diagrams are used to describe the behaviour.

It is desirable to express the acceptance tests in terms of the domain model so that domain experts who are not familiar with the formal notations can easily create and validate them.

iUML-B [13,16,17], an extension of the Rodin Platform, provides a 'UML like' diagrammatic modelling notation for Event-B in the form of class-diagrams and state-machines, with automatic generation of Event-B formal models. iUML-B is a formal notation which is much closer to the domain model and makes therefore the formal models more visual and thus easier to comprehend.

Class diagrams provide a way to visually model data relationships. Classes, attributes and associations are linked to Event-B data elements (carrier sets, constants, or variables) and generate constraints on those elements. Methods elaborate Event-B events and contribute additional parameter representing the class instance.

A state-machine automatically generates Event-B data elements (sets, constants, axioms, variables, and invariants) to implement the states, and contributes additional parameters representing the state machine instance, as well as guards and actions representing state changes to existing events elaborated by transitions. State-machines support nested states (hierarchical state machiness) and may be also *lifted* to the instances of a class so that the behaviour of each instance of the class is modelled by an independent instance of the state-machine (see example in Fig. 2).

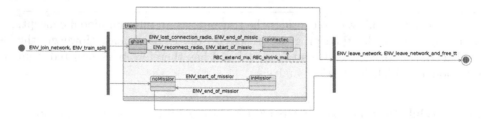

Fig. 2. iUML-B state machine diagram – Train states

Cucumber for iUML-B. Cucumber for. iUML-B provides a collection of step definitions translating the iUML-B constructs into the corresponding underlying Event-B model elements (events and variables), allowing the acceptance tests to use the notation provided by iUML-B. The acceptance tests can then refer to domain elements like classes and their methods, attributes and associations as well as state machine states and transitions.

However, this requires a great deal of discipline on the part of modelers, as only the strict adherence to the Domain Driven Design principles, especially a rigorous compliance to an ubiquitous language shared between the domain experts and the formal modeling experts is crucial, as each deviation leads to failed tests and hence to manual rectifications.

The following steps are defined for validating state-machines:

Given *state machine* " «name»:«inst»"
   Preset the given instance of the given state machine.
When *trigger transition* " «trans»"
   Trigger the given state machine transition.
Then *transition* " «trans»" *is enabled/disabled*
   Check if the given state machine transition is enabled/disabled.
Then *is in state* " «state»"
   Check if the state machine is in the given state.

The following steps are defined for validating class diagrams:

Given *class* " «name»:«inst»"
   Preset the given class with the given instance.
When *call method* " «name»" *with* " «formula»"
   Call the given class instance method.
Then *method* " «name»" *with* " «formula»" *is enabled/disabled*
   Check if the given class instance method is enabled/disabled.
Then *attribute* " «attr»" *is* " «value»"
   Check if the given class instance attribute is equal to the given value.

In general, class attributes and associations can be any binary relation (i.e., not necessarily functional), hence further checks can be defined accordingly.

4 Conclusion

Many works have been done to ensure that the formal model represents the desired behaviour. For this reason, some works focused on modelling control flow explicitly in state-based formalisms, such as [6,10] and [5,14], which have explicitly specified and verified control flow in Event-B and its predecessor the B-method [1]. Control flow is implicitly modelled in B and Event-B machines, making the validation and model checking of complex control systems cumbersome.

In [18], the authors define a methodology to support the formal development and verification of railway interlocking systems. They use a combination of formal methods and domain specific language (DSL), where a generator takes the

DSL and a generic model to provide a concrete behavioural model as an input to the model checker. While [11], presents some of the challenges of model based testing and propose a solution based on static model analysis to the automatic generation of requirements-based test cases. All the previously mentioned efforts improve the verification and validation process.

In this paper we have discussed how BDD principles can be utilized for formal model validation and also demonstrated the applicability of this approach by applying the Gherkin scenarios to an Event-B/iUML-B formal model of a 'fixed virtual block' approach to train movement control. In summary, we have confirmed the benefits of validating the formal models using the acceptance tests.

In addition we also pointed out, how to close the gap between the informal domain specification and the formal model, thus enabling the domain expert to write acceptance tests in a high-level language matching the formal specification.

Finally, we analysed the advantages of such an approach and proposed measures to mitigate identified drawbacks.

Once validated, the acceptance tests can also be used in order to show the conformity of the implementation with respect to the formal model. This transition has been left for the future work.

Recommendations. We recommend to adopt the BDD methodology already during requirement elicitation phase before modeling activities, as the subsequent adaptation of tests to the existing model is tedious and costly.

Furthermore, we intend to enhance the Cucumber for Event-B framework according to the aforementioned proposals and also integrate it tightly with the iUML-B plugin.

Acknowledgements. This work has been conducted within the ENABLE-S3 project that has received funding from the ECSEL Joint Undertaking under Grant Agreement no. 692455. This Joint Undertaking receives support from the European Union's HORIZON 2020 research and innovation programme and Austria, Denmark, Germany, Finland, Czech Republic, Italy, Spain, Portugal, Poland, Ireland, Belgium, France, Netherlands, United Kingdom, Slovakia, Norway.

ENABLE-S3 is funded by the Austrian Federal Ministry of Transport, Innovation and Technology (BMVIT) under the program "ICT of the Future" between May 2016 and April 2019. More information https://iktderzukunft.at/en/.

References

1. Abrial, J.R., Hoare, A., Chapron, P.: The B-Book: Assigning Programs to Meanings. Cambridge University Press, New York (1996)
2. Abrial, J.R.: Modeling in Event-B: System and Software Engineering, 1st edn. Cambridge University Press, New York (2010)
3. Abrial, J.R., Butler, M., Hallerstede, S., Hoang, T.S., Mehta, F., Voisin, L.: Rodin: an open toolset for modelling and reasoning in Event-B. Int. J. Softw. Tools Technol. Transf. **12**(6), 447–466 (2010). https://doi.org/10.1007/s10009-010-0145-y
4. Adzic, G.: Specification by Example: How Successful Teams Deliver the Right Software, 1st edn. Manning Publications Co., Greenwich (2011)

5. Butler, M., Leuschel, M.: Combining CSP and B for specification and property verification. In: Fitzgerald, J., Hayes, I.J., Tarlecki, A. (eds.) FM 2005. LNCS, vol. 3582, pp. 221–236. Springer, Heidelberg (2005). https://doi.org/10. 1007/11526841_16

6. Dghaym, D., Butler, M., Fathabadi, A.S.: Extending ERS for modelling dynamic workflows in Event-B. In: 22nd International Conference on Engineering of Complex Computer Systems, 08 November 2017, pp. 20–29, February 2018 https:// eprints.soton.ac.uk/413608/

7. Dghaym, D., Poppleton, M., Snook, C.: Diagram-led formal modelling using iUML-B for Hybrid ERTMS Level 3. In: Butler, M., Raschke, A., Hoang, T.S., Reichl, K. (eds.) ABZ 2018. LNCS, vol. 10817, pp. 338–352. Springer, Cham (2018). https:// doi.org/10.1007/978-3-319-91271-4_23

8. EEIG ERTMS Users Group: Principles: Hybrid ERTMS/ETCS Level 3. Ref. 16E042 Version 1A, July 2017. http://www.ertms.be/sites/default/files/2018-03/ 16E0421A_HL3.pdf

9. Hoang, T.S.: An introduction to the Event-B modelling method. In: Romanovsky, A., Thomas, M. (eds.) Industrial Deployment of System Engineering Methods, pp. 211–236. Springer, Heidelberg (2013)

10. Iliasov, A.: Use case scenarios as verification conditions: Event-B/Flow approach. In: Troubitsyna, E.A. (ed.) SERENE 2011. LNCS, vol. 6968, pp. 9–23. Springer, Heidelberg (2011). https://doi.org/10.1007/978-3-642-24124-6_2

11. Peleska, J., Brauer, J., Huang, W.: Model-based testing for avionic systems proven benefits and further challenges. In: Margaria, T., Steffen, B. (eds.) ISoLA 2018. LNCS, vol. 11247, pp. 82–103. Springer, Cham (2018). https://doi.org/10.1007/ 978-3-030-03427-6_11

12. Reichl, K., Fischer, T., Tummeltshammer, P.: Using formal methods for verification and validation in railway. In: Aichernig, B.K.K., Furia, C.A.A. (eds.) TAP 2016. LNCS, vol. 9762, pp. 3–13. Springer, Cham (2016). https://doi.org/10.1007/978-3-319-41135-4_1

13. Said, M.Y., Butler, M., Snook, C.: A method of refinement in UML-B. Softw. Syst. Model. 14(4), 1557–1580 (2015). https://doi.org/10.1007/s10270-013-0391-z

14. Schneider, S., Treharne, H.: Communicating B machines. In: Bert, D., Bowen, J.P., Henson, M.C., Robinson, K. (eds.) ZB 2002. LNCS, vol. 2272, pp. 416–435. Springer, Heidelberg (2002). https://doi.org/10.1007/3-540-45648-1_22

15. Smart, J.F.: BDD in Action: Behavior-Driven Development for the Whole Software Lifecycle. Manning Publications, Shelter Island (2014)

16. Snook, C.: iUML-B statemachines. In: Proceedings of the Rodin Workshop 2014, Toulouse, France, pp. 29–30 (2014). http://eprints.soton.ac.uk/365301/

17. Snook, C., Butler, M.: UML-B: formal modeling and design aided by UML. ACM Trans. Softw. Eng. Methodol. 15(1), 92–122 (2006). https://doi.org/10.1145/ 1125808.1125811

18. Vu, L.H., Haxthausen, A.E., Peleska, J.: Formal modelling and verification of interlocking systems featuring sequential release. Sci. Comput. Program. 133, 91–115 (2017). http://www.sciencedirect.com/science/article/pii/S0167642316300570. Formal Techniques for Safety-Critical Systems (FTSCS 2014)

19. Wynne, M., Hellesøy, A.: The Cucumber Book: Behaviour-Driven Development for Testers and Developers. Pragmatic Programmers, LLC, Raleigh (2012)

Modelling

A Separation of Concerns Approach for the Verified Modelling of Railway Signalling Rules

Yves Ledru[1,2(✉)], Akram Idani[1,2], Rahma Ben Ayed[2],
Abderrahim Ait Wakrime[2], and Philippe Bon[2,3]

[1] Univ. Grenoble Alpes, CNRS, Grenoble INP, LIG, 38000 Grenoble, France
{yves.ledru,akram.idani}@imag.fr
[2] Institut de Recherche Technologique Railenium, 59300 Famars, France
{rahma.ben-ayed,abderrahim.ait-wakrime}@railenium.eu
[3] Univ Lille Nord de France, IFSTTAR, COSYS, ESTAS,
59666 Villeneuve d'Ascq Cedex, France
philippe.bon@ifsttar.fr

Abstract. This paper proposes a modelling approach for railway signalling rules. It adopts a separation of concerns approach similar to the one used in information systems security. It first models the effect of operations, and then specifies permissions involving the agent performing the action and the conditions that must be satisfied before performing this action. These models are expressed in SecureUML diagrams enhanced with B assertions. It then takes advantage of the B4MSecure tool to translate these diagrams into B machines. It finally relies on the ProB tool to verify the model using model-checking and animation. Model-checking assesses the reachability of desired states, and verifies the absence of accidents. The approach proceeds by introducing human errors, checking their consequences, and deploying counter-measures.

1 Introduction

Railway systems are critical systems whose safety has been studied for a long time. Safety results from a combination of physical devices (e.g. brakes, lights, ...), policies (e.g. signalling rules) and cooperation between agents (e.g. train driver, traffic agent, ...). New technologies are considered to improve railway systems. For example, GNSS (Global Navigation Satellite System) is based on GPS to acquire the position of the train. New standards such as the European ERTMS/ETCS (European Rail Traffic Management System/European Train Control System) have emerged to replace signalling systems. New signalling rules must be designed to take this new equipment into account. Their critical character requires verification and validation efforts to guarantee their safety.

Formal methods, especially the B method [1], have been used for more than 25 years in the field of railway systems. In Chap. 17 of [2], Abrial describes the requirements for an interlocking system, and its formal specification, structured

© Springer Nature Switzerland AG 2019
S. Collart-Dutilleul et al. (Eds.): RSSRail 2019, LNCS 11495, pp. 173–190, 2019.
https://doi.org/10.1007/978-3-030-18744-6_11

by four refinement steps. Success stories of the use of the B method in this field [18] include the development of the Météor subway line in Paris [4] or modernisation of the New York Subway [19]. Over the years, a community has grown in European projects such as FMERail, and conferences such as RSSRail [10]. In 2018, the ABZ conference [8], which gathers amongst others the B community, proposed a case study to model ERTMS/ETCS level 3.

Recently, we have proposed [5,6] to structure B specifications of signalling rules in the same way as secure information systems are described in SecureUML [17]. In [5], exchange of information between a train, and the traffic control center, is described as a class diagram associated with a security model where agents (human or software agents) must have permissions to access the objects. This approach promotes a separation of concerns between the objects involved in the system, and the rules allowing the agents to manipulate these objects. In this approach, the B4MSecure tool [12] provides support to translate SecureUML diagrams into B specifications. The ProB tool [15] is then used as an animator to validate the model [5] and the AtelierB prover is used to discharge the proof obligations linked to railway safety invariants [6].

In this paper, we propose an approach for the modelling and verification of signalling rules in a railway system. This approach improves the approach adopted in our previous work with respect to the following topics:

1. *Lightweight formal method.* Our approach involves several verification steps, corresponding to reachability assessment and invariant preservation. These verifications are performed with the ProB model-checker. In this study, reachability was verified in a few minutes, while invariant preservation may last several hours.
2. *Impact of human errors.* The railway system involves human agents. Hence, human errors may happen (e.g. because the agent is tired) and lead the agents to violate the rules. In this paper, we model such behaviours and evaluate their potential consequences.
3. Our previous studies [6] focused on the protocols between the train and the traffic agent. Here we consider a more global system which includes the track layout. Moreover, verification is performed here using model-checking instead of animation and proof.

This paper is organized as follows. Section 2 introduces an illustrative example. Section 3 surveys the steps of our modelling and verification approach. Section 4 details its application on the example. Finally, Sect. 5 discusses model-checking to verify our models. Section 6 compares our contribution to related work, and Sect. 7 draws the conclusions and perspectives of this work.

2   An Illustrative Example

This paper will be illustrated by the track layout of Fig. 1. This track layout is composed of 10 track portions (also called "sections"). Two of these portions (3 and 6) correspond to railroad switches (also called "points"). We make the

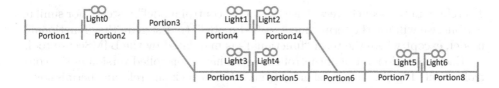

Fig. 1. Track layout

simplifying hypothesis that, at a given time, a train occupies a single portion, i.e. the whole train moves instantly from one portion to the next one. This simplification can be avoided by handling operations to move the head and the tail of the train, as was done by Abrial [2] or Vu [11]. Also, we assume that train integrity is guaranteed (i.e. the train does not separate from several passenger cars). In our initial state, we will systematically deploy two trains: *train1* on *Portion1* and *train2* on *Portion8*.

Although simple, this railway system leaves space for accidents. We consider several cases for accidents, including:

– the case where two trains occupy the same portion of the track (collision),
– the case where a railroad switch is changed while a train is on the switch (derailment),
– the case where the train goes over the end of the track (collision with the buffer stop).

In order to prevent accidents, a signalling system is deployed. It is based on lights located at the beginning of some portions. For example, Light0 is located at the beginning of portion 2. It is applicable to trains traveling from the left hand side of the figure to its right hand side. Trains coming from the right hand side do not see the state of the light.

A signalling rule requires the driver of a train to stop when the light is off, and grants him permission to move to the next portion if the light is on.

There are two kinds of human agents in this system: train drivers who move the trains and traffic agents who switch the lights on and off.

3   Modelling Approach

Separation of Concerns. Our modelling approach is based on separation of concerns between an uncontrolled model only governed by the laws of physics, where accidents may happen (step 1 of Fig. 2), and a model controlled by signalling rules, where bad things should not happen (step 4 of Fig. 2).

This is similar to the distinction made in secure information systems between data and associated functions, described in a so-called "functional" model, and the permissions that rule the accesses of users to these data, described in a "security" model. It must be noticed that the use of the term "security model" in this study is confusing, since we worry about safety rather than security.

Therefore, in the sequel, we will use the term "control model" instead. For similar reasons, we will use the term "uncontrolled model" to designate the "functional" model, except where the term "functional" is mandated by the B4MSecure tool.

Each operation of the uncontrolled model has a controlled version in the control model (Fig. 3). This version adds guards to check the relevant permissions. In our example, trains, tracks, lights and their associated operations correspond to the uncontrolled model. Train drivers and traffic agents must follow the rules that constrain the call to these operations, as modelled by the controlled version of these operations. It must be noted that separation of concerns allows to experiment with several sets of rules, i.e. several control models, while the uncontrolled model remains unchanged.

Verification. The ProB model-checker is used to verify several properties:

- The possibility of accidents should be shown in the uncontrolled model, using model-checking (step 2). In this model, signalling rules do not apply, so the train located in *Portion1* can move and collide with the train in *Portion8*, provided that the railroad switches are positioned appropriately.
- Reachability of a desired state without causing accidents (step 3) is the next property to establish. Before designing the control model, one may check that the uncontrolled model allows to avoid accidents while performing useful tasks. In our example, we show that the train in *Portion1* can cooperate with train 2 and move to *Portion8* without causing accidents.
- In the control model, agents must follow the rules, and we expect that the rules governing the management of lights and train movements guarantee the absence of accidents (step 5).
- Reachability of a desired state is the final property to establish. A trivial way to prevent accidents is to forbid movements of the trains, resulting in a useless railway system. Therefore, one must show that train movements are possible when the signalling rules are followed (step 6). In our example, we check that the signalling rules still allow train 1 to move to *Portion8*. In the control model, this requires to switch appropriate lights on and off, to position the railroad switches appropriately and to move both trains, according to the signalling rules.

ProB can verify both kinds of properties. Reaching a given state is a classical task for model-checkers. This corresponds to steps 2 (reaching an accidental

1. Build an **uncontrolled model** of the physical world
2. *Check that accidents are possible*
3. *Check reachability without accidents*
4. Build a **control model** with signalling rules
5. *Check that the model forbids accidents*
6. *Check reachability*

Fig. 2. The modelling and verification process

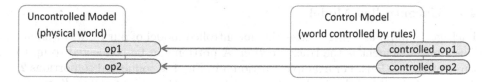

Fig. 3. Uncontrolled and control models

state), 3 and 6 (reaching a desired state). Step 5, i.e. proving that signalling rules do not lead to accidents, requires to explore the whole state space of the model. This is usually out of the scope of model-checking, due to the state space explosion problem. But if the state space is small enough, invariants can be proven by exhaustive coverage of the state space, as it is the case in our example.

Human Errors. The control model does not only introduce permissions, it also features agents. The safety of the railway system assumes that agents follow the rules. But human errors can lead to rule violations. E.g. a tired train driver can forget to stop at a light and hence enter a portion occupied by another train. The "irresponsive" behaviour of agents can be described in the control model, and animation or model-checking can be used to check the possibility of accidents. In our example, it will show that accidents are possible if a train driver does not follow the rules. This highlights the responsibilities and the impact of each agent on the safety of the railway system.

In order to mitigate the consequences of human errors, additional devices may be deployed on the track. For example, automatic train stop systems (ATS) can be installed on the same portions as lights. When a train enters a portion where an ATS is armed, the ATS will trigger an emergency brake of the train, and the train will no longer move until the ATS is disarmed. The behaviour of these additional devices should be modeled as an extension of the uncontrolled model, and signalling rules should be adapted. This is where verification activities such as model-checking will bring benefits. Although animation is sufficient to show that a driver who does not follow the rules can cause an accident in the original model, model-checking or proof is necessary to show that an irresponsive driver cannot cause accidents in a modified model, featuring ATS and appropriate signalling rules. Verification activities should also be performed on these modified models to show that reachability remains.

4   Formal Modelling and Verification

Our work takes advantage of several tools, associated with the B method: B4MSecure and ProB. B4MSecure [12] transforms a graphical SecureUML model into B. ProB [15] is a model-checker used to animate and verify B specifications.

4.1   Uncontrolled Model

Package *Functional* in Fig. 4 gives the uncontrolled model of our railway system. The central element is the track *Portion*. A portion can be connected to up to three other portions. For example, portion 3 in Fig. 1 is connected to portions 2, 4 and 15. This is recorded in the attributes *A_main*, *B_straight* and *C_divergent* of class *Portion*. The direction of the portion (ie. whether connection A is on the left or on the right) is also recorded. If the portion is a railroad switch, its current status (straight or divergent) is recorded.

Our model does not support diamond crossings. It could be modeled as two straight portions with mutual exclusion, which requires to add this mutual exclusion notion in the UML model. This would have impact on the uncontrolled model, but our overall approach remains valid.

Accidents is a static attribute associated to class *Portion*. It records the set of portions where an accident happened. We consider that there is an accident as soon as two trains occupy the same track portion. Accidents also result from changing a switch while a train is on the switch, or when a train tries to exit the portion through an end which is not connected to another portion (e.g. moving to the left while in portion 1). Variable *Accidents* will be updated by operations *Move* and *ChangeSwitch* if needed.

The *Train* class features the *Move* operation which moves the train to the next portion according to the current direction of the train (*odd* for left to right, *even* for right to left). Operation *ChangeDirection* changes the direction of the train, e.g. when it has reached the last track portion.

A train is located on a single track portion, as described in Sect. 2. The association between trains and portions allows several trains to occupy the same portion, leaving the possibility of accidents. Class *Light* corresponds to signalling equipment. A light may be in state *on* or *off*. A light can only be seen by the trains moving in the same direction as the light, recorded in attribute *direction*. Lights are associated with the portion where they are located. They are located at the start of the portion to prevent a train from entering it.

Portions, lights and trains are physical objects of our model. Class *Route*, discussed in Sect. 4.2, introduces a necessary notion to express signalling rules.

Translation of the Uncontrolled Model. B4MSecure translates this uncontrolled model into a single B machine. Each class is translated to an abstract set, including all possible objects of the class, and a variable including all objects of the class currently created. For example, class *Train* is translated as:

MACHINE
   Functional

SETS
   TRAIN; ...

ABSTRACT_VARIABLES
   Train, ...

INVARIANT
   $Train \in \mathcal{F}\,(TRAIN)\; \wedge \ldots$

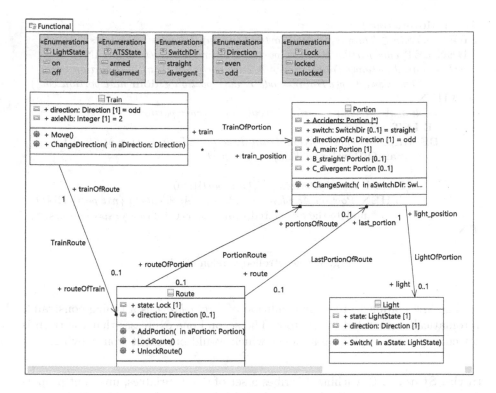

Fig. 4. Uncontrolled model

Associations between classes, and attributes of the classes are translated as functions or relations. For example, the association between trains and portions is translated as a total function which links a train to its current position:

$$TrainOfPortion \in \ Train \ \rightarrow \ Portion \ \wedge \dots$$

By default, the translation includes the synthesis of basic operations (setters and getters) for the attributes of each class, and the associations. Basic operations can be used to build structurally correct instances of the class diagram.

The user may also define specific operations, like *Move* in class *Train*. In this case, the body of the operation and specific preconditions are added as annotations to the graphical model. Figure 5 gives the B specification of *Move*.

The body of *Move* is user-defined. It first computes *curr_portion*, the current portion occupied by the train. It then checks that this current portion has a neighbour when traveling in the direction of the train. If there is no such neighbour, then moving the train in this direction leads to an accident, and the current portion is added to *Portion_Accidents*, the static attribute of class *Portion*. Else, if there is a neighbour, it is stored in *nxt_port*, and the position of the train is updated. In parallel, the operation checks that the neighbour was not already occupied by a train, which leads to an accident.

Train_Move(a $Train$) =
PRE a $Train \in Train \land TrainOfPortion(a Train) \notin Portion\_Accidents$
THEN LET $curr\_portion$ **BE** $curr\_portion = TrainOfPortion(a Train)$ **IN**
   IF ($Train\_direction(a Train) = even \land curr\_portion \notin \textbf{dom}(next\_portion\_even)$)
      $\lor$ ($Train\_direction(a Train) = odd \land curr\_portion \notin \textbf{dom}(next\_portion\_odd)$)
   THEN
      $Portion\_Accidents := Portion\_Accidents \cup \{curr\_portion\}$
   ELSE LET nxt_port
     BE $nxt\_port = (next\_portion(Train\_direction(a Train)))(curr\_portion)$ **IN**
        TrainOfPortion(a $Train$) := nxt_port
        ||
       IF card($TrainOfPortion^{-1}[\{nxt\_port\}]$)>0
          THEN $Portion\_Accidents := Portion\_Accidents \cup \{nxt\_port\}$ **END**
       || ... /* update the associated route (not detailed here for space reasons) */
END;

Fig. 5. Uncontrolled version of *Move*

The first conjunct of the precondition of *Train_Move* is a typing constraint, automatically generated by the tool. The second one expresses that the train is not currently involved in an accident which would prevent it from moving.

Initial State. A B machine describes a set of state variables, invariant properties and operations. It also describes the initial state of the machine. B4MSecure generates an empty initial state. E.g. it generates empty sets of trains, portions, lights, and the B functions corresponding to attributes and associations are also empty. In order to reason on the track layout of Fig. 1 with 10 portions and 2 trains, it must either be constructed manually from this empty initial state using the setters of these classes, or be captured in a manually defined initial state as follows:

INITIALISATION
    $Portion := \{PORTION1, PORTION2, ... PORTION15\}$ ||
    $Train := \{TRAIN1, TRAIN2\}$ ||
    ...
    $TrainOfPortion := \{(TRAIN1 \mapsto PORTION1), (TRAIN2 \mapsto PORTION8)\}$ ||
    $Portion\_switch := \{(PORTION3 \mapsto straight), (PORTION6 \mapsto divergent)\}$ ||
    $Train\_direction := \{(TRAIN1 \mapsto odd), (TRAIN2 \mapsto even)\}$ ||
    ...

We have also developed a tool, named Meeduse, which helps us construct such initialisations through a graphical user interface [13].

One must take care that this initial state features several properties that are not expressed in the invariant and hence not shared by all possible initial states (see Sect. 5 for a discussion of this point).

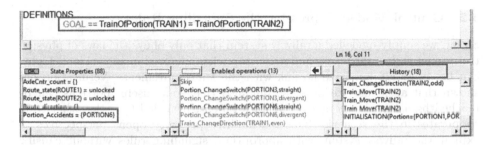

Fig. 6. ProB finds a sequence leading to an accident

Verification of the Uncontrolled Model. Verification of the uncontrolled model corresponds to steps 2 and 3: one must check that accidents are possible, and that desired states can be reached. Otherwise, it would be useless to design signalling rules to prevent accidents.

Possibility of Accidents. Showing that accidents are possible can be done by animating the model and playing a scenario which leads to an accident, or by providing an appropriate goal to the ProB model-checker. Here the goal expresses that both trains may end up in the same portion:

$$GOAL == TrainOfPortion(TRAIN1) = TrainOfPortion(TRAIN2)$$

In the *Functional* machine, the track portions are not expected to change. Therefore we remove the getters, setters, constructors and destructors of the class from the model. We keep only the *Move* and *ChangeDirection* operations for class *Train*, and the *ChangeSwitch* operation for class *Portion*. Figure 6 shows that ProB easily finds a scenario where this accident happens after 18 steps. It finds this scenario in about 2.1 s, using the default strategy (mixed depth-first/breadth-first), on a 16 Gb machine with Intel Core i7 CPU 2.80 GHz. ProB also reports that the search went through 342 states and 4857 transitions.

Reachability. Checking reachability of a desired state on the uncontrolled model will guarantee that this goal is within the reach of this model, and that its failure on the control model would result from the permission rules. In our example, we checked reachability of the following goal:

$$GOAL == TrainOfPortion(TRAIN1) = PORTION8 \wedge Portion\_Accidents = \emptyset$$

This goal ensures that there exists a scenario where *TRAIN1* will reach portion 8, on the right hand side of the tracks. This also requires that the other train will leave portion 8 and move to a place that *TRAIN1* will not visit.

ProB finds a 37 steps scenario, reaching this goal, by checking 1723 states and 24549 transitions of the *Functional* machine in 11 s.

4.2   Control Model: Expressing the Signalling Rules

So far, we simply modelled a railway system that only obeys the laws of physics: trains must follow the tracks and must stop when involved in an accident. Lights can be *on* or *off* but have no link with the train movements. Verification has shown that accidents are possible, but also that some useful portions can be reached by a train without causing an accident, provided that the other train cooperates in the scenario. This reachability property opens perspectives to exploit the railway system with appropriate signalling rules without causing accidents.

Signalling rules involve two kinds of actors: (1) the train *driver* executes the *Move* and *ChangeDirection* operations and pays attention to the state of the lights; (2) the *traffic agent* has a global view of the position of trains and can modify the state of lights to coordinate train movements. He can also act on the railroad switches to guide a train to a given portion. These two kinds of actors will correspond to the roles of our control model. This model expresses the permissions granted to roles to access the operations of the uncontrolled model's classes.

The Notion of Route. A naive attempt to define signalling rules is to only rely on the position of the trains and the state of lights. A light may be switched on when there is no train between the light and the next off-light in the direction of the train. Unfortunately, this naive approach is not safe, because trains move in both directions and the railroad switches can be modified while a train moves towards it.

A more robust approach is to make reservations on track portions and to lock these reservations. This is expressed in our uncontrolled model by the notion of route. A route is a set of contiguous portions between a train and an *off* signal. These portions are reserved for the train. The route is constructed incrementally by adding adjacent portions. It can be locked as soon as the next signal has been reached, provided that this signal is in the *off* state.

Routes are objects that are managed by the traffic agent. The traffic agent first draws the routes by adding portions and positioning railroad switches. The agent then locks the route and uses its information to switch lights on.

The train driver has no direct access to the information of the routes. He has only to follow the instructions of the lights.

Graphical Model of the Control Policy. Figure 7 shows that role *Driver* has permission to operate *Move* of class *Train*. This permission is conditioned by an authorisation constraint, expressed in the B language, stating that:

– the train is in a portion which has a neighbour in the direction of the train;
– either this neighbour portion has no light,
– or the light is oriented in the opposite direction,
– or the light is *on*.

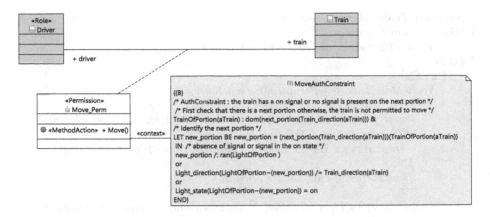

Fig. 7. Permission to move the train

From this model, B4MSecure generates the specification of the controlled version of *Move* (Fig. 8). Its precondition is the same as the one of the uncontrolled version of *Move*. Its *SELECT* clause includes the check that the current role has permission to execute *Move*, and the authorisation constraint expressed in B in the permission diagram. If the *SELECT* clause is satisfied, the operation executes the uncontrolled version of *Move*.

Permissions are expressed for all operations of the uncontrolled model. Then, the B4MSecure tool generates a B machine, named *RBAC_Model* which includes the *Functional* machine and defines a controlled version of its operations.

Initialisation. The initial state of this control model features two users: *Alice* is a traffic agent, and *Dan* is a driver. Please note that the model allows this single driver to drive both trains. A more realistic model would associate each train with its driver, and authorisation constraints would take it into account. The initial state also assigns a single empty route to each train.

Verifying the Absence of Accidents. It should now be shown that the signalling rules of machine *RBAC_Model* prevent accidents. This can be expressed as an invariant in this machine stating the absence of accidents:

$$Portion\_Accidents = \emptyset$$

Unfortunately, the current version of B4MSecure does not allow to express invariants in the control model. They can only be expressed in the uncontrolled model. So instead of expressing this property as an invariant, we express its negation as a goal for the model checker:

$$GOAL == Portion\_Accidents \neq \emptyset$$

ProB searches through the entire state space for a path to this goal and reports that the goal was not found. This exhaustive search proves that the

controlled_Train_Move($aTrain$) =
PRE $aTrain \in Train \wedge$
         $TrainOfPortion(aTrain) \not\subseteq Portion\_Accidents$
THEN
   SELECT
      $Train\_Move\_Label \in isPermitted[currentRole] \wedge$
      $(Driver \in currentRole \Rightarrow$
         $TrainOfPortion(aTrain) \in \mathbf{dom}(next\_portion(Train\_direction(aTrain))) \wedge$
         LET $new\_portion$ **BE** $new\_portion =$
            $(next\_portion(Train\_direction(aTrain)))(TrainOfPortion(aTrain))$
         IN
            $new\_portion \not\subseteq \mathbf{ran}(LightOfPortion)$
            $\vee$
         $Light\_direction(LightOfPortion^{-1}(new\_portion)) \neq Train\_direction(aTrain)$
            $\vee$
            $Light\_state(LightOfPortion^{-1}(new\_portion)) = on$
         END)
      THEN
         Train_Move($aTrain$)
      END
   END;

Fig. 8. Controlled version of *Move*

model will not allow accidents when started from the initial state. We performed this experiment with three variants of the track layout of Fig. 1 (see Table 1). Each variant keeps the same topology of track portions, but the number of lights varies. Each of the three searches reports the absence of accidents, but the state space clearly suffers state explosion. The third example, which corresponds to the layout of Fig. 1 with its 7 lights, takes 9 h and seems representative of the limits of our model-checking approach to prove the absence of accidents. The verification of larger state spaces will require to decompose the layout as proposed by Limbrée [16] or Winter [20]. It may also benefit from the use of advanced model-checking techniques: for example, Vu [11] used Bounded Model-Checking combined with k-induction to verify larger track layouts (46 portions, 23 points, 49 signals and 59 routes).

Table 1. Exhaustive search for an accident using ProB (using Depth-First strategy, on a 16 Gb machine with Intel Core i7 CPU 2.80 GHz)

Lights present in the track layout	Time to perform exhaustive search	Number of states visited	Number of transitions visited
$0, 1, 4, 5$	34 min	77 471	693 787
$0, 1, 2, 3, 4, 5$	3 h 40 min	553 487	5 429 529
$0, 1, 2, 3, 4, 5, 6$	9 h	1 384 747	14 208 413

We also experimented that the model-checker is an efficient tool to rapidly find errors in new versions of the signalling rules or to discard an erroneous initial state. For example, if we change the direction of *Light0* in Fig. 1, which leaves too much freedom to train 1, ProB finds a counter-example leading to an accident in 34 steps and 92 s (checking 3768 states and 42486 transitions).

Reachability of Desired States. We can also check that the rules are not too strict and still allow a scenario where *TRAIN1* reaches *PORTION8*. The model-checker finds a scenario of 49 steps after exploring 6577 states and 72651 transitions in 166 s. This reachability scenario is slightly more complex than the one of the uncontrolled model because it must alternate the current user between *Alice*, who positions the point switches, makes portion reservations and changes the lights, and *Dan* who moves the train.

4.3   Human Errors

The verification of the signalling rules assumes that users follow the rules, i.e. they only access operations that are permitted, and follow authorisation constraints. These assumptions are not valid in the case of human errors. In our example, there can be several kinds of human errors: (1) the train driver can overlook an *off* light and enter a forbidden track portion, ignoring the authorisation constraint; (2) the traffic agent can switch *on* a light ignoring the corresponding authorisation constraint. Such human errors can be the consequence of tiredness. In 2016, Infrabel, the Belgian railway company, reported that 91 trains (out of 1,3 million) ignored a red light [14].

Our models can be adapted to take into account errors of these agents. We add a state variable, named *irresponsive*, which records the set of users who do not follow the rules. E.g., in the initial state, *Dan* appears as irresponsive.

VARIABLES
  irresponsive
INVARIANT
  irresponsive $\subseteq$ *USERS*
INITIALISATION
  irresponsive := { *Dan* }

We can then modify the *Move* operation to take into account the irresponsive character of the current user (Fig. 9). This version checks that the role of the current user has permission to execute *Move*, i.e. that it is a train driver. But it bypasses the authorisation constraint for irresponsive users, calling the uncontrolled version of *Move* instead of the controlled one.

It must be noted that, in the controlled model, the train driver have only access to *Move* through *controlled_Train_Move2*. As a result, the train driver must either follow the rules or be irresponsive to execute *Move*.

The current version of B4MSecure does not support the modelling of irresponsive users. In order to experiment with these concepts, we have modified manually the specifications of a simpler signalling model. Model-checking has

```
controlled_Train_Move2(aTrain)=
  PRE
  aTrain ∈ Train
  ∧ TrainOfPortion(aTrain) ∉ dom(Portion_Accidents )
  THEN SELECT
          Train__Move_Label ∈ isPermitted[currentRole]
      THEN IF currentUser  ∈ irresponsive
          THEN Train_Move(aTrain)
          ELSE controlled_Train_Move(aTrain) END
      END
  END
```

Fig. 9. Controlled version of *Move*, taking irresponsive users into account

shown that irresponsive users may cause accidents. In order to prevent such human errors, additional devices, such as automatic train stop systems, can be deployed on the track, and block a train which overlooks an off signal. The model, equipped with these counter-measures, can be model-checked to show the absence of accidents and the reachability of desired states.

5   Model-Checking

In this work, we have adopted a lightweight approach to formal methods, replacing theorem proving by model-checking.

Verification was aimed at guaranteeing the absence of accidents and finding scenarios which establish the reachability of desired states.

Checking reachability was successful. The goals are reached in a few minutes by the model-checker. When the search becomes more difficult, it is still possible to guide the ProB model-checker by providing CSP specifications which rule the sequence of operations. Using these CSP specifications, it is possible to instruct the model-checker to perform the connection of users at the beginning of the sequence, and to avoid connection operations after this initial sequence. This directed model-checking accelerates reachability searches.

Checking the unreachability of a goal or establishing an invariant property requires to explore the whole state space. This is subject to the state explosion problem and in our case, it limits the number of objects involved in the track layout. A promising approach is to decompose the track layout into sub-layouts and verify the correctness of each sub-layout, and the interactions between sub-layouts. This approach has been experimented successfully by Limbrée [16] and Winter [20]. We intend to experiment with a similar approach as future work.

Influence of the Initial State. Model-checking guarantees that all states reachable from the initial state preserve the invariant. But other initial states can still lead to dangerous situations. For example, an initial state with two trains, and without lights allows accidents to take place. So model-checking only proves the correctness of signalling rules for a given initial state. Given a track layout, model-checking should be performed several times varying the number of trains involved, the initial state of lights and railroad switches.

This also means that there exist implicit properties of the initial state that were not identified in our model. Some initial states verify these properties and lead to a safe behaviour. Others do not and may lead to accidents. These properties should be identified and captured as invariants.

Nevertheless, we have noticed that erroneous rules or erroneous initial states are rapidly detected by the model-checker, typically in a few minutes. We have reported on a mutation of the track layout of Fig. 1 which was detected in 92 s. So, model-checking appears as an efficient tool to find errors, and when the search for accidental states lasts longer, it usually indicates that the model is correct, but that its state space exploration takes a long time.

6   Related Work

The B method has been successfully used to model real railways systems. [18] reports on 4 studies where safety properties were modeled and proven. The combination of UML and B or Event-B has already been experimented to model such systems. For example, [7] reports on the use of iUML-B to generate Event-B specifications from UML class and state diagrams. That study uses refinement steps to structure the model. In our group, [3] used B4MSecure to translate a class diagram model of the ERTMS/ETCS signaling system level 3. The resulting model was completed with event-B specifications and the whole was verified using animation and model-checking.

None of the above mentioned works used the separation of concerns approach presented in this paper. This approach was initially experimented by our group in [5,6] to model the exchange of information between the traffic agent, the train and its driver. The current study considers a larger system which includes the track layout. It also discusses the case of irresponsive agents, which is a new contribution.

The present work uses model-checking for verification purposes. Numerous teams have used various model-checking tools to verify railway systems. For example, Fantechi [9] proposed and modelled a distributed organisation of interlocking, and verified the absence of collision and derailments on a track layout with up to 10 stations. It must be noted that this work focuses on routes and does not model the trains. Another formalisation is proposed by Vu [11] who uses Bounded Model-Checking and k-induction to address large track layouts (46 portions, 23 points, 49 signals and 59 routes).

Our work is closer to the work of Winter [20] who models the routes and the trains, and model-checks the control tables using ASM and NuSMV. Since that model suffers the state explosion problem, [20] proposes to decompose the layout, taking each route into account. This is an interesting approach to scale up model-checking, but it requires a predefined set of routes, which is not the case in our model. [16] also decomposes the track layout in order to support model-checking. This decomposition is not based on the notion of route, but on the identification of connection points between sublayouts. We intend to study both works in order to scale up model-checking in our modelling approach.

7   Conclusion

We have presented an approach which uses formal methods to model and verify railway signalling systems. The novelty of this approach is to use concepts from the Access Control domain to separate concerns between an uncontrolled model, which describes the behaviour of the railway system in the absence of rules, and a control model, which describes the signalling rules which control this railway system. The control model also introduces users of the railway system and associates them to roles. This allows to take into account human actors and their potential errors.

We have shown how irresponsive behaviours can be expressed in our control model. Additional work is needed to further detail these irresponsive behaviours. For example, a tired train driver may miss an off signal, but will not arbitrarily perform a change of direction which requires several conscious actions.

Verification of these models exploits model-checking to show the presence of accidents in uncontrolled models, their absence in the control model. It also shows that the uncontrolled model allows to reach some desired states, and that signalling rules do not prevent the trains from reaching their destination.

ProB allowed us to adopt a lightweight approach to formal methods where proof is not necessary to establish invariant preservation for a given initial state. For other initial states, the exhaustive search must be performed again.

Further work will address the state space explosion problem by the decomposition of a given track layout into sublayouts which can be verified independently and in reasonable time. It will also consider the modelling of further equipment, like Automatic Train Stop systems, or the detection of the position of the train using the ERTMS Eurobalise, or GNSS (Global Navigation Satellite System).

Acknowledgments. This work is funded by the NExTRegio project of IRT Railenium. The authors would like to thank SNCF Réseau for its support. We also thank German Vega for his support of B4MSecure.

References

1. Abrial, J.R.: The B-Book: Assigning Programs to Meanings. Cambridge University Press, Cambridge (1996)
2. Abrial, J.R.: Modeling in Event-B: System and Software Engineering, 1st edn. Cambridge University Press, New York (2010)
3. Ait Wakrime, A., Ben Ayed, R., Collart-Dutilleul, S., Ledru, Y., Idani, A.: Formalizing railway signaling system ERTMS/ETCS using UML/Event-B. In: Abdelwahed, E.H., Bellatreche, L., Golfarelli, M., Méry, D., Ordonez, C. (eds.) MEDI 2018. LNCS, vol. 11163, pp. 321–330. Springer, Cham (2018). https://doi.org/10.1007/978-3-030-00856-7_21

4. Behm, P., Benoit, P., Faivre, A., Meynadier, J.-M.: Météor: a successful application of B in a large project. In: Wing, J.M., Woodcock, J., Davies, J. (eds.) FM 1999. LNCS, vol. 1708, pp. 369–387. Springer, Heidelberg (1999). https://doi.org/10.1007/3-540-48119-2_22

5. Ben Ayed, R., Collart-Dutilleul, S., Bon, P., Idani, A., Ledru, Y.: B formal validation of ERTMS/ETCS railway operating rules. In: Ait, A.Y., Schewe, K.D. (eds.) ABZ 2014. LNCS, vol. 8477, pp. 124–129. Springer, Heidelberg (2014). https://doi.org/10.1007/978-3-662-43652-3_10

6. Ben Ayed, R., Collart-Dutilleul, S., Bon, P., Ledru, Y., Idani, A.: Formalismes basés sur les rôles pour la modélisation et la validation des règles d'exploitation ferroviaires. Technique et Science Informatiques **34**(5), 495–521 (2015). https://doi.org/10.3166/tsi.34.495-521

7. Butler, M.J., et al.: Formal modelling techniques for efficient development of railway control products. In: Fantechi, A., Lecomte, T., Romanovsky, A. (eds.) RSSRail 2017. LNCS, vol. 10598, pp. 71–86. Springer, Cham (2017). https://doi.org/10.1007/978-3-319-68499-4_5

8. Butler, M., Raschke, A., Hoang, T.S., Reichl, K. (eds.): ABZ 2018. LNCS, vol. 10817. Springer, Cham (2018). https://doi.org/10.1007/978-3-319-91271-4

9. Fantechi, A., Haxthausen, A.E., Nielsen, M.B.R.: Model checking geographically distributed interlocking systems using UMC. In: PDP 2017, pp. 278–286. IEEE Computer Society (2017). https://doi.org/10.1109/PDP.2017.66

10. Fantechi, A., Lecomte, T., Romanovsky, A. (eds.): RSSRail 2017. LNCS, vol. 10598. Springer, Cham (2017). https://doi.org/10.1007/978-3-319-68499-4

11. Vu, L.H., Haxthausen, A.E., Peleska, J.: Formal modeling and verification of interlocking systems featuring sequential release. In: Artho, C., Ölveczky, P.C. (eds.) FTSCS 2014. CCIS, vol. 476, pp. 223–238. Springer, Cham (2015). https://doi.org/10.1007/978-3-319-17581-2_15

12. Idani, A., Ledru, Y.: B for modeling secure information systems - the B4MSecure platform. In: Butler, M., Conchon, S., Zaïdi, F. (eds.) ICFEM 2015. LNCS, vol. 9407, pp. 312–318. Springer, Cham (2015). https://doi.org/10.1007/978-3-319-25423-4_20

13. Idani, A., Ledru, Y., Ait Wakrime, A., Ben Ayed, R., Bon, P.: Towards a tool-based domain specific approach for railway systems modeling and validation. In: Collart-Dutilleul, S., et al. (Eds.) RSSRail 2019. LNCS, vol. 11495, pp. 23–40. Springer, Heidelberg (2019)

14. Infrabel: Stabilisation du nombre de dépassements de signaux sur le rail en 2016, Januray 2017. https://www.infrabel.be/fr/presse/stabilisation-du-nombre-depassements-signaux-rail-2016

15. Leuschel, M., Butler, M.J.: ProB: an automated analysis toolset for the B method. STTT **10**(2), 185–203 (2008). https://doi.org/10.1007/s10009-007-0063-9

16. Limbrée, C., Cappart, Q., Pecheur, C., Tonetta, S.: Verification of railway interlocking - compositional approach with OCRA. In: Lecomte, T., Pinger, R., Romanovsky, A. (eds.) RSSRail 2016. LNCS, vol. 9707, pp. 134–149. Springer, Cham (2016). https://doi.org/10.1007/978-3-319-33951-1_10

17. Lodderstedt, T., Basin, D., Doser, J.: SecureUML: a UML-based modeling language for model-driven security. In: Jézéquel, J.-M., Hussmann, H., Cook, S. (eds.) UML 2002. LNCS, vol. 2460, pp. 426–441. Springer, Heidelberg (2002). https://doi.org/10.1007/3-540-45800-X_33

18. Sabatier, D.: Using formal proof and B method at system level for industrial projects. In: Lecomte, T., Pinger, R., Romanovsky, A. (eds.) RSSRail 2016. LNCS, vol. 9707, pp. 20–31. Springer, Cham (2016). https://doi.org/10.1007/978-3-319-33951-1_2

19. Sabatier, D., Burdy, L., Requet, A., Guéry, J.: Formal proofs for the NYCT line 7 (flushing) modernization project. In: Derrick, J., et al. (eds.) ABZ 2012. LNCS, vol. 7316, pp. 369–372. Springer, Heidelberg (2012). https://doi.org/10.1007/978-3-642-30885-7_34

20. Winter, K., Robinson, N.J.: Modelling large railway interlockings and model checking small ones. In: ACSC2003, pp. 309–316. Australian Computer Society (2003). http://crpit.com/confpapers/CRPITV16Winter.pdf

RBS2HLL
A Formal Modeling of Relay-Based Interlocking

Naïm Aber[✉], Benjamin Blanc, Nathalie Ferkane, Mohand Meziani[✉],
and Julien Ordioni

RATP, ING/STF/QS, 54 rue Roger Salengro, 94724 Fontenay-sous-Bois, France
{naim.aber,benjamin.blanc,nathalie.ferkane,
Mohand-ameziane.meziani,julien.ordioni}@ratp.fr

Abstract. The safety of railway systems is a major challenge due to the
serious consequences that may result from a design error in the context
of a growing complexity. Formal methods play a more and more important role to tackle these issues. A key part of the safety strategy relies
on the rules and procedures embedded in the interlocking and signaling system. RATP already applied formal methods for computer-based
implementation of such systems. However a large part of current interlocking systems are still relay-based. This paper presents a translation
tool, called RBS2HLL (for Relay Based System To HLL) aiming at providing RATP with a formal specification of a relay based interlocking
system. The main features of our tool are: first, the formal modelisation is based on the minimal set of guaranteed safety requirements, and
second, the translation result allows the verification of generic properties parameterized by application data. This tool was initially developed
for the new RATP product named PHPI, and successfully applied on a
section of Paris Metro Line 6.

Keywords: Interlocking · Formal methods ·
Safety-critical railway system · HLL

1 Introduction

RATP is one of the most important operator in Paris by carrying more than 3
billions of passengers per year. RATP has in charge the operation and the maintenance of the 16 urban lines of the Metro in Paris, 8 lines of Tramway, more than
350 lines of Bus and part of the most busiest suburban lines of Europe (RER A
& B, resp. more than 1,200 k and 900 k passengers/day). About 150 interlocking
installations controlling more than 3,000 routes are necessary to manage this
Metro and RER network. To ensure sustainability of those interlocking systems,
RATP started a renewal program in 2001: several Computer Based Interlocking (CBI) systems were commissioned between 2001 and 2014. These systems
allowed to avoid a lot of night work (needed to perform final tests safely relating
to the passengers) and to formally demonstrate a part of the safety of the interlocking using a model checking approach. This work led to co-develop the very

© Springer Nature Switzerland AG 2019
S. Collart-Dutilleul et al. (Eds.): RSSRail 2019, LNCS 11495, pp. 191–201, 2019.
https://doi.org/10.1007/978-3-030-18744-6_12

first version of HLL (High Level Language). HLL [10] is a synchronous data-flow language used today in our formal PERF Workshop [3]. The main issue met with digital embedded technologies is the lifespan of the hardware components. On the contrary, relay based technologies were in revenue service for a long period of time. For instance some of interlocking systems on the RATP network are still running today and this for more than 50 years. The CBIs commissioned in the world and in particular at RATP are not this aged today but some issues have already to be addressed concerning hardware availability. For instance the CBIs installed in Japan since the middle of the 80s were planned to be changed right after 20 years of service.

This is one of the reasons why RATP developed an hybrid interlocking system, called PHPI, picking up the advantages of both technologies: the robustness and long lifespan of electro-mechanical embedded components and the computerized formal safety demonstration performed during office hour. Using formal methods is almost natural for RATP because of our engagement in the domain for more than 25 years [5] The PHPI safety validation is totally included in this formal approach allowing to perform deep analysis leading to a very confident safety level. Nevertheless, reaching a formal proof on a relay-based system is not exactly the same as performing a formal verification on an interlocking software. In the latter there is no physical issues due to the intangibility of the software. To prove a PHPI system, RATP had to develop a specific translator to model the whole electro-mechanical components of a project and, more difficult, to model electricity behavior, mechanical phenomena and continuous time. This translator, named RBS2HLL (for Relay Based System to HLL), builds its model only on the safety guaranteed behavior of the relays. This is possible due to the fact that all the interlocking principles used by RATP are based on the NS1-like relays intrinsic safety characteristics (cf. French standards NF F 70-030).

Modeling such a system leads to make choices: not all physical phenomenons would be part of the model. The work done here allowed RATP to achieve its main goal: prove the safety properties of an interlocking system and exhibit the different modeling assumptions and hypothesis used to do that. The latter should be treated by other means than RBS2HLL. This paper explains how we choose to model a relay-based system in HLL to perform a formal safety verification.

The paper is organized as follows: Sect. 2 gives a brief introduction of HLL language and Sect. 3 some reminders about relay-based systems. The proposed tool is described in Sect. 4. Section 5 is devoted to giving a case study of how the tool can be used to validate an interlocking. Finally, in Sect. 6 we present the main results that have been obtained and the future work currently in progress.

2   HLL

HLL [10] (*High Level Language*) is a formal declarative and synchronous data flow language in the tradition of Lustre. HLL has been developed for certification purposes for RATP and has recently been released as an open-source language. An HLLmodel follows a cyclic execution: at each cycle, the set of inputs are updated, and outputs are computed according to their data-flow definitions.

This synchronous behavior is standard in control models that require a highly regulated real-time response to their environment.

```
Inputs:
int i;
Declarations:
int tmp;
Definitions:
o = ...;
tmp = ... ;
Proof Obligations:
...
```

Models in HLL are defined by an unordered set of sections. Streams, representing the traces of variables over time, are declared in *Declarations*, *Inputs*, or *Outputs* blocks with type checking information; their values are given as expressions in the *Definitions* blocks. The *Proof Obligations* block contains a set of properties related to streams for verification purpose. *Constraints* block contains expressions used to reduce the behavior of inputs streams. Expressions are composed above boolean and integer streams with usual logical and arithmetic operators, following a pointwise semantics: if $a = (a_1, a_2, \ldots)$ and $b = (b_1, b_2, \ldots)$ are infinite streams, then $a + b$ represents the stream $(a_1 + b_1, a_2 + b_2, \ldots)$. Temporal operators can be used to refer to initial, past, or next values of streams. The declarative nature of the language makes it suitable for the definition of formal models as well as safety properties whose status must be true at every cycle of the execution.

3   Relay-Based Systems Background

3.1   Safety Studies and Formal Modelling with Relays

The safety of a system is defined by the lack of unacceptable risks. Once these risks have been identified, some failure reduction measures could be defined to prevent or mitigate them through a deductive analysis (through experiences feedback, domain knowledge, etc.).

On the other hand, an inductive method could define safety properties the system has to ensure in order to prevent some faulty events. A safety property is written to ensure that something unsafe will never happen. A property states the absence of some observable outputs (signal states, route locking, track circuit occupations) in a definite situation.

Due to the complexity of railways system, an automatization of the safety assessment of the properties provides many benefits [3]. To be effective, the formalization process shall guarantee that all possible means to trigger an unsafe state are effectively reflected in the formal model (safe abstraction). Therefore, when a proof is completed on the formal model, the proof can be applied to the real system.

On the contrary, when a proof fails, a counter example scenario can be exhibited as a sequence of inputs that leads to an unsafe state, following the internal computations of the model. This scenario could be performed on the real system in order to exhibit the problematic behavior. But reaching this reproducibility may be very difficult, especially when it comes to physical systems. Multi-physics phenomena may be involved in the realization of a scenario.

These two outcomes of the proof process have different importance: the first one is mandatory for the safety validation, while the second is helpful for the functional validation. For its safety assessor role treated here, RATP is interested in the first constraint.

3.2   Relay Based Systems

The proof process can be applied at different levels of the development process: specification, conception or implementation. In order to gain the most confidence on the safety demonstration, it must be performed on the lowest level possible. When applied to a relay-based implementation, the circuit diagram encompasses a view of the system before its realization and is therefore a good candidate for the modeling. Before presenting these diagrams, let us first introduce basic knowledge on relays.

Relays. A relay is an electrically operated or electromechanical switch composed of an electromagnet, an armature, a spring and a set of electrical contacts. The electromagnetic switch is operated by a small electric current (its command) that turns a larger current on or off by either releasing or retracting the armature contact, thereby cutting or completing the circuit.

When the electromagnet (1 in Fig. 1) is powered, it will break the initial connection between the left (2) and the middle (3) pin and create a new connection between the middle (3) and the right (4) pin. Pins (2) and (3) create normally closed (NC) contacts; pins (3) and (4) normally open (NO) contacts.

Fig. 1. Basic electromechanical relay

Actual relays involve several devices in order to provide a more complex though more reliable output: diodes or snubber circuits to smooth the transition from one state to the other, spring or gravity to relax the electromagnet when deactivated, choice of material for contacts according to their electrical resistance. Similarly, the fine-grain study of a relay may reveal non-linear or faulty behaviors (rebounds, undesired arcing between contacts, contacts welding shut, temperature sensitivity).

Circuit Diagrams. A circuit diagram as shown in Fig. 2 describes the electrical wires connecting the command of the relays with their power supplies. The diagram includes the following syntactic elements:

- Positive and negative power supplies: noted $P+$ and $P-$ respectively;
- Physical adresses in the cabinet, allowing a unique identification (HA0.B3, HA0.F10);

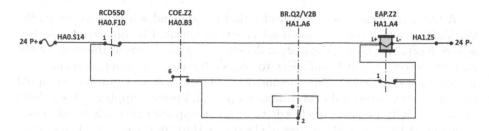

Fig. 2. Execution diagram for the command of relay EAP.Z2

- Electric devices: relays, bistable relays, etc, with their command pins (positive $L+$ and negative L-). RCDV550 is a track circuit receptor, COE.Z2 corresponds to the confirmation light of signal Z2, etc.;
- Contacts of relays, either NO/NC, or left/right/translators for bistable relays, with a unique identifier for each device. For instance, the NO contact of relay RCDV550 is just next to the $P+$ supply, and is noted RCDV550_T1;
- Wires between them, either single or multiple.

4   RBS2HLL

RBS2HLL is a tool that provides an automatic translation of circuit diagrams into an HLL model. The underlying formal model must capture enough information about the circuit to allow its safety validation and capture the logic it is implementing. The objective of the model is to find out what is the sequential logic implemented by a given circuit. To do so we need to adopt a discrete and relevant point of view on the electrical behavior to express it in HLL. Besides capturing the logic, the model needs to allow a modular translation of a circuit. Modular means here that we want to separate the expression of the circuit topology from the description of components behavior. This separation has the advantage of allowing the introduction of new components without having to modify the tool that translates the circuit description. Due to the complexity of relay-based systems, building a formal model of such system is a big challenge. In addition, the formal proof must be feasible with the model thus obtained.

4.1   A Model of Circuit Diagrams

Considering a circuit diagram, we can intuitively identify inputs, outputs, and internal states needed to produce them:

Outputs: Wires used to provide current to an external actuator (a railway switch point, a signal).
Internal States: Commands of devices that control these wires.
Inputs: Power supplies that are involved in commands.

A first approximation is to consider that a command is a Boolean value: the threshold at which the electromagnet is actually excited is considered a perfect square function. This approximation does not take into account the value of the current, especially if it is sufficient to trigger the electromagnet as specified in its technical description. The command is true when there is an uninterrupted flow of current between its two command pins and power supplies. This reflects the connectivity property of electricity. A second approximation is to introduce no timing delay to model the flow of electricity through the circuit. The electric current is considered to flow instantaneously from one of a wire to the other.

Similarly, contacts along the path between the command pins and power supplies are modeled as perfect switches, and therefore take Boolean values: *True* means that the switch is closed or the power supply is present, *False* meaning the opposite. A command is therefore defined by combining all the wire paths that come out of the pins to the power supplies. A sequential path corresponds to a conjunction of contacts and power supplies, while a parallel path corresponds to a path disjunction. An HLL representation of the equation of command for relay EAP.Z2, noted as the internal variable EAP.Z2_Cmd will be:

```
EAP.Z2_Cmd := ((RCDV550_T1 & HAO.S14)
              #(EAP.Z2_T1 & COE.Z2_R6 & HAO.S14)
              #(BR.Q2/V2B_G2 & COE.Z2_R6 & HAO.S14)) & ((HA1.Z5));
```

Indeed, the command is active when at least one of the paths to positive power supply identified by its address HAO.S14 is true, and its path to the negative one HA1.Z5 also is. Each path is composed of a conjunction (operator &) of contacts switches ending on a power supply. The three possible paths from the positive pin of the relay are obtained by a graph traversal of the graphical representation of the circuit and combined by a logical disjunction (operator #).

Note that this traversal does not rely on a specific direction for the electrical current. For instance, when coming upon the right pin of the NC contact of relay COE.Z2, the algorithm shall not only allow to go to its left pin, but also to the bottom pin of the BR.Q1/V2B left contact. This path is finally discarded since it encounters an already visited node.

4.2 A Simple Model of Relays

From this model of circuits, one has to add a logical model for every kind of devices encountered in the system. For relays, the model shall explain the constraints between NO/NC contacts and command. A functional view of a relay would state that a NO contact shall be equal to its command, delayed by a tiny amount of time (time needed for electromagnet to be energized plus for the rebounds to stop, for instance). A NC contact would do the exact opposite. This can be performed in HLL by using the temporal delay operator pre:

```
EAP.Z2_T1 = pre(EAP.Z2_Cmd);
EAP.Z2_R1 = ~ EAP.Z2_T1;
```

The delay operator refers to the previous value of the infinite stream. It allows the wellformedness of recursive definition like the one for EAP.Z2, since one of the energizing path contains the NO contact T1 of the same relay. In the second equation, the HLL ~ operator (tilde) stands for the Boolean negation.

However, this functional view does not take into account failure modes, mandatory for the safety analysis. Moreover, actual relays used in railway systems cannot ensure such a strong functional relationship. The normative description of relays, encoded in the French normative document NF F 70-030, only states the following constraints:

- NO contacts shall be opened when the command is set to False;
- NO contacts and NC contacts shall not be set to True at the same time

The first constraint is a weakening of the previous equation. Indeed, it allows a failure in contact switching on even though a command is set to True, but does not allow the contrary (contacts welding shut). In this more general model, contacts are declared as inputs and are only constrained by the HLL representation of these constraints. The second constraint is also a weakening of the second equation since it only forbids contacts to be true altogether, while allows them to be false at the same time. For instance, for relay EAP.Z2, the two constraints are:

```
EAP.Z2_T1 -> pre(EAP.Z2_Cmd);
~(EAP.Z2_T1 & EAP.Z2_R1);
```

These requirements describe the minimum guaranteed expected behavior of a device outputs, as stated by a normative description, and that could be ensured by other means. These requirements provide safe-states of the device, and thus of the system. They can be established for every device involved in a relay-based implementation of an interlocking system.

The drawback of such a loose model is that it may fail to prove any property, due to a lack of relationship between inputs and outputs. On the contrary, when a proof is completed, it allows a strong confidence in the system robustness for the given property.

5   Application: PHPI Interlocking

The RBS2HLL tool is part of a generic software validation process applied by RATP for interlocking systems. In this section, a case study of how this tool can be used to validate a PHPI interlocking will be presented. Before presenting this validation method, a brief description of the PHPI solution will be given.

5.1   PHPI Interlocking

PHPI (*Poste Hybride à Procédé Informatique* in French) is a new RATP interlocking product designed to embrace the advantages of both relay-based and computer-based interlocking. As any interlocking system, the main function of PHPI is to set train routes on railway networks. The logic of signaling functions can be implemented by electromechanical relays or processed by computer. The solution introduced by PHPI is a hybrid system involving two parts:

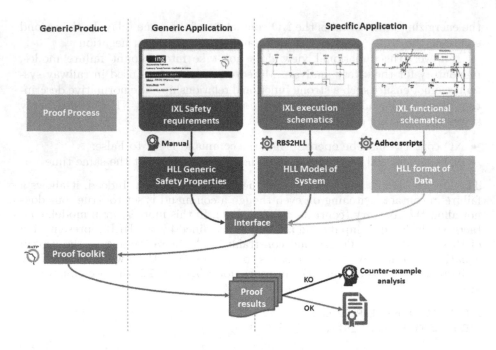

Fig. 3. PHPI validation process

- the relay-based part implements interlocking functions;
- the computer-based part implements safety validation (formal proof) and functional validation.

5.2 PHPI Validation Process

Figure 3 describes the validation process applied for the PHPI interlocking. This process is an instance of the *EN 50129* [2] generic approach which can fall under 3 categories: *Generic Product, Generic Application* and *Specific Application*.

Generic Product. The proof process is performed with *RATP Proof Toolkit* (see [3] and [6]). This engine checks if a safety property is satisfied by an interlocking model. If the property is violated, the proof engine provides a counter-example showing a possible scenario leading to the violation of the property.

Generic Application. In our study case, this generic application is the signaling application for RATP network. The safety properties are obtained from preliminary hazard analysis: trains collision and train derailment. These properties are subsequently refined into more detailed requirements according to different configurations such as front collision, rear collision, derailment due to a badly set point, etc. These refined requirements constitute the database of *IXL Safety Requirements*. Property P, given as example, is extracted from this database.

Property P:
Dangerous high-level situation: Train derailment
Refinement: Derailment on a point
Refined Property: If signal 's' origin of a route 'r' which includes
point 'p' is permissive, then point 'p' is not in motion.

Each generic safety requirement is formally modeled in HLL. This activity is performed manually and leads to HLL *Generic Safety Properties*. The proof obligations (PO) are independent from application data and design, they are expressed only with signaling devices (routes, point, signals, etc) and generic functions. The HLL PO of property P, called PO_P, is given as follows:

```
PO_P := ( ALL p : point__tab, s: signal__tab, r: route__tab
          (   route_signal_origin__param(r,s)
           & point_on_route__param(p,r)
           & signal_open__func(s))
        -> ~( point_left__func(p) & point_right__func(p)));
```

The parameters and the functions appearing in PO_P will be described below with the corresponding phase.

Specific Application. The formal modeling of an interlocking system is completely automatic thanks to the RBS2HLL tool presented in this paper. This tool takes the circuit diagrams as input and yields an HLL model as result. As mentioned above, the tool was developed bearing in mind that its output file would be used to perform formal proof. The data tables arising from the *IXL functional schematics* are transformed into HLL format by ad-hoc scripts developed for the specific needs of the application (in the case of PHPI, these tables were in Microsoft Excel format). The application data lists all instantiations of:

1. The track devices such as routes, points, signals, etc.
   As an illustration, point__tab, signal__tab and route__tab are tables that respectively lists points, signals and routes;
2. The links between these devices.
   For example, route_original_signal__param(r,s) associates each route to its original signal.

For each specific application, only a subset of the overall generic properties will need to be proven. These are identified by analyzing the track configuration, or the kind of trains running on it (automatic or manual). However, since the properties are generic, an interface file is required to link each object from the generic description to the actual names. For instance, property PO_P uses the following interface functions:

- signal_open__func(s) reads the state of the relay commanding the signal opening s in the HLL model. It returns true if s is open and false otherwise;
- point_right__func(p) reads the state of the relay controlling if the point p is positioned on the right in the HLL model. It returns true if p is positioned on the right and false otherwise;

- `point_left_func(p)` reads the state of the relay controlling if the point p is positioned on the left in the HLL model. It returns true if p is positioned on the left and false otherwise.

6 Conclusion

This paper presented RBS2HLL, the new RATP tool for relay based interlocking system formal modelisation. It explained how an HLL model of the system can be automatically generated, based on a minimal set of guaranteed safety requirements.

Related Works. Using formal methods in order to assess the safety of interlocking systems gains more and more attractivity. It has been reported in many applications and research papers (eg. [4,7,9,11]). More specifically, Haxthausen and al. present in [8] a tool for formal modeling relay based interlocking systems. The tool takes the circuit diagrams of a relay-based interlocking system as input and gives as result a transition system. The resulting model is expressed in the SAL language and uses the SAL model checker to verify required properties. The tool has been applied to the circuit diagrams of Stenstrup station in Denmark. However, the internal relay model used in this work has not been fully described.

RBS2HLL Validation Process. RBS2HLL is the result of a multi-disciplinary collaboration: a real effort has been made to write the RBS2HLL specification. Collaborations were set up with PHPI project manager Nazim Benaissa, safety manager David Bonvoisin, signaling experts, hardware experts and formal method experts to formally define the safety criteria guaranteed for each family of relays. The RBS2HLL tool was developed according to the European standard NF EN 50128:2011 [1] recommendations for a T2 class tool, since it must be used in RATP industrial context. The RBS2HLL tool contains two independent translation chains which have been developed by two independent teams with different technologies. The RBS2HLL tool is internally validated at RATP and is currently being assessed as part of the PHPI project's certification by an external and independent certification authority.

First Application. RBS2HLL was applied to a section of Paris Metro line 6 with the following metrics: 11 routes, 17 track circuits, 4 points and 9 signals. The obtained HLL model has 1974 lines of code, 1050 variables, 164 equations, 153 constraints and 100 devices.

Building the HLL model of the system with RBS2HLL merely took a few seconds. Using the resulting model of the system, along with specific track data in HLL format, a large variety of generic safety properties were proven (the project contains 20 applicable properties). No new system shortcoming was identified, but all our purposefully injected faults were detected.

Future Works. This paper allowed to demonstrate the feasibility of automating the formal modelisation of relay based interlocking systems. The next challenge is to assess the capability of our tool to deal with larger interlocking systems. RBS2HLL performance is currently being tested on the considerably more complex system: Paris Metro line 14 end of line interlocking system which contains 35 routes, 16 track circuits, 9 points and 16 signals. The resulting model has 152500 lines of code, 79000 variables, 73000 equations, 1422 constraints and 468 devices.

This project is just starting, and yet the use of the RBS2HLL tool already allowed us to detect two wiring failures in the IXL execution schematics.

References

1. 50128:2011, C.E.: Railway applications communications, signalling and processing systems - software for railway control and protection systems (2011)
2. 50129:2003, C.E.: Railway applications - communications, signalling and processing systems - safety related electronic systems for signalling, February 2003
3. Benaissa, N., Bonvoisin, D., Feliachi, A., Ordioni, J.: The PERF approach for formal verification. In: Lecomte, T., Pinger, R., Romanovsky, A. (eds.) RSSRail 2016. LNCS, vol. 9707, pp. 203–214. Springer, Cham (2016). https://doi.org/10.1007/978-3-319-33951-1_15
4. Bonacchi, A., Fantechi, A., Bacherini, S., Tempestini, M.: Validation process for railway interlocking systems. Sci. Comput. Program. **128**, 2–21 (2016)
5. Bonvoisin, D.: 25 years of formal methods at RATP. In: IRSC, 2–7 October 2016
6. Breton, N., Fonteneau, Y.: S3: proving the safety of critical systems. In: Lecomte, T., Pinger, R., Romanovsky, A. (eds.) RSSRail 2016. LNCS, vol. 9707, pp. 231–242. Springer, Cham (2016). https://doi.org/10.1007/978-3-319-33951-1_17
7. Busard, S., Cappart, Q., Limbrée, C., Pecheur, C., Schaus, P.: Verification of railway interlocking systems. In: Proceedings 4th International Workshop on Engineering Safety and Security Systems, ESSS 2015, Oslo, Norway, 22 June 2015, pp. 19–31 (2015)
8. Haxthausen, A.E., Kjær, A.A., Le Bliguet, M.: Formal development of a tool for automated modelling and verification of relay interlocking systems. In: Butler, M., Schulte, W. (eds.) FM 2011. LNCS, vol. 6664, pp. 118–132. Springer, Heidelberg (2011). https://doi.org/10.1007/978-3-642-21437-0_11
9. Vu, L.H., Haxthausen, A.E., Peleska, J.: Formal modeling and verification of interlocking systems featuring sequential release. In: Artho, C., Ölveczky, P.C. (eds.) FTSCS 2014. CCIS, vol. 476, pp. 223–238. Springer, Cham (2015). https://doi.org/10.1007/978-3-319-17581-2_15
10. Ordioni, J., Colaço, N.B.J.L.: Hll vol 2.7 modelling language specification (2018)
11. Sun, P., Dutilleul, S.C., Bon, P.: A model pattern of railway interlocking system by petri nets. In: 2015 International Conference on Models and Technologies for Intelligent Transportation Systems (MT-ITS), Budapest, Hungary, 3–5 June 2015, pp. 442–449 (2015)

Property-Based Modelling and Validation of a CBTC Zone Controller in Event-B

Mathieu Comptier[1], Michael Leuschel[2(✉)], Luis-Fernando Mejia[3],
Julien Molinero Perez[1], and Mareike Mutz[2]

[1] ClearSy System Engineering, Aix-en-Provence, France
{mathieu.comptier,julien.molineroperez}@clearsy.com
[2] Institut für Informatik, Universität Düsseldorf, Düsseldorf, Germany
{michael.leuschel,mareike.mutz}@hhu.de
[3] Alstom, St-Ouen, France
luis-fernando.mejia@alstomgroup.com

Abstract. This paper describes a formal analysis method applied at the software design level. The objective is to prove that a software specification and its implementation satisfy the expected system properties. In our case the analysed design is that of the Zone Controller of a CBTC developed using B. The B-Method is used to ensure that the implementation is correct wrt the software specification, but it does not guarantee that the algorithms described in the specification are correct wrt the system level requirements.

Our analysis overcomes this shortcoming, providing a stronger assurance that the designed software meets its objectives. In particular, we prove that the implemented algorithms ensure that the track portion actually occupied by a train is covered by a protection envelope on the software side. The analysis is formalised with an Event-B model that is subject to tool-based inspections: animation with PROB and formal proof with Atelier B. In contrast to the existing B-Method model, our Event-B model links environment variables (the real position of the trains) with software variables (protection envelopes) and models the assumptions about the possible evolution of the environment.

This analysis was carried out on an industrial scale software, consisting of 12000 lines of executable code, with immediate concrete results. This paper shows that, in addition to demonstrating compliance, this approach is clearly of interest from an industrial point of view.

Keywords: B-Method · Event-B · CBTC · Zone controller · Proof · Animation · Model checking

---

This research has been conducted within the project AMASS, that has received funding from the ECSEL JU under grant agreement No 692474. This Joint Undertaking receives support from the European Union's Horizon 2020 research and innovation programme and from Spain, Czech Republic, Germany, Sweden, Italy, United Kingdom and France.

© Springer Nature Switzerland AG 2019
S. Collart-Dutilleul et al. (Eds.): RSSRail 2019, LNCS 11495, pp. 202–212, 2019.
https://doi.org/10.1007/978-3-030-18744-6_13

1 Motivation

In this work we analyzed a CBTC (Communication-Based Train Control) system whose functional part was developed with the B-Method. A formal model of the software components was created, then formally refined and finally formally implemented. The actual code was generated from B-Method implementations in Atelier B [4]. This obviates the need for module and integration testing and results in a very robust product. This approach to code generation has been successful for other CBTC products [7,8]. However, while this formal approach avoids errors in the coding process, it does not prevent errors made at the level of the requirements specification. Thus it is important to also validate the high-level specification of each component of a CBTC. In particular, we want to guarantee system-wide safety properties

- in light of evolving requirements specification of the components,
- and taking into account optimisation to increase availability of the system.

In this paper we propose an approach to tackle these challenges:

- by developing a system model of one CBTC component and its relevant environment.
- by using a property-driven approach, where a component has to maintain and guarantee a clear set of formal properties and
- by translating these properties to the software level of the CBTC component under consideration.

In this paper we present a property-based methodology which allows to ensure safety of a system while improving its availability and flexibility. This formal system modelling approach is validated through the analysis of one particular vital CBTC component: the zone controller (ZC). The presented process and its associated tooling helps the future evolution of ZC and increases the confidence in its correct functioning.

2 CBTC Background

A CBTC is a safety-critical system for automatic train operation on metro lines and rail yards. It can deal with both driver-less and driver-operated trains. It is composed of several communicating subsystems (ZC, CC, CBI, ATS) which aim at ensuring safe passenger traffic and optimal service. To ensure the required safety level, subsystems must exchange reliable information, and thus, must be considered together in the safety demonstration.

For instance, the global system must ensure that there is **no train derailment**. This function is mainly performed by the interlocking component (CBI), which must guarantee for instance that no switch can move under a train. The mechanisms implemented within the CBI are based on its knowledge of the track occupancy. The occupancy status is gathered by equipment set along the track. However, in some cases, it can be improved by taking advantage of the ZC's knowledge obtained via direct communication with talkative trains. This occupancy status transmitted by the ZC to the CBI must thus be correct in order to be able to perform safety functions (and so must be the locations communicated by the carborne controller (CC) to the ZC).

Establishing a safe occupancy of the track is one of the main goals of the ZC. It is called the "train tracking" function. The algorithms implemented to achieve it are eminently safety critical, they represent the main complexity of the software and can spread over several thousand lines of code. The study carried out focuses on this specific feature of the ZC which is based on computation of envelopes covering every possible track portion occupied by a train.

Specific Notions. *An envelope* is a ZC software concept represented by two locations delimiting a continuous portion of the track. Envelopes cover the areas that are (potentially) occupied by trains. They are transmitted to the CBI who will declare an area *free* if no envelope intersects this area. When the ZC knows the identity of the train covered by an envelope it associates these two entities. In other cases the envelope is called a *Non Identified Envelope*.

A train is considered as *talkative* when ZC has recently received a valid message from this train indicating its certified position on the track. Otherwise it is considered as *non talkative* and its position is tracked only using specific wayside equipment.

3   Methodology

The aim of this section is to describe the four methodological steps (Sects. 3.1–3.4) and illustrate them on a concrete example.

3.1   Step 1: Inputs and Main Properties

The first step is to define the main property the system shall respect when operating in its environment. To illustrate this on our real analysis, the main property concerns the track occupancy information sent by the ZC to the CBI which uses this information to lock/release portions of tracks and switches. More precisely the property is the following:

"At any time, every location of the track beneath a train
is covered by at least one envelope."

Then, the implementation is studied to understand how it guarantees the property. This requires a good representation of the implementation, which can be obtained either from: the specification (in natural language), the (B) abstract models of the implementation, the code of the implementation itself, or experts' knowledge of the system implementation.

3.2   Step 2: Key Sentences Identification

During this phase, the implementation's founding principles, on which the main property relies on, are identified. Indeed, the main property uses generic system notions which are difficult to link to the implementation. Hence, this property has to be refined in key principles closer to the implementation. These principles are sub-properties connecting the software variables to the environment. They must be:

1. sufficient to guarantee the main property (Sect. 3.1);
2. satisfiable by an initial state when starting the software;
3. preserved by the implemented functions of the system.

These sub-properties (or invariants) may be found during this analysis and/or directly provided by experts depending on the project. In our concrete study, the sub-properties obtained are:

– "Any talkative train, physically located on the CBTC controlled area, has to be integrally covered by its own envelope "
– "Any non-talkative train, physically located on the CBTC controlled area, has to be integrally covered by a set of specific non-identified envelopes."

This example illustrates that these sub-properties contain details specific to the implementation which were not in the main property definition (talkative trains, non-identified envelopes, . . .). At the end of this phase a list of "key sentences" are obtained. These are sufficient to ensure the main property and all implemented functions must preserve them, which is the aim of the following section.

3.3   Step 3: Systematic Use and Manual Justifications

Once the key sentences have been found, the method becomes systematic. For each function of the system, we develop a semi-formal reasoning in natural language to justify that the invariants are preserved. In other words, starting from a correct situation the function shall not violate the sub-properties. The reasoning may use additional hypotheses which are exported as requirements to different sub-systems (CBI, ZC, CC...). For example in our case, the location reports sent by CC must be correct.

As the reasoning is formalised, an irrefutable demonstration is obtained based on well-defined and non-ambiguous notions. The advantage is that the reasoning is based on properties and not on the scenario anymore. This is preponderant since the scenario based analysis cannot be guaranteed to be complete.

Concrete Example. Let us illustrate this approach on a specific function that deals with a train becoming talkative and associating an identified envelope to it. Figure 1 illustrates this function of the ZC. Before the execution of the function the concerned train was associated with a non-identified envelope also covering, for instance, two other non-talkative trains. This function modifies the status of several notions used in the definition of the key sentences:

- Talkative and non-talkative trains.
- Identified and non-identified envelopes.

As the status of these notions are updated, we have to argue how and why the key sentences are preserved. This requires us to prove that when this ZC function associates a train to an identified envelope:

- The concerned train is physically located in this envelope.
- All other non-talkative trains are still covered by non-identified envelopes.

As several non-talkative trains may have been covered by the initial non-identified envelope which becomes identified, non-identified envelopes have to be created over these potential non-talkative trains. The creation of the two new non-identified envelopes is mandatory. Indeed, without it the proof in the AtelierB (presented in the next subsection) will not succeed.

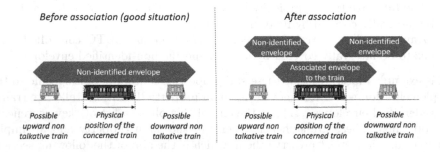

Fig. 1. Talkative train envelope association

3.4   Step 4: Tooled Verification

The method is tooled as well. Indeed, nothing prevents errors in manual proofs hence certified automatic provers are required. A powerful tool containing both modelling environment and provers is AtelierB. It allows to model the reasoning in B language and is able to prove that the sub-properties are preserved by all the functions modelled. When all the functions of the system are "completely proved" the system is proven safe. Another advantage of the B-Model is the possibility of using a second convenient tool: PROB [10]. This tool allows to check and animate the reasoning to check that the model matches the expected system behaviour. The application on our study is presented in Sect. 4.

3.5   Illustration

Figure 2 illustrates the different phases of the method described above: It emphasises that when the reasoning or the proof cannot be concluded this can be due to two reasons:

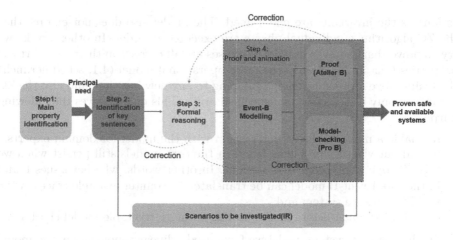

Fig. 2. Property-driven approach to ensure safety and availability of systems.

- either the reasoning/model is at fault and we have to go back to the previous step with additional hypotheses (corrections)
- or a fault is detected which leads to scenarios to be investigated. In this case, new key sentences may have to be derived or a safety investigation needs to be carried out.

4   Proof and Animation

In this section we illustrate how tooling has supported our methodology.

4.1   Abstract System Model

The formal development used in our activities contains three types of models:

1. core Event-B models for **proof**, containing relevant ZC operations (i.e., phases of the ZC algorithm) and environment events. They contain the key sentences as invariants.
2. instantiated core models for **animation** and model checking by PROB. These "extend" the core Event-B models and fix the size of the track and the maximum number of trains,
3. a more operational model (scheduler.mch) which enforces a cyclic sequencing of the ZC operations and limits environment train movements to more "natural" progressions.

In the core Event-B models we use two types of events: those which are phases of the ZC's algorithm, e.g., insert_talkative_train corresponding to Fig. 1, and the events which relate to the environment. The core model itself behaves in a very non-deterministic way: any environment evolution is allowed as long as the invariants are maintained. The model also does not enforce that the ZC algorithm's individual phases are executed in order. In other words, we try to prove that the ZC's individual phases are all correct on their own, wrt the properties (aka invariants). In the more operational model (4.1, scheduler.mch) the trains move forward instead of jumping to any new location, and also the ZC events can only be triggered in a specified order. This model serves the following purposes:

- to enable a more "realistic" interaction with the model for domain experts,
- to find out whether problems found in the core models still persist when we take ZC operation order into account. In other words, whether issues found in the core Event-B model can be translated to counter example traces of the real ZC software system and
- to restrict the non-determinism, leading to more tractable model checking.

In the abstract system model we have used a linear topology, i.e. the model focuses on one particular path through the topology and puts particular emphasis on chaining breakings (points), as a lot of complexity in the ZC's operation stems from dealing with chaining breakings. The topology is modelled as an interval (i.e., a set of abscissas). Possible chaining breakings are a subset of said abscissas.

4.2   Validation Tools

We applied animation and model checking in addition to and ideally before proof. This way we could provide concrete scenarios, detect missing invariants, well-definedness errors, and deadlocks before attempting the (time-consuming) proof. For these validations we used the animator and model checker PROB [10]. We used both the command-line version of PROB as well as a new graphical interface (called ProB2-UI) based on JavaFX.

Visualization. To enable animation we extended PROB to support more of Atelier B's Event-B syntax.[1] To provide a graphical visualisation of the state of the model we wrote a ProB2-UI plugin, shown in Fig. 3. In the top row the occupation status of the secondary detection devices is shown. Below we see the trains on the track, including their status (talkative or not talkative). For talkative trains we also see the minimum and maximum locations representing the location error (shown as the yellow area surrounding the red train). The track including a switch is shown, in the example given we have an active chaining breaking over the switch (represented by the star), i.e. the switch is either in reverse position or its position is unknown to the ZC. Below the track all envelopes within their external extremities are shown: colour and text depict the kind of envelope. The last line is reserved for the ZC itself: we can see the last command executed by the ZC, the colour shows the status of the ZC, i.e. if it is busy or not. Figure 3 actually shows an invariant violation uncovered by model checking (on a faulty, preliminary version of our model).

---

[1] PROB did already support Event-B within the Rodin platform, but for this development we used Event-B as supported by Atelier-B.

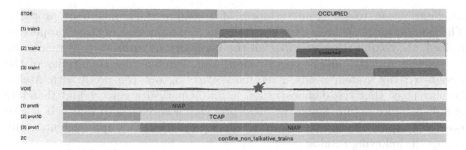

Fig. 3. JavaFX visualisation of the state of the ZC model

Model Checking. Model checking was used as means of an additional validation before the proof. Exhaustive verification, however, was only possible for very small topologies. For example, for 3 trains, 6 protections and a topology with one point and abscissas from 0..4, and fixing many parameters to one particular value, exhaustive verification results in 66,056,638 states. But even small increases in the above parameters the state spaces becomes so large as to be intractable for explicit state model checking. Still, non-exhaustive model checking was useful to detect well-definedness errors, errors before proof, and find concrete scenarios leading to certain desired (or undesired states). In particular, we have implemented a new directed model checking feature to extend a given scenario to a full fledged counter example if it exists.

Proof. The formal proof has been performed using Atelier B release 4.5.0 which will be made public during the second semester of 2019. Atelier B generates proof obligations every time a variable is modified; its new value must satisfy the expressed invariants. Atelier B verifies the systematic principle described in Sect. 3.2: starting from a valid situation, every event in the model should preserve the invariants.

In our case, the developed model results in a few hundred proof obligations, around 55% of which are automatically proved. The others had to be done manually. This part of the activity consists in transmitting the reasoning that has been done "on paper" before, in order to validate that it does not contain logical mistakes or implicit assumptions. This part of the project detected several errors leading to invariants adjustment.

Once an event is proved (i.e., a ZC function), we know that it doesn't create any unsafe situation. Otherwise a scenario that violates the property can be given. Once the entire model is proved, we know that the main property is always true: the design is compliant with the system expectation.

5   Results

The presented formal analysis provides a fresh look at design, by isolating each involved concept, whether internal or from another subsystem, and associating its contribution to safety in the form of a clear and unambiguous property. The overall safety of the system results from a combination of these properties. Indeed, the combination provides all the necessary hypotheses to demonstrate the safety property under consideration, and therefore the conformity of the design wrt the system needs. Eventually, carrying out the proof with Atelier B guarantees that the demonstration is mathematically correct and therefore is indisputable. In our study, the main property was related to safety. It is also possible to apply the approach for functional properties. This approach naturally brings the following results:

- Retrieve and/or explain clearly the fundamental design principles.
- Exhibit and explain formally the assumptions made about the studied function inputs.
- Retrieve and formalise the historical reasoning of the designers and keep track of their justification.
- Identify complexity that is not necessary to maintain the properties and has become useless or obsolete, providing opportunities for functional improvements and performance gains.
- Possibly detect corner cases where the properties are not fulfilled, providing the safety teams the elements necessary to analyse the consequences.
- Propose design improvements.

Industrial Relevance. Beyond the results presented above, this approach constitutes a real alternative to "traditional" design and safety analysis methods based on scenario analysis.

From the point of view of the system teams at the origin of the design, the key phrases are an aid: just remember that each function that can be executed preserves these properties. It is no longer necessary to try to imagine all possible combinations of functions. In return, any newly developed function must preserve the invariant properties.

From the safety point of view, an implemented function (or an association of functions) is safe as long as it preserves the key invariant properties as exhibited by this study. To validate the safety of an evolution, it is therefore sufficient to require a formal demonstration, and to ensure that it doesn't contain logical errors. For this part, the study already carried out is accompanied by models supported by Atelier B in which any evolution can be mathematically proven even before it enters the traditional software development cycle.

From a practical point of view, it does not seem reasonable to ask the domain experts to produce this proof, but rather to a formal team working in parallel and in collaboration with them.

Integrating this type of approach into an industrial development process amounts to moving the analysis effort towards the upstream phase of development. The goal is to disclose as soon as possible safety defects that otherwise would be disclosed later (during the validation phase, or worse during commissioning) and thus significantly reduce development costs.

6 Conclusion, Related and Future Work

Related Work. Several examples using Event-B for system modelling, notably one railway example, can be found in Abrial's book [2]. Several Event-B models were developed for the ETCS hybrid level 3 principles [1,6,9,11]. ClearSy has used Event-B in two previous projects [5,12] (Flushing Line for NYCT and Octys for RATP) to perform a safety analysis of CBTC systems. These were system-wide safety analyses and did not make the link to a software component, such as in the presented case. We have applied a combination of proof, animation and model checking, not just proof alone. This has helped us uncover some subtle issues, and avoid positing axioms which cannot be satisfied in practice.

Future Work. In this work we have linked the Event-B system model of a ZC component of a CBTC with its software model. In future, we would like to examine the correctness of distributed system functions, which require to examine at least two software components (such as the CC and the ZC). On the tooling level, we want to improve the integration of proof and validation activities: certain properties are important for proof but disturb animation and vice-versa. We want to make it easier in PROB to hide certain axioms from the animator, so that the animation and proof teams can work on the same formal model. We also think about developing a tool for exploration of the CBTC specification by domain experts without requiring B knowledge. In other words, we would like to allow domain experts to formalise and check properties by direct interaction with a graphical representation of the model. We want to use PROB to generate MC/DC tests from the Event-B specification to test that the B software model is a correct implementation of the ZC component.

Conclusion. We presented a new methodology which allows us to formally prove that a system design and implementation are correct with relation to a given property. This methodology was validated through consequent industrial application: The train tracking function of Alstom CBTC representing around 12000 code lines and hundred pages of specifications.

We emphasise that our property based is an alternative to the scenario approach. The main advantages and industrial relevance of this approach were discussed in Sect. 5 and are summarised here:

- It is complete. Contrary to the scenario approach, no cases can be forgotten. Indeed, we do not need to think about all possible failure cases, but only need to show that the invariants are preserved.
- The methodology brings immediate, concrete and understandable results.
- It could easily be integrated into an existing design process. It can also be conducted independently.
- It is useful both for system validation and for system evolution.

In addition this method can be supported with tools for automatic proving (such as AtelierB) and for model exploration (such as PROB).

Up to our knowledge this method is the first, applied on a real industrial system, which links real entities (such as e.g. physical train positions) and variables in executable software.

Acknowledgements. We would like to thank David Deharbe, Etienne Prun and Fabien Belmonte for useful contributions to this research. We thank David Schneider for developing the visualisation plugin seen in Fig. 3.

References

1. Abrial, J.: The ABZ-2018 case study with Event-B. In: Butler et al. [3], pp. 322–337
2. Abrial, J.-R.: Modeling in Event-B: System and Software Engineering. Cambridge University Press, Cambridge (2010)
3. Butler, M., Raschke, A., Hoang, T.S., Reichl, K. (eds.): ABZ 2018. LNCS, vol. 10817. Springer, Cham (2018). https://doi.org/10.1007/978-3-319-91271-4
4. ClearSy: Atelier B, User and Reference Manuals. Aix-en-Provence, France (2009). http://www.atelierb.eu/
5. Comptier, M., Déharbe, D., Molinero-Perez, J., Mussat, L., Thibaut, P., Sabatier, D.: Safety analysis of a CBTC system: a rigorous approach with Event-b. In: Fantechi, A., Lecomte, T., Romanovsky, A.B. (eds.) RSSRail 2017. LNCS, vol. 10598, pp. 148–159. Springer, Heidelberg (2017). https://doi.org/10.1007/978-3-319-68499-4_10
6. Dghaym, D., Poppleton, M., Snook, C.F.: Diagram-led formal modelling using iUML-B for hybrid ERTMS level 3. In: Butler et al. [3], pp. 338–352
7. Dollé, D., Essamé, D., Falampin, J.: B dans le transport ferroviaire. L'expérience de Siemens Transportation Systems. Technique et Science Informatiques **22**(1), 11–32 (2003)
8. Essamé, D., Dollé, D.: B in large-scale projects: the canarsie line CBTC experience. In: Julliand, J., Kouchnarenko, O. (eds.) B 2007. LNCS, vol. 4355, pp. 252–254. Springer, Heidelberg (2006). https://doi.org/10.1007/11955757_21
9. Hansen, D., et al.: Using a formal B model at runtime in a demonstration of the ETCS hybrid level 3 concept with real trains. In: Butler et al. [3], pp. 292–306
10. Leuschel, M., Butler, M.J.: ProB: an automated analysis toolset for the B method. STTT **10**(2), 185–203 (2008)
11. Mammar, A., Frappier, M., Fotso, S.J.T., Laleau, R.: An Event-B model of the hybrid ERTMS/ETCS level 3 standard. In: Butler et al. [3], pp. 353–366
12. Sabatier, D.: Using formal proof and B method at system level for industrial projects. In: Lecomte, T., Pinger, R., Romanovsky, A. (eds.) RSSRail 2016. LNCS, vol. 9707, pp. 20–31. Springer, Cham (2016). https://doi.org/10.1007/978-3-319-33951-1_2

Formal Verification

Interlocking Formal Verification at Alstom Signalling

Camille Parillaud[1]([✉]), Yoann Fonteneau[2], and Fabien Belmonte[1]

[1] Alstom Transport SA., 48 rue Albert Dhalenne, Saint-Ouen, France
camille.parillaud@alstomgroup.com
[2] Systerel, Toulouse, France

Abstract. Over the past decade, the growing number of safety-critical software in the railway signalling industry has led customers and industrials to look for efficient, cost-effective, verification and validation techniques. Formal methods, which have proven to be applicable and beneficial in terms of accuracy and completeness, are good candidates. However, they are still far from being used systematically for the verification of all safety-critical railway signalling systems. In order to evaluate their applicability, Alstom successfully experimented on its interlocking systems the model checking methods and tools developed by Systerel. This article describes the methodology used to industrialize this experimental model checking application process.

Keywords: Railway signalling · Formal verification · Industrial usage · Interlocking · Safety-critical systems

1 Introduction

This article presents the interlocking formal verification performed at Alstom Signalling using Systerel Smart Solver (S3) model checking solution. Applying formal verification to interlocking systems is not new, several use cases are well known in the railway signalling domain (as shown in previous communication made by Systerel [2]). However, formal methods are neither used for all interlocking systems nor for all signalling applications. This article argues that formal verification of interlocking system is a step forward to introduce the recent development of formal methods (such as optimization of model checking tools) in railway signalling applications. This is a first step towards building an industry-specific methodology. It starts with a presentation of the industrial issues of applying model checking to interlocking systems (Sect. 2), followed by a brief state-of-the-art (Sect. 3). Then the technical issue is described in Sect. 4. Section 5 explains how model checking has been introduced in Alstom's interlocking verification process before presenting the results in Sect. 6 and concluding in Sect. 7.

© Springer Nature Switzerland AG 2019
S. Collart-Dutilleul et al. (Eds.): RSSRail 2019, LNCS 11495, pp. 215–225, 2019.
https://doi.org/10.1007/978-3-030-18744-6_14

2   Industrial Issues

Alstom's signalling systems span from wayside equipment such as track circuits to complete signalling solutions such as Communication Based Train Control (CBTC) systems. The number of installed equipment since the 1970s grows each year and in particular the number of integrated solutions. For instance, the Urbalis 400 CBTC solution equips 56 lines around the world today and will soon be deployed on another 54 lines. This extensive number of systems in operation increases the risk exposure to safety-related hazards and potential accidents; hence the need for efficient verification and validation techniques.

Software development of signalling subsystems has intensively benefited from formal methods such as the B-Method which was used by Alstom to develop the safety critical software of its mainline and urban Automatic Train Protection Systems. However, formal methods have not been used at Alstom to develop legacy subsystems such as interlocking since they rely on old principles inherited from relay logic. Verification and validation of these old principles are performed by highly skilled individuals and knowledge management of these skills is hard to maintain. Moreover, several projects require the installation of CBTC systems interfaced with pre-existing relay-based interlocking systems which must be adapted to the CBTC features. Alstom looked for a way to capture and formalize critical knowledge of such systems, as well as an efficient method to validate the new and the pre-existing interlocking systems.

2.1   Limits and Difficulties of Classical Verification and Validation Process

The classical verification and validation process of interlocking subsystems relies on wide testing campaigns performed on virtual stations. These stations are conceived so that as many functional scenarios as possible are included. Their design and implementation are difficult and time-consuming activities. It is especially hard to demonstrate that all safety-related scenarios have been correctly tested. Indeed, some ripple effects due to modifications can be hard to foresee and test on a virtual station. When dealing with existing relay-based interlocking systems which have been improved and optimized over the years, extracting the principles and the associated safety concepts is a challenging task. The assessment of the potential impact on the global system functions and safety requires important effort.

2.2   Expected Results from Formal Verification

For these reasons, Alstom is introducing formal methods in the verification and validation process of its interlocking systems. Indeed, these methods are based on mathematical logic and they ensure an exhaustive and sound verification of the system. The objective is to formally verify conventionally developed interlocking systems whether they are computer-based or relay-based, prior to site operation. Model checking is particularly suitable to verify that systems always satisfy a set of properties and since the development of the interlocking system is already performed, formal development is not adapted. This is why model checking has been favoured to other formal methods. The use of model checking in Alstom's interlocking verification process will be presented in the following sections of this article. The expected benefits are numerous and they will improve the competitiveness of the system on which the formal methods were used.

Exhaustive and Unambiguous. As previously mentioned, formal methods are founded on mathematical theories. They aim at building precise models of the system or software under development. Their common objective is to eliminate any ambiguity or imprecision which may come from the use of natural language in order for the results to be unambiguous. They are sound and ensure that the system is exhaustively verified or proved. Consequently, using formal methods eases the approval process of the system.

Shortened Time-to-Market and Costs Reduction. In the railway domain, the majority of safety-related faults which are discovered late in the lifecycle of the project (which are therefore problematic) are linked to unlikely scenarios that were not foreseen beforehand. The completeness of the proof or verification obtained with the use of formal methods allows discovering these safety-related scenarios early in the development lifecycle. The necessary modifications can then be made earlier and the amount of required rework will be limited. This implies a substantial amount of time saved and costs reduction at project level.

2.3 Limitations

Despite the significant advantages they present, formal methods also have their limitations. The first limitation is that the proof (or verification) performed formally is based on a set of safety properties that are manually determined beforehand. If this set of properties is erroneous or incomplete, the value of the formal proof (or verification) is of little use. It is therefore crucial to establish a robust process to list the necessary and sufficient safety properties to be proven. The process Alstom uses is presented in Sect. 5. Moreover, formal methods are efficient when they contribute to the safety demonstration of the system. However, when it comes to proving non safety-related properties, these are very complicated to determine as they must include all possible functional requirements cases to be provable.

3 State of the Art

Interlocking systems, with their inherent boolean nature and overwhelming combinational complexity have been a privileged target of model checking techniques. Pioneering work started as soon as sufficiently powerful model-checker software came into existence in the early 2000s (*e.g.* [1,3,8]). All these contributions were analyzing manually crafted models of interlocking systems, somewhat distant from the real installed safety critical systems. Moreover, at that time, it had always been concluded that the huge state space of these systems could not be handled without over-simplifications and/or splitting and compositional verification techniques.

Over the past decade, model checking techniques have matured, increasing the analysis power. After 2010, a renewed interest arose, leading to novel attempts to solve the problem (e.g. [4–6]). Great progress has been made that demonstrates the feasibility of the formal safety verification of real-world interlocking systems.

In this article, following the Systerel Smart Solver (S3) workflow presented in a previous article (see [2]), we describe the use of these techniques in an industrial and normative context.

4 Technical Issue

The formal safety verification of an interlocking system requires both a solution to perform the analyses and the safety properties to be analysed under a number of environment constraints. This section focuses on the formal verification solution, and Sect. 5 describes the safety properties.

Following the description given in [2], an S3 formal safety verification solution involves the development of a translator from a given interlocking application (given in its specific language/format) to a model of this application in HLL, the S3 tool-chain input modelling language [7]. This model of the safety critical application shall be *sound*, in that it shall preserve the semantics of the real application, so that any property proved on this model is valid on the real application. A second translator is also needed to translate a description of the track layout controlled by the given interlocking application. These data, usually given in some form of database, contain the objects present on the tracks (e.g. signals, points, routes, ...), and relations between these objects (e.g. origin signal of a route, points of a route, ...). They are translated in HLL as hierarchical enumerations of objects, and predicates on these objects. These two translators are specific to the given family of interlocking applications.

The obtained HLL models can then be concatenated with the desired safety properties and environment constraints formalized in HLL to obtain the analysis model. This model can then be analyzed by the standard S3 tool-chain. It is first given to an expander tool that transforms the HLL model into a semantically equivalent model in LLL, a purely boolean subset of HLL suitable for S3 analysis. Two main types of analyses may be performed.

Bounded Model Checking (BMC). In this type of analysis, scenarios of increasing length are investigated in order to find counter-examples of some of the provided safety properties. Such a scenario, exercising the inputs of the interlocking application (i.e. its sensors) in a way compatible with the provided environment constraints, leads the application from its initial state to a state violating a safety property. For each safety property, the result of this analysis is thus either a scenario violating the property, or the assurance that this property holds for every scenario up to a given length (the higher the length, the longer the analysis will take). This type of analysis is the first one to be attempted on a new system or a new property, until no more counter-examples can be found, and the BMC has reached a length large enough to have an intimate conviction that the non-violated properties hold.

Induction over Time. In this mode, the analysis engine attempts to prove that some safety property is valid, which means that there exist no scenario, whatever the length, that leads the interlocking application to a violation of this safety property (e.g [2,4]). This is performed using standard induction over the length of the scenario. A first analysis shows that the property holds for every scenario of length 1, and a second shows that if the property holds in some state of the system, it will hold in any state reachable from this state in one transition of the interlocking application. When these two analyses are successful, the property is proved valid. If the first analysis fails, a counter-example to the property has been found (similarly to the BMC analyses). However, when the second analysis fails it either means that the property can be falsified with a long scenario (longer than the length reached by a BMC on this property), or more often, that the property is non-inductive. This means that the analysis engine has found a scenario (called a step-counter-example) starting from a state of the system in which the property holds, and which leads with a single transition of the interlocking application to a state violating this property. This means that this starting state is unreachable from the initial state of the system. The way to deal with these non-inductive properties is by developing induction enforcing lemmas, as explained in Sect. 5.

The analysis process starts by using the BMC strategy repeatedly and correcting either the expression of the safety properties or the bugs found in the interlocking application until no more counter-examples are found for a large length. The process then reverts to an induction strategy, used iteratively to find all lemmas until all properties are proved.

However, in the EN50128 normative context, this is not sufficient. This standard asks for some insurance on the results of the verification (T2) tool.

To achieve a high degree of confidence compatible with EN50128, a second set of translators is developed in an independent way (different development team and different programming language), a second independent expander from HLL to LLL is also used. The resulting LLL models of the two translations expanded by the two expanders are combined by a tool that creates a new LLL file expressing that the two models are *sequentially-equivalent* (*i.e.* provided with the same inputs sequences, they produce the same output sequences). This resulting LLL file is then given to the S3 analysis engine to prove the equivalence. Moreover, the S3 analysis engine is equipped with a proof-log/proof-check mechanism, such that for each proof that it finds (proofs of equivalence and of the safety properties), it outputs a proof-log file containing this proof expressed in a formalized proof system, and the correctness of each proof-log is independently verified by a simple proof-checker software.

Therefore, the S3 solution is compatible with an EN50128 T2 verification tool certification.

5 Industrial Process

5.1 Determination of Safety Properties

The first step towards proving that an interlocking system is safe through model checking is to determine the safety properties that this system must satisfy. These safety properties must be as high-level as possible in order to maintain a black box approach and remain independent from the design of the interlocking system. Thus, the safety properties are less likely to be biased and to hide a possibly dangerous scenario. The identification of the adequate safety properties is performed through the "Deductive Identification of Safety Properties" which is a three-step process.

Deductive Tree Analysis. First, a top-down analysis is conducted. It aims at identifying a comprehensive set of high-level functional safety properties to be satisfied by the interlocking system. It is performed independently from the detailed design, i.e. with a black-box approach, knowing only the external interfaces of the interlocking. Thanks to a user-level knowledge of the functions the system must implement and to the definition of its scope, the influence of the system on its external environment is studied based on the two following criteria: What are the hazards that are likely to occur in the scope of the interlocking system? How can the interlocking protect against these hazards by use of its means of interaction with its external environment? This identification of prohibited scenarios allows modelling the hazards associated with the functional behaviour of the interlocking system. The properties, thus specified, ensure that the system does prevent these hazards from occurring.

Failure Modes and Effects Analysis (FMEA). The previous deductive approach has the advantage of being completely independent from the product. However, some risks can originate from the design choices. This is why a FMEA, which is inductive (or bottom-up), is performed. Instead of focusing on the hazards and looking for the possible causes, it aims at determining the possible effects of a failure of each function performed by the interlocking system and defining mitigations should the risk be safety-related.

Convergence. In order to ensure the completeness of the list of safety properties, the two sets of requirements coming both from the deductive and the inductive analyses are traced. This ensures that the high level properties of the system do cover all possible hazards related to the interlocking system.

The safety properties are the result of this traceability. They are based on the wording of the requirements coming from the deductive analysis. Should there be a requirement from the inductive analysis that cannot be traced with any requirement of the deductive analysis, a new safety property is added, based on the formalization of this requirement. Once this last task is performed, the output is a complete set of safety properties expressed in natural language that will be proven with model checking after being formalized.

5.2 Modelling

Environment. In order to adequately simulate the inputs of the interlocking system, a model of its environment is created. This model describes the behaviour of the systems interfaced with the interlocking by constraining their outputs which are inputs of the interlocking system. This prevents impossible scenarios from being considered and allows the proof to focus on realistic ones. For instance, an impossible scenario could be a train not moving continuously along the track.

The environment of the model can also include a similar system to the one that is being proved (two systems managing different geographical parts of the track). In that case, each system is proved separately. If some hypotheses must be made on the behaviour of the first system to prove the second, they must be proved when performing the proof of the first system. As the interlocking conditions are different in the two systems, this methodology does not create any reasoning loop and the proof of both systems stands. The asymmetrical conditions come from track layout deployment rules.

Safety Properties. The model also includes the safety properties that have been previously established. These properties rely on refined concepts that must be formally modelled in order to rigorously remove any ambiguity that could be introduced by using natural language.

Interlocking System. The model of the interlocking application and the track layout data are obtained as described in Sect. 4.

Modelling Risks. In order for the proof to be effective and reliable, some precautions must be taken during the modelling phase. It is necessary for the model to be as permissive as possible. It must allow all possible scenarios to occur, otherwise a safety-related hazard could be missed during the proof process. Thus, the constraints on the inputs must be carefully defined and checked with this risk in mind.

5.3 Proof Process

The proof process is described in the Fig. 1. In this process there are two manual tasks:

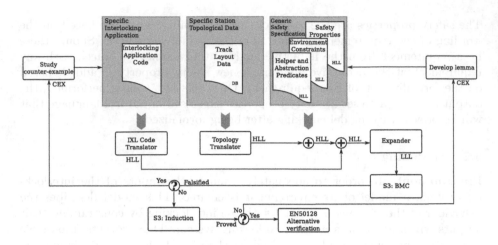

Fig. 1. S3 formal verification process implemented at Alstom

Study of Counter-Examples. This task consists in exploring the counter-example step by step to understand why a property is falsified. The bounded model checking can find problems of three different categories:

- Environment modelling error: the model of the railway environment is too abstract. The error is not reproducible on the track. Some constraints have to be added to remove this behavior. In this case, the environment model has to be fixed.
- Data error: there is an error in the data (chaining error, definition of flanking, ...) or the data of the interlocking are not compatible with some interlocking principles usage restrictions. In this case, the track layout data has to be fixed.
- Principles errors: error in the interlocking principles or the principles are not compatible with the specific track configurations. In this case, the Specific interlocking application has to be fixed.

Development of Lemmas. When a property is not proved, a step-counter-example is generated. This counter-example is used to develop a lemma. A lemma is a relation that holds between variables of the system. It is thus similar in essence to a safety property, except that a property is usually expressed only in terms of the inputs and outputs of the system whereas a lemma may also rely on internal variables. Also, a safety property characterizes some aspect of the safety of the system, whereas a lemma may be more general. Looking at the unreachable state found in a step-counter-example, together with the knowledge of the system design and especially of the principles ensuring its safety, it is usually rather simple to express a relation between variables of the model that eliminates this unreachable state.

5.4   Insertion of Model Checking into Alstom's Pre-existing Process

Interlocking Development Process. Alstom's classical interlocking development process is based on the development of a generic product which is then customized through data to the different specific applications required by commercial projects. This separation between generic product and specific application ensures a high level of reusability of the different activities involved in the development of the specific application (design, validation, safety demonstration). Regarding formal verification, it means that the model of the environment and safety properties, which is based only on the generic product principles and functions, is applicable to all specific applications based on the same version of the generic product. When the interlocking principles are updated, usually in order to incorporate a new functional gap for a client, so is the generic product which in turn means the model has to be adapted as well. The proof, however, is always performed on a specific application as it requires the instantiated principles of the interlocking system.

Occurrence in the Lifecycle of the Interlocking System. The proof is performed on instantiated principles. It can therefore occur as soon as the first version of these instantiated principles is available. The modelling phase can start earlier though, during the design phase, as long as the principles and functions of the system have been defined. The proof must then be repeated for each update of the instantiated principles and system data.

6   Results

6.1   Technical Results

The S3 formal verification solution has been applied on several Smartlock 400 GP interlocking applications on multiple subway lines (Amsterdam, Lusail, Guadalajara...). On the larger stations (1312 routes, 235 points, 398 signals, and 587 secondary detection devices), the analysis took up to 24 h of CPU time on an intel i5-4670. While this duration is acceptable for the long BMC runs used to find falsification of the safety properties, it reveals a burden when it comes to the development of lemmas. For this phase of the project, a custom utility tool has been developed to allow the splitting of a station on a small sub-region of its track layout to allow for faster analysis time. However the final proofs are obviously performed on the whole track-layout.

A total of 114 properties have been formalized, and 533 lemmas were needed to ultimately prove these properties. During the analysis, a total of 5 iterations have been needed to mature the environment modelling (driven by 5 environment modelling errors). The various long BMC runs have unveiled 3 data errors (mainly around the definition of the flanking of points), and a single unlikely principle error. After correction of all these errors, all considered interlocking applications have been proved to respect the safety properties.

6.2   Related to the Industrial Process

As implemented, model checking allows a non intrusive verification of the system design. Thus, the design process of the interlocking system is not impacted by the introduction of formal verification in the safety demonstration process. It is only the verification and validation activities that are impacted as the model checking proof can replace the safety-related tests performed for the interlocking system, that is to say about 30% of the required tests. Indeed, the model of the interlocking system is obtained by two independant translators and a proof of equivalence between the two translations is established, ensuring the model is totally compliant with the source code. Incidentally, the safety demonstration can be provided more quickly when using model checking compared to the classical verification process. This compensates the additional modelling work required by the model checking process.

Moreover, the use of model checking has proven to be beneficial as valid counter-examples (whether they were related to the data or the interlocking principles) were found earlier than with the classical process on the different lines it was tested on. This confirms that introducing model checking in the interlocking system verification and validation process does have added value.

7   Conclusion

Introducing model checking in Alstom's verification and validation process of interlocking systems has proven to be efficient as safety-related counter-examples have been discovered more quickly than with the traditional process. In addition, model checking is performed on a set of instantiated interlocking principles, whereas the traditional verification process uses the generic principles. Therefore, using model checking provides additional confidence in the safety demonstration compared to the traditional process because the proof uses the real data of the specific application. Today, this approach is applied on Alstom's largest interlocking project and the computation time is shorter than a day.

However, the sensibility to complex stations is linked to the lemmas identification for reuse. Indeed, the lemmas that must be defined for the inductive proof can be difficult to find as they must be adequate for all track configurations existing in the specific application. This means they could have to be modified when switching from one application to another.

Overall, this new process was deemed beneficial and will be used on new Alstom interlocking systems in the future.

References

1. Bernardeschi, C., Fantechi, A., Gnesi, S., Mongardi, G.: Proving safety properties for embedded control systems. In: Hlawiczka, A., Silva, J.G., Simoncini, L. (eds.) EDCC 1996. LNCS, vol. 1150, pp. 321–332. Springer, Heidelberg (1996). https://doi.org/10.1007/3-540-61772-8_46

2. Breton, N., Fonteneau, Y.: S3: proving the safety of critical systems. In: Lecomte, T., Pinger, R., Romanovsky, A. (eds.) RSSRail 2016. LNCS, vol. 9707, pp. 231–242. Springer, Cham (2016). https://doi.org/10.1007/978-3-319-33951-1_17

3. Eisner, C.: Using symbolic model checking to verify the railway stations of Hoorn-Kersenboogerd and Heerhugowaard. In: Pierre, L., Kropf, T. (eds.) CHARME 1999. LNCS, vol. 1703, pp. 99 100. Springer, Heidelberg (1999). https://doi.org/10.1007/3-540-48153-2_9

4. Haxthausen, A.E., Peleska, J., Pinger, R.: Applied bounded model checking for interlocking system designs. In: Counsell, S., Núñez, M. (eds.) SEFM 2013. LNCS, vol. 8368, pp. 205–220. Springer, Cham (2014). https://doi.org/10.1007/978-3-319-05032-4_16

5. James, P., et al.: Verification of solid state interlocking programs. In: Counsell, S., Núñez, M. (eds.) SEFM 2013. LNCS, vol. 8368, pp. 253–268. Springer, Cham (2014). https://doi.org/10.1007/978-3-319-05032-4_19

6. Mota, J.L., et al.: Safety demonstration for a rail signaling application in nominal and degraded modes using formal proof. In: Formal Methods Applied to Industrial Complex Systems, pp. 71–113, July 2014. https://doi.org/10.1002/9781119004707.ch4

7. Ordioni, J., Breton, N., Colaço, J.L.: HLL vol 2.7 modelling language specification. Other STF-16-01805, RATP, May 2018. https://hal.archives-ouvertes.fr/hal-01799749

8. Winter, K.: Model checking railway interlocking systems, February 2002. https://doi.org/10.1145/563857.563836

Survey on Formal Methods and Tools in Railways: The ASTRail Approach

Alessio Ferrari[1]([envelope]) [iD], Maurice H. ter Beek[1] [iD], Franco Mazzanti[1] [iD],
Davide Basile[1,2] [iD], Alessandro Fantechi[1,2] [iD], Stefania Gnesi[1] [iD],
Andrea Piattino[3], and Daniele Trentini[3]

[1] ISTI–CNR, Pisa, Italy
{alessio.ferrari,m.terbeek,f.mazzanti,s.gnesi}@isti.cnr.it
[2] Università di Firenze, Florence, Italy
{davide.basile,alessandro.fantechi}@unifi.it
[3] SIRTI S.p.A., Genoa, Italy
{a.piattino,d.trentini}@sirti.it

Abstract. Formal methods and tools have been widely applied to the
development of railway systems during the last decades. However, no universally accepted formal framework has emerged, and railway companies
wishing to introduce formal methods have little guidance for the selection of the most appropriate methods and tools to adopt. A work package (WP) of the European project ASTRail, funded under the Shift2Rail
initiative, addresses this problem, by performing a survey that considers
scientific literature, international projects, and practitioners' perspectives to identify a collection of formal methods and tools to be applied
in railways. This paper summarises the current results of this WP. We
surveyed 114 scientific publications, 44 practitioners, and 8 projects to
come to a shortlist of 14 methods considered suitable for system modelling and verification in railways. The methods and tools were reviewed
according to a set of functional, language-related, and quality features.
The current paper extends the body of knowledge with a set of publicly
available documents that can be leveraged by companies for guidance on
formal methods selection in railway system development.

Keywords: Formal methods · Model-based development · Railways

1 Introduction

The railway field is characterised by its rigorous development processes and
its robust safety requirements. During the last decades, formal methods and
tools have been widely applied to the development of railway systems (cf.,
e.g., [1,4–6,8,9,11,12,14,15,17,18,20–25,28,29]). Formal methods are mentioned as highly recommended practices for SIL 3–4 platforms [10,14] by the
CENELEC EN 50128 standard for the development of software for railway control and protection systems. The extensive survey on applications of formal methods by Woodcock et al. [30], which includes a structured questionnaire submitted

© Springer Nature Switzerland AG 2019
S. Collart-Dutilleul et al. (Eds.): RSSRail 2019, LNCS 11495, pp. 226–241, 2019.
https://doi.org/10.1007/978-3-030-18744-6_15

to the participants of 56 projects, also identified the transport domain, including railways, as the one in which the largest number of projects including applications of formal methods has been performed. Relevant examples are the usage of the B method for developing railway signalling systems in France, like, e.g., Line 14 of the Paris Métro and the driverless Paris–Roissy Airport shuttle [1]. Another is the usage of Simulink/Stateflow for formal model-based development, code generation, model-based testing, and abstract interpretation in the development of the Metrô Rio ATP system [12]. Many projects have been also carried out, often in collaboration with national railway companies, for the verification of interlocking systems [7,16,18,27–29].

Also the EU's Shift2Rail initiative[1] considers formal methods to be fundamental to the provision of safe and reliable technological advances to increase the competitiveness of the railway industry. In particular, a specific call was issued asking for an analysis of the suitability of formal methods in supporting the transition to the next generation of ERTMS/ETCS signalling systems, which will include satellite-based train positioning, moving block distancing, and automatic driving. The Horizon 2020 Shift2Rail-RIA-777561 project ASTRail[2] (SAtellite-based Signalling and Automation SysTems on Railways along with Formal Method and Moving Block Validation) responds to this call. As partners of this project, we are involved in a specific work package (WP) of the ASTRail project, focussing on the contribution of formal methods to address this challenging transition; this WP operates in the following two phases:

1. An *analysis phase* dedicated to a comparison and evaluation of the main formal methods and tools that are currently being used in the railway industry to guarantee that software bugs do not jeopardise safety;
2. An *application phase* in which selected formal methods are used to model and analyse two main goals addressed by the project, namely moving block distancing and automatic driving, in order to validate that the methods are not only able to guarantee safety issues, but also—more in general—the long term reliability and availability of the software.

This paper reports on the first phase. It illustrates the results from a survey based on 114 publications and 8 projects, and a questionnaire filled in by 44 practitioners. Based on the results of the survey, a set of 14 formal tools have been analysed according to a set of functional, language-related, and quality features. Given the extensive amount of work, this paper only summarises the results. The interested reader can refer to our public deliverable [13] for further insights.

The remainder of the paper is structured as follows. In Sect. 2, an overview of the approach is provided. In Sects. 3–5, the results of a literature review, projects review, and questionnaire are presented. In Sect. 6, the tools review is presented. Section 7 provides final remarks.

---

[1] shift2rail.org.
[2] astrail.eu.

2   Context: Formal Methods and Tools in ASTRail

In this section, we briefly describe the context of our paper, namely the ASTRail project and its specific concern for formal methods and tools.

2.1   ASTRail Objectives

ASTRail is one of the Shift2Rail initiatives to increase the competitiveness of the European railway industry, in particular concerning the transition to the next generation of ERTMS/ETCS signalling systems, which will include satellite-based train positioning, moving block distancing, and automatic driving. ASTRail aims to introduce recent scientific results and methodologies as well as cutting-edge technologies from other transport sectors, in particular avionics and automotive, in the railway sector, leveraging on formal methods and tools for careful analyses of the resulting novel applications and solutions in terms of safety and performance.

One of the main focuses of ASTRail concerns the usage of the global navigation satellite system (GNSS) [26] for onboard train localisation. While satellite-based positioning systems have been in use for quite some time now in the avionics and automotive sectors to provide accurate positioning and distancing, the current train separation system is still based on fixed blocks (a block is the section of the track between two fixed points), implemented by specific equipment along the lines. One of ASTRail's aims is to define a *moving block* signalling [2] (according to which a safe zone around the moving train can be computed, thus optimising the line's exploitation) and to perform its hazard analysis. For this solution to work, it requires the precise absolute location, speed, and direction of each train, to be determined by a combination of sensors: active and passive markers along the track, as well as train-borne speedometers. One of the current challenges in the railway sector is to make such moving block signalling systems as effective and precise as possible, leveraging on an integrated solution for signal outages (think, e.g., of tunnels) and the problem of multipaths [26]. A related aim of the project is to study the possibility of deploying the resulting precise and reliable train localisation to improve *automatic driving* technologies in the railway sector.

2.2   Formal Methods and Tools in ASTRail

WP4 of the ASTRail project—discussed in this paper—aims to identify, on the basis of an analysis of the state of the art, of the past experiences of the involved partners and on work done in previous projects, the candidate set of formal and semi-formal techniques that appear as the most adequate to be used in the different phases of the conception, design, and development of railway systems in general, and of the class of signalling systems that is the subject of the ASTRail project in particular. In the following, when we will use the general term formal method, we will implicitly include also semi-formal methods, i.e., those methods that use languages for which the semantics is not formally defined but depends

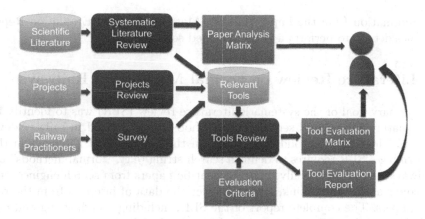

Fig. 1. Overview of the approach adopted in the analysis phase of WP4

on its execution engine. Furthermore, given that in practice a formal method always needs a support tool to be practically applicable, we will use the terms formal methods and formal tools interchangeably.

Figure 1 presents the overall approach applied in the context of this analysis phase. To address the goal of identifying the most mature formal/semi-formal languages and tools to be applied for the development of railway systems, we first performed a benchmarking task, by gathering information from three different sources: Scientific Literature, information from other Projects, and Railway Practitioners. Information from these sources were gathered through a Systematic Literature Review (SLR), a Projects Review and a Survey submitted to practitioners in the form of a questionnaire. The information was used to identify a set of main formal and semi-formal tools that appear to have been used in the railway domain (Relevant Tools in Fig. 1). Specifically, scientific literature was used as a primary source, since it provides more extensive information for guidance in the selection of relevant formal methods, while other projects and railway practitioners were used as sources to complement the information from the literature review. Furthermore, Evaluation Criteria for the different tools were defined based on collaboration between academic and industrial partners. These were applied to carefully evaluate the selected tools in a Tools Review.

The SLR produced a Paper Analysis Matrix (included as Annex 1 in our deliverable [13]), which may support the identification of the possible tools to be used depending on the specific railway system to be developed, and depending on the life-cycle phase to address. Furthermore, a Tool Evaluation Matrix (Annex 2) was defined for the different tools based on the tools review, and a Tool Evaluation Report (Annex 3), which provides details about the evaluated tools. The Tool Evaluation Matrix aims to support the selection of a formal or semi-formal tool for the railway problem at hand, based on specific preferences selected by the user of the matrix, concerning different evaluation criteria (e.g., functionalities supported by the tool, flexibility, usability) and guided by the information from the Paper Analysis Matrix. The Tool Evaluation Report provides details to perform a more informed selection.

3   Literature Review on Formal Methods in Railways

The primary goal of the systematic literature review (SLR) was to identify the most mature formal and semi-formal methods to be applied in railway development. The SLR was conducted based on the guidelines of Kitchenham [19]. Performing a SLR requires to define a search string (e.g., "formal methods" and "railways") to automatically retrieve scientific papers from search engines, such as Scopus and SpringerLink, and to extract the data of interests from the relevant papers. The complete report of the SLR, including search string and data analysis procedures, can be found in the project's deliverable. Here, we present the most relevant results.

The search was conducted on the 7th of December, 2017, while the analysis and data extraction were performed during the following months. From the initial search, and a first analysis of the abstracts of the papers, we identified a set of 411 potentially relevant papers to use for data extraction. Given the large amount of literature, and given that the focus of ASTRail is not on interlocking systems, we decided to focus solely on studies that do not deal exclusively with interlocking (hence, 124 papers focussing mainly on interlocking were excluded from our analysis). We manually analysed 294 papers to check their quality and to identify shorter versions of other papers in the set. We excluded 180 studies of low quality, according to our quality checklist, or which turned out to be shorter versions of other papers from the set. In the end, a set of 114 papers was used for data extraction. Therefore, in the following, we report on the data extracted from 114 high-quality, and non-interlocking studies.

When appropriate, the statistics in the following sections will distinguish between the total number of papers considered in the review, and the papers that had either an industrial evaluation, or that led to actually developed products. These papers, identified as IND/DEV in the statistics, were considered more important, since they show evidence of industrial maturity of a certain method or tool.

3.1   Languages from the Literature Review

Figure 2 reports the results in terms of number of papers that use certain semi-formal and formal languages. The list of languages is extensive, and, in the statistics, we do not report on languages that appeared in only one non-industrial paper. The most used input language, according to the analysed papers, is UML. This is a semi-formal language, which is often used in the early phases of system design, and it is typically translated into a formal language, like, e.g., the B language, in the considered studies. State Machines or Statecharts, in their different dialects, such as Simulink/Stateflow, are also frequently used. Also more formal

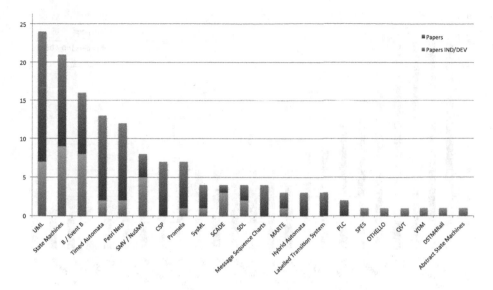

Fig. 2. Languages cited in the literature

languages, like Timed Automata, Petri Nets, CSP and Promela occur in a non-negligible amount of papers. However, these formal languages are mainly used in academic papers, while few industrial papers use them. Indeed, industrial papers tend to privilege State Machines, UML and B/Event B, or the SCADE language. It is also worth noticing that some industrial papers use several specific modelling languages, e.g. DSTM4Rail, that are used only in the context of the paper, but not in purely academic papers.

3.2 Tools from the Literature Review

Figure 3 reports the results in terms of number of papers that use a certain support tool. The list of tools mentioned in these papers is extremely extensive and each paper uses a different combination of methods and tools. Therefore, in the statistics we consider solely those tools for which there are at least two papers using the tool. The most used tools are those that belong to the B family: by summing up the contributions of Atelier B and ProB, we have 13 papers using these tools (Rodin is normally used in combination with Atelier B or ProB). By summing up the contribution of the two tools, they also dominate in industrial studies. These B method tools are followed by Simulink, UPPAAL, NuSMV, SPIN and other tools. We do not report the complete list of identified tools, since this is particularly long, and because here we are interested in identifying the most used tools for industrial studies in railways.

Interestingly, tools such as UPPAAL and SPIN, which appear frequently in the papers, are less frequent in industrial papers, in which, besides Atelier B, we see a greater usage of NuSMV, Simulink, Statemate and SCADE. We also see

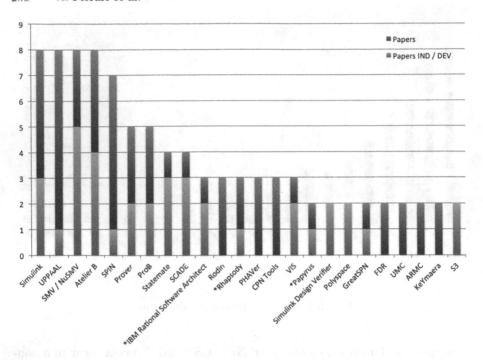

Fig. 3. Tools cited in the literature (tools marked with * support semi-formal modelling only, and do not have formal verification capabilities).

that, among the industrial papers, NuSMV appears to be more frequently used than other tools, such as, e.g., Simulink, which is inherently more industry oriented. We argue that this may be related to the particular capability of NuSMV to deal with the formal verification of large, realistic systems. Simulink is more oriented to modelling and simulation, and its formal verification tool, Simulink Design Verifier, although used in industrial works, has been rarely used for formal verification of large systems, but more of sub-components [12]. It should be noted, however, that in the inspected industrial papers, modelling and formal verification with NuSMV was not performed by railway practitioners, but by formal methods experts [9]. This suggests that the usage of state-of-the-art formal verification in industry still requires the support of formal methods experts to be actually effective in practice.

Overall, we notice that there is a large fragmentation of the papers in terms of used tools, and even the most used tools appear in no more than eight papers. This indicates that in the literature there is no clear, indisputable evidence or direction about which tools to employ in railway system development, and many tools may be adequate for the same purpose.

3.3 Maturity of Formal Methods for Railways

To identify the most mature tools, we consider the papers that are marked as IND/DEV, which indicate studies with industrial participation. We recall that the answer to this question is given for the railway context, and for non-interlocking systems. If we consider solely the tools and languages used in industrial papers, the most mature languages appear to be State Machines/Statecharts, UML and B/Event B. The literature shows an acceptable amount of evidence in this sense, with more than five industrial scientific publications for each language. Furthermore, non-industrial works also confirm the dominance of these languages. Less evidence is available for tools. If we arguably consider a tool to be industrially mature if it is used in at least two industrial studies, then the tools that can be considered mature are: Simulink, NuSMV, Atelier B, Prover, ProB, SCADE, IBM Rational Software Architect, Polyspace, and S3. Statemate also appears to be mature, but there is no recent work using the tool, and the tool appears not to be maintained anymore by IBM. A similar situation occurs for VIS, which does not appear to be used in recent publications, and does not appear to be currently maintained.

As mentioned, these considerations on tools are based on fragmented evidence from the literature, and no empirically grounded answer can be given on the most appropriate tools to employ for railway software development. However, in the context of ASTRail, this information was considered sufficient to be used as first guidance for selecting relevant tools to be evaluated during the tool review. It should also be noticed that these conclusions are applicable solely based on the published evidence, and do not take into account possible experience performed in industry with formal tools, if they do not have an associated scientific publication. To have an insight on tools that may be neglected by the literature, we complement the SLR with a Projects Review and a Survey with railway practitioners, which are presented in the following sections.

4   Projects on Formal Methods and Railways

The projects review has been based on the identification of projects from the last twenty years that have addressed the use of formal methods and tools in railway applications. The list of projects was identified based on pointers from the papers analysed in the SLR, and based on the knowledge of the authors. The available documentation for each project, like papers and web pages, has been examined in order to list the formal methods used. We found 14 projects which, starting from 1998 to this day, have addressed the use of formal methods and tools in railway applications. Among those projects, only 8 are not dealing solely with interlocking-related applications, namely: CRYSTAL, Deploy, DITTO, EuRailCheck, MBAT, OpenCOSS, OpenETCS-ITEA2, and PERFECT.

Figure 4 shows the adopted modelling languages, while Fig. 5 shows the tools used. The two figures substantially confirm the information extracted by the SLR, with a prominence of the "B eco-system", but otherwise confirming the

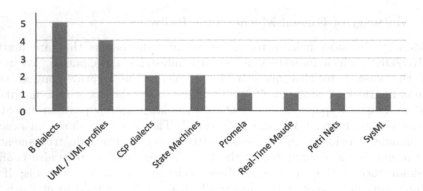

Fig. 4. Languages used in the projects

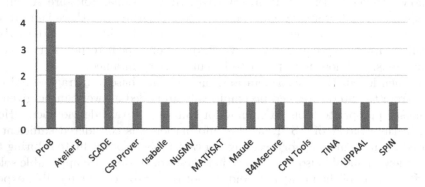

Fig. 5. Tools used in the projects

industrial preference to UML/SySML as modelling languages, followed by different state machine-based languages, and the importance of a commercial tool such as SCADE, emerging from a number of academic tools, mostly dedicated to formal verification.

5   Survey with Practitioners

For the non-trivial task of obtaining a significant amount of data from industrial stakeholders, a survey was carried out by means of a structured questionnaire, submitted to the participants of the RSSRail'17 conference[3], which is normally attended by academics and practitioners interested in applying formal methods in railways, and as such a promising source for a population sample that might be able to provide a well-informed judgment. We have reported and discussed the detailed results from the questionnaire in a recent paper [3]. Here, we report the ones that are more relevant in the context of this paper.

---

[3] http://conferences.ncl.ac.uk/rssrail/.

One of the goals of the questionnaire was to identify the current uptake of formal and semi-formal methods and tools in the railway sector according to the experience of practitioners. The first part of the questionnaire was dedicated to identify the respondents in terms of affiliation and experience in railways and in using formal/semi-formal methods and tools. The 44 respondents are balanced between academics (50%) and practitioners (50%, of which 47.7% from railway companies and 2.3% from aerospace and defense). A large percentage of respondents had several years of experience in railways (68% more than 3 years and 39% more than 10 years) and in formal methods (75% more than 3 years, 52% more than 10 years), which confirms that the sample provides informed opinions on the proposed questions.

Tools. Among the various questions, the respondents were also asked to list the tools used in the context of their projects. We believe it is interesting to separate the results of industrial respondents from those of academics. In Fig. 6, we can see that the large majority of industrial and academic respondents mentioned tools belonging to the B method family (e.g. B, ProB, Atelier B, Event B, RODIN). Actually, there are only slightly more industrial users than academic users in our sample, but we recall that the academic users were asked to report on their collaborative projects with industry. Other methods and tools mentioned by both groups are the Matlab toolsuite, including Simulink and Stateflow, SCADE, Petri nets/CPN tools and Monte Carlo Simulation: the overlap between tools used in industry and in academia is actually limited to these five. Industrial

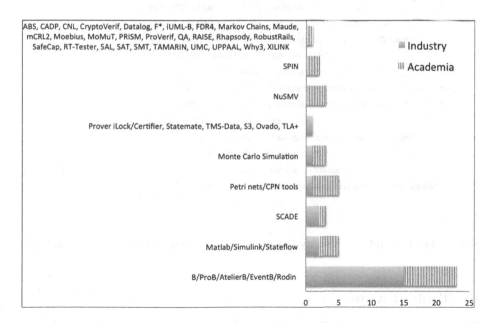

Fig. 6. Tools cited in the questionnaire (from [3])

users named a few other tools as well, whereas a large list of other tools has been named by academics, with popular model checkers like NuSMV and SPIN leading this list. An interpretation of this can be that a frequent pattern of collaboration between academia and industry includes the academic support in adopting advanced formal verification techniques inside a collaborative project.

Quality Aspects. Figure 7 reports the most relevant quality aspects that a tool should have to be applied in railways. The maturity of the tool (stability and industry readiness) is considered to be among the most relevant quality aspects by 75% of the respondents, followed by learnability by a railway software developer (45.5%), quality of documentation (43.2%), and ease of integration in the CENELEC process (36.4%). Overall, the most relevant quality aspects are associated with the usability of the tool. Less relevant are deployment aspects, such as platforms supported (9.1%) and flexible license management (11.4%). Interestingly, also the low cost of the tool (13.6%) appears to be a not so relevant feature. This is a reasonable finding. Indeed, the development and certification cost of railway products is high and, hence, if a company expects to reduce these costs through a formal tool, it can certainly tolerate the investment on the tool.

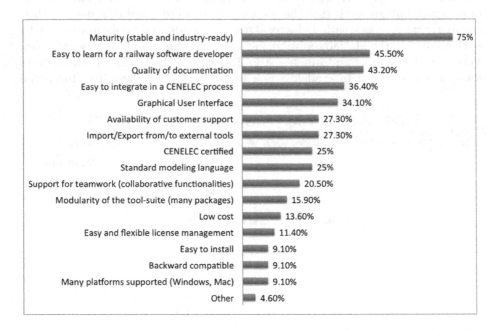

Fig. 7. The most relevant quality aspects a (semi-)formal tool should have (from [3])

6   Tools Review

The main goals of the SLR was to identify the most mature formal and semi-formal methods to be applied in railways. From the analysis of the papers, we derived the following list: Simulink, NuSMV/nuXmv (latest version of NuSMV), Atelier B, Prover, ProB, SCADE, IBM Rational Software Architect, Polyspace, and S3. From this list, we discarded IBM Rational Software Architect because it is just a design tool that does not allow any kind of formal verification, Polyspace because it is a static analysis tool that does not support any kind of behavioural verification, and Prover as well as S3 because of difficulties in finding sufficient documentation and inability to access a demo version within the time allocated to this project task. Thus, the subset of tools that have been selected for a further, more specific evaluation are Simulink, NuSMV/nuXmv, Atelier B, ProB, and SCADE. Furthermore, the results of the Survey with Practitioners indicate two additional tools sometimes used in railway-related industrial projects, namely SPIN and CPN Tools. Therefore, these tools have been also selected for further specific evaluation. Additionally, we are aware of other relevant tools and frameworks used in industrial projects, even if not widely used within the railway sector so far. Without the ambition to make an exhaustive coverage, and without any negative bias towards unselected tools, we wanted to experiment with a spectrum of tools and verification techniques (e.g. Logical approaches, Process Algebras, Statistical approaches) wider than that of the mainstream approaches. Therefore, we have decided to extend our specific evaluations adding to our list UPPAAL, FDR4, CADP, mCRL2, SAL, and TLA+. Finally, we have also taken into consideration one more tool, namely UMC, which—even if lacking a solid background in terms of industrial usage—has the uncommon feature of allowing a direct verification of UML-based models. We recall that, according to the SLR, UML is the most common semi-formal language used for the high-level specification of railway systems. Hence, the final list of 14 tools or frameworks selected for a deeper evaluation is as follows:

> Simulink, nuXmv, Atelier B, ProB, SCADE, SPIN, CPN Tools, UPPAAL, FDR4, CADP, mCRL2, SAL, TLA+, and UMC.

Each of these tools, with the exception of SCADE[4], has been downloaded, installed, and experimented with the design and verification of simple railway-related cases studies. Part of the results were published in recent works [2,22]. The corresponding available tool documentation has been analysed with the depth allowed by the project timeline. To evaluate the tools, a set of 34 evaluation features was considered, including functional features (e.g., formal verification, code generation), language-related aspects (e.g., support for concurrency, non-determinism), and the quality aspects also considered in the questionnaire (e.g., maturity, ease of use). The complete list of features is reported in the deliverable [13].

---

[4] In the case of SCADE, due to licensing issues, it was not possible to gain a hands-on experience within the limited timespan of the project. Hence, our evaluation is based on the analysis of the available official tool documentation and presentations, and on the experiences reported in students' assignments at the University of Florence, carried out under the ANSYS SCADE Academic Program.

6.1   Results and Discussion

The tools review produced two main reference documents. A Tool Evaluation Report, in which for each feature a qualitative evaluation is given, together with the motivation for the assigned evaluation, and a Tool Evaluation Matrix, which summarises the evaluation for the tools. An excerpt of the matrix focussing on quality aspects is presented in Fig. 8 (the matrix is reported in its entirety in our deliverable). Overall, the majority of tools offer formal modelling and verification through model checking, and they generally offer simulation in textual or graphical form. Less frequent are features such as code generation, model-based testing, and traceability. With few exceptions, such as SCADE and Simulink, graphical user interfaces (GUIs) for these different tools are rather limited. Furthermore, in terms of learnability, the tools mainly require medium to advanced competences in formal methods, and, in the majority of the cases, require the support of an expert to be successfully used. This is in contrast with the demands of practitioners (Fig. 7), who primarily require tools that are easy to learn. It is also worth noticing that only SCADE is fully certified according to CENELEC.

Category	Name	SPIN	Simulink	nuXmv	ProB	AtelierB	UPPAAL	SCADE
Tool Flexibility	Backward Compatibility	LIKELY	LIKELY	LIKELY	LIKELY	MODERATE	LIKELY	LIKELY
	Standard Input Format	YES	PARTIAL	YES	YES	YES	PARTIAL	PARTIAL
	Import/Export	MEDIUM	LOW	MEDIUM	HIGH	MEDIUM	LOW	LOW
	Modularity of the Tool	LOW	HIGH	LOW	LOW	MEDIUM	LOW	HIGH
	Team Support	NO	NO	NO	NO	YES	NO	NO
Maturity	Industrial Diffusion	MEDIUM	HIGH	MEDIUM	RAILWAY	RAILWAY	MEDIUM	RAILWAY
	Stage of Development	YES	YES	YES	YES	YES	YES	YES
Usability	Customer Support	PARTIAL	YES	PARTIAL	YES	YES	YES	YES
	Graphical User Interface	LIMITED	YES	NO	PARTIAL	PARTIAL	PARTIAL	YES
	Easy to Use	MEDIUM	BASIC	MEDIUM	MEDIUM	ADVANCED	MEDIUM	BASIC
	Quality of Documentation	GOOD	EXCELLENT	GOOD	GOOD	EXCELLENT	GOOD	EXCELLENT
Company Constraints	Cost	FREE	PAY	MIX	FREE	FREE	MIX	PAY
	Supported Platforms	Windows, Linux, macOS	Windows, Linux, macOS	Windows, Linux, macOS	Windows, Linux, macOS	Windows, Linux, macOS	Windows, Linux, macOS	Windows
	Complexity of License Management	EASY	ADEQUATE	EASY	EASY	EASY	MODERATE	ADEQUATE
	Easy to Install	YES	YES	YES	YES	YES	YES	YES
Railway-specific Criteria	CENELEC Certification	NO	PARTIAL	NO	NO	NO	NO	YES
	Integration into the CENELEC Process	MEDIUM	YES	MEDIUM	YES	YES	MEDIUM	YES

Fig. 8. Tool Evaluation Matrix (Excerpt)

7   Conclusion

The current paper reports ongoing results from WP4 of the ASTRail project. We presented a number of activities aimed at supporting the identification of the most suitable formal and semi-formal methods to be used for railway system development. Specifically, a SLR was conducted to categorise 114 scientific publications on formal methods and railways according to features such as the type of system and the phase of the development process addressed by the experience considered in the publication. The SLR was complemented with a projects review and a survey with practitioners, to identify the most mature formal and semi-formal methods and tools to be used in a railway context. This analysis has shown a dominance of the UML modelling language for high-level representation of system models, and a large variety of formal tools being used, with a dominance of the tools from the B family (ProB and Atelier B), followed by several other tools, including Simulink, NuSMV/nuXmv, Prover, SCADE, IBM Rational Software Architect, Polyspace, S3, SPIN, CPN Tools, etc. The projects review and the survey with practitioners confirmed this scattered landscape. As part of a tools review, tools supporting both modelling and formal verification were considered for accurate experimentation and evaluation. A set of 14 tools, considered to be the most promising, was carefully reviewed by means of a systematic evaluation based on a set of 34 evaluation features. The final product of these activities is a set of informative documents to support the ranking and selection of formal and semi-formal methods for railways, based on (a) the information retrieved from the literature, summarised in a Paper Analysis Matrix, (b) the information available from the tools evaluation, and (c) the Tool Evaluation Matrix, which allows practitioners to perform a fine-grained selection of the most appropriate formal methods and tools, suitable to their specific needs.

Based on the results presented in this paper, we are currently conducting the application phase of the project. In this phase, we first model the moving block distancing principles by means of 8 formal tools, namely Simulink, SCADE, NuSMV/nuXmv, SPIN, Atelier B, ProB, UPPAAL and UMC, selected based on the previous results. We then perform a usability evaluation of the tools together with railway practitioners. Finally, we further assess the applicability of the tools, involving our industrial partners in the modelling of automated driving principles.

Acknowledgements. This work has been partially funded by the ASTRail project. This project received funding from the Shift2Rail Joint Undertaking under the European Union's Horizon 2020 research and innovation programme under grant agreement No. 777561. The content of this paper reflects only the authors' view and the Shift2Rail Joint Undertaking is not responsible for any use that may be made of the included information.

References

1. Abrial, J.R.: Formal methods: theory becoming practice. J. Univers. Comput. Sci. **13**(5), 619–628 (2007). https://doi.org/10.3217/jucs-013-05-0619
2. Basile, D., ter Beek, M.H., Ciancia, V.: Statistical model checking of a moving block railway signalling scenario with UPPAAL SMC. In: Margaria, T., Steffen, B. (eds.) ISoLA 2018. LNCS, vol. 11245, pp. 372–391. Springer, Cham (2018). https://doi.org/10.1007/978-3-030-03421-4_24

3. Basile, D., et al.: On the industrial uptake of formal methods in the railway domain – a survey with stakeholders. In: Furia, C.A., Winter, K. (eds.) IFM 2018. LNCS, vol. 11023, pp. 20–29. Springer, Cham (2018). https://doi.org/10.1007/978-3-319-98938-9_2

4. ter Beek, M.H., Gnesi, S., Knapp, A.: Formal methods for transport systems. Int. J. Softw. Tools Technol. Transf. **20**(3), 237–241 (2018). https://doi.org/10.1007/s10009-018-0487-4

5. Berger, U., James, P., Lawrence, A., Roggenbach, M., Seisenberger, M.: Verification of the European rail traffic management system in real-time maude. Sci. Comput. Program. **154**, 61–88 (2018). https://doi.org/10.1016/j.scico.2017.10.011

6. Bjørner, D.: New results and trends in formal techniques and tools for the development of software for transportation systems – a review. In: Tarnai, G., Schnieder, E. (eds.) Proceedings of the 4th Symposium on Formal Methods for Railway Operation and Control Systems, FORMS 2003. L'Harmattan, Hungary (2003)

7. Bosschaart, M., Quaglietta, E., Janssen, B., Goverde, R.M.P.: Efficient formalization of railway interlocking data in RailML. Inf. Syst. **49**, 126–141 (2015). https://doi.org/10.1016/j.is.2014.11.007

8. Boulanger, J.L. (ed.): Formal Methods Applied to Industrial Complex Systems—Implementation of the B Method. Wiley, Hoboken (2014). https://doi.org/10.1002/9781119002727

9. Chiappini, A., et al.: Formalization and validation of a subset of the European Train Control System. In: Proceedings of the 32nd ACM/IEEE International Conference on Software Engineering, ICSE 2010, vol. 2, pp. 109–118. ACM, USA (2010). https://doi.org/10.1145/1810295.1810312

10. European Committee for Electrotechnical Standardization: CENELEC EN 50128—Railway applications – Communication, signalling and processing systems – Software for railway control and protection systems, 1 June 2011. https://standards.globalspec.com/std/1678027/cenelec-en-50128

11. Fantechi, A.: Twenty-five years of formal methods and railways: what next? In: Counsell, S., Núñez, M. (eds.) SEFM 2013. LNCS, vol. 8368, pp. 167–183. Springer, Cham (2014). https://doi.org/10.1007/978-3-319-05032-4_13

12. Ferrari, A., Fantechi, A., Magnani, G., Grasso, D., Tempestini, M.: The Metrô Rio case study. Sci. Comput. Program. **78**(7), 828–842 (2013). https://doi.org/10.1016/j.scico.2012.04.003

13. Ferrari, A., et al.: Survey on formal methods and tools in railways technical report on the activities performed within ASTRail, Deliverable D4.1. Technical report 396822, ISTI-CNR (2018). https://doi.org/10.5281/zenodo.2573921

14. Ferrari, A., Fantechi, A., Gnesi, S., Magnani, G.: Model-based development and formal methods in the railway industry. IEEE Softw. **30**(3), 28–34 (2013). https://doi.org/10.1109/MS.2013.44

15. Flammini, F. (ed.): Railway Safety, Reliability, and Security: Technologies and Systems Engineering. IGI Global, Hershey (2012). https://doi.org/10.4018/978-1-4666-1643-1

16. Haxthausen, A.E., Peleska, J., Kinder, S.: A formal approach for the construction and verification of railway control systems. Formal Aspects Comput. **23**(2), 191–219 (2011). https://doi.org/10.1007/s00165-009-0143-6

17. Iliasov, A., Taylor, D., Laibinis, L., Romanovsky, A.: Formal verification of signalling programs with SafeCap. In: Gallina, B., Skavhaug, A., Bitsch, F. (eds.) SAFECOMP 2018. LNCS, vol. 11093, pp. 91–106. Springer, Cham (2018). https://doi.org/10.1007/978-3-319-99130-6_7

18. James, P., Moller, F., Nguyen, H.N., Roggenbach, M., Schneider, S., Treharne, H.: Techniques for modelling and verifying railway interlockings. Int. J. Softw. Tools Technol. Transf. **16**, 685–711 (2014). https://doi.org/10.1007/s10009-014-0304-7
19. Kitchenham, B.: Procedures for performing systematic reviews. Technical report TR/SE-0401. University of Keele, UK, July 2004. https://goo.gl/vYU8Fu
20. Lecomte, T., Deharbe, D., Prun, E., Mottin, E.: Applying a formal method in industry: a 25-year trajectory. In: Cavalheiro, S., Fiadeiro, J. (eds.) SBMF 2017. LNCS, vol. 10623, pp. 70–87. Springer, Cham (2017). https://doi.org/10.1007/978-3-319-70848-5_6
21. Leuschel, M., Falampin, J., Fritz, F., Plagge, D.: Automated property verification for large scale B models with ProB. Formal Aspects Comput. **23**(6), 683–709 (2011). https://doi.org/10.1007/s00165-010-0172-1
22. Mazzanti, F., Ferrari, A.: Ten diverse formal models for a CBTC automatic train supervision system. In: Gallagher, J.P., van Glabbeek, R., Serwe, W. (eds.) Proceedings of the 3rd Workshop on Models for Formal Analysis of Real Systems and the 6th International Workshop on Verification and Program Transformation, MARS/VPT 2018. EPTCS, vol. 268, pp. 104–149 (2018). https://doi.org/10.4204/EPTCS.268.4
23. Mazzanti, F., Ferrari, A., Spagnolo, G.O.: Towards formal methods diversity in railways: an experience report with seven frameworks. Int. J. Softw. Tools Technol. Transf. **20**(3), 263–288 (2018). https://doi.org/10.1007/s10009-018-0488-3
24. Mazzanti, F., Spagnolo, G.O., Della Longa, S., Ferrari, A.: Deadlock avoidance in train scheduling: a model checking approach. In: Lang, F., Flammini, F. (eds.) FMICS 2014. LNCS, vol. 8718, pp. 109–123. Springer, Cham (2014). https://doi.org/10.1007/978-3-319-10702-8_8
25. Moller, F., Nguyen, H.N., Roggenbach, M., Schneider, S., Treharne, H.: Defining and model checking abstractions of complex railway models using CSP‖B. In: Biere, A., Nahir, A., Vos, T. (eds.) HVC 2012. LNCS, vol. 7857, pp. 193–208. Springer, Heidelberg (2013). https://doi.org/10.1007/978-3-642-39611-3_20
26. Rispoli, F., Castorina, M., Neri, A., Filip, A., Di Mambro, G., Senesi, F.: Recent progress in application of GNSS and advanced communications for railway signaling. In: Proceedings of the 23rd International Conference Radioelektronika, RADIOELEKTRONIKA 2013, pp. 13–22. IEEE (2013). https://doi.org/10.1109/RadioElek.2013.6530882
27. Vanit-Anunchai, S.: Modelling and simulating a Thai railway signalling system using Coloured Petri Nets. Int. J. Softw. Tools Technol. Transf. **20**(3), 243–262 (2018). https://doi.org/10.1007/s10009-018-0482-9
28. Vu, L.H., Haxthausen, A.E., Peleska, J.: Formal modelling and verification of interlocking systems featuring sequential release. Sci. Comput. Program. **133**, 91–115 (2017). https://doi.org/10.1016/j.scico.2016.05.010
29. Winter, K., Robinson, N.J.: Modelling large railway interlockings and model checking small ones. In: Oudshoorn, M.J. (ed.) Proceedings of the 26th Australasian Computer Science Conference, ACSC 2003. Conferences in Research and Practice in Information Technology, vol. 16, pp. 309–316. Australian Computer Society, Australia (2003). http://crpit.com/confpapers/CRPITV16Winter.pdf
30. Woodcock, J., Larsen, P.G., Bicarregui, J., Fitzgerald, J.S.: Formal methods: practice and experience. ACM Comput. Surv. **41**(4), 19:1–19:36 (2009). https://doi.org/10.1145/1592434.1592436

B-Specification of Relay-Based Railway Interlocking Systems Based on the Propositional Logic of the System State Evolution

Dalay Israel de Almeida Pereira[1]($\boxtimes$) (ID), David Deharbe[2] (ID), Matthieu Perin[3] (ID),
and Philippe Bon[1]

[1] Univ. Lille Nord de France, IFSTTAR, COSYS/ESTAS,
59650 Villeneuve d'Ascq, France
dalay-israel.de-almeida-pereira@ifsttar.fr
[2] ClearSy S.A., Aix-en-Provence, France
[3] Institut de Recherche Technologique Railenium, 59300 Famars, France

Abstract. In the railway signalling domain, a railway interlocking system (RIS) is responsible for controlling the movement of trains by allowing or denying their routing according to safety rules. Relay diagrams are a commonly used abstraction in order to model relay-based RIS, describing these systems by graph-like schemata that present the connections between electrical components. The verification of these diagrams regarding safety, however, is a challenging task, due to their complexity and the lack of tools for the automatic proof and animation. The analysis of relay diagrams by a specialist is the main method to verify the correctness and the safety of these systems. Nonetheless, human manual analysis is error prone. This paper presents an approach for formally specifying the behaviour of the systems described in relay diagrams in the B-method formal language. Considering that each relay has only two states, it is possible to describe the rules for the state evolution of a system by logical propositions. Furthermore, it is possible to use ProB in order to animate and model-check the specification.

Keywords: Railway interlocking systems · Relay diagrams · B-method · Propositional logic

1 Introduction

Railway Interlocking Systems (RIS) are built with the objective of controlling the movement of trains by allowing and denying their movements in specific tracks in order to avoid the occurrence of problems like collisions, for instance. The first built RIS was purely mechanical, than it evolved to use new technologies, becoming electrical mechanical systems, relay-based systems and, more recently,

Supported by the LCHIP (Low Cost High Integrity Platform) project.

© Springer Nature Switzerland AG 2019
S. Collart-Dutilleul et al. (Eds.): RSSRail 2019, LNCS 11495, pp. 242–258, 2019.
https://doi.org/10.1007/978-3-030-18744-6_16

computer controlled systems [10]. As critical systems, these RIS must be specified and safety proved in order to guarantee the absence of critical errors, which, in this case, may lead to the loss of people lives.

Despite the existence of new computer technologies, many old companies still implement RIS as relay-based systems, which are electrical circuits containing relays. However, the safety proof of these systems is a challenging task, since they are modelled by electrical circuits drawings (relay diagrams) and the only way to verify them is by manually inspecting and drawing conclusions, which is error prone [11]. Consequently, the railway domain needs new methodologies for the specification and verification of railway interlocking systems.

In this context, formal methods arises as a useful tool for the specification, proof and analysis of RIS. Among many formal methodologies, the B-method has excelled in the railway field. The work presented in [6] compares the applicability of different formal methods to railway signalling and the B-method was shown to be one of the strongest approaches that may be used in the verification of such systems. Some of the reasons of this success are: the existence of rigorous mathematical foundations, the well-developed underlying methodology and the existence of reasonably advanced support tools, which allows the specification, refinement and implementation of B-machines with automatic code generation and performing verifications at each stage.

This paper presents a methodology for the specification of relay-based RIS behaviours in B-method based on the preconditions for the state evolution of the system electrical components. These conditions may be written in propositional logic based solely on the specific behaviour of each component. From the specification of these preconditions, it is possible to specify the complete behaviour of a RIS in B, which allows the proof of safety properties and the animation of the system by using the B-method supporting tools. Another contribution of this paper is to provide a non-exhaustive dictionary for the specification of state evolution preconditions for each type of electrical components described in relay diagrams, which is the basis of the specification of these systems in B.

There are many different formalisms and patterns that may be used in order to model relay diagrams. In this work, we focus on the models used by SNCF (the French National Railway Company) in order to implement their relay-based RIS. The choice of using B-method as a targeting language is explained by the success of the application of this language for the specification and proof of railway systems [3,9,12]. Besides, B-method disposes of a complete set of supporting tools that allows its specification, verification, refinement and automatic code generation, which may be used in the future in order to transform theses systems from relay-based to computer controlled RIS. Regarding components failures, they are not taken into account in our approach, since it requires a complete RIS failure model that is subject for a future work.

Many existing works have presented approaches for the formal specification and verification of RIS in order to verify safety properties [8,10,17]. However, only some of them focused on the specification of relay-based RIS [4,7,11,16], which is a technology that is still used by many railway companies. Despite the fact that these works are in the same field, the context is a differentiating factor, since each company uses different notations, patterns and languages in order to model relay-based RIS.

In [11] it is presented an approach for the formal specification and verification of relay-based RIS applied for the danish RIS specification. Unlike SNCF RIS models, the relay diagrams presented in [11] use different patterns and notations, besides the fact that it contains fewer different types of components, which makes these systems less complex. Consequently, this work allows the behavioural translation of a smaller set of electrical components in comparison to our work, since their context (danish systems) is different from ours context (SNCF systems).

Furthermore, although the proximity with our work, [11] focuses on the specification of the temporal logic of the system based on the process description allowed by LTL [2] and our work focuses on the specification of the stable states of the RIS in order to find possible unsafe states. A stable state is defined as a moment when the system "waits" for an interaction (input changes) in order to change its own state. Furthermore, B-method allows the specification of abstract machines that can be refined in order to generate code. Our work represents a first step towards a transformation from relay-based RIS towards computer-controlled RIS, which may be supported by the B-method refinement and automatic code generation processes.

The Sect. 2 of this paper presents some details about the modelling of RIS in relay diagrams, followed by the formal methodology of specification, B-method, in Sect. 3. Then, based on these specification languages, it is possible to discuss about the specification of RIS behaviour in B-method based on relay diagrams in Sect. 4. The last Section of this paper concludes our work and presents some perspectives.

2   Relay-Based Modelling

Interlocking systems are the signalling functions controlling the trains movements in a particular location in order to meet safety requirements [17]. Many railways interlocking systems implemented by railway companies are relay-based systems, which is formed by electrical circuits containing relays. Responsible for the transmission, reception and use of information, a relay is an electromechanical switching element comprised by electromagnets (coils) and contacts [14]. In a relay-based RIS, an electrical circuit is composed by a source of energy, a command element (like contacts or levers, for instance) and a receiver (like relays or outputs, for instance), which are connected by conductive wires. A component or wire is electrified if it is connected to the positive and negative sources of energy poles.

2.1   Relay-Based Railway Interlocking Systems Modelling

Relay-based RIS are usually modelled by relay diagrams, which are graph-like representations of how the electrical elements are connected by wires. This section presents some details about the modelling of RIS in industry, more specifically, how SNCF uses relay diagrams in order to model railway interlocking systems. An example of a relay diagram is presented in the Fig. 1 (detailed in Sect. 2.2). Some graphical notations that may be used in a relay diagram are presented in Table 1.

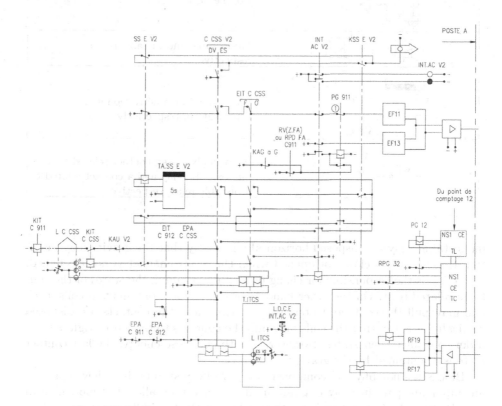

Fig. 1. Relay-based system model of the signalling control point A

Originally, a contact has two different states in a RIS: closed or opened. The former state allows the electrical current to flow from a wire to another. In the latter state, the contact is not connected to both wires, so it does not allow the electrical current to flow. A contact may be closed or opened by the influence of the gravity or by the electromagnetic influence of a relay. Furthermore, a contact is "normally closed" if it is necessary a magnetic influence to open it (the gravity maintains it closed otherwise). Following the same principle, a contact is "normally opened" when the gravity maintains it opened as a way that it is necessary a magnetic influence in order to close it.

There are two different types of relays: monostable and bistable. A monostable relay contains only one electromagnet that is responsible for attracting or repulsing one or more movable contacts. In this case, the contacts related to a

Table 1. Elements that may be used in a Relay-based diagram.

—⊚— + ⊚—	Electrical sources of energy poles (negative and positive, respectively).
ES V2 / DV	Couple button-lever.
	Monostable and bistable relays, respectively.
5s 15s	Blocks for timed activation and deactivation, respectively.
	A normally closed contact related to a monostable relay and a contact related to a bistable relay, respectively.

monostable relay are disposed horizontally in a way that the gravity may maintain these contacts closed or opened when the electromagnet is not electrified. The relay is the responsible for changing and maintaining the states of the contacts related to it. On the other hand, a bistable relay contains two coils, each one may pull the contacts to one side. In this case, the contacts are disposed vertically as a way that the coils may pull the contacts to the left or right side in order to change their states. However, if both coils lose energy, the last contact state is maintained by the gravity.

Blocks are not physical components in a railway system, but they represent an important part in relay diagram models, since they allow the modelling of timed relays. A block with a black thicker line on the top indicates that it delays the activation of a relay. On the other hand, a block with a thicker black line on the bottom is responsible for retarding the deactivation of a relay. Inside the white part of the block it is indicated the time spent on these delays, which is normally indicated in seconds.

There are many types of inputs that may be used in the relay diagrams modelling, which represent the interface between these diagrams and the environment. Some examples of inputs that allows the human intervention inside the system are buttons and levers. A button acts like a contact since it may connect two different wires. However, its states are controlled by the environment, which means that it is not magnetically connected to a relay. A lever is similar to a button, since it needs a physical force in order to change its states. However, a lever controls the flow of electrical current in more than one pair of wires. Furthermore, if a lever allows the current flow in one pair of wires and at the same time it blocks the current in another pair, it will maintain these states alternated after the external intervention by changing all the states together.

An input may also be represented by a contact whose associated relay is not presented in the diagram. The behaviour of this abstracted relay is considered as an input since it controls the state of the contact. As an example, the detection of the position of a train may be modelled by abstracting the relay in the diagram, since the train (environment) is the responsible for the activation of the relay, which controls the state of the contacts represented inside the diagram.

The outputs of the RIS can be generally understood as a permission or denial for a train to enter in a determined track. These outputs must be verified in order to avoid giving permission to two different trains entering in the same track, for instance, which may cause a collision. An industrial example of a model that can be verified in order to avoid collisions is presented in the next subsection. This model is used as an example throughout this paper.

2.2   Industrial Example

This subsection presents details about an example that is used in industry. The diagram presented in Fig. 2 represents a track plan containing two tracks (one for each direction) and the space between the signalling control point A and C. In this example, we consider that a train that arrives in the point A may change to the track below because of problems on its own track. In this case, this train will start going on the "wrong way", which may cause a frontal collision with a train that may come from the point C. In order to avoid this type of collision, there must exist a signalisation that indicates if a train may enter or not in this portion of the tracks. In this example we focus on the signalisation existing in the point A.

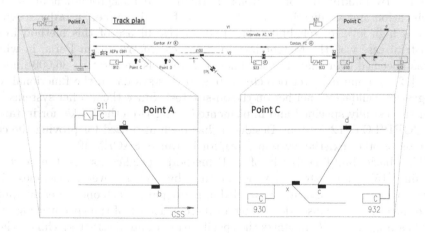

Fig. 2. Track plan from the signalling control point A to C

In order to control the signalisation in the signalling control point A, a relay-based RIS must be implemented according to the model presented in Fig. 1. In this system, the pair button-lever L $ITCS$ is responsible for indicating if the tracks are working normally (DV - "Double Voie") or if it is necessary to use only one track (ES - "En Service"), which is a situation that may cause a collision if not safety proved. After switching L $ITCS$ to the ES state, it also changes the bistable relay C CSS $V2$ to the ES state, which allows the train that arrives in the point C to enter in the dangerous zone (activation of the output $EF11$), since it refuses a train that arrives in point A to enter (KIT C 911 deactivated). If L $ITCS$ is set to DV, it means that the two tracks are working normally and the signal is never closed.

If a train aim to enter in the dangerous zone from the point A, a permission may be given by changing the state of the lever L C CSS to O, which also changes the relay EIT C CSS to the O state. This action will deactivate the output $EF11$, which no longer gives permission to trains in the point C to enter in the dangerous zone. If the point C agrees with these changes, it may allow a train in the point A to enter by activating the relay KSS E $V2$. These sequence of actions may activate the relay SS E $V2$ after a delay of five seconds, counted by the block $TA.SS$ E $V2$.

After the activation of the relay KSS E $V2$, a permission is granted to a train in the point A to enter in the dangerous zone by the activation of the relay KIT C 911. This permission must be given only if $EF11$ is deactivated and vice versa. This is a condition that must be guaranteed.

3   B-Method

According to [1], B is a method for specifying, describing and coding software systems. By making use of a strong mathematical background, it allows the specification and verification of systems in a formal manner in order to guarantee a high level of reliability. The first successful use of this method in an industrial case was the Meteor line 14 drive-less metro [3], in Paris, in which it was specified over than 110,000 lines of B-models, generating 86,000 lines of code [12]. No one has ever detected a bug in this system in the functional and integration validation, neither on the on-site test. Since then, other systems has been successfully specified and implemented using B-method, like, for instance, the COPPILOT [12] system. Besides, B has been also used for proving the correctness of other existing systems, like, for instance, SACEM [9].

The basic building block of a B-method specification is the abstract machine [15]. One system may be specified by one or several machines. The specification inside a machine is divided in many parts, each one under an appropriate heading (or clause) describing a different aspect of the specification. The first heading, $MACHINE$, starts the specification of an abstract machine, whose name must be described under this heading.

The local state of a machine is kept by the variables which are defined under the $VARIABLES$ clause and whose details are defined under the $INVARIANT$

heading. These details comprise variables typing and properties that must be satisfied by the specification. The initial state of the machine must be described in the *INITIALISATION* clause. It is also possible to describe constant information, like, for instance, sets of constant information that can be used inside the machine, which are described under the *SETS* heading.

It is also possible to define operations for a machine inside the *OPERATIONS* clause. These operations may receive inputs, provide outputs and change the state of the machine by changing the values of the variables. In order to define an operation it is required to define the preconditions that must be met in order to execute this operation.

```
 5  MACHINE
 6      example
 7
 8  SETS ANSWERS = {yes, no}
 9
10  VARIABLES answer
11  INVARIANT answer : ANSWERS
12  INITIALISATION answer :: ANSWERS
13  OPERATIONS
14
15      ans <-- set_answer(input) =
16      PRE input : ANSWERS
17      THEN answer := input || ans := input
18      END
19
20  END
```

Fig. 3. Example of a simple B-machine

A small example of a B-machine is depicted on Fig. 3. This example presents how the clauses can be used in order to specify a machine that allows the storage of an information of the type defined by the set **ANSWERS**. The information that can be stored inside the variable **answer** are the elements **yes** or **no**. More details about the clauses and notations used in order to specify a B-machine can be found in [1].

4   B-Specification of Relay-Diagrams Behaviours

A relay-based RIS is composed of many components, each one with an independent specific behaviour. The specification of an entire RIS may be described as a combination of the behaviours of all the components that constitutes it. Furthermore, in order to activate a component, an electrical current is required (precondition) and the flux of electrical current may be controlled by other components with other preconditions. This type of reactive behaviour can be described inside a B-method abstract machine, which may be used for proof and animation purposes, as it is presented in this section.

4.1 Relay-Diagram Behavioural Logic

The most important components of a relay-based RIS are the relays. This component is responsible for opening and closing the contacts, which controls the flux of electrical current inside the wires. Therefore, the activation and deactivation of relays commands the activation and deactivation of other components by controlling the flow of electrical current inside the wires. Before specifying any component behaviour, it is important to understand the precondition for a component to be activated.

Definition 1 *(Component Activation Precondition). An electrical component is activated if both of its wires are connected to a different pole (positive and negative) of energy sources as a way to allow the flow of electrical current inside the component. This means that all contacts, buttons and levers between the component and both poles of energy sources must be closed.*

It is clear that a component is activated if there is electrical current flowing inside it, however, the precondition for having electrical current is that each wire connected to a component must be connected to a different pole of sources of energy. A precondition for the component deactivation can also be defined.

Definition 2 *(Component Deactivation Precondition). An electrical component is deactivated if its wires are not connected to different poles (positive and negative) of energy sources as a way that there does not exist a flow of electrical current inside it. This means that at least one contact, button or lever between the component and one pole of energy source must be opened (considering that there is no other connection to the same type of pole).*

A monostable relay has two states: TRUE (activated) or FALSE (deactivated). The former represents the state where there is current passing through the coil and the latter represents the state where the coil is not electrified (according to Definitions 1 and 2, respectively). The consequence of its activation or deactivation is the state evolution of the contacts related to this relay. The state of a monostable relay changes as soon as the precondition of this state is no longer met.

A bistable relay has also two states: right or left, representing the activation of the right and left coils, respectively. Generally, the two coils will not be activated at the same time, however, both coils may be deactivated. If the right coil activates, the relay assumes the "right" state and it changes the state of the contacts related to this relay. Then, this may change to "left" if, and only if, the right coil is deactivated and the left coil activates, which changes the state of the contacts as well. The main difference between a monostable and a bistable relay relies on the fact that the latter may maintain its last state even if the coils are no longer activated.

Considering that the contacts states are directly defined by the relays related to them, the states of the contacts in the relay diagrams can be completely abstracted by means of the relays states. As an example, the precondition for the relay *KIT C CSS* to be activated in the relay diagram depicted on Fig. 1 is that *SS E V2* must be activated (in order to close the normally opened contact), *EIT C CSS* must be set to the right (which closes the bistable contact) and *INT AC V2* must be activated (in order to close the normally opened contact).

Furthermore, there are two special cases concerning the logic of relays: timed activated/deactivated and self-alimented relays. In the former case, the Definitions 1 and 2 changes in the presence of a block. A relay connected to a block that retards the activation will be activated if the block is activated (according to Definition 1) after the time represented by the block. In this case the relay deactivation occurs right after the deactivation of the block (not timed). Contrarily, a relay connected to a block that retards the deactivation activates right after the activation of the block, however, this relay deactivates only after the time defined inside the block when the block is deactivated. The relay *SS E V2* is an example of timed-activation relay.

A relay can also be self-alimented when it controls a contact that may activate it. In a case that the activation of a relay closes a contact that also aliments it with energy (like the relay *PG 911*, for instance), this contact may never activate the relay by itself, so it is not considered as a precondition for the relay activation. Furthermore, this contact does not open unless the relay is deactivated, so it is also not considered in the precondition for the deactivation of the relay either. However this contact has a high importance in order to maintain the activated state of the relay after its activation.

Similar to contacts, buttons and levers are responsible for the activation or deactivation of other components, since they control the electrical current flow inside the wires. However, the states of buttons and levers cannot be abstracted, since they are controlled directly by the environment. So, these components may be treated as inputs and the information inserted in the system by these inputs are important for the definition of the system state.

Furthermore, the outputs are part of the general state of the diagram, representing an important part on the safety analysis, since they represent the response given to the environment calculated based on the inputs. In a relay-diagram, an output may be connected to only one energy source pole (like *EF11*, for instance), or to two different poles (like the *INT.AC V2* lights, for instance) in order to be activated. Besides, it may be depicted as another component, like relays (*KIT C 911*, for instance). One verification that is possible to make in our running example in order to analyse its safety is that it there must never exist a state where the component *KIT C 911* (permission for the train in the point A to enter in the dangerous zone) and the component *EF11* (permission for the train in the point C to enter in the dangerous zone) are activated at the same time, since it may cause a collision.

4.2   Relay-Based Logic Specification in B

Based on the relay diagrams and on the logic for the state evolution of the electrical components, it is possible to specify the behaviour of the RIS in B-method. In order to specify these systems, it is necessary to define what is inside each header of the B specification. After the *MACHINE* header, which contains the machine, one must define sets containing the special states related to levers or bistable relays under the *SETS* clause. Regarding the example used throughout this paper, It is necessary to define the special states *POS_O* and *POS_F* for the components *EIT C CSS* and *L C CSS* as well as the states *POS_DV* and *POS_ES* for the component *C CSS V2*. When related to bistable relays, these states represent the left (DV, F) or right (ES, O) state of these components. These states represent the positions that these components may assume. Hence, our running example can be initially specified as shown in Fig. 4.

```
MACHINE                        VARIABLES
    itcs                           KIT_C_CSS,
SETS                               SS_E_V2,
    O_OU_F = {POS_O, POS_F};        TA_SS_E_V2,
    DV_OU_ES = {POS_ES, POS_DV}     EIT_C_CSS,
                                    C_CSS_V2,
                                    PG_911,
                                    EF11,
                                    KIT_C_911
```

Fig. 4. B-method MACHINE, SET and VARIABLES clauses

In a B-method specification the variables (listed inside the *VARIABLES* clause) define the state of a machine. In the RIS context, this state is defined by the state of each component. Hence, in our methodology, the variables must represent components. However, in order to simplify the specification and decrease a significantly number of variables and, by consequence, the number of possible states, inputs and contacts are not treated as variables. As presented before, the state of the contact is directly linked to the state of the relay in a way that contact states can be easily abstracted. Furthermore, since inputs are responsible for directly or indirectly changing the states of all other components, we chose to specify them as the inputs for the operation responsible for the state evolution. In other words, these components affect the system, but their states are not maintained by the system, since they may be changed at any time by the environment. This option does not affect negatively the safety verification and neither the animation of the specification. In fact, by avoiding the specification of inputs as variables we decrease the number of specified states, which allows a faster and lighter model-checker verification.

A special case regarding variables is the specification of blocks. The state of this component is maintained by the system because they are nor directly activated by the environment. However, the environment has an effect over the blocks, since the time has an important part on its behaviour. In this work, time is considered as an environmental factor. So, this type of component must not only be specified as a variable, but it must also be specified as an input of the state evolution. This input represents the passing of time. In our running example, the *VARIABLES* clause is specified as presented in Fig. 4.

Inside the *INVARIANT* clause, one must define the type of the variables. In this case, regarding RIS components, the types represent the possible states that the components may assume. As presented before, monostable relays may assume the states *TRUE* or *FALSE*, in other words, they have the Boolean type. Since the outputs may also be activated or deactivated, they also must be Boolean. However, bistable relays may have special types defined inside the diagrams in order to indicate the left and the right states. In our running example, for instance, we have the types *O_OU_F* and *DV_OU_ES* for the relays *EIT C CSS* and *C CSS V2*, respectively.

Moreover, inside the *INVARIANT* clause, it is also possible to define conditions that must be respected at any possible state of the machine. In the case of RIS specification, one may describe safety properties in order to guarantee that the system will never reach a dangerous state. In our running example, for instance, a safety property that must be always met is that the components *KIT C 911* and *EF11* must never be activated at the same time in order to avoid collision. The specification of this property and the complete *INVARIANT* clause of our example are depicted in Fig. 5.

```
INVARIANT                              INITIALISATION
    KIT_C_CSS : BOOL &                     KIT_C_CSS := FALSE ||
    SS_E_V2 : BOOL &                       SS_E_V2 := FALSE ||
    TA_SS_E_V2 : BOOL &                    EIT_C_CSS := POS_F ||
    EIT_C_CSS : O_OU_F &                   C_CSS_V2 := POS_DV ||
    C_CSS_V2 : DV_OU_ES &                  PG_911 := TRUE ||
    PG_911 : BOOL &                        TA_SS_E_V2 := FALSE ||
    EF11 : BOOL &                          EF11 := FALSE ||
    KIT_C_911 : BOOL &                     KIT_C_911 := FALSE

    not(KIT_C_911 = TRUE &
        EF11 = TRUE)
```

Fig. 5. B-Machine INVARIANT and INITIALISATION clauses

The initial state of the system is defined by the relay diagram drawing, since it shows the initial position of the levers, bistable relays, and if the monostable relays are connected to the energy or not. In our running example, the *INITIALISATION* clause is defined as presented in Fig. 5.

The state evolution of a railway interlocking system sheet may be specified inside a B-method operation. The use of a unique operation allows us to reach all the stable states only by changing the inputs given by the environment. Since the inputs are the responsible for triggering the state evolution, they are the inputs of the operation. Inside the precondition clause of the operation, all the inputs must be typed. The operation must also be able to change the state of all variables considering that the state of one variable may affect the final state of another. This type of behaviour can be specified in B by the following notation:

`<<variables>>:(<<variables typing>> & <<variables information>>)`

By using this expression, it is possible to change the value of a set of variables (`<<variables>>`) by informing their types (`<<variables typing>>`) and the conditions they must meet after the execution of this expression (`<<variables information>>`). Inside the conditions, it is possible to define the values of the variables according to the inputs and other variables states (activation and deactivation preconditions). As an example, the state evolution of the variable *KIT_C_CSS* that must be described inside the `<<variables information>>` part of the notation is the activation condition presented in Fig. 6.

```
KIT_C_CSS = bool(SS_E_V2 = TRUE & EIT_C_CSS = POS_O &
    INT_AC_V2 = TRUE & L_C_CSS = POS_O)
```

Fig. 6. Example of a state evolution

So, in order to activate the component *KIT_C_CSS*, *SS_E_V2* and *INT_AC_V2* must be electrified at the same time that *EIT_C_CSS* and *L_C_CSS* are in the *O* position (*POS_O*). Furthermore, it is possible to specify the same type of expression for each variable. The complete operation defined for our running example can be defined as presented in Fig. 7, where all variables are represented in red and all the inputs are represented in green for sake of clarification.

In some cases, in order to define the sate evolution of a relay, it is necessary to consider its previous state (before the execution of the operation), which may be specified by using the notation *$0* after the name of the variable [5]. This rule applies for the specification of bistable, self-alimented or timed relay behaviours. In case of bistable relays (as for the relays *EIT_C_CSS* and *C_CSS_V2*, for instance), one must consider that the previous state must be maintained if there is no electricity inside the coils, since gravity maintains the contacts closed.

Regarding self-alimented relays, the component *PG_911* is one example of it. The contact related to this relay may never be responsible for changing the relay state. However, although this contact does not directly interfere in the relay activation and deactivation, it "blocks" other contacts that could be related to the relay activation. For instance, although the contacts of the relays *KAG_a_G* and *RPD_FA_C_911* may deactivate the relay *PG_911*, they are not able to activate it, since the *PG_911* contact is not able to activate the relay.

In the last special case, timed relays, as the relay *SS_E_V2*, for instance, one must consider the state of the blocks that they are related to. In order to activate or deactivate timed relays, the input related to the block time must be considered. This means that these relays can only be activated or deactivated it the time has passed (input set to *TRUE*). In our operation responsible for

```
mise_a_jour_poste_A(L_C_CSS, INT_AC_V2, EPA_C_CSS, EIT_C_912, KAG_a_G, RPD_FA_C_911, L_ITCS, KAU_V2,
    KSS_E_V2, EPA_C_911, TA_SS_E_V2_echue) =
PRE
    L_C_CSS : O_OU_F & INT_AC_V2 : BOOL & EPA_C_CSS : BOOL & EIT_C_912 : BOOL & KAG_a_G : BOOL &
    RPD_FA_C_911 : BOOL & L_ITCS : DV_OU_ES & KAU_V2 : BOOL & KSS_E_V2 : BOOL & EPA_C_911 : BOOL &
    TA_SS_E_V2_echue : BOOL
THEN
    KIT_C_CSS, PLUS_KIT_C_911, EIT_C_CSS, PG_911, C_CSS_V2, EF11, TA_SS_E_V2, SS_E_V2:(

    KIT_C_CSS : BOOL & PLUS_KIT_C_911 : BOOL & EIT_C_CSS : O_OU_F & PG_911 : BOOL &
    C_CSS_V2 : DV_OU_ES & EF11 : BOOL & SS_E_V2 : BOOL & TA_SS_E_V2 : BOOL &

    KIT_C_CSS = bool(SS_E_V2 = TRUE & EIT_C_CSS = POS_O & INT_AC_V2 = TRUE & L_C_CSS = POS_O) &

    PLUS_KIT_C_911 = bool(KIT_C_CSS = TRUE & KAU_V2 = TRUE & C_CSS_V2 = POS_ES & PG_911 = TRUE) &

    (EIT_C_CSS$0 = POS_O =>
        EIT_C_CSS = { TRUE |-> POS_F, FALSE |-> POS_O }(bool(L_C_CSS = POS_F & EPA_C_CSS = TRUE))) &
    (EIT_C_CSS$0 = POS_F =>
        EIT_C_CSS = { TRUE |-> POS_O, FALSE |-> POS_F }(bool(L_C_CSS = POS_O & C_CSS_V2 = POS_ES &
        EIT_C_912 = FALSE))) &

    (PG_911$0 = FALSE => PG_911 = bool(INT_AC_V2 = FALSE)) &
    (PG_911$0 = TRUE => PG_911 = bool(RPD_FA_C_911 = TRUE or KAG_a_G = TRUE or INT_AC_V2 = FALSE)) &

    (C_CSS_V2$0 = POS_ES =>
        C_CSS_V2 = { TRUE |-> POS_DV, FALSE |-> POS_ES }(bool(L_ITCS = POS_DV & EPA_C_CSS = TRUE &
        EPA_C_911 = TRUE))) &
    (C_CSS_V2$0 = POS_DV =>
        C_CSS_V2 = { TRUE |-> POS_ES, FALSE |-> POS_DV }(bool(L_ITCS = POS_ES & EPA_C_CSS = TRUE &
        EPA_C_911 = TRUE))) &

    EF11 = bool(SS_E_V2 = FALSE & C_CSS_V2 = POS_ES & EIT_C_CSS = POS_F & INT_AC_V2 = TRUE &
        PG_911 = TRUE) &

    (SS_E_V2$0 = TRUE =>
        SS_E_V2 = bool(
            (C_CSS_V2 = POS_ES & (EIT_C_CSS = POS_O or PG_911 = FALSE or INT_AC_V2 = FALSE)) or
            (C_CSS_V2 = POS_ES & EIT_C_CSS = POS_O & KSS_E_V2 = TRUE))
        ) &
    (SS_E_V2$0 = FALSE =>
        SS_E_V2 = bool(TA_SS_E_V2$0 = TRUE & TA_SS_E_V2_echue = TRUE & (C_CSS_V2 = POS_ES &
        EIT_C_CSS = POS_O & KSS_E_V2 = TRUE))) &

    TA_SS_E_V2 = bool(SS_E_V2$0 = FALSE & (C_CSS_V2 = POS_ES & EIT_C_CSS = POS_O &
        KSS_E_V2 = TRUE) & TA_SS_E_V2_echue = FALSE)
    )
END
```

Fig. 7. State evolution of the signalling control point A specified in B-method

the state evolution, the input *TA_SS_E_V2_echue* represents the passing of time related to the block *SS_E_V2*. In this case, this input is only considered for the activation of the relay.

4.3   Animation and Verification

Many tools have been developed in order to support the B-method. One example of these tools is the ProB [13], which allows not only the animation of the machines but also their specification and model-checking. In this work, ProB may be useful in order to animate the specification as a way to analyse the system behaviour. During the animation, the tool allows operations to be called and it always verifies if the machine state is valid according to the invariant.

Regarding the machine verification, ProB contains a model-checker that allows the verification of each possible state of the machine in order to find the existence of a state that does not meet the invariant. If an invalid state is found, the tool presents it as an counter example.

In order to analyse the machine representing our running example, it is possible to animate and verify it. The animation provide an overview of the execution of the system when implemented, and, in this case, the animation of the specification has shown to be accurate with the reality. Furthermore, the verification of the system by the model-checker guaranteed that, in a case where all components are working normally, two trains must not have the permission to go in opposite ways in the same track at the same time, meaning that the invariant not(KIT_C_911 = TRUE & EF11 = TRUE) is false in every possible machine state. The model-checking process took 3031 milliseconds, verifying the 36,865 possible transitions between the 18 existing states in order to analyse if any transition may lead to an inconsistent state. The verification was made by a 64 bits Intel(R) Core(TM) i7-7600U 2.80 GHz CPU with 16 Gb RAM and running the Windows 10 operating system in its professional version.

However, although this strategy of specification is able to guarantee the absence of states that may lead to a collision, it is important to admit that the verification is not enough in order to guarantee the complete absence of collisions in the real field. The execution of the system in reality contains many other variables related to the context that are not specified in this work. These variables are related, for example, to the position of the trains in the tracks, the decisions made by the driver or even the well functioning of each component. This type of contextual information may be considered in the specification in order to prove the safety of the system. The specification and use of context variables in the B-method relay-based RIS specification are in our near future agenda.

5   Conclusion

This paper presented a strategy for the formal specification of relay-based railway interlocking systems in B-method based on the behavioural logic of the relay diagram electrical components. Since the complete behaviour of a system is comprised by the behaviour of each of its components, it is possible to specify the complete RIS system by using the specification of its components behaviours. Furthermore, as a reactive system based on the activation and deactivation of the components (boolean states), it is possible to specify the conditions for each component to be activated and the effect of their activation by using propositional logic, which is supported by B-method. Moreover, by using B-method, it is possible to animate and prove safety properties that should be enforced by the relay diagrams by the use of the tools that supports B-method.

By using the strategy presented in this paper, an example of relay diagram used in industry was specified in B and a safety property about this diagram was proved. The Prob model-checker was used in order to verify the B-specification and, as specified in the INVARIANT of the B-machine, the tool was able to prove that two trains may not have the permission to enter in the same track in opposite directions at the same time. Although this property is important in order to avoid frontal collisions, it is not enough, since there are many contextual variables that must be considered in order to prove the safety of the system.

In our upcoming agenda, we aim to be able to specify contextual variables related to the environment of the RIS system. These variables may specify information that must be considered in order to prove the safety of the system, like the position of the train or the possibility of the driver to make unsafe decisions. Besides, we aim to specify relay-based RIS based on the possibility of the components to failure. By analysing this specification, we intend to demonstrate the impact of these failures on the safety of the system and provide methodologies in order to avoid dangerous states.

Furthermore, B-method disposes of methods for system refinement and implementation, which may be explored in order to implement RIS as computer-controlled systems in the future. This paper presents a first step towards the possibility of evolving relay-based RIS into computer-controlled RIS by specifying the logic of relay diagrams in B-method based on propositional logic. This specification presents how the inputs affects the system in order to produce outputs, which may be refined in order to generate code that can be executed. Once compiled, the implementation of this system may be used inside small computers which are able to receive electrical inputs, process them based on the implemented system and emit outputs also in the form of electrical signals that manages the movement of the trains in the tracks.

References

1. Abrial, J.R.: The B-Book: Assigning Programs to Meanings. Cambridge University Press, New York (1996)
2. Beer, H.: The LTL Checker Plugins: A Reference Manual. Eindhoven University of Technology, Eindhoven (2004)
3. Behm, P., Benoit, P., Faivre, A., Meynadier, J.-M.: Météor: a successful application of B in a large project. In: Wing, J.M., Woodcock, J., Davies, J. (eds.) FM 1999. LNCS, vol. 1708, pp. 369–387. Springer, Heidelberg (1999). https://doi.org/10.1007/3-540-48119-2_22
4. Cavada, R., Cimatti, A., Sessa, M.: Analysis of relay interlocking systems via SMT-based model checking of switched multi-domain Kirchhoff networks. In: The Eighteenth in a Series of Conferences on the Theory and Applications of Formal Methods in Hardware and System Verification (FMCAD 2018), vol. 18, pp. 179–187. IEEE (2018)

5. ClearSy: B Language Reference Manual, version 1.8.5
6. Fantechi, A., Fokkink, W., Morzenti, A.: B-specification of relay-based railway interlocking systems based on the propositional logic of the system state evolution. In: Formal Methods for Industrial Critical Systems: A Survey of Applications, pp. 61–84 (2013)
7. Ghosh, S., Das, A., Basak, N., Dasgupta, P., Katiyar, A.: Formal methods for validation and test point prioritization in railway signaling logic. IEEE Trans. Intell. Transp. Syst. **18**(3), 678–689 (2017)
8. Gjaldbæk, T., Haxthausen, A.E.: Modelling and verification of interlocking systems for railway lines. IFAC Proc. Vol. **36**(14), 233–238 (2003)
9. Guiho, G., Hennebert, C.: SACEM software validation. In: 1990 Proceedings of the 12th International Conference on Software Engineering, pp. 186–191. IEEE (1990)
10. Hansen, K.M.: Formalising railway interlocking systems. In: Nordic Seminar on Dependable Computing Systems, pp. 83–94. Citeseer (1998)
11. Haxthausen, A.E., Le Bliguet, M., Kjær, A.A.: Modelling and verification of relay interlocking systems. In: Choppy, C., Sokolsky, O. (eds.) Monterey Workshop 2008. LNCS, vol. 6028, pp. 141–153. Springer, Heidelberg (2010). https://doi.org/10.1007/978-3-642-12566-9_8
12. Lecomte, T., Servat, T., Pouzancre, G., et al.: Formal methods in safety-critical railway systems. In: 10th Brasilian Symposium on Formal Methods, pp. 29–31 (2007)
13. Leuschel, M., Butler, M.: ProB: a model checker for B. In: Araki, K., Gnesi, S., Mandrioli, D. (eds.) FME 2003. LNCS, vol. 2805, pp. 855–874. Springer, Heidelberg (2003). https://doi.org/10.1007/978-3-540-45236-2_46
14. Rétiveau, R.: La signalisation ferroviaire. Presse de l'école nationale des Ponts et Chaussées (1987)
15. Schneider, S.: The B-Method: An Introduction. Palgrave, Basingstoke (2001)
16. Sun, P., Collart-Dutilleul, S., Bon, P.: A model pattern of railway interlocking system by Petri nets. In: 2015 International Conference on Models and Technologies for Intelligent Transportation Systems (MT-ITS), pp. 442–449. IEEE (2015)
17. Winter, K.: Model checking railway interlocking systems. In: Australian Computer Science Communications, vol. 24, pp. 303–310. Australian Computer Society, Inc. (2002)

Security

Threat Modeling in the Railway Domain

Christoph Schmittner[1]([✉])([iD]), Peter Tummeltshammer[2], David Hofbauer[3],
Abdelkader Magdy Shaaban[1], Michael Meidlinger[2], Markus Tauber[3],
Arndt Bonitz[1], Reinhard Hametner[2], and Manuela Brandstetter[3]

[1] AIT Austrian Institute of Technology GmbH, Giefinggasse 4, 1210 Vienna, Austria
christoph.schmittner@ait.ac.at
[2] Thales Austria GmbH, Handelskai 92, 1200 Vienna, Austria
[3] Fachhochschule Burgenland GmbH, Campus 1, 7000 Eisenstadt, Austria

Abstract. Connected and intelligent railway technologies like the European Rail Traffic Management System (ERTMS) introduce new risks in cybersecurity. Threat modeling is a building block in security engineering that identifies potential threats in order to define corresponding mitigation. In this paper, we show how to conduct threat modeling for railway security analysis during a development life cycle based on IEC 62443. We propose a practical and efficient approach to threat modeling, extending existing tool support and demonstrating its applicability and feasibility.

Keywords: Railway · Cybersecurity · Threat modeling · IEC 62443 · Cybersecurity analysis

1 Introduction

The railway system is changing towards an Internet of Things (IoT)-based system with an increased usage of Components of the Shelf (COTS) [21] and wireless communication technologies [11]. With the transition to information and communication systems, the cyber-attack surface has increased tremendously. Evaluations showed vulnerabilities and weaknesses in European Rail Traffic Management System (ERTMS) [4,16] and a rail based honeypot setup showed an active threat landscape [15].

In order to address cybersecurity concerns, different existing standards have been examined [5] and the IEC 62443 series [13] was selected. A pre-norm from the German standardization committee DKE [8] provides guidance on how to apply IEC 62443 in the railway domain. IEC 62443-3-2 [3] does not prescribe or propose a methodology for the identification of cybersecurity risk.

In this paper, we present a novel Threat Modeling approach for identifying threats in the safety critical railway domain. To the best of the authors' knowledge, no previous works exist that treats threat modeling in the railway domain in a systematic and concise manner. The remainder of this paper is structured as follows. Section 2 gives an overview about the Railway Domain, existing

© Springer Nature Switzerland AG 2019
S. Collart-Dutilleul et al. (Eds.): RSSRail 2019, LNCS 11495, pp. 261–271, 2019.
https://doi.org/10.1007/978-3-030-18744-6_17

approaches towards security and Threat Modeling. Section 3 describes our approach of Threat Modeling and a proof-of-concept. Finally, Sect. 4 concludes the paper.

2 State of the Art

This section presents the State of the Art of the railway system based on ERTMS and summarizes the current framework regarding safety. The focus was on the already existing coverage of security. Section 2.3 presents the IEC 62443 series as a security framework for the railway domain. The section is concluded by presenting existing approaches towards railway security assessment and the existing work for threat modeling.

2.1   Overview of the Railway System

ERTMS is a European Union initiative to create a common standard for train signaling, control, communication and management. The goal is to increase efficiency, especially for cross-border traffic [23].

The two main components of ERTMS are ETCS (European Train Control System) and GSM-R (Global System for Mobile Communications – Railway) or LTE-R (Long Term Evolution – Railway). ETCS is intended for safety-critical signaling and control systems. In ETCS Level 3, trains find their positions themselves with the help of onboard sensors (tachometer, radar) and absolute position reference (APR) beacons, called eurobalise, located on the track. The trains continuously transmit their signals (position and speed) to the Radio Block Center (RBC) which is further connected to a Control Centre. Based on the high-resolution information which is received from all trains in the zone, the limit of movement authority[1] and speed is determined and fed back to the vehicle via the GSM-R or LTE-R radio link, alongside some additional route information.

2.2   Safety Framework

In the railway domain, safety engineering is guided mainly by the following standards.

EN 50126: *The specification and demonstration of Reliability, Availability, Maintainability and Safety (RAMS).* This document defines security as the resilience of a system to "vandalism and unreasonable human action", but the aspect of protection against cyber threats is outside the scope of this standard. However, "security hazards" are listed in system hazard analysis [9].

EN 50128: *Software for railway control and protection systems.* This standard does not consider security because it is out of the scope of this standard [7].

---

[1] i.e. the section on the tracks which is pre-approved for the train.

EN 50129: *Safety related electronic systems for signalling.* This standard addresses "protection against unauthorized access" and the 2018 edition was extended to include additional sections on IT security [10].

EN 50159: *Safety-related communication in transmission systems.* This standard is aimed at the safety-related usage of transmission systems which might be endangered by security threats. The focus is on ensuring the integrity of the communication, availability and confidentiality is excluded [6].

2.3 Security Framework

Based on an evaluation of different security standards [5], the IEC 62443 [13] series was identified as a suitable security framework for the railway domain. The IEC 62443 series "Security for industrial automation and control systems" is divided into four groups. Note that not all parts of the standard have been released yet, and the development is still ongoing.

The standard defines the following roles "Asset Operator", "System Integrator" and "Product Supplier". Depending on the role, different parts of the standard apply.

IEC 62443-1-x: *General* describes overarching concepts, terms and metrics for secure IACS systems.

IEC 62443-2-x: *Policies & Procedures* present the management framework for implementation, patching and operation.

IEC 62443-3-x: *System* is aimed at "Asset Operator" and "System Integrator" and describes necessary activities and processes during the system engineering.

IEC 62443-4-x: *Component* is for "Product supplier" and describes how to develop secure components for the integration in IACS.

IEC 62443 uses the following Security Level (SL).

Security Level Target (SL-T): Desired level of security, usually based on a risk assessment.

Security Level Capability (SL-C): Level of security achievable if a system or component is properly configured and installed.

Security Level Achieved (SL-A): Achieved level of security, based on an assessment of system design or deployment.

The Asset Owner uses Part 3-2 to determine the security needs of the system while considering safety and business criticality. Based on the security needs and logical and functional distribution a security architecture is developed which divides the system into zones and conduits. A zone collects systems with a similar criticality level or security needs and has a SL-T assigned.

The System Integrator can use Part 3-3 to design a system which achieves SL-A. For this, components and systems with a suitable SL-C have to be chosen.

The Product Supplier can use Part 4-1 and 4-2 to develop secure components with SL-C. Part 4-1 describes security development life cycle and the required capabilities for the process. Part 4-2 describe technical security requirements for components.

2.4   Existing Railway Risk Analysis Approaches

For both, the detailed and the high-level risk assessment, it is suggested to use the same risk assessment methodology [3]. In [25], fault trees are used to analyze safety and security in a Communication Based Train Control (CBTC) system of urban railways. Security events are added as additional nodes in the fault tree. There are however some drawbacks to that approach. First of all, this approach requires all relevant security events to be identified beforehand. The threat modeling approach presented in this paper provides a systematic methodology to do so and can be used to resolve this issue. Additionally, once the events have been identified, they need to be weighted by the probability of their occurrence, which is difficult to assess.

More specifically, [24] extends hazard and operability studies (HAZOP) to also take into account security threats in a Train Leader Telephone System. The HAZOP guide-word driven system is used to formulate a set of generic expressions which are then used to examine the system for potential threats. This is similar –but less formal– than the approach of using an explicit "threat model" with corresponding knowledge base of threats and vulnerabilities.

Another line of work [4] puts more focus on developing approaches towards risk assessment, e.g. how to rate and classify identified threats.

The American Public Transportation Association published a Recommend Practice [1] which already referred to the Microsoft Secured Development Life-cycle (MS-SDL) [12] and listed STRIDE. Threat modeling is not mentioned as method, instead attack trees are recommended. We assume one of the reasons is that this Recommend Practice was published, before a threat modeling tool was available, which could be adapted to different domains.

2.5   Threat Modeling

Our approach proposed in Sect. 3 is based on threat modeling. Threat modeling is a technique for the identification of security risks and has been promoted as part of the MS-SDL [12]. It defines an abstract model of potential threats, which is applied to the system model in order to identify representations of the threats. In general, threat modeling can be divided into the following steps:

1. Model the system with all security related assumptions and necessary information.
2. Model potential adversaries with capabilities, actions, tactics, techniques, and procedures.
3. Apply the threat model to the system model to identify potential threats
4. Evaluate all identified threats and decide on the risk treatment
5. Update the system model with the security countermeasures
6. Repeat step 3 in order to identify missed or new threats

Systems are modeled in a Data- ow Diagram (DFD). There are five basic elements in a DFD:

Processes are elements that, based on their input, perform actions and/or generate outputs.

Data stores are sinks or sources of data. Examples are databases or internal storage.

Data flows represent the flow of information between elements. A data flow can be a protocol specific communication link such as HTTPS or UDP.

External interactors are elements whose influence should be taken into account, but which are outside the scope of the analysis.

Trust boundaries divide the elements in the diagram into different trust zones, e.g. elements in open networks vs elements in internal networks.

Depending on the available system details and threat identification needs, a high-level process can be further decomposed into multiple lower-level components in a hierarchical way. One can use Spoofing, Tampering, Repudiation, Information disclosure, Denial of Service, and Elevation of privilege (STRIDE) to define a generic threat model (see Table 1). As an example, a Data Flow can be tampered with, the transmitted information can be disclosed or a denial of service can impact the Data Flow. Since a data flow is not an entity, it cannot be spoofed.

Table 1. STRIDE threat model

	Spoofing	Tampering	Repudiation	Inf. disclosure	DoS	Elev. of priv.
Data flows		×		×	×	
Data store		×		×	×	
Processes	×	×	×	×	×	×
Interactors	×		×			

Depending on the level of granularity and available information, threat models can contain more specific descriptions of threats. For example, if the Data Flow is wireless one can define subcategories for Denial of Service like Jamming.

Research regarding threat modeling in the mobility domain has been carried out in [22]. There, components are modeled for connected cars, which are then used to derive a threat and vulnerability catalogue. With regards to the automotive domain, threat models have been employed successfully in [14,17].

Consequently, we propose to use this approach also for modeling components, threats and vulnerabilities in the railway domain, e.g. for autonomous trains. One benefit of using threat modeling is the availability of tools which support the method [20]. Microsoft developed a Threat Modeling Tool (TMT) which is available as a free plugin for Microsoft Visio [18]. With the 2016 release of the tool, it is possible to create own and domain specific templates. This allows for the TMT to be applied to new domains such as rail, as we will present in the upcoming Sect. 3.

3 Railway Threat Modeling

In order to conduct a cybersecurity risk assessment according to IEC 62443, we need a systematic approach to identify threats to a system. As Sect. 2.4 has shown, the current approaches are either based on already identified threats or rely on expert judgment and brainstorming for the identification of threats. We developed a railway specific template, which allows the modeling of railway systems and a railway threat model and integrate the Railway threat modeling process with the IEC 62443 workflow.

3.1 Railway Template

The template is the central storage of modeling elements, threats, and corresponding mitigation. It should be periodically updated with external information regarding vulnerabilities and mitigation and experiences from applying threat modeling. A Template describes in the threat modeling tool a collection of stencils and corresponding threat types.

- **Stencils:** A collection of modelling elements with their properties. In Fig. 4 all the elements used (red boxes, round circles, connections) need to be defined as stencils. A part of this collection is shown on the right of Fig. 4. Each of this modeling elements has a set of properties which can be used to describe its security relevant behavior.
- **Threat types:** A collection of rules, describing when a specific threat is relevant. This rules are defined, using names and properties of stencils, and stored in a threat database. A threat type can be extended with additional information, an example would be potential mitigation and comments. A example for a rule is: *source is [stencilname] and target is [stencilname] and target.[property] is 'Yes'.*

When creating a new template, the most important parts are stencils for drawing DFDs and threat types that define threat and mitigation catalogues. We created stencils for railway components such as RBC or GSM-R. For each stencil, different properties and values are defined. Once defined, they can be used during the threat modeling to define already known security relevant information.

The threat model in the template consists of threat types, classified based on the STRIDE categories. Each threat type is described by title, threat description, potential mitigation and *include* and *exclude* rule. The rules describe when a threat is generated for an element in a data flow diagram. The grammar for the rules can be found in the documentation of the threat modeling tool [19].

Threat modeling can be performed in further phases of the lifecycle as monitoring activity to identify if new threats are relevant for a certain system. This requires updating the data flow diagram to mirror the real system and re-analyzing it with an updated threat database.

As an example, based on [16], we add the property Cipher Algorithm to the GSM-R stencil (see Fig. 1). We can add different potential values for this

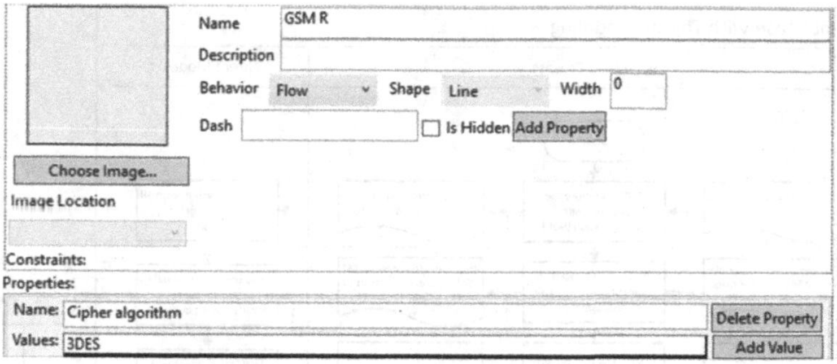

Fig. 1. Extensions of stencil properties and rules

property, to denote which cipher algorithm is used. The next step is to extend the rule set accordingly. We can either extend an existing rule or add an rule. Figure 2 shows the rule definition interface with the additional rule. This rule checks if a communication flow uses the insecure Cipher Algorithm and if this flow is potentially susceptible to eavesdropping. The second part is checked with the condition if the flow crosses a physical boundary, e.g. is transferred over a public (or wireless) communication. Based on this in further evaluation of existing models we will receive a warning that there are potential threats with 3DES. If there are more concerns or real world attacks we can increase the suggested impact and justification. Doing this allows us to document new concerns in existing systems and monitor for new risks.

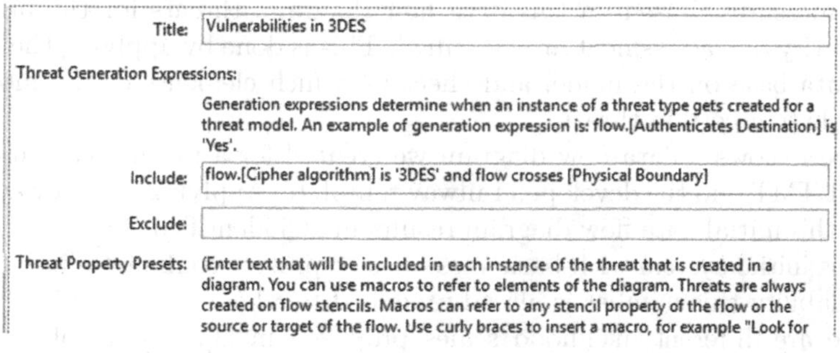

Fig. 2. New rule for 3DES

3.2 Proposed Process

Figure 3 shows our proposal how threat modeling can be used in the IEC 62443 workflow.

The specification of the system under consideration and the security related properties is done by defining a data flow diagram of the system. The elements

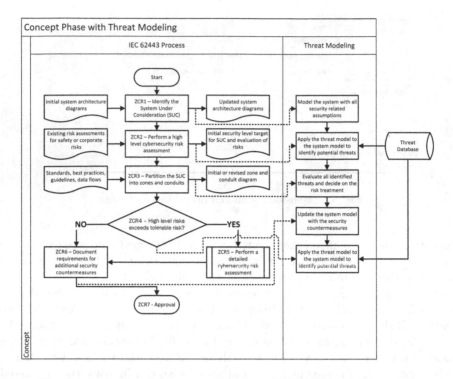

Fig. 3. Integration of threat modeling into IEC 62443 security analysis

in the data flow diagram need to be able to represent already implemented security measures. Based on this data flow diagram, threats for the high level cybersecurity risk assessment are identified. This is done by applying the railway threat data base on the model and checking which elements of the model are susceptible to a certain threat.

Figure 4 shows a data flow diagram we created for a rail use case using the Microsoft TMT and the developed railway template. Applying the railway threat types to this initial data flow diagram results in 103 identified threats. If we configure this initial system with basic measures to protect confidentiality, integrity and availability this number is already reduced to 82.

There are different likelihood scales proposed in [3], but all of them rely on expert judgment to rate risks. We use the approach from Common Criteria (ISO/IEC 15408) [2]. This approach is well established and has the additional benefit that most of the factors are more or less stable over time. This means that a risk analysis which is repeated or conducted by a different set of experts should deliver similar results. In addition we can apply this analysis on different levels of granularity without changing the likelihood scale.

The considered factors "Time taken to identify and exploit (Elapsed Time)", "Specialist technical expertise required (Specialist Expertise)", "Knowledge of the TOE design and operation (Knowledge of the TOE)", "Window of

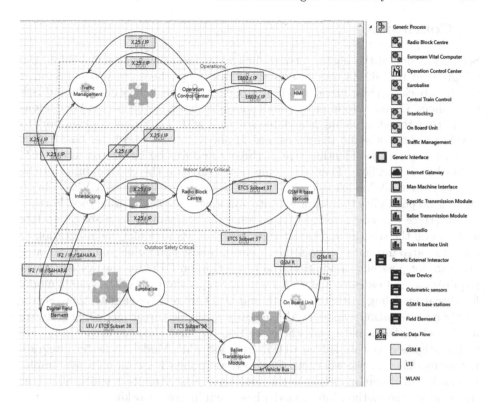

Fig. 4. Data flow diagram with a sub set of available stencils (Color figure online)

opportunity", "IT hardware/software or other equipment required for exploitation". Based on this factors a attack potential is calculated (into five defined levels), which is used to determine the likelihood of a successful attack. [3] proposes a severity scale, considering Operational, Financial and HSE, divided into three levels. Both qualitative values are be combined in a risk matrix to conduct the risk assessment. The risk matrix can be tailored to the risk acceptance of the organisation, legal and regulatory requirements. If no adjustments are planned, the example of a 3×5 risk matrix in Annex B of IEC 62443-3-2 [3] can be used to determine the SL.

Based on its outcome, the system is partitioned into zones and conduits and initial security measures are assigned. The zones are modeled by adding corresponding trust boundaries and security measures into the diagram. Repeating the threat modeling shows if the applied measures resolved the threats, or if new threats are introduced. If the risks are still not tolerable additional threat modeling for subsets of the first data flow diagram can be conducted. When all threats are either accepted or resolved, the identified cybersecurity requirements are documented and approved.

4   Conclusion

Security is one of the biggest new challenges in the railway domain. While the adoption of IEC 62443 was an important first step, there are still many open points especially regarding detailed approaches to threat identification and risk assessment. One step to improve the situation is shown in this paper: We demonstrate that threat modeling is a viable solution with a sufficient tool support to develop railway specific templates and apply it to real world use cases. This enables a systematic identification of threats and can be integrated into a IEC 62443 based workflow. There are some restrictions on the expandability of the Microsoft Threat Modeling tool. Due to the implementation as a Visio plugin there is no possibility to integrate it into a model-based engineering tool. Further the interface was not developed for ongoing maintainability to manage, update and extend the stencils and threat rules. Further features like the integration of an automated interface between the threat database and vulnerability databases are also not possible. In addition, the restriction on DFD for the system model requires, in most cases, to maintain a separate representation of the system model for threat modeling. Although SysML and DFD are relative similar, there is currently no translation available. All currently available threat modelling software are based on DFD and it was therefore also our first choice. Further steps are to investigate if we can deduce a DFD from a SysML Model, to better integrate threat modeling in the workflow. Due to these points we work on a new implementation of threat modeling in the tool Enterprise Architect which allows us to integrate the method into a model-based engineering workflow.

Acknowledgments. This work is partially supported by the ECSEL projects Productive4.0 and SECREDAS (contract no. 737459, 783119) and Austrian Research Promotion Agency (FFG).

References

1. Securing Control and Communications Systems in Rail Transit Environments Part II: Defining a Security Zone Architecture for Rail Transit and Protecting Critical Zones. RECOMMENDED PRACTICE APTA-SS-CCS-RP-002-13, American Public Transportation Association, June 2013
2. Common Methodology for Information Technology Security Evaluation. Technical report, CCMB-2017-04-004, April 2017
3. IEC 62443 Security for industrial automation and control systems - Part 3-2: Security risk assessment and system design. Committee Draft for Vote (CDV) IEC 62443-3-2 ED1, France (2018)
4. Bloomfield, R., Bendele, M., Bishop, P., Stroud, R., Tonks, S.: The risk assessment of ERTMS-based railway systems from a cyber security perspective: methodology and lessons learned. In: Lecomte, T., Pinger, R., Romanovsky, A. (eds.) RSSRail 2016. LNCS, vol. 9707, pp. 3–19. Springer, Cham (2016). https://doi.org/10.1007/978-3-319-33951-1_1
5. Braband, J.: Towards an IT Security Framework for Railway Automation. Toulouse, February 2014

6. CENELEC: EN 50159:2010: Railway applications - communication, signalling and processing systems - safety-related communication in transmission systems

7. CENELEC, European Committee for Electrotechnical Standardization: EN 50128 Railway applications - Communication, signalling and processing systems - Software for railway control and protection systems (2011)

8. DKE Deutsche Kommission Elektrotechnik Elektronik Informationstechnik: Electric signalling systems for railways – Part 104: IT Security Guideline based on IEC 62443 (2014)

9. European Committee for Standardization: EN 50126-1 Railway applications - The specification and demonstration of Reliability, Availability, Maintainability and Safety (RAMS) - Part 1: Basic requirements and generic process (2010)

10. European Committee for Standardization: EN 50129, Railway applications - Communication, signalling and processing systems - Safety related electronic systems for signalling (2010)

11. He, R., et al.: High-speed railway communications: from GSM-R to LTE-R. IEEE Veh. Technol. Mag. **11**(3) (2016). https://doi.org/10.1109/MVT.2016.2564446. http://ieeexplore.ieee.org/document/7553613/

12. Howard, M., Lipner, S.: The Security Development Lifecycle, vol. 8. Microsoft Press, Redmond (2006)

13. International Electrotechnical Commission: IEC 62443: Industrial communication networks - Network and system security

14. Karahasanovic, A., Kleberger, P., Almgren, M.: Adapting Threat Modeling Methods for the Automotive Industry, p. 11 (2017)

15. Koramis, Sophos: Whitepaper Project HoneyTrain. Technical report, September 2015

16. Lopez, I., Aguado, M.: Cyber security analysis of the European train controlsystem. IEEE Commun. Mag. **53**(10), 110–116 (2015)

17. Ma, Z., Schmittner, C.: Threat modeling for automotive security analysis. Adv. Sci. Technol. Lett. **139**, 333–339 (2016)

18. Microsoft: Microsoft Threat Modeling Tool (2016). https://www.microsoft.com/en-us/download/details.aspx?id=49168

19. Microsoft - SDL Team: Introducing Microsoft Threat Modeling Tool 2014 (2014). https://www.microsoft.com/security/blog/2014/04/15/introducing-microsoft-threat-modeling-tool-2014/

20. Meland, P.H., Spampinato, D.G., Hagen, E., Baadshaug, E.T.: SeaMonster: providing tool support for security modeling, p. 10 (2008)

21. Rong, H., Liu, W.: Development and research of train operation control system and safety computer platform based on COTS. Boletín Técnico **55**(18), 7 (2017)

22. Strobl, S., Hofbauer, D., Schmittner, C., Maksuti, S., Tauber, M., Delsing, J.: Connected cars—threats, vulnerabilities and their impact. In: 2018 IEEE Industrial Cyber-Physical Systems (ICPS), pp. 375–380. IEEE (2018)

23. unife: From Trucks to Trains - How ERTMS Helps Making Rail Freight More Competitive (2018)

24. Winther, R., Johnsen, O.-A., Gran, B.A.: Security assessments of safety critical systems using HAZOPs. In: Voges, U. (ed.) SAFECOMP 2001. LNCS, vol. 2187, pp. 14–24. Springer, Heidelberg (2001). https://doi.org/10.1007/3-540-45416-0_2

25. Yi, S., Wang, H., Ma, Y., Xie, F., Zhang, P., Di, L.: A safety-security assessment approach for communication-based train control (CBTC) systems based on the extended fault tree. In: 2018 27th International Conference on Computer Communication and Networks (ICCCN), pp. 1–5. IEEE (2018)

Integration Approach for Communications-Based Train Control Applications in a High Assurance Security Architecture

Thorsten Schulz$^{(\boxtimes)}$ ⓘ, Frank Golatowski ⓘ, and Dirk Timmermann ⓘ

Institute of Applied Microelectronics and CE, University of Rostock,
Rostock, Germany
{thorsten.schulz,frank.golatowski,dirk.timmermann}@uni-rostock.de

Abstract. The secure integration of model-based, safety-critical applications implemented in the programming suite Ansys SCADE is explained with the help of a demonstrator. The interoperability between the embedded devices of the demonstrator is achieved using the new TRDP middleware. Remote connections are secured using the WireGuard secure network channel. The demonstrator security concept addresses the different life cycles of its heterogeneous components by adoption of the robust MILS separation architecture. The goal of this open demonstrator is to show how these essential technologies can be composed to a secure safety-critical system.

Keywords: MILS · Security · Formal modeling · Railway · CPS

1 Introduction

From a systematic viewpoint, an application or device in a distributed system has inputs, the application logic and outputs. For a physical system, the application is hosted on hardware, typically abstracted from the application with a hardware abstraction layer and an operating system. In an interoperable, networked system, the inputs and outputs and their connection fabric are abstracted by a middleware using a standardized network protocol. Networks can range from dedicated, local connections to remote connections over untrusted networks. Untrusted access must be secured with adequate measures, defined by norms such as IEC 62443 or Common Criteria. Depending on the requirements of the application, certain levels of security assurance require different security measures. Railway devices must be maintainable with regards to EN 50126. Even on a dedicated network, they must secure their maintenance access and update features. The update/maintenance provider may not part a certified of the system.

This puzzle of heterogeneous technologies potentially induces three pitfalls: different life cycles, mismatching interfaces, complex integration. In this paper,

© Springer Nature Switzerland AG 2019
S. Collart-Dutilleul et al. (Eds.): RSSRail 2019, LNCS 11495, pp. 272–283, 2019.
https://doi.org/10.1007/978-3-030-18744-6_18

we describe our approach for an educational technology demonstrator that addresses these issues by applying the Multiple Independent Levels of Security (MILS) architecture on a separation kernel [11,14].

A real-world device is based on technologies, e.g., network protocols and hardware, with shorter life cycles compared to its core application logic. Different levels of modularity and a separation architecture are required to achieve a composed system certification. Such a separation architecture with different levels of security and safety can sustain security patches or updates to components without invalidating the safety certification of the application. This paper describes the security architecture in the next Sect. 2, showing its feasibility with the help of a demonstrator in Sect. 3.

In comparison to earlier approaches of our OpenETCS[1] On-Board-Unit (OBU) demonstrator [6], we have upgraded a basic middleware implementation with the new IEC 61375 standard based reference implementation of the Train Real Time Data Protocol (TRDP) from the TCNopen consortium. The adaptations and extensions to the TRDP Light library, we deemed necessary for a smooth integration with the critical application's interfaces, will be explained in Sect. 4. Within the MILS architecture, the demonstrator also applies a novel, state of the art encryption mechanism with minimal additional overhead for embedded systems. We have selected this data encryption tunnel for communication between, in terms of the use-case, "non-local" devices. The motivation will be discussed in Sect. 5.

2   Security Architecture for Critical Systems

Railway applications are required to be reliable, available, maintainable and safe (RAMS) according to accepted and governing standards, in Europe EN 50126. The properties are a result of qualified processes and guided methods, requiring specially trained engineers, operators and maintainers to minimize application risks. The processes specifically require that access is limited to that qualified and authorized group to assure the integrity of the processes and the system. Physical access barriers, e.g., locked cabinets, typically have a constant ratio between cost of securing and effort to bypass, largely due to the required physical attendance of the intruder with the specific knowledge to that barrier.

The introduction of networked or remote access to critical systems as Cyber-Physical Systems (CPS), in principle, has not changed this paradigm, but removed the latter physical appearance of an intruder. This has introduced negative scaling effects making even well secured systems with only a small security vulnerability cheap for large-scale attacks. The current mitigation trend in IT systems is to automate and improve testing methods, and to shorten time to update, i.e., patch vulnerabilities. In contrast, critical systems have stricter update policies and typically run on non-standardized hardware. Consequently,

---

[1] ETCS, European Train Control System. OpenETCS was a research project fostering an open reference implementation.

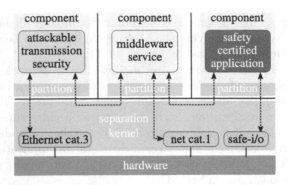

Fig. 1. Architecture of a base MILS system with a separation kernel, a safety application and additional services. Components like the security protocol (green) and the middleware must be instantiated separated to assure non-interference and correct behaviour of the safety application. (Color figure online)

testing requires more effort for a much smaller number of operative products. Modifying a critical system's software requires re-certification – even for security patches.

Current research is developing methodologies to reduce the fore-said re-certification effort through dependable partitioning of a system, applying the Multiple Independent Levels of Security (MILS) architecture (Fig. 1).

The demonstrator's system design splits the system into a safe control component, a communication middleware and an independent security component with remote authorization, authentication and encryption. The safety function within the control application is unaffected of corruptions within the transmission component, if it can continue operation in degraded mode without that transmission data, e.g., safely issue an emergency command. The data flow between the components is guarded by the MILS separation kernel, see Fig. 1, allowing only predefined data flows between the partitions, i.e., application domains. This approach is also covered by IEC 62443 as conduits connecting zones [9]. Depending on attack vectors, system and application design, the security relevant transmission components could then also be of lower software confidence level and classified with a low Software Safety Integrity Level (SSIL), being less susceptible to re-certification requirements.

The separation kernel (SK) of a MILS system connects and controls the components within its partitions. There are different kinds and implementations of SK. For our demonstrator's OBU we use Sysgo's PikeOS. A different approach following the same MILS architecture is implemented in Thales' TAS platform [7] building on a Linux KVM-hypervisor setup for security. The kernel security development process follows different strategies to prove high assurance assumptions claiming interference-free execution of the composed system. Some rely on rigorous testing, using different testing techniques such as systematic and robustness testing (fuzz-testing), others rely on formal methods and a mixture of these techniques [13].

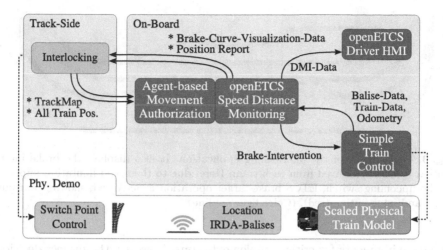

Fig. 2. Demonstrator concept view. On the left, the trackside control device has a GUI and is connected to the demonstrator model. On the right are the On-Board components, which are instantiated for each train. (Color figure online)

An additional security measure that is applied within the demonstrator design is a cryptography data tunnel. This component can ensure the CIA properties of confidentiality, integrity and authenticity of external data access via untrusted networks (i.e., IEC 62443 cat. 3). Most state-of-the-art encryption protocols provide these properties. However, they strongly differ in algorithmic and integration complexity. Some technology choices are less desirable for carrying process data of safety-critical systems. We will discuss our choice in Sect. 5.

In the next section, we will introduce the system structure of the demonstrator and its applications. The safety-critical application has a longer life cycle compared to a network-connected middleware or encryption tunnel. These need to be able receive regular security patches, which is supported by the MILS architecture. Therefore, we also separate the middleware described in Sect. 4.

3   Demonstrator Overview

The demonstrator show in Fig. 2 has three parts: The trackside control application, termed "interlocking". Then, for each train, the on-board components and last, but not least, the physical demonstrator with model-trains. Larger parts of the on-board application logic (see dark-red boxes in Fig. 2) are implemented using the programming language Scade for safety-critical systems. Scade is an extension of Lustre, a synchronous dataflow programming language for reactive systems. It is graphically defined in the ANSYS SCADE Suite modeller. A code generator creates C code for compilation into executable binaries. The advantages of Scade are proofs towards causality errors, graphical verification, immanent bounds checking and well defined behaviour. There exist other

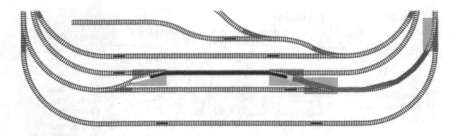

Fig. 3. GUI output of the interlocking application. It also displays the brake intervention locations received from each train. Here, due to the speed limitation imposed by the upcoming switch, ETCS brake-target operation is activated, showing warning (org.) and intervention (red). (Color figure online)

viable environments for critical implementations. However, the project decision for Scade was based on the existing OpenETCS models.

The demonstrator use-case is a simplified distributed Communications-based Train Control (CBTC) application: It consists of an interlocking, movement authorization, movement supervision (OpenETCS), a driver-machine interface (OpenETCS) and a train control with movement simulation or emulation on the model railway. While the implemented approach is applying state-of-art technology with real-world performance requirements, it is nevertheless, a technology showcase with an uncommon use-case – the *distributed* calculation of the train's movement authorization. Nonetheless, the goal is to integrate practical components in a MILS system for evaluation and education.

The dataflow is found in Fig. 2. The interlocking GUI application controls the physical switches of the demonstrator model and communicates the current track segments to all train instances. It also receives and broadcasts all train positions. The "On-Board" devices are instantiated for each train, for both, simulated or connected to a physical model train. The devices are a train control instance, an ETCS Driver HMI (DMI) and the ETCS On-Board-Unit (OBU). All these on-board applications are implemented as a Scade model. However, for simplification of the demonstrator, the OBU application uses a subset of the OpenETCS OBU with only the core module for Speed and Distance Monitoring (SDM, [15]). The SDM reads a movement authorization, which is the reserved track up to the next stopping point, and a track segment list with speed limits, ascent-profile and special prohibitions. With this data, the SDM calculates safe speed limits that need to be obeyed at upcoming locations. This data is sent back to the interlocking GUI. The GUI captured Fig. 3 visualizes the ETCS data for the demonstrator. If the derived deceleration curves are crossed, they trigger brake commands, which are sent as intervention commands to the train control. In a real ETCS application the movement authorization and the track information is received from track data elements (balises), as well as the radio block centre (RBC) via a mobile communication channel. In our demonstrator, each train receives only the track map with the current switch settings and the

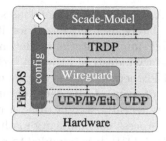

Fig. 4. Overview of the combined technologies in the OBU device of the demonstrator. All SW components are separated into partitions (see Fig. 1). The configuration for each component, the scheduling setup and the regulated information flow is sourced from a coordinated config pool.

locations of all trains (Fig. 2). The on-board application generates the necessary data: the safe movement authorization and the track atlas, for a safe movement of the train on the demonstrator.

The following sections focus on the integration of the SDM + movement authorization application together with the networking components within a MILS system.

4 Lightweight Middleware

A middleware is required to connect the interfaces of separate applications. The most basic communication channels exist on the same hardware as Inter-Process-Communication (IPC) techniques like message queues and shared memories with signalling. However, basic IPC are not regarded as middleware, as they are provided and governed by the operating system kernel. Strictly defined IPC are also one of the key features of the MILS system architecture, which will be discussed in the following section. Middleware typically abstracts application's interfaces in a standardized way, independent of the underlying operating system or hardware architecture to enable interoperability. For example, in the demonstrator setup (Fig. 2), the OpenETCS component Speed and Distance Monitoring passes a uniform data structure to the DMI, which is connected via Ethernet. The first approach copied the output of one into a UDP packet and sourced it to the ScadeDisplay DMI application on the other side. This worked, as long as both ran the same hardware, same OS, same compiler, etc. When we changed one device a from 32 to a 64 bit CPU architecture, the memory addresses of the fields within the data structure changed due to specific memory alignments. This is a typical issue addressed by middleware referred to as "marshalling". We will return to this later in this section.

Middleware nowadays are based on web services, XML, SOAP and other service-oriented architectures. These are often not targeted for real-time applications on embedded, resource-constrained systems. More fitting alternatives for machine-to-machine communications in industrial automation (IIoT) are CoAP,

MQTT, DDS and OPC UA. Despite its tremendous success in factory process automation, OPC UA has lately been criticized for its standard's complexity leading to non-interoperable implementations. Beyond these open protocols, there are also many proprietary industrial Ethernet technologies, like ProfiNET, EtherCAT, SERCOS III, TTEthernet, which can provide safe data transmission up to SIL 3, but this is out of scope of this demonstrator.

The railway industry has recently standardized a network protocol tailored towards efficient on-board process communication, the Train Real Time Data Protocol (TRDP, IEC 61375-2-3 [1]). It is intended to replace vendor proprietary solutions based on legacy buses or numerous incompatible custom solutions. It implements pull requests and cyclic push messages, as well as filtering based on a publish-subscribe scheme. The accompanying TCN standards (Train Communication Network) also define discovery, topology and direction based services. The payloads are predefined, immutable binary data structures. This makes it a perfect fit interfacing with the Scade applications, which, in the generated code, provide bare C-structures.

For the demonstrator, we used the open TRDP Light from the TCNopen consortium. It provides a reference implementation of the core functionality of TRDP. The Light implementation also provides the XML configuration functionality ([1] Annex C), for memory, process and message ("telegram") configuration for TRDP. Typically, TRDP functions are linked from a library to the application code. However, following the MILS separation approach we integrate TRDP as a generic component in our demonstrator. It obtains its specializing configuration from the embedded operating system's (here PikeOS) central data provider, see Fig. 4.

For transferring the inputs and outputs of the Scade application component with the TRDP component, we use a small shared-memory area. To ensure synchronicity between the Scade application's interface and TRDP's related telegram definition, we implemented a small "type bridge" tool that converts between the data model descriptions. Coming back to the motivation of this section, TRDP Light also provides dataset marshalling based on the provided XML configuration. Different memory alignments and architecture endianness (big endian vs. little endian) are taken care of. The IEC 61375 standard defines 16 basic types, considering character, integer, float and time types with different bit-widths and, for integers, signedness. These data types can be combined to custom dataset structures making up a telegram.

However, we could not use the stock marshalling function and had to implement a refined version. This is due to the OpenETCS applications being implemented in a former version of Scade (6.4) that is limited to a single integer flow type, e.g., int32 or int64. Our modified marshalling function can be configured to take these type mappings into account, i.e., inflate an incoming int8 to the Scade-defined type and vice-versa. This approach maybe also required for other specialized programming environments.

To transport safety-critical SIL-2 process payloads, the Safe Data Transmission extension ([1] Annex B) has to be used. The application-to-application safety channel needs implementation of the safety code (checksum) calculation in the same safety context as the application, hence in Scade. This is, however, still work in progress. Security assurance is achieved by having TRDP as a separate component as discussed. The MILS approach simplifies security patching in case of a discovered weakness in the network protocol.

5   Secure Data Encryption Tunnel

Network traffic encryption for security can be applied on different layers of the common ISO-OSI (Open Systems Interconnection model). The tunnelled traffic of security protocols ranges from data link layer (2) up to the application layer (7). When the data link layer, such as Ethernet, can be abstracted, as well as application specific higher schemes are out of scope, OSI layer 3 layer encryption (L3-VPN) is the most versatile choice to be used as a component. The section will thus look at the choice of the Transport Layer Security protocol (TLS) as used in OpenVPN, as well as the WireGuard protocol, a VPN implementation using one specific configuration of the Noise protocol. Since IPsec is of even greater complexity than TLS, according to evaluation by Schneier and Ferguson [5], we do not consider it here. However, partner projects dealing with Distributed MILS (D-MILS) approaches have well analysed this technology for deterministic networking, see their results in [8]. Algorithms used within L3-VPNs are also known from tunnel specific higher-level application protocols. For example, TLS is used to turn the Hypertext Transport Protocol (HTTP) into its secured version HTTPS and the Noise protocol is used by the widespread WhatsApp messaging service.

TLS itself is standardized and can tunnel payload and higher level protocols in many ways. For this reason, we will only refer to TLS in general in the following paragraphs. In comparison, "Noise" rather is a protocol framework that describes a protocol and requires a specific application implementation to exist. Therefore, we will refer to WireGuard implementing exactly one crypto algorithm and one protocol scheme.

For cryptography algorithms and security protocols, it is generally advisable to stick to proven solutions ([16]). Even small weaknesses turn the whole implementation vulnerable. For this reason, TLS has been widely adopted. However, a matured solution like TLS that has received continuous updates and adoptions to many applications, also grows in complexity and becomes more susceptible to implementation flaws, for example the infamous Heartbleed Bug published in 2014. The implementation of TLS is accompanied by over 20 extensional internet standards (RFC). E.g., the informational RFC 7457 exists alone to list known vulnerabilities and weaknesses to TLS implementations. Common sources of weaknesses in TLS are protocol downgrades to a broken cryptographic algorithm, buffer overruns of message parser, weak implementations of algorithms and dubious interpretation of certificates [17].

Some of those weaknesses of TLS are addressed in the latest version 1.3 [10], which is now a proposed standard, RFC 8446. Major changes listed in the RFC:

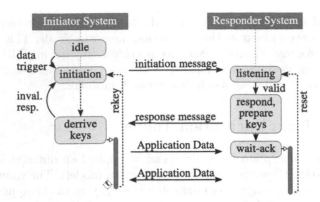

Fig. 5. The WireGuard state-machine has few states. The initiator starts rekeying after 120 s. Otherwise, the responder discards its transport keys after a maximum of 180 s.

- Legacy encryption algorithms were removed.
- Only Authenticated Encryption with Associated Data (AEAD) alg.
- Static RSA and Diffie-Hellman (DH) suites were removed for ephemeral var.
- Key-exchange suites provide Perfect Forward Secrecy.
- The handshake state machine has been significantly restructured to be more consistent and to remove superfluous messages.
- Elliptic curve algorithms move to base specification; signature algorithms Ed25519 and Ed448 were added. Point format negotiation was removed.

As a result, current TLS Compliance Requirements (see Sect. 9 of the RFC [10]) can be considered smaller than previous versions. The Subsect. 9.1 of the RFC lists one mandatory and two optional to implement cipher suites for AEAD and two Diffie-Hellman key exchanges. Which cipher suite is used for the application data, is negotiated in the handshake process. The TLS handshake messages have optional and mandatory extensions, e.g., the "KeyShare", the certificate, etc. As a result, the handshake messages are of variable length and of varying complexity, which has led to vulnerabilities and implementation mismatches in the past [17].

The WireGuard protocol [2] on the other hand, uses a much more simplified approach. Only one cipher suite is specified and certificates are not part of the protocol. The control-flow in Fig. 5 has an untangled structure. Peer selection and verification is solely based on public keys. A more or less sophisticated Public-Key-Infrastructure (PKI) may be implemented separately, but only if the overall application requires this. Like in TLS 1.3, two message types are sent in the handshake: the initiation and the response. A third message type can be sent by the responder instead of a response msg., with low computational effort, if the replying responder is unable to serve the costly Diffie-Hellman key calculation. This may be due to exhausting the real-time scheduling budget, when the component is under heavy load (e.g., in an adversary attack), avoiding denial of service complications. The fourth message type transports the application data.

Fig. 6. The physical demonstrator component. Shown are the modified model trains with the Bluetooth-LE (red PCB) back-channel to notify balise detection for odometry. The IRDA balises are seen in the foreground tracks between the white ribbon-cables connected to the IR-PCB. (Color figure online)

All four message types have a fixed length and a fixed structure. Hence, the parser is immune against length and buffer-overrun vulnerabilities.

Recently in 2018, the authors of WireGuard have published their results of the formal security verification of the protocol in [3]. The verification efforts are based on the tool Tamarin, and assert the security properties of the modelled protocol according to key agreement, key secrecy, session uniqueness and identity hiding. Beyond these properties, due to numerous static data structures and avoidance of dynamic memory allocations, the main C implementation of WireGuard claims low risk of unsafe behaviour and was recently accepted as a mainline Linux kernel driver module. The Linux implementation uses formally verified implementations of the X25519 algorithm published in [18] and [4], applying formal methods of F* and Coq.

As an alternative for use in safety-critical systems, we have also approached implementing the WireGuard protocol as a Scade model based on previous work in [12]. While the implementation reached proof-of-feasibility status for the demonstrator within the OBU component, it is still work in progress. We can conclude that the straightforward protocol state-machine and clear algorithmic choices of WireGuard make such an implementation feasible with hard real-time requirements. On the other hand, it must still be analysed whether a special implementation in Scade is necessary or, if the mainline implementation together with the anyway necessary security measures supported by the MILS architecture provide enough assurance. The MILS separation architecture does ensure non-interfering separation in terms of CPU time and memory space, for each component independent of its assurance level.

6   Conclusion

In the previous sections, we argued our choice of components and the applied system architecture to build a secure demonstrator composed of network-connected devices hosting model-based safety-critical applications.

When used together with TRDP as a middleware, the Scade-generated code does not require much boilerplate code, other than memory initialization and cycle timing. TRDP needs only minor adaptations in terms of a modified Scade-type dataset marshalling function and operating system layer modification. PikeOS is not directly supported in TRDP Light, but via the POSIX adaptation layer. After modification, sourcing the TRDP-XML configuration from the PikeOS rom-image property file system (pfs) unifies overall configuration and removes the need for a full-blown file system. The WireGuard component was also adapted to source the configuration for peer-public-keys and endpoint addresses from the pfs. Building these components on the base of the MILS separation architecture ensures security assurance for different software integrity- and assurance levels throughout the whole life cycle accommodating security updates for individual components.

Ongoing work in the certMILS project will guide the discussed MILS system architecture towards an accomplished certification methodology for secure safety-critical products. This will be demonstrated on real-world pilots, such as a power-grid control unit, a platform approach for SIL-4 railway applications and a demonstrator for the Prague subway system. Our educational railway demonstrator (Fig. 6) will also benefit from those pilot projects, applying developed testing techniques, improving integration tooling and fixing bugs that still need special procedures. In the short term, we also like to integrate the TRDP-SDT extension with Scade models, as well as evaluate the performance of our formalized WireGuard implementation and find an answer whether it is beneficial for secure data transport in safety-critical applications. A vital part of this ongoing work is to discuss the current real-time performance of the demonstrator on competitive, i.e., related industrial hardware.

Acknowledgments. This work is part of the certMILS project, funded by the European Union's Horizon 2020 research and innovation programme under grant agreement No. 731456.

References

1. CENELEC: Electronic railway equipment – train communication network (TCN) – part 2-3: TCN communication profile (IEC 61375-2-3:2016). Technical report, IEC (2017)
2. Donenfeld, J.A.: Wireguard: next generation kernel network tunnel. In: NDSS Symposium (2017). https://www.wireguard.com/papers/wireguard.pdf
3. Donenfeld, J.A., Milner, K.: Formal verification of the wireguard protocol. Technical report, Oxford University (2018). https://www.wireguard.com/papers/wireguard-formal-verification.pdf

4. Erbsen, A., Philipoom, J., Gross, J., Sloan, R., Chlipala, A.: Systematic generation of fast elliptic curve cryptography implementations. Technical report, MIT, Cambridge, MA, USA (2017)

5. Ferguson, N., Schneier, B.: A cryptographic evaluation of IPsec. Counterpane Internet Security, Inc. (2000). http://www.cs.fsu.edu/~yasinsac/Papers/ipsec.pdf

6. Gorski, P., Özer, M., Schulz, T., Golatowski, F.: A modular train control system through the use of certified COTS HW/SW and qualified tools. Elektronik **18**, 42–49 (2016)

7. Hametner, R., Resch, S.: A platform approach for fusing safety and security on a solid foundation. In: 4th International Workshop on MILS. Zenodo (2018). https://doi.org/10.5281/zenodo.1306081

8. Hirschler, B., Jakovljevic, M.: Secure deterministic L2/L3 ethernet networking for integrated architectures. resreport, SAE Technical Paper (2017)

9. IEC TC65 WG10: IEC TS 62443-2-4 Industrial communication networks - Network and system security - Part 2-4: Requirements for IACS solution suppliers (2015)

10. Rescorla, E.: The transport layer security (TLS) protocol version 1.3. Technical report, IETF (2018). https://datatracker.ietf.org/doc/rfc8446/

11. Rushby, J.: A trusted computing base for embedded systems. In: Proceedings of the 7th D/NBS Computer Security Conference (1984)

12. Schulz, T., Golatowski, F., Timmermann, D.: Evaluation of a formalized encryption library for safety-critical embedded systems. In: IEEE International Conference on Industrial Technology (ICIT) (2017). https://doi.org/10.1109/ICIT.2017.7915525

13. Schulz, T., Griest, C., Golatowski, F., Timmermann, D.: Strategy for security certification of high assurance industrial automation and control systems. In: IEEE 13th International Symposium on Industrial Embedded Systems (SIES) (2018). https://doi.org/10.1109/SIES.2018.8442081

14. Tverdyshev, S.: Security by design: introduction to mils. In: MILS Workshop Embedded World Conference (2017). https://doi.org/10.5281/zenodo.571164

15. UNISIG: SUBSET-026 - System Requirements Specif. SRS 3.3.0, ERA (2012)

16. Victors, J.: TLS 1.3 and the future of cryptographic protocols. Technical report, Synopsys (2016). https://www.synopsys.com/blogs/software-security/tls-1-3/

17. Walz, A., Sikora, A.: Exploiting dissent: towards fuzzing-based differential black box testing of TLS implementations. IEEE Trans. Dependable Secure Comput. 1 (2017). https://doi.org/10.1109/TDSC.2017.2763947

18. Zinzindohoué, J.K., Bhargavan, K., Protzenko, J., Beurdouche, B.: HACL*: a verified modern cryptographic library. In: Proceedings of the 2017 ACM SIGSAC Conference on Computer and Communications Security, CCS 2017 (2017). https://doi.org/10.1145/3133956.3134043

Merging Worlds – Aligning Safety and Security

Christian Schlehuber[1]([⊠]) and Dominik Renkel[2]([⊠])

[1] DB Netz AG, Weilburger Str. 22, 60326 Frankfurt am Main, Germany
christian.schlehuber@deutschebahn.com
[2] NEXTRAIL GmbH, Schaumainkai 91, 60596 Frankfurt am Main, Germany
dominik.renkel@nextrail.com

Abstract. Safety and security are important domains in current industrial control systems. While safety protects the human and the system itself from failures, security protects the system from malicious entities and their activities. One is static, admitted, and is not allowed to change over years, the other has to adopt dynamically to changes in the threat landscape. Due to digitalization and the need for more performance and a better maintainability, isolated systems, responsible for controlling signals in the railway domain or a power plant in the energy sector, are connected to large networks, using standard protocols and commercial-off-the-shelf components. Because of this change suddenly IT-Security becomes an important topic and it must be integrated in safety components, which due to the contradicting requirements of the domains can be challenging.

In a first approach one could think of designing the safety system and applying security to it as a shell afterwards. Although this approach may be applicable and lead to a useable result, better methods may exist, which result in a more efficient design process and a more secure solution. In our integrated approach security and safety lifecycles are merged and several activities like estimating the impact of an error only must be performed once for both domains. Especially in risk analysis, the derivation of security requirements and the maintenance phase, several processes can be combined and will be shown in this work.

Keywords: Safety · Security · Engineering · Industrial experience

1 Introduction

Control and safety systems take a central role in the safe operation of trains in European rail networks since a long time. In the early days, around 1900, the safety of trains was ensured by the usage of mechanical interlockings. Since then, the interlocking systems have experienced a steady evolution, which resulted in the current electronic interlockings (ESTW). ESTWs are computerized systems, on which the safety logic of the interlocking is implemented. As a part of this evolution, also the general architecture and behavior of the interlockings evolved; while only a minimum of interaction with external systems was required in the beginning, modern electronic interlockings or operations control centers are connected to a wide variety of systems. Partly also public communication links are used for these connections.

© Springer Nature Switzerland AG 2019
S. Collart-Dutilleul et al. (Eds.): RSSRail 2019, LNCS 11495, pp. 284–295, 2019.
https://doi.org/10.1007/978-3-030-18744-6_19

Each new interlocking design introduced improvements to the protective functions in response to previous incidents. This continuous improvement process resulted in the situation, that railway transportation is considered one of the safest public transports. However, in recent years new challenges for the control and safety systems arose, which are the result of a change in social structures and behavior. In 1900, the greatest threats for the railway transportation were technical or human errors, this means errors that are caused from actors of the system itself. Only in rare cases errors have been caused intentionally by system-external actors.

With this recent change in social structures and behavior, it had to be observed, that the railway is attacked more and more by external actors [1–3]. These types of deliberate attacks on control and safety systems have only be considered in a certain extent yet. Due to the increasing amount of such attacks and the potential degree of damage, which may be caused by such an attack, these are no longer negligible and must be treated properly to achieve adequate protection.

In the area of safety analysis standards, which define proper requirements and safety levels (e.g. SIL), for critical systems have been introduced over the last decades. Based on these safety levels a concrete implementation of a system can be evaluated for a given level. In the area of security analysis, no experienced method for the analysis of security requirements has been established so far, which may be a result from the nature of security analysis itself. While for safety analyses you may decide on relatively simple empirical values for the occurrence of an event or by targeted long-term tests, it is very difficult to achieve a similar measure in the security area. That is because this area is dependent on the actions of external actors and a simulation of possible attackers' behavior is almost impossible to develop.

This work is structured as follows: Sect. 2 gives an overview over related work in standards. Afterwards Sect. 3 compares the areas of security and safety and tries to show the differences in their processes. It is also shown how security for a safety system can be assured. In Sect. 4 it is shown, how the shell design for securing a safety system works and where the advantages and disadvantages are. Afterwards Sects. 5 and 6 show how an integrated approach could work and how this could result in a secure and safe system using virtualization. Afterwards Sect. 7 concludes this paper.

2 Related Work

For current CCS systems (Control and command systems) a wide variety of safety standards exists, for example [4] defines general requirements on reliability, availability, maintainability and safety (RAMS) of such systems. Additionally, to this standard, several more specific standards like EN 50159 for setting up safety-related communication channels over closed or open communication networks exist. A vendor for interlocking systems therefore can prove the safety of his system by fulfilling the requirements and advices in the given standards.

Security has not been covered to this point by now, which means that around security no railway specific standards are existent. The security of common IT systems has been covered by several national and international standards. For instance, the German Federal Office for Information Security defined a process for security management in its

"IT-Grundschutzhandbuch" (a basic protection manual on IT Security) and on the international level the ISO defined its 2700x series of standards. These form a good basis for securing a common IT system, but the domain of rail transportation has several specialties, which are hard to handle with the former mentioned processes.

Most CCS systems in rail transportation are very persistent, e.g. interlockings from the beginning of the 20th century are still in use, and if they are safety relevant, they are required to fulfil strong admission requirements by the local authorities. This also applies to updates to such systems. If a vendor discovers some vulnerability and provides a patch for it, the patch also must be checked by the local authorities. Due to these and other points general IT security standards are only partly applicable to the rail domain.

Asides from these, ISA (International Society of Automation) is currently working on its standard IEC 62443, which deals with IT security in automation systems. This standard covers some of the former mentioned points, but lacks guidance on several specialties of the rail domain.

3 Comparison of Safety and Security

While security in the area of railways is a quite new topic, processes for safety have been defined over years and mature standards already exist for their application in the railway domain. In general, for the development of a safety relevant system the V-Development Cycle of [4] is applied. Within this lifecycle it is clearly stated, which phases must be fulfilled, and which documents must be presented before the beginning of the next phase.

The development always starts with a Concept in Phase 1, this should describe, what the system should do in general. Afterwards this concept is elaborated to a System Definition during Phase 2. In this phase the functional blocks of the system and the behavior to different operating conditions are described. In Phase 3 a risk analysis is performed based on the system design, which results in RAMS requirements on specific parts of the system.

During the next phases the vendor of the system implements the system itself, evaluates its functionality and afterwards hands the product to the operator. From there on the system is evaluated and afterwards set into operation.

After these phases, the system gets maintained in specific intervals but in usual cases it is not changed over several years, as the safety requirements on the system normally will not change. Besides this also changes to the configuration of the system could result in the need for a new admission. From a safety point of view these long patch intervals may be completely acceptable, but if we consider the different context of security it becomes obvious, that the processes are not sufficient.

For security the life cycle has lots of similarities to the safety development cycle, but there also exist several differences. Before starting with the first phase of the security process (Fig. 1), which namely is the definition of system requirements, the engineer should become familiar with the domain and the values of the system.

Therefore, an analysis of the system assets should be performed, and the identified assets should be used during the future steps, especially during the risk analysis.

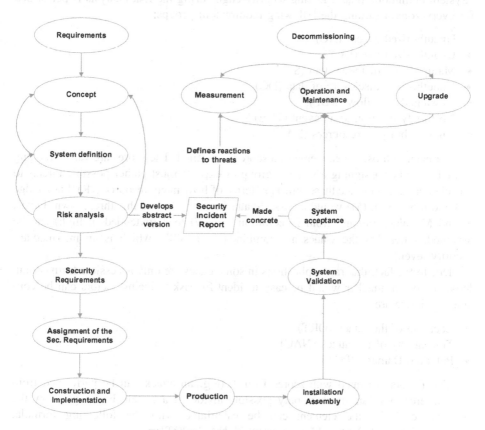

Fig. 1. Security development process

In the requirements phase the information about functional and non-functional requirements of the system are gathered. The operational environment and the affected assets should be collected. Afterwards during the concept phase a security system design is developed, which fulfils the former defined requirements. In addition, all systems in this design must be documented.

During the System definition the system should be defined in terms of desired functions and contained subsystems. The first part of this step is like every other system concept phase, but afterwards the system must be parted into zones and conduits. In this context a zone is an aggregation of similar devices and subsystems (similar according to the required security level for those systems). Conduits act as connections between different zones. At the end of this phase every object in the system design must be assigned to a zone or a conduit. In an upcoming step each of these zones is assigned different security requirements, which must be fulfilled. These are dependent on the security analysis of the zone.

For identification of relevant threats and according security requirements a security Risk analysis must be performed for every zone, which has been identified during the "System definition" phase. During security engineering the risk analysis is performed for every zone regarding the following requirement groups:

- Unauthorized access (AC)
- Unauthorized use (UC)
- Manipulation of the system (SI)
- Unauthorized disclosure of data (DC)
- Unwanted data flow (RDF)
- No timely reaction to an event (TRE)
- Unavailability of resources (RA)

For each of those seven elements a score is assigned. The scores are values ranging from 1 to 4. For assigning a value, a group of experts must gather possible threats to this element and then rate these threats in terms of how many resources (R), knowledge (K) and motivation (M) would a possible attacker, which uses this threat, own. For R, K and M values ranging from 2 (common or low) to 4 (extended or high) can be assigned. After this the values are combined to a VSL, which is an intermediary security level.

Due to the fact, that rail applications in some cases are only accessible from certain locations or an attacker would be easy to identify, risk reducing factors can be considered. These are:

- Location of the attack (ORT)
- Traceability of the attack (NAC)
- Potential Damage (POT)

The factors are rated with scores from 0 (e.g. an attack can be performed from everywhere) to 1 (an attack is only possible inside of a certain building). Now the security level for the element can be calculated with the following formula: SL = Maximum (1, VSL − Maximum{ORT, NAC, POT})

As a result, the risk analysis step finishes with a SL for each of the former mentioned 7 elements for every zone, which was defined earlier. The estimated SL-Vector is afterwards used to select the necessary security requirements. In [5] lists with security requirements (SR) have been defined for every requirement group with different requirements. An additional railway specific list of SRs can be found in [6]. In the following construction phase, it must be ensured, that the vendor fulfils the requirements, which are defined in the IEC 62443. Which means that several security processes at the vendor must be in place.

In the domain of railway transportation systems validation and acceptance is strongly related to admission by local authorities. Therefore, it is advised to include the validation and acceptance process into the already existing processes from the EN 50128/50129 to keep the overhead as low as possible. Afterwards additional security requirements for operation and maintenance are defined, which should be taken into consideration by operators of such systems. There should be update features for the security software on each system and a method for continuous measurement of the elements must be available.

During the operation phase of the device life cycle a system should be able to deal with potential incidents during normal operation. At this point the security cycle (Fig. 2) takes place. It is a wishful dream that a system is free of any vulnerabilities or bugs, which an attacker may use for performing an attack. In reality there is always an entry point, which an ambitious attacker might use to compromise the system. Therefore, the system should can deal with possible incidents. The phases, which may occur if an attack happens, can be seen in the security cycle below.

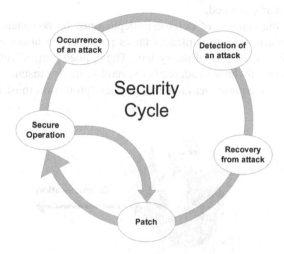

Fig. 2. Security cycle (part of operation and maintenance phase).

During decommissioning of a security relevant system, it should be ensured, that all sensitive data is removed from the system before it is sent in for repair or its complete disposal. If the systems design may reveal information useful for an attacker, the system should be securely disposed.

As it should have become obvious there are several similar points in both processes, but also differences, because security requires jumps to former phases at several points to ensure a secure solution.

4 Security by Shell

In a first approach to bring security into signaling systems the security shell was introduced [7]. The shell approach aims at securing safety relevant systems without interfering with the safety functions and the admission of those systems. This is done by wrapping the safety core of a system within a security shell. After this all communication to the system must pass through the security shell, which at least provides encryption, authentication and filtering of data, and only valid data is passed to the safety core of the system. There may also be other security functions implemented within the security shell, but the former mentioned are essential. This approach can be seen in Fig. 3. This concept assumes, that a safety communication protocol is in use between the safety core and the interlocking system, which cannot be altered by accident by the security components in the communication channel. All communication must pass a security shell before it is passed to the safety part of the system (marked red).

If now a new threat to the system is discovered a mitigation can be set in place within the security shell, because the admission of the safety part is decoupled from the security side. In this context it is important, that the interfaces and the performance (e.g. minimum bandwidth and latency) indicators between the safety core and the security shell have been clearly defined.

Nevertheless, the concept of defense-in-depth must be considered, which means that safety and security are decoupled as far as possible, but also some elements are implemented to the safety core of the system. The applied parts should be more static defenses, which will only have to adapt after several years (for instance input validation methods). Also, some countermeasures like physical protection must be implemented.

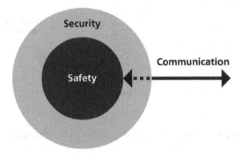

Fig. 3. Security shell around the safety core.

While this concept has the clear advantage, that incidents can be distinguished between the security and the safety part and the parts can be developed mostly independent of each other there are also several disadvantages. As the safety and the security team can work independently, they may work with different assumptions on the system and the results could be conflicting. For instance, zones could be inappropriately defined during the security risk analysis because the results of the safety risk analysis are not known and not aligned. In general, it can be stated, that this process results in a duplication of work and an increased cost due to the duplication of tasks. During the safety engineering process requirements on the system could be defined, which also affect the security risk analysis positively and by this could result in lesser additional security requirements. Also, during safety risk analysis, the impact of failures in functional blocks is defined and could be reused during the security engineering process because the potential impact of a security or a safety problem is the same.

Nevertheless, the shell methodology can be used for securing already defined systems or even already built systems.

5 Security for Safety: Integrating Processes

As it was shown during the previous section the security shell may be a pragmatic and applicable solution. Although this concept may be applicable for almost all systems it still has several disadvantages, which could be – at least for new systems – avoided by an integrated approach, which interconnects safety and security engineering. We will now draft how such a process could look.

Figure 4 shows the interconnection between safety and security during the development phases of the system lifecycle. On the left side the classic safety activities can be seen and on the right side the security elements can be found. The system is defined during phase 2 of [4] and during this work also security best practices should be included. Afterwards there are 2 negative influences on the system that have to be taken into account. From the safety perspective hazards can cause harm to the system and the environment. Due to this fact a risk analysis is performed during phase 3, which results in RAMS requirements. From a security perspective the system can also be influenced by vulnerabilities, which are exploited by threats. These vulnerabilities then can have a negative influence on the RAMS requirements of the system (e.g. availability can be influenced by the ability to perform a denial-of-service attack on the system). To react on this a Security Level (SL) is derived based on the risk analysis. This SL can be mapped to foundational requirements afterwards, which then reduce the possibility to exploit vulnerabilities to an acceptable level. RAMS requirements and Foundational Requirements are then formulated as System Requirements and assigned to parts of the System.

For the Security Engineering process, a more detailed view can be seen in Fig. 5. The process is divided in specific and general steps. The general ones must be performed on a regular basis without being in a specific development process and the outcomes can then be used for all projects. The specific ones must be performed for every system.

The Security Engineering process starts with a system definition, which is used as a base for performing a high-level risk analysis to derive zones and conduits. After this we analyze the operational assets of the system under consideration. The results from the safety analysis can be taken as a base for this. Afterwards assumptions on the system must be defined, for instance that all components are deployed in secured housings and are only maintained by controlled and trained personnel. In those assumptions we also must consider the RAMS requirements, because those can potentially be able to mitigate certain forms of attacks. For instance, input validation may be required by RAMS and can then be assumed to be effective by the security team. The information gathered by now results into a basic documentation of the zones and conduits.

For all the defined zones and conduits, we must check the potential threats. For doing so we derive the threats from several resources. On the one hand we have general mature threat landscaped to be considered, like the threats from ISO 27005 and from national catalogues, like the "Grundschutzkatalog" in Germany. On the other hand, railway specific threats should be considered, which must be derived from earlier logged security incidents on existing systems. With the now derived list of threats we start an evaluation process against a railway specific attacker model to filter the relevant threats. With those in mind a Security Level gets defined, which results in a certain set of requirements. With those requirements we check our relevant threats again and try to find attacks on the system that are still possible. Afterwards the SL gets refined. This process continues until an acceptable level of risk is achieved.

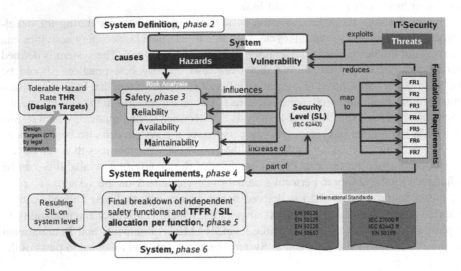

Fig. 4. Interconnection between IT-security and safety.

6   Integration of Security and Safety on a Single Platform

A system developed by the previously described process offers a state-of-the-art solution for protecting safety by security. An implementation on a single platform can be seen in Fig. 6. The shown system has been crafted taking security and safety into account. The base is built by a hardened and ruggedized hardware platform for railway usage, which is developed to RAMS standards. On the one hand this hardware platform offers the interfaces to a network and on the other hand the physical interfaces to the field elements to be controlled. Besides this, hardware security features like a Trusted Platform Module have been included.

On top of this a special SIL 4 operating system is implemented, which provides virtualization technologies. Due to these virtualization technologies and a Separation Kernel, which ensures that the virtual compartments are completely independent of each other various improvements become possible. First, it is possible to bring safety and security components on the same platform. Each component becomes its own compartment and the traffic flows can be clearly defined. Besides this it is also possible to create temporary compartments, which can be used during the update of the needed compartments. The new software is deployed to a temporary compartment and afterwards active and temporary compartments are changed. If something does not behave as expected it is also possible to switch back to the last working compartment.

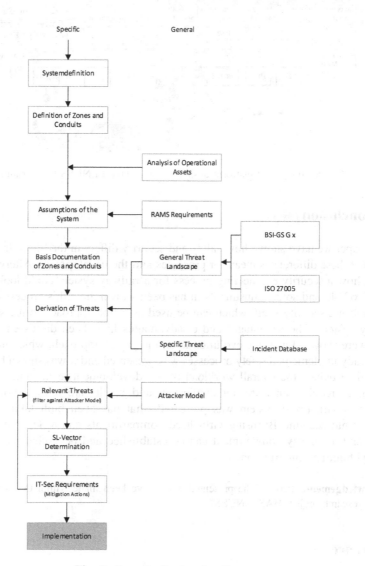

Fig. 5. Security Engineering Process.

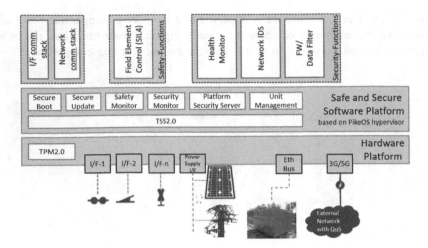

Fig. 6. Integrated platform design (Source: HASELNUSS Consortium).

7 Conclusion

In the paper we have shown how safety and security differs in the lifecycle of a system and what these differences mean for processes and the development. Afterwards it was shown how a security engineering process for a railway system could look like based on IEC 62443 and some adjustments. It has been shown, how this process can be used to establish a security shell, which can be used as a first approach to the security of a railway system. The advantages and disadvantages have been discussed and the use cases were shown. Later, the evolution to an integrated approach, which makes use of the already implemented safety processes was presented and it was shown how this can be used to reduce the overall workload of the development teams and the cost of a system, as requirements are not duplicated, and results are reused. Following this process, a virtualized system was presented, that has been built taking safety and security into account. By using virtualized compartments and a Separation Kernel a safety and a security compartment can be established and be exchanged by updated ones without any interruption.

Acknowledgement. Parts of the presented work have been made within the German BMBF funded research project HASELNUSS.

References

1. Ballard, J.D.: A preliminary study of sabotage and terrorism as transportation risk factors associated with the proposed Yucca Mountain high-level nuclear facility. Technical report, School of Criminal Justice - Grand Valley State University, July 1998
2. Riley, J.: Terrorism and rail security. Technical report, RAND Corporation, March 2004

3. S. A. I. of India: Report no. 14 of 2011-12 (Railways) - Security Management in Indian Railways. Technical report (2011)
4. Railway Applications - The Specification and Demonstration of Reliability, Availability, Maintainability and Safety (RAMS), EN 50126 (2015)
5. Security for Industrial Automation and Control Systems, ISA/IEC 62443 (2017)
6. DKE: Elektrische Bahn-Signalanlagen – Teil 104: Leitfaden für die IT-Sicherheit auf Grundlage der IEC 62443 (DIN VDE V 0831-104) (2014)
7. Schlehuber, C., Heinrich, M., Vateva-Gurova, T., Katzenbeisser, S., Suri, N.: A security architecture for railway signalling. In: Tonetta, S., Schoitsch, E., Bitsch, F. (eds.) SAFECOMP 2017. LNCS, vol. 10488, pp. 320–328. Springer, Cham (2017). https://doi.org/10.1007/978-3-319-66266-4_21

Author Index

Printed in the United States
By Bookmasters

Printed in the United States
By Bookmasters